LADY DAY'S DIARY

THE LIFE OF BILLIE HOLIDAY 1937-1959

WRITTEN BY KEN VAIL

Published by Castle Communications plc,
A29 Barwell Business Park, Leatherhead Road,
Chessington, Surrey KT9 2NY.

ISBN 1 86074 131 2

Printed and bound in the UK by Staples Printers Rochester Limited

While the publishers have made every reasonable effort to
trace the copyright owners for any or all of the photographs
in this book, there may be some omissions of credits for which
we apologise.

Acknowledgements

My grateful thanks to:
Beryl Bryden for her recollections and wonderful photographs;
Rolf Dahlgren for his generosity in sharing his vast collection of
photographs;
Franz Hoffmann for his amazing series of books, *Jazz Advertised*;
Bob Inman for his radio logs and a very rare photograph;
Ken Jones of the National Jazz Foundation Archive at Loughton;
Jack Millar of the Billie Holiday Circle for his generosity in sharing
his knowledge and providing precious record labels;
Brian Peerless for sharing his collection of *Metronomes* and *Down Beats*
and much more besides;
Tony Shoppee for sharing his *Down Beat* collection;
Andrew Simon of the National Sound Archive for a previously
unpublished photograph and an original poster;
Bobby Tucker for patiently recalling his time with Billie and for some
sensational photographs;
Bozy White of the IAJRC Library for allowing me to use his article
'Billie and Artie' in *IAJRC Journal* Vol 21, No2;
and David Stonard, a Billie Holiday completist, for his diligent proof-
reading and pertinent observations.
I would also like to acknowledge the kind assistance of
Ray Avery, John Chilton, Donald Clarke, Eddie Cook, Stanley Crouch,
Roger Dalleywater, Dave Green, David Griffiths, John Jeremy, Nick
Jones, Don Lawson, Don Luck, Stuart Nicholson, Hank O'Neal, Jack
Parnell, Annie Ross, Charles Saunders, Duncan Schiedt, Klaus
Stratemann, Jack Surridge, Denny Termer, Peter Vacher and Bob Weir

I have also been grateful for the writings of Frank Buchmann-Møller,
John Chilton, Donald Clarke, Stanley Crouch, William Dufty,
Leonard Feather, Burnett James, Max Jones, Bud Kliment, Jack
Millar, Stuart Nicholson, Robert O'Meally, Phil Schaap, Bob Weir and
John White

Photographs from the collections of Ray Avery, Rolf Dahlgren, Frank
Driggs, Bob Inman, Max Jones, Bengt H. Malmquist, Hank O'Neal,
Brian Peerless, Charles Peterson, Redferns (Beryl Bryden/William
Gottlieb/Bob Willougby), Hal Reiff, Duncan Schiedt, Andrew Simon,
Jack Surridge, Bobby Tucker, Peter Vacher and the author

Preface

Lady Day's Diary sets out to provide a fascinating insight into the life and times of the most soulful and influential singer in jazz… Miss Billie Holiday… Lady Day. Using contemporary photographs, newspaper reports, advertisements and reviews, I have attempted to chronicle her life month-by-month from the day she joined Count Basie's Orchestra in March 1937 to her death on 17 July 1959, preceded by a brief resumé of her life up to March 1937. I have tried to include all known club, concert, television, film and jam session appearances as well as her recordings, although this is not intended to be a discography. For that, I urge you to read Jack Millar's excellent *Fine and Mellow*.

I hope that you, the reader, will find this book an informative accompaniment when listening to Billie's records or reading any of her fine biographies. I am grateful to Penny Braybrooke of Castle Books for the faith she has shown in the project, and to Carolyn Begley for her dedication and energy in the exacting task of sourcing the photographs.

Ken Vail, Cambridge, February 1996

7 APRIL 1915

Billie Holiday is born in the Philadelphia General Hospital at
2.30 a.m. She is the illegitimate daughter of Sadie Gough
(19) and Clarence Holiday (16) of Baltimore. Sadie had
moved to Philadelphia to find work. Billie is named
Eleanora Gough.

She is taken back to Baltimore by Robert Miller, the
husband of Sadie's half-sister Eva, to be raised by Robert's
mother, Martha.

20 OCTOBER 1920

Sadie marries Philip Gough in Baltimore. Eleanora (5) starts
at Public School 102, The Thomas E. Hayes Elementary
School.

NOVEMBER 1920

Eleanora is taken out of the public school system and sent
to a Catholic school.

5 JANUARY 1925

9 year old Eleanora appears before the Juvenile Court for
truancy. She is described as a 'minor without proper care
and guardianship' and is sent to the House of Good
Shepherd for Colored Girls.

19 MARCH 1925

Eleanora is baptised.

3 OCTOBER 1925

Eleanora is paroled and goes to live with Sadie in East
Baltimore.

24 DECEMBER 1926

Eleanora (11) is raped by a neighbour, Wilbert Rich. Philip
and Sadie Gough burst in on the act and Eleanora is
immediately sent back to the House of Good Shepherd to be
held in protective custody.

18 JANUARY 1927

Wilbert Rich is found guilty of carnal knowledge of a 14–16
year old and sentenced to 3 months in a House of
Correction.

2 FEBRUARY 1927

Eleanora is released into the care of Sadie. Money is scarce
and she is soon running errands and doing jobs for the
madame of a local whorehouse. Eleanora enjoys the
opportunity to hear records by Bessie Smith and Louis
Armstrong on the whorehouse Victrola.

Right: Harlem in the 1930s.

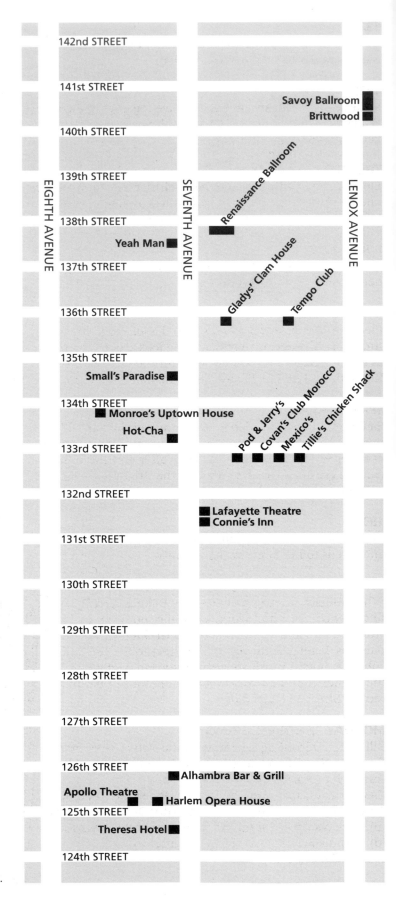

1928

At the end of 1928 Sadie leaves Eleanora in the care of Martha Miller to seek work in Harlem.

1929

Sadie sends for Eleanora and they live together in Florence Williams' whorehouse at 151 W140th Street, between Lenox and Seventh, in Harlem.

THURSDAY 2 MAY 1929

Eleanora and Sadie are among the girls arrested in a police raid on prostitutes. Eleanora is sent to hospital, to be followed by 100 days in the workhouse.

9 JULY 1929

Eleanora is discharged from hospital and sent to complete her sentence in the workhouse.

OCTOBER 1929

Eleanora (14) is released and she and Sadie go to live in Brooklyn. She begins to take singing jobs around Brooklyn in the company of a young neighbourhood tenor saxist, Kenneth Hollon. She begins using the name Billie Holiday.

SPRING 1930

Sadie gets a job at Mexico's in Harlem and she and Billie move to W127th Street. Billie helps out, waiting and singing at tables for tips. Soon she is singing after hours at other clubs in Harlem – Small's Paradise, the Bright Spot and the Alhambra Bar & Grill.

1932

Record producer John Hammond becomes aware of Billie, and listens to her at every opportunity.

1933

When Mexico's changes ownership, Billie and Sadie find themselves out of work, but Billie soon goes to work at Pod's and Jerry's Log Cabin Grill for $2 a night plus tips. Later, she moves up the street to the Hot-Cha. John Hammond is still an enthusiastic fan, and when the chance comes, he arranges for her to make her first record. She is 18 years old.

MONDAY 27 NOVEMBER 1933

Billie's first recording session with the Benny Goodman Orchestra for Columbia at 55 Fifth Avenue in NYC. The session is produced by John Hammond.
CHARLIE TEAGARDEN, SHIRLEY CLAY (t), BENNY GOODMAN (cl), ARTHUR KARLE (ts), JACK TEAGARDEN (tb), BUCK WASHINGTON (p), DICK MCDONOUGH (g), ARTIE BERNSTEIN (b), GENE KRUPA (d), ARTHUR SCHUTT (arr), BILLIE HOLIDAY (v)
Your Mother's Son-in-Law

MONDAY 4 DECEMBER 1933

Recording session with the Benny Goodman Orchestra for Columbia at 55 Fifth Avenue in NYC. The session is produced by John Hammond.
CHARLIE TEAGARDEN, SHIRLEY CLAY (t), BENNY GOODMAN (cl), ARTHUR KARLE (ts), JACK TEAGARDEN (tb), JOE SULLIVAN (p), DICK MCDONOUGH (g), ARTIE BERNSTEIN (b), GENE KRUPA (d), BILLIE HOLIDAY (v)
Riffin' the Scotch (2 takes)
Both takes are rejected, and they try again two weeks later.

MONDAY 18 DECEMBER 1933

Recording session with the Benny Goodman Orchestra for Columbia at 55 Fifth Avenue in NYC. The session is produced by John Hammond.
CHARLIE TEAGARDEN, SHIRLEY CLAY (t), BENNY GOODMAN (cl), ARTHUR KARLE (ts), JACK TEAGARDEN (tb), JOE SULLIVAN (p), DICK MCDONOUGH (g), ARTIE BERNSTEIN (b), GENE KRUPA (d), BILLIE HOLIDAY (v)
Riffin' the Scotch

25 MARCH 1934

Lester Young (24) joins the Fletcher Henderson Orchestra at the Cotton Club in Harlem. Billie meets Lester, they become friends and he soon moves in with Billie and Sadie. Billie continues singing on the bar circuit in Harlem, often with Lester in tow.

JULY 1934

Lester Young leaves the Fletcher Henderson Orchestra and returns to Kansas City.

FRIDAY 23 NOVEMBER 1934

Billie (19) makes her debut at the Apollo Theatre, working as a duo with her lover, pianist Bobbie Henderson.

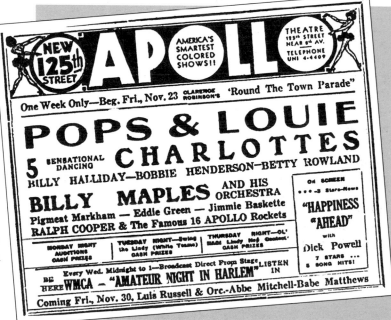

15 FEBRUARY 1935

Billie is offered a try-out with the Mills Blue Rhythm Band at the Lincoln Theatre in Philadelphia, however the engagement is cancelled because of a management dispute.

TUESDAY 12 MARCH 1935

Recording session with the Duke Ellington Orchestra for the film soundtrack of *Symphony in Black* at the Paramount Film Studios, Astoria, Long Island, New York.
ARTHUR WHETSOL, FREDDIE JENKINS, COOTIE WILLIAMS (t), MARSHALL ROYAL (cl/as), Barney Bigard (cl/ts), JOHNNY HODGES (as), Harry Carney (bar), JOE NANTON, JUAN TIZOL, LAWRENCE BROWN (tb), DUKE ELLINGTON (p), FRED GUY (g), WELLMAN BRAUD (b), SONNY GREER (d), BILLIE HOLIDAY (v)
Big City Blues (aka *Saddest Tale*)

FRIDAY 12 APRIL 1935

Billie returns to the Apollo Theatre, as featured vocalist with Ralph Cooper's Big Band. The whole cast is held over for a second week after doing stand-out business.

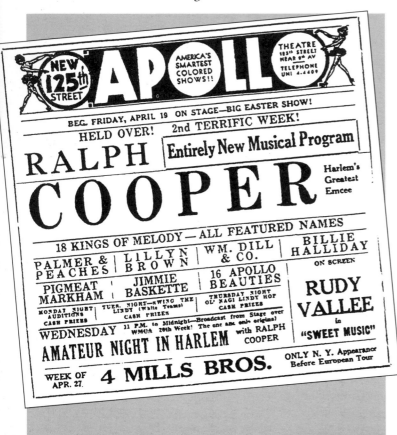

2 JUNE 1935

Billie has moved from the Hot-Cha to Clark Monroe's Uptown House when John Hammond approaches her with an offer to record for Brunswick.

TUESDAY 2 JULY 1935

Recording session with the Teddy Wilson Orchestra for Brunswick at 1776 Broadway in NYC. The session is produced by John Hammond with ROY ELDRIDGE (t), BENNY GOODMAN (cl), BEN WEBSTER (ts), TEDDY WILSON (p), JOHN TRUEHEART (g), JOHN KIRBY (b), COZY COLE (d), BILLIE HOLIDAY (v)
I Wished on the Moon / What A Little Moonlight Can Do / Miss Brown To You / A Sun Bonnet Blue

WEDNESDAY 31 JULY 1935

Recording session with the Teddy Wilson Orchestra for Brunswick at 1776 Broadway in NYC. The session is produced by John Hammond with ROY ELDRIDGE (t), CECIL SCOTT (cl), HILTON JEFFERSON (as), BEN WEBSTER (ts), TEDDY WILSON (p), LAWRENCE LUCIE (g), JOHN KIRBY (b), COZY COLE (d), BILLIE HOLIDAY (v)
What A Night, What A Moon, What A Girl / I'm Painting The Town Red / It's Too Hot For Words

FRIDAY 3 AUGUST 1935

Billie (billed as Billy Halliday) appears at the Apollo on a bill with Willie Bryant and his Band, The Berry Brothers, Pearl Baines, The Five Percolators, John Mason, Pigmeat Markham, George Wiltshire, and Bobbie Evans.

SUNDAY 15 SEPTEMBER 1935

Billie opens at the Famous Door on 52nd Street, her first downtown engagement. She is backed by Teddy Wilson and also on the bill is the George Brunis Band with Max Kaminsky on trumpet and Joe Bushkin on piano. Billie's style does not go down well with the patrons, and she is fired after only four nights.

SUNDAY 29 SEPTEMBER 1935

Billie opens in Montreal, Canada for a one-week engagement secured by Irving Mills.

FRIDAY 25 OCTOBER 1935

Recording session with the Teddy Wilson Orchestra for Brunswick at 1776 Broadway in NYC. The session is produced by John Hammond with ROY ELDRIDGE (t), CHU BERRY(ts), BENNY MORTON (tb), TEDDY WILSON (p), DAVE BARBOUR (g), JOHN KIRBY (b), COZY COLE (d), BILLIE HOLIDAY (v)
Twenty Four Hours A Day / Yankee Doodle Never Went To Town / Eeny Meeny Miney Mo / If You Were Mine

SUNDAY 29 OCTOBER 1935

Billie opens in the Broadway revue *Stars Over Broadway* at Connie's Inn, which has moved downtown to W48th Street between Seventh Avenue and Broadway. Louis Armstrong is the star, backed by the Luis Russell Orchestra and featuring Ted Hale, Earl 'Snakehips' Tucker, Chuck & Chuckles, and Sonny Woods.

TUESDAY 3 DECEMBER 1935
Recording session with the Teddy Wilson Orchestra for Brunswick at 1776 Broadway in NYC. The session is produced by John Hammond with DICK CLARK (t), TOM MACEY (cl), JOHNNY HODGES (as), TEDDY WILSON (p), DAVE BARBOUR (g), GRACHAN MONCUR (b), COZY COLE (d), BILLIE HOLIDAY (v)
These 'n' That 'n' Those / You Let Me Down / Spreadin' Rhythm Around

JANUARY 1936
Billie leaves *Stars Over Broadway* and is replaced by Bessie Smith.

THURSDAY 30 JANUARY 1936
Recording session with the Teddy Wilson Orchestra for Brunswick at 1776 Broadway in NYC. The session is produced by John Hammond with GORDON 'CHRIS' GRIFFIN (t), RUDY POWELL (cl), TED McRAE (ts), TEDDY WILSON (p), JOHN TRUEHEART (g), GRACHAN MONCUR (b), COZY COLE (d), BILLIE HOLIDAY (v)
Life Begins When You're In Love

FEBRUARY 1936
Eddie Condon invites Billie to join in the regular Sunday afternoon jam sessions he is initiating at the Famous Door.

MARCH 1936
Billie works briefly with the Jimmie Lunceford Band on some theatre dates in upstate New York.

JUNE 1936
Billie opens at the Grand Terrace in Chicago with Fletcher Henderson's Band. The club manager, Ed Fox, hates Billie's singing and keeps telling how to sing. Billie eventually explodes, and is fired.

TUESDAY 30 JUNE 1936
Recording session with the Teddy Wilson Orchestra for Brunswick at 1776 Broadway in NYC. The session is produced by John Hammond with JONAH JONES (t), HARRY CARNEY (cl/bar), JOHNNY HODGES (as), TEDDY WILSON (p), LAWRENCE LUCIE (g), JOHN KIRBY (b), COZY COLE (d), BILLIE HOLIDAY (v)
It's Like Reaching For The Moon / These Foolish Things / I Cried For You (2 takes) / *Guess Who*

FRIDAY 10 JULY 1936
Recording session as Billie Holiday and her Orchestra for Vocalion in NYC. The session is produced by Bernie Hanighen with BUNNY BERIGAN (t), ARTIE SHAW (cl), JOE BUSHKIN (p), DICK McDONOUGH (g), PETE PETERSON (b), COZY COLE (d), BILLIE HOLIDAY (v)
Did I Remember? / No Regrets (2 takes) / *Summertime / Billie's Blues*

SATURDAY 11 JULY 1936
Billie makes her first appearance on CBS radio's popular *Saturday Night Swing Club* with Bunny Berigan.

WEDNESDAY 2 SEPTEMBER 1936
Billie opens at the Onyx Club on 52nd Street. Also on the bill is Stuff Smith, a long-term favourite at the club. Smith objects to Billie's success and she is forced to leave.

TUESDAY 29 SEPTEMBER 1936
Recording session as Billie Holiday and her Orchestra for Vocalion in NYC. The session is produced by Bernie Hanighen with BUNNY BERIGAN (t), IRVING FAZOLA (cl), CLYDE HART (p), DICK McDONOUGH (g), ARTIE BERNSTEIN (b), COZY COLE (d), BILLIE HOLIDAY (v)
A Fine Romance / I Can't Pretend / One, Two, Button Your Shoe / Let's Call A Heart A Heart

SUNDAY 4 OCTOBER 1936
Billie opens at the Renaissance Casino in Harlem with the Louis Metcalf Band. Billie's father Clarence plays guitar in the band, and Lester Young who was on a brief sabbatical from the Count Basie Band in Kansas City.

WEDNESDAY 21 OCTOBER 1936
Recording session with the Teddy Wilson Orchestra for Brunswick at 1776 Broadway in NYC. The session is produced by John Hammond with IRVING 'MOUSE' RANDOLPH (t), VIDO MUSSO (cl), BEN WEBSTER (ts), TEDDY WILSON (p), ALLAN REUSS (g), MILT HINTON (b), GENE KRUPA (d), BILLIE HOLIDAY (v)
Easy To Love / With Thee I Swing / The Way You Look Tonight (2 takes)

WEDNESDAY 28 OCTOBER 1936
Recording session with the Teddy Wilson Orchestra for Brunswick at 1776 Broadway in NYC. The session is produced by John Hammond with IRVING 'MOUSE' RANDOLPH (t), VIDO MUSSO (cl), BEN WEBSTER (ts), TEDDY WILSON (p), ALLAN REUSS (g), MILT HINTON (b), GENE KRUPA (d), BILLIE HOLIDAY (v)
Who Loves You? (2 takes)

THURSDAY 19 NOVEMBER 1936

Recording session with the Teddy Wilson Orchestra for Brunswick at 1776 Broadway in NYC. The session is produced by John Hammond with JONAH JONES (t), BENNY GOODMAN (cl), BEN WEBSTER (ts), TEDDY WILSON (p), ALLAN REUSS (g), JOHN KIRBY (b), COZY COLE (d), BILLIE HOLIDAY (v)
Pennies From Heaven (2 takes) / *That's Life I Guess* (2 takes) / *I Can't Give You Anything But Love*

DECEMBER 1936

The Count Basie Band arrive in New York for their Christmas Eve opening at the Roseland Ballroom. Lester Young and Billie soon renew their friendship and he moves into Billie and Sadie's apartment at 9 West 99th Street. Billie is now working at Clark Monroe's Uptown House.

TUESDAY 12 JANUARY 1937

Recording session as Billie Holiday and her Orchestra for Vocalion in NYC. The session is produced by Bernie Hanighen with JONAH JONES (t), EDGAR SAMPSON (cl/as), BEN WEBSTER (ts), TEDDY WILSON (p), ALLAN REUSS (g), JOHN KIRBY (b), COZY COLE (d), BILLIE HOLIDAY (v)
One Never Knows, Does One? / *I've Got My Love To Keep Me Warm* (2 takes) / *If My Heart Could Only Talk* / *Please Keep Me In Your Dreams*

MONDAY 25 JANUARY 1937

Billie makes her first recordings with members of the Count Basie band.
Recording session with the Teddy Wilson Orchestra for Brunswick at 1776 Broadway in NYC. The session is produced by John Hammond with BUCK CLAYTON (t), BENNY GOODMAN (cl), LESTER YOUNG (ts), TEDDY WILSON (p), FREDDY GREEN (g), WALTER PAGE (b), JO JONES (d), BILLIE HOLIDAY (v)
He Ain't Got Rhythm / *This Year's Kisses* / *Why Was I Born?* / *I Must Have That Man*

FEBRUARY 1937

John Hammond has been pulling strings to get Billie into the Count Basie Band. Early in February Billie travels by train to Philadelphia, where Basie is appearing at the Chatterbox, to audition with the band.

THURSDAY 18 FEBRUARY 1937

Recording session with the Teddy Wilson Orchestra for Brunswick at 1776 Broadway in NYC. The session is produced by John Hammond with HENRY 'RED' ALLEN (t), CECIL SCOTT (cl), PRINCE ROBINSON (ts), TEDDY WILSON (p), JIMMY McLIN (g), JOHN KIRBY (b), COZY COLE (d), BILLIE HOLIDAY (v)
The Mood That I'm In / *You Showed Me The Way* / *Sentimental and Melancholy* / *This Is My Last Affair*

TUESDAY 23 FEBRUARY 1937

Billie's father, Clarence Holiday (37), dies of influenzal pneumonia in Dallas, Texas, where he is touring with the Don Redman Band.

MONDAY 1 MARCH 1936

Billie is working at Clark Monroe's Uptown House when she receives a telephone call informing her of Clarence's death. Clark Monroe makes the funeral arrangements. Sadie refuses to ride in a car with Clarence's wife, Fanny, or his unofficial wife Atlanta, makes her own arrangements, gets lost and misses the funeral altogether.

MON	**1**
TUES	**2**
WED	**3**
THUR	**4**
FRI	**5**
SAT	**6**
SUN	**7**
MON	**8**
TUES	**9**
WED	**10**
THUR	**11**
FRI	**12**
SAT	**13**
SUN	**14**
MON	**15**
TUES	**16**
WED	**17**
THUR	**18**
FRI	**19**
SAT	**20**
SUN	**21**
MON	**22**
TUES	**23**
WED	**24**
THUR	**25**
FRI	**26**
SAT	**27**
SUN	**28**
MON	**29**
TUES	**30**
WED	**31**

SATURDAY 13 MARCH 1937
Billie Holiday joins the Count Basie Orchestra at Energetic Park, Scranton, Pennsylvania on a salary of $70 a week.

SUNDAY 14 MARCH 1937
Billie and the Basie Band at New York Hot Club, NYC and Emma Jettick Park, Binghamton, NY

FRIDAY 19 MARCH 1937
Billie and the Basie Band open at the Apollo Theatre, on 125th Street in Harlem for a one-week engagement. A newspaper review of the opening says:

The sensation of the show is statuesque and effervescent Billie Holiday, and braving controversy we dare to place her in superior position to Ella Fitzgerald. When the rhythm-wise redhead swings 'I Cried For You' and sings of her 'Last Affair', the Apollo, the audience and the fixtures truly belong to her. But it was not until she came across with the beautiful 'One Never Knows, Does One?' does she rate tops. There is more force, personality and sparkle in the Holiday voice than we ever noticed in La Fitzgerald's, and that's going some, for Fitzgerald can sing for us anytime of the day.

WEDNESDAY 24 MARCH 1937
The Amateur Hour at the Apollo is broadcast on station WMCA.

THURSDAY 25 MARCH 1937
Billie and the Basie Band close at the Apollo Theatre, Harlem.

FRIDAY 26 MARCH 1937
Billie and the Basie Band embark on a short tour which includes Cincinnati Cotton Club, Adams Theatre in Newark, NJ and Hartford, Connecticut.

WEDNESDAY 31 MARCH 1937
Recording session with the Teddy Wilson Orchestra for Columbia in NYC. The session is produced by John Hammond at 1776 Broadway and the band comprises COOTIE WILLIAMS (t), HARRY CARNEY (cl/bs), JOHNNY HODGES (as), TEDDY WILSON (p), ALLAN REUSS (g), JOHN KIRBY (b), COZY COLE (d)
Carelessly / How Could You? / Moanin' Low
The session is completed with an instrumental version of *Fine and Dandy*.

THUR	**1**
FRI	**2**
SAT	**3**
SUN	**4**
MON	**5**
TUES	**6**
WED	**7**
THUR	**8**
FRI	**9**
SAT	**10**
SUN	**11**
MON	**12**
TUES	**13**
WED	**14**
THUR	**15**
FRI	**16**
SAT	**17**
SUN	**18**
MON	**19**
TUES	**20**
WED	**21**
THUR	**22**
FRI	**23**
SAT	**24**
SUN	**25**
MON	**26**
TUES	**27**
WED	**28**
THUR	**29**
FRI	**30**

THURSDAY 1 APRIL 1937
Recording session as Billie Holiday and her Orchestra for American Vocalion in NYC. The session is produced by Bernie Hanighen and the band is: EDDIE TOMPKINS (t), BUSTER BAILEY (cl), JOE THOMAS (ts), TEDDY WILSON (p), CARMEN MASTREN (g), JOHN KIRBY (b), ALPHONSE STEELE (d)
Where Is The Sun? / Let's Call The Whole Thing Off / They Can't Take That Away From Me (2 takes) / *Don't Know If I'm Comin' Or Goin'* (2 takes)

In the evening Billie joins the Basie Band for their opening at the Savoy Ballroom in Harlem.

WEDNESDAY 7 APRIL 1938
Billie's 22nd birthday.

SUNDAY 11 APRIL 1937
Billie and the Basie Band are again at the Savoy Ballroom in Harlem where the packed house includes Louis Armstrong, Ella Fitzgerald, Benny Goodman, John Hammond, Lionel Hampton, Allan Reuss, Dave Tough and Chick Webb.

Billie (left) at the Savoy Ballroom. Also in the group are Bob Bach, Dave Tough, Eddie Stein and companion, Mrs Dave Tough and Ruby Helena. Ruby Helena was living with Billie and Sadie and was often referred to as Billie's sister.

WEDNESDAY 14 APRIL 1937
Billie and the Basie Band close at the Savoy Ballroom in Harlem.

THURSDAY 15 APRIL 1937
Billie and the Basie Band open a week's engagement at the Nixon Grand Theatre, Philadelphia closing on Wednesday 21 April.

SATURDAY 17 APRIL 1937
Billie and the Basie Band broadcast from the Nixon Grand Theatre, Philadelphia. Billie sings *This Year's Crop Of Kisses*.

WEDNESDAY 21 APRIL 1937
Billie and the Basie Band close at the Nixon Grand Theatre, Philadelphia

FRIDAY 23 APRIL 1937
Billie and the Basie Band start a week at the Howard Theatre, Washington.

THURSDAY 29 APRIL 1937
Billie and the Basie Band close at the Howard Theatre, Washington.

SAT	**1**
SUN	**2**
MON	**3**
TUES	**4**
WED	**5**
THUR	**6**
FRI	**7**
SAT	**8**
SUN	**9**
MON	**10**
TUES	**11**
WED	**12**
THUR	**13**
FRI	**14**
SAT	**15**
SUN	**16**
MON	**17**
TUES	**18**
WED	**19**
THUR	**20**
FRI	**21**
SAT	**22**
SUN	**23**
MON	**24**
TUES	**25**
WED	**26**
THUR	**27**
FRI	**28**
SAT	**29**
SUN	**30**
MON	**31**

MONDAY 3 MAY 1937
Billie's photograph appears on the cover of Flash magazine.

TUESDAY 11 MAY 1937
Recording session with the Teddy Wilson Orchestra for Columbia in NYC. The session is produced by John Hammond with BUCK CLAYTON (t), BUSTER BAILEY (cl), JOHNNY HODGES (as), LESTER YOUNG (ts), TEDDY WILSON (p), ALLAN REUSS (g), ARTIE BERNSTEIN (b), COZY COLE (d)
Sun Showers / Yours and Mine / I'll Get By (2 takes) / *Mean To Me* (2 takes)

SUNDAY 30 MAY 1937
Billie makes a solo appearance at a midnight benefit concert for the Harlem Children's Center at the Apollo Theatre.

TUES	1
WED	2
THUR	3
FRI	4
SAT	5
SUN	6
MON	7
TUES	8
WED	9
THUR	10
FRI	11
SAT	12
SUN	13
MON	14
TUES	15
WED	16
THUR	17
FRI	18
SAT	19
SUN	20
MON	21
TUES	22
WED	23
THUR	24
FRI	25
SAT	26
SUN	27
MON	28
TUES	29
WED	30

TUESDAY 1 JUNE 1937

Recording session with the Teddy Wilson Orchestra for Columbia in NYC. The session is produced by John Hammond with BUCK CLAYTON (t), BUSTER BAILEY (cl), LESTER YOUNG (ts), TEDDY WILSON (p), FREDDIE GREEN (g), WALTER PAGE (b), JO JONES (d)
Foolin' Myself / Easy Living / I'll Never Be The Same
The session is completed by an instrumental – *I Found A New Baby.*

FRIDAY 4 JUNE 1937

Billie and the Basie Band commence a week at the Apollo Theatre, Harlem. Also on the bill are Radcliffe & Rogers, and Leonard Harper.

WEDNESDAY 9 JUNE 1937

The Amateur Hour at the Apollo is broadcast on station WMCA.

THURSDAY 10 JUNE 1937

Billie and the Basie Band close at the Apollo Theatre, Harlem.

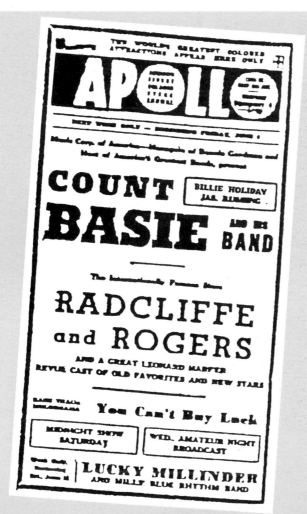

TUESDAY 15 JUNE 1937

Recording session as Billie Holiday and her Orchestra for Columbia in NYC. Bernie Hanighen is the producer and the band is BUCK CLAYTON (t), EDMOND HALL (cl), LESTER YOUNG (ts), JAMES SHERMAN (p), FREDDIE GREEN (g), WALTER PAGE (b), JO JONES (d)
Me, Myself And I (2 takes) / *A Sailboat In The Moonlight / Born To Love / Without Your Love* (2 takes)

TUESDAY 22 JUNE 1937

Billie and the Basie Band open at the Savoy Ballroom, Harlem opposite Billy Hicks' Sizzling Six.

WEDNESDAY 23 JUNE 1937

Bob Inman, a young swing fan, describes his visit to the Savoy in his diary: *After a twenty minute subway ride we arrived at the Savoy Ballroom at 9:30 p.m. and paid the fifty cent admission fee. ... Count Basie was one of the best bands; it's so relaxed with a driving rhythm section behind all the great soloists ... and the sensational singer, Billie Holiday. Basie's band played Sometimes I'm Happy (Evans), I Surrender Dear (Rushing), House Hop, Boo Hoo, My First Thrill, Riffin' at the Ritz, I've Got My Eye On You (Young, Evans), Pennies From Heaven (Rushing), Jam Session, Always, Louise (Evans), Me Myself And I (Holiday), Blue Ball, Dreamboat, Mayflower (Moore, Young). Too bad Billie Holiday didn't sing more numbers. After having a very enjoyable evening at the Savoy, we 16-yr-olds had to catch the 1:15 train from 138th Street to our homes in Bronxville, N.Y.*

MONDAY 28 JUNE 1937

Billie and the Basie Band broadcast from the Savoy Ballroom, Harlem.

WEDNESDAY 30 JUNE 1937

Billie and the Basie Band broadcast direct from the Savoy Ballroom on the last night of their engagement. The broadcast is recorded by John Hammond and is the first broadcast by Billie with the Basie Band which has so far come to light. The announcer is Howard Doyle and the personnel of the Basie Orchestra is ED LEWIS, BOBBY MOORE, BUCK CLAYTON (t), DAN MINOR, GEORGE HUNT (tb), EARLE WARREN (as), LESTER YOUNG (cl/ts), HERSCHEL EVANS (ts), JACK WASHINGTON (bs), COUNT BASIE (p), FREDDIE GREEN (g), WALTER PAGE (b), JO JONES (d), JIMMY RUSHING, BILLIE HOLIDAY (v)
Theme – Moten Swing / Shout and Feel It /The You and Me That Used To Be (v JIMMY RUSHING) / *The Count Steps In / They Can't Take That Away From Me* (v BILLIE HOLIDAY) / *I'll Always Be In Love With You / When My Dreamboat Comes Home* (v JIMMY RUSHING) / *Swing, Brother, Swing* (v BILLIE HOLIDAY) / *Bugle Blues / I Got Rhythm / Theme – Moten Swing*

THUR	**1**
FRI	**2**
SAT	**3**
SUN	**4**
MON	**5**
TUES	**6**
WED	**7**
THUR	**8**
FRI	**9**
SAT	**10**
SUN	**11**
MON	**12**
TUES	**13**
WED	**14**
THUR	**15**
FRI	**16**
SAT	**17**
SUN	**18**
MON	**19**
TUES	**20**
WED	**21**
THUR	**22**
FRI	**23**
SAT	**24**
SUN	**25**
MON	**26**
TUES	**27**
WED	**28**
THUR	**29**
FRI	**30**
SAT	**31**

SATURDAY 3 JULY 1937
Billie broadcasts on CBS Radio's 'Saturday Night Swing Club' with Duke Ellington and members of his band. She sings 'Swing, Brother, Swing'. The station announcer is Paul Douglas. *New York Amsterdam News* reports: 'Twas swell'

WEDNESDAY 7 JULY 1937
The Basie Orchestra record four tunes in New York – *Smarty / One O'Clock Jump / Listen, my Children, And You Shall Hear* (v JIMMY RUSHING) / *John's Idea* – for Decca. Billie is not included but, the same evening, Billie and the Basie Band play a 'Battle of the Bands' with Jimmie Lunceford in Hartford, Connecticut.

THURSDAY 8 JULY 1937
Billie and the Basie Band open at the Hotel Ritz-Carlton in Boston for an extended residency.

SUN	**1**
MON	**2**
TUES	**3**
WED	**4**
THUR	**5**
FRI	**6**
SAT	**7**
SUN	**8**
MON	**9**
TUES	**10**
WED	**11**
THUR	**12**
FRI	**13**
SAT	**14**
SUN	**15**
MON	**16**
TUES	**17**
WED	**18**
THUR	**19**
FRI	**20**
SAT	**21**
SUN	**22**
MON	**23**
TUES	**24**
WED	**25**
THUR	**26**
FRI	**27**
SAT	**28**
SUN	**29**
MON	**30**
TUES	**31**

MONDAY 9 AUGUST 1937
The Basie Orchestra, without Billie, record at the Decca Studios in New York. BENNY MORTON (tb) replaces GEORGE HUNT and EDDIE DURHAM (tb/g) is added.
Good Morning Blues (v JIMMY RUSHING) / *Our Love Was Meant To Be* (v EARLE WARREN) / *Time Out / Topsy*

FRIDAY 13 AUGUST 1937
Billie and the Basie Band broadcast from the Hotel Ritz-Carlton in Boston.

MONDAY 16 AUGUST 1937
Billie and the Basie Band broadcast from the Hotel Ritz-Carlton in Boston.

FRIDAY 20 AUGUST 1937
Billie and the Basie Band broadcast from the Hotel Ritz-Carlton in Boston.

SATURDAY 21 AUGUST 1937
Billie and the Basie Band broadcast from the Hotel Ritz-Carlton in Boston.

MONDAY 23 AUGUST 1937
Billie and the Basie Band broadcast from the Hotel Ritz-Carlton in Boston.

FRIDAY 27 AUGUST 1937
Billie and the Basie Band broadcast from the Hotel Ritz-Carlton in Boston.

MONDAY 30 AUGUST 1937
Billie and the Basie Band broadcast from the Hotel Ritz-Carlton in Boston.

WED	1	FRI	1
THUR	2	SAT	2
FRI	3	SUN	3
SAT	4	MON	4
SUN	5	TUES	5
MON	6	WED	6
TUES	7	THUR	7
WED	8	FRI	8
THUR	9	SAT	9
FRI	10	SUN	10
SAT	11	MON	11
SUN	12	TUES	12
MON	13	WED	13
TUES	14	THUR	14
WED	15	FRI	15
THUR	16	SAT	16
FRI	17	SUN	17
SAT	18	MON	18
SUN	19	TUES	19
MON	20	WED	20
TUES	21	THUR	21
WED	22	FRI	22
THUR	23	SAT	23
FRI	24	SUN	24
SAT	25	MON	25
SUN	26	TUES	26
MON	27	WED	27
TUES	28	THUR	28
WED	29	FRI	29
THUR	30	SAT	30
		SUN	31

FRIDAY 3 SEPTEMBER 1937
Billie and the Basie Band broadcast from the Hotel Ritz-Carlton in Boston.

MONDAY 6 SEPTEMBER 1937
Billie and the Basie Band broadcast from the Hotel Ritz-Carlton in Boston.

MONDAY 13 SEPTEMBER 1937
Recording session as Billie Holiday and her Orchestra in New York. Bernie Hanighen is the producer and the band is: BUCK CLAYTON (t), BUSTER BAILEY (cl), LESTER YOUNG (ts), CLAUDE THORNHILL (p), FREDDIE GREEN (g), WALTER PAGE (b), JO JONES (d)
Getting Some Fun Out Of Life / Who Wants Love? / Trav'lin' All Alone / He's Funny That Way

WEDNESDAY 13 OCTOBER 1937
The Basie Orchestra, without Billie record at the Decca Studios in New York. BOBBY HICKS (t) replaces Bobby Moore.
I Keep Remembering (v JIMMY RUSHING) / *Out The Window / Don't You Miss Your Baby?* (v JIMMY RUSHING) / *Let Me Dream* (v EARLE WARREN)

Count Basie "Clicks" On Baltimore Stage
BALTIMORE, Md., Nov. 4 — Count Basie and his orchestra with James Rushing and Billie Halliday doing the vocals made a hit on their recent appearance at the Royal Theatre here. Press agents gave the band several hundred words of praise.

THURSDAY 21 OCTOBER 1937
Billie and the Basie Band begin a two-week stint at the Meadowbrook Lounge, Cedar Grove, New Jersey.

SUNDAY 31 OCTOBER 1937
Billie and the Basie Band broadcast from the Criterion Theatre, New York at 11am on Sunday Swing Concert.

Billie in action in front of the Count Basie Band during their two-week stint at Frank Dailey's Meadowbrook Lounge in Cedar Grove, New Jersey.

MON	**1**	WED	**1**
TUES	**2**	THUR	**2**
WED	**3**	FRI	**3**
THUR	**4**	SAT	**4**
FRI	**5**	SUN	**5**
SAT	**6**	MON	**6**
SUN	**7**	TUES	**7**
MON	**8**	WED	**8**
TUES	**9**	THUR	**9**
WED	**10**	FRI	**10**
THUR	**11**	SAT	**11**
FRI	**12**	SUN	**12**
SAT	**13**	MON	**13**
SUN	**14**	TUES	**14**
MON	**15**	WED	**15**
TUES	**16**	THUR	**16**
WED	**17**	FRI	**17**
THUR	**18**	SAT	**18**
FRI	**19**	SUN	**19**
SAT	**20**	MON	**20**
SUN	**21**	TUES	**21**
MON	**22**	WED	**22**
TUES	**23**	THUR	**23**
WED	**24**	FRI	**24**
THUR	**25**	SAT	**25**
FRI	**26**	SUN	**26**
SAT	**27**	MON	**27**
SUN	**28**	TUES	**28**
MON	**29**	WED	**29**
TUES	**30**	THUR	**30**
		FRI	**31**

MONDAY 1 NOVEMBER 1937

Teddy Wilson and his Orchestra recording session in New York for Brunswick. John Hammond is the producer and the band is: BUCK CLAYTON (t), PRINCE ROBINSON (cl/ts), VIDO MUSSO (cl/ts), TEDDY WILSON (p), ALLAN REUSS (g), WALTER PAGE (b), COZY COLE (d)
Nice Work If You Can Get It / Things Are Looking Up / My Man / Can't Help Lovin' Dat Man

WEDNESDAY 3 NOVEMBER 1937

On the last night of the Meadowbrook Lounge engagement the CBS broadcast direct from the club is recorded by John Hammond. The Basie Orchestra now comprises: ED LEWIS, BOBBY MOORE, BUCK CLAYTON (t), DAN MINOR, BENNY MORTON, EDDIE DURHAM (tb), EARLE WARREN (as), LESTER YOUNG (cl/ts), HERSCHEL EVANS (ts), JACK WASHINGTON (bs), COUNT BASIE (p), FREDDIE GREEN (g), WALTER PAGE (b), JO JONES (d), JIMMY RUSHING, BILLIE HOLIDAY (v)
Theme – Moten Swing / One O'Clock Jump / I Can't Get Started (v BILLIE HOLIDAY) */ A Study In Brown / Rhythm In My Nursery Rhymes* (v JIMMY RUSHING) */ John's Idea / Good Morning Blues* (v JIMMY RUSHING) */ Dinah* (v JIMMY RUSHING)

FRIDAY 5 NOVEMBER 1937

Billie and the Basie Band begin a week at the Apollo Theatre in Harlem. Also appearing on the bill are Butterbeans & Susie, The Three Miller Brothers, Big Time Crip, Hilda Rogers, Paul Bass, Honey Brown, John Mason and John Vigal.

WEDNESDAY 10 NOVEMBER 1937

The Amateur Hour at the Apollo is broadcast on station WMCA.

THURSDAY 11 NOVEMBER 1937

Closing night at the Apollo.

FRIDAY 12 NOVEMBER 1937

Billie and the Basie Band begin a week at the Howard Theatre, Washington.

THURSDAY 18 NOVEMBER 1937

Closing night at the Howard Theatre.

FRIDAY 19 NOVEMBER 1937

Billie and the Basie Band play at a dance organised by Elsa Maxwell at Princeton University, Princeton, New Jersey.

The rest of the year consists of a tour of one-nighters including 1 week at Fox Theatre in Detroit in early December and the last two weeks of December at the Grand Theatre, Philadelphia.
On the road heading for Philadelphia, some of the band play dice. Jo Jones recalls:

BILLIE WAS LEFT-HANDED AND SHE NEVER SHOT DICE IN HER LIFE. LESTER YOUNG HAD ONE DOLLAR AND HE SAID, "COME ON, BILLIE, SHOOT THIS DOLLAR FOR ME." SHE'S IN THE BACK OF THE BUS … SHE BROKE UP EVERYBODY. SHE JUST TOOK EVERYBODY'S MONEY BECAUSE THEY TOLD HER WRONG AND SHE SHOT THE DICE WRONG AND BROKE THE WHOLE BAND … THIS WAS A VERY CUTE THING … YOU'RE TELLING SOMEBODY WRONG AND SHE DIDN'T KNOW WHAT SHE'S DOING BUT SHE'S WINNING!

SAT	1
SUN	2
MON	3
TUES	4
WED	5
THUR	6
FRI	7
SAT	8
SUN	9
MON	10
TUES	11
WED	12
THUR	13
FRI	14
SAT	15
SUN	16
MON	17
TUES	18
WED	19
THUR	20
FRI	21
SAT	22
SUN	23
MON	24
TUES	25
WED	26
THUR	27
FRI	28
SAT	29
SUN	30
MON	31

SATURDAY 1 JANUARY 1938
Billie and the Basie Band play at a dance at Roseland in Boston.

SUNDAY 2 JANUARY 1938
Billie and the Basie Band play at a dance in Hamilton Park, Waterbury, Connecticut.

MONDAY 3 JANUARY 1938
The Basie Orchestra, without Billie, record for Decca in New York. Billie is unable to record with Basie as she is under contract to ARC/Columbia.
Georgianna (v Jimmy Rushing) / *Blues In TheDark* (v Jimmy Rushing)
Billie has four days off.

THURSDAY 6 JANUARY 1938
Recording session with the Teddy Wilson Orchestra for Columbia in NYC. The session is produced by John Hammond with Buck Clayton (t), Lester Young (ts), Benny Morton (tb), Teddy Wilson (p), Freddie Green (g), Walter Page (b), Jo Jones (d)
My First Impression Of You (2 takes) / *When You're Smiling* (2 takes) / *I Can't Believe That You're In Love With Me* (2 takes) / *If Dreams Come True* (2 takes)

FRIDAY 7 JANUARY 1938
Billie and the Basie Band open a two-night engagement at the Astor Theatre on Times Square in New York.

SATURDAY 8 JANUARY 1938
Billie and the Basie Band close at the Astor Theatre.

WEDNESDAY 12 JANUARY 1938
Recording session for Columbia in New York as Billie Holiday and her Orchestra. The producer is Bernie Hanighen and the band is: Buck Clayton (t), Lester Young (ts), Benny Morton (tb), Teddy Wilson (p), Freddie Green (g), Walter Page (b), Jo Jones (d)
Now They Call It Swing (3 takes) / *On The Sentimental Side* (2 takes) / *Back In Your Own Backyard* (2 takes) / *When A Woman Loves A Man* (2 takes)

FRIDAY 14 JANUARY 1938
Billie and the Basie Band at Johnson City, New York.

SATURDAY 15 JANUARY 1938
Billie and the Basie Band at Scranton, Pennsylvania.

The poster announces the 20–26 January appearance of Billie and the Basie Band in the stage show at Loew's State in Times Square, New York City.

SAT	1
SUN	2
MON	3
TUES	4
WED	5
THUR	6
FRI	7
SAT	8
SUN	9
MON	10
TUES	11
WED	12
THUR	13
FRI	14
SAT	15
SUN	16
MON	17
TUES	18
WED	19
THUR	20
FRI	21
SAT	22
SUN	23
MON	24
TUES	25
WED	26
THUR	27
FRI	28
SAT	29
SUN	30
MON	31

SUNDAY 16 JANUARY 1938

Members of the Basie Band appear at the famous Benny Goodman Carnegie Hall Concert in New York. Afterwards, the band and Billie appear at the Savoy Ballroom in Harlem, in a Battle of the Bands with Chick Webb's Orchestra.

Down Beat described the event:

The affair drew a record attendance and hundreds were turned away at the box office with the crowd tying up traffic for several blocks in that vicinity. Applause for both bands was tremendous and it was difficult to determine which band was the more popular.

Nevertheless, the ballot taken showed Chick Webb's band well in the lead over Basie's and Ella Fitzgerald well out in front over Billie Holliday (sic) and James Rushing...

Feeling ran very high between the supporters of the two bands, and it was a fight to the finish. Both bands played magnificently, with Basie having a particular appeal for the dancers, and Webb consistently stealing the show on the drums. Ella caused a sensation with her rendition of 'Loch Lomond', and Billie Holiday thrilled her fans with 'My Man'. When Ella sang she had the whole crowd rocking with her. James Rushing had everybody shouting the blues right along with him. Handkerchiefs were waving, people were shouting, the excitement was intense...

General consensus of opinion agreed that both bands played magnificently making the decision a very close one.

MONDAY 17 JANUARY 1938

Billie and the Basie Band play a one-nighter at The Ritz, Pottsville, Pennsylvania.

THURSDAY 20 JANUARY 1938

Billie and the Basie Band begin a week at Loew's State Theatre, New York City.

WEDNESDAY 26 JANUARY 1938

Billie and the Basie Band complete their week at Loew's State Theatre.

FRIDAY 28 JANUARY 1938

Billie and the Basie Band play a one-nighter at The Casino, Washington DC.

SUNDAY 30 JANUARY 1938

Billie and the Basie Band play a one-nighter in Harrisburg, Pennsylvania.

TUES	1
WED	2
THUR	3
FRI	4
SAT	5
SUN	6
MON	7
TUES	8
WED	9
THUR	10
FRI	11
SAT	12
SUN	13
MON	14
TUES	15
WED	16
THUR	17
FRI	18
SAT	19
SUN	20
MON	21
TUES	22
WED	23
THUR	24
FRI	25
SAT	26
SUN	27
MON	28

WEDNESDAY 2 FEBRUARY 1938
Billie and the Basie Band play a Battle of the Bands with Lucky Millinder's Orchestra at The Armory, Baltimore, Maryland. Harry Edison is playing trumpet with Lucky Millinder, impresses Basie, and joins the Basie Band shortly afterwards.

THURSDAY 3 FEBRUARY 1938
Billie and the Basie Band play a one-nighter at the High School in Red Bank, New Jersey – Basie's home town.

FRIDAY 4 FEBRUARY 1938
Billie and the Basie Band play a one-nighter at Williamstown College, Williamstown, Massachusetts.

SATURDAY 5 FEBRUARY 1938
Billie and the Basie Band play a one-nighter in Portland, Maine.

THURSDAY 10 FEBRUARY 1938
Billie and the Basie Band play a one-nighter at Cornell University, Ithaca, New York.

FRIDAY 11 FEBRUARY 1938
Billie and the Basie Band play a one-nighter in Rochester, New York.

SATURDAY 12 FEBRUARY 1938
Billie and the Basie Band play a return one-nighter at Cornell University, Ithaca, New York.

WEDNESDAY 16 FEBRUARY 1938
The Count Basie Orchestra, without Billie, record for Decca in New YorkCity.
Buck Clayton, Ed Lewis, Harry Edison (t), Benny Morton, Dan Minor, Eddie Durham (tb), Earle Warren (as), Lester Young (cl/ts), Herschel Evans (cl/ts), Jack Washington (as/bs), Count Basie (p), Freddie Green (g), Walter Page (b), Jo Jones (d), Jimmy Rushing (v)
Sent For You Yesterday And Here You Come Today (v Jimmy Rushing) / *Every Tub* / *Now Will You Be Good?* (v Jimmy Rushing) / *Swinging The Blues*

THURSDAY 17 FEBRUARY 1938
Billie and the Basie Band play a one-nighter in Wilmington, Delaware.

FRIDAY 18 FEBRUARY 1938
Billie and the Basie Band play a one-nighter at The Strand in Philadelphia.

SUNDAY 20 FEBRUARY 1938
Billie and the Basie Band play a one-nighter at Club Fordham in the Bronx, New York.

TUESDAY 22 FEBRUARY 1938
Billie and the Basie Band play a one-nighter at the Roseland Ballroom, New York City. Also involved in the Battle of the Bands are Don Redman, Zinn Arthur and Gene Kardos.

FRIDAY 25 FEBRUARY 1938
Billie and the Count Basie Orchestra begin a week at the Apollo Theatre, Harlem, New York City.

SATURDAY 26 FEBRUARY 1938
Billie and the Count Basie Orchestra at the Apollo Theatre, Harlem, New York City.
Bob Inman, a young swing fan, is at the 2.15pm show where Billie sings five numbers: *Underneath The Stars* / *Nice Work If You Can Get It* / *I Can't Get Started* / *Living For You* / *One Never Knows*. He notes:
'Holiday's hair used to be red, but now is black!'

SUNDAY 27 FEBRUARY 1938
Billie and the Basie Band appear at the Criterion Theatre, New York at 11am on Sunday Swing Concert.

TUES	**1**
WED	**2**
THUR	**3**
FRI	**4**
SAT	**5**
SUN	**6**
MON	**7**
TUES	**8**
WED	**9**
THUR	**10**
FRI	**11**
SAT	**12**
SUN	**13**
MON	**14**
TUES	**15**
WED	**16**
THUR	**17**
FRI	**18**
SAT	**19**
SUN	**20**
MON	**21**
TUES	**22**
WED	**23**
THUR	**24**
FRI	**25**
SAT	**26**
SUN	**27**
MON	**28**
TUES	**29**
WED	**30**
THUR	**31**

Billie Thru With Basie, In New Spot

NEW YORK CITY, Mar. 3—Fresh from a sensational engagement at the Apollo Theatre and her last with Count Basie and his orchestra Billie Holiday, one of the modern delineators of swing songs, will go into Clark Monroe's Uptown House in Harlem for an indefinite engagement.

Others in the Uptown House revue are: Clarence Weems, emcee; Joe Smothers, Mae Arthur, Bernice Robinson, Toy (Mad Genius) Wilson and Clark Monroe himself, whose ability as a dancer, is second to his ability as a host.

BILLIE HOLIDAY TO BE FEATURED IN ALL-WHITE BAND

NEW YORK, March 17–Billie Holiday, who ranks third in the top list of the nation's singers of swing songs, this week moves into history-making channels of coloured theatricals, having become the second coloured girl to be chosen to feature in an all-white band. Signed last week, Miss Holiday departed for Boston last Saturday where she will join the all-white aggregation of Artie Shaw, who, this week, opened a three months engagement at the Roseland State Ballroom there. The contract given Billie to act as a part of this outfit is an indefinite one, and unless racial prejudices intervene, she will remain with the band from now on.

WEDNESDAY 2 MARCH 1937
The Amateur Hour at the Apollo is broadcast on station WMCA.

THURSDAY 3 MARCH 1938
The closing night at the Apollo is also Billie's last engagement with the Basie Band. She leaves after the final show.

WEDNESDAY 9 MARCH 1938
Billie sings with Artie Shaw as a tryout at the Harvest Moon Ball in Madison Square Garden.

SATURDAY 12 MARCH 1938
Billie leaves for Boston to join Artie Shaw.

TUESDAY 15 MARCH 1938
Billie joins the Artie Shaw Orchestra and opens at Roseland-State Ballroom, Boston for a three-month engagement.

Art Shaw set for next three months at Roseland-State Ballroom, Boston.
Plays Tuesdays and Saturdays. Plays Cy Shribman's string of New England ballrooms other nights. Broke all box office records opening night. Capacity ever since.

SATURDAY 17 MARCH 1938
Billie and the Artie Shaw Orchestra appear at Roseland-State Ballroom, Boston.

TUESDAY 22 MARCH 1938
Billie and the Artie Shaw Orchestra appear at Roseland-State Ballroom, Boston.
The orchestra do a 30 minute broadcast on WABC at midnight.

SATURDAY 26 MARCH 1938
Billie and the Artie Shaw Orchestra appear at Roseland-State Ballroom, Boston.

SUNDAY 27 MARCH 1938
Billie travels to New York to visit her mother, Sadie, who is ill.

TUESDAY 29 MARCH 1938
Billie and the Artie Shaw Orchestra appear at Roseland-State Ballroom, Boston.
The orchestra do a 30 minute broadcast on WABC at midnight.

FRI	**1**
SAT	**2**
SUN	**3**
MON	**4**
TUES	**5**
WED	**6**
THUR	**7**
FRI	**8**
SAT	**9**
SUN	**10**
MON	**11**
TUES	**12**
WED	**13**
THUR	**14**
FRI	**15**
SAT	**16**
SUN	**17**
MON	**18**
TUES	**19**
WED	**20**
THUR	**21**
FRI	**22**
SAT	**23**
SUN	**24**
MON	**25**
TUES	**26**
WED	**27**
THUR	**28**
FRI	**29**
SAT	**30**

SATURDAY 2 APRIL 1938
Billie and the Artie Shaw Orchestra appear at Roseland-State Ballroom, Boston.

TUESDAY 5 APRIL 1938
Billie and the Artie Shaw Orchestra appear at Roseland-State Ballroom, Boston.
The orchestra do a 30 minute broadcast on WABC at midnight.

THURSDAY 7 APRIL 1938
Billie's 23rd birthday.

FRIDAY 8 APRIL 1938
Artie Shaw makes a guest appearance on the Paul Whiteman/Chesterfield radio show (WABC 8.30–9.00pm).

SATURDAY 9 APRIL 1938
Billie and the Artie Shaw Orchestra appear at Roseland-State Ballroom, Boston.

TUESDAY 12 APRIL 1938
Billie and the Artie Shaw Orchestra appear at Roseland-State Ballroom, Boston.
The orchestra do a 30 minute broadcast on WABC at midnight.

SATURDAY 16 APRIL 1938
Billie and the Artie Shaw Orchestra appear at Roseland-State Ballroom, Boston.

EASTER SUNDAY 17 APRIL 1938
Billie and the Artie Shaw Orchestra appear at Reade's Casino, Asbury Park, New Jersey.

TUESDAY 19 APRIL 1938
Billie and the Artie Shaw Orchestra appear at Roseland-State Ballroom, Boston.
The orchestra do a 30 minute broadcast on WABC at midnight.

SATURDAY 23 APRIL 1938
Billie and the Artie Shaw Orchestra appear at Roseland-State Ballroom, Boston.

TUESDAY 26 APRIL 1938
Billie and the Artie Shaw Orchestra appear at Roseland-State Ballroom, Boston.
The orchestra do a 30 minute broadcast on WABC at midnight.

SATURDAY 30 APRIL 1938
Billie and the Artie Shaw Orchestra appear at Roseland-State Ballroom, Boston.

A rare picture (courtesy of Bob Inman) of Billie with Artie Shaw and the Orchestra at the Roseland State Ballroom in Boston.

SUN	1
MON	2
TUES	3
WED	4
THUR	5
FRI	6
SAT	7
SUN	8
MON	9
TUES	10
WED	11
THUR	12
FRI	13
SAT	14
SUN	15
MON	16
TUES	17
WED	18
THUR	19
FRI	20
SAT	21
SUN	22
MON	23
TUES	24
WED	25
THUR	26
FRI	27
SAT	28
SUN	29
MON	30
TUES	31

TUESDAY 3 MAY 1938

Billie and the Artie Shaw Orchestra appear at Roseland-State Ballroom, Boston.
The orchestra do a 30 minute broadcast on WABC at midnight.

The May issue of *Metronome* reports:

Boston news – The Back Bay section of the Hub city has been rockin' solid for the past few weeks to the rhythm of Chick Webb and Art Shaw. Chick and his great swingstress Ella Fitzgerald are still packing them in at Levaggi's while right next door at the State, the new Shaw-Holiday combo is drawing record gates. The addition of Billie Holiday to Shaw's band has put this outfit in top brackets. Band is plenty solid with leader Shaw stealing the show with his clarinet work. 'Wee Maxie' Kaminsky, Tony Pastor and Les Burness are the most consistent performers in the band. Drummer Cliff Leeman, the nucleus of a very solid rhythm section is getting plenty of attention from the fans with his wild man act. Most interested of all seems to be Nita Bradley, who drops over from her Hi Hat spot at every chance. Some of Webb's band sneak in more than often to catch Shaw's music. Webb has been NBC'd twice weekly and Shaw is filling CBS ether.

SATURDAY 7 MAY 1938

Billie and the Artie Shaw Orchestra appear at Roseland-State Ballroom, Boston.

TUESDAY 10 MAY 1938

Billie and the Artie Shaw Orchestra appear at Roseland-State Ballroom, Boston.
The orchestra do a 30 minute broadcast on WABC at midnight.

WEDNESDAY 11 MAY 1938

Recording session as Billie Holiday and her Orchestra for Columbia in NYC. The band is: BERNARD ANDERSON (t), BUSTER BAILEY (cl), BABE RUSSIN (ts), CLAUDE THORNHILL (p), JOHN KIRBY (b), COZY COLE (d)
You Go To My Head (2 takes) / *The Moon Looks Down And Laughs* (2 takes) / *If I Were You* / *Forget If You Can*

SATURDAY 14 MAY 1938

Billie and the Artie Shaw Orchestra appear at Roseland-State Ballroom, Boston.

MONDAY 16 MAY 1938

Billie and the Artie Shaw Orchestra appear at Nuttings on the-Charles, Waltham, Massachusetts opposite the Red Norvo Band and Mildred Bailey.

Metronome reports:

The greatest attraction of the month was the battle staged at Nuttings between Art Shaw and Red Norvo. Shaw who had previously nicked Tommy Dorsey at Dartmouth also edged Norvo who was making his initial New England stand. Billie Holiday and Mildred Bailey waged a war within a war with Nita Bradley re-engaged by Shaw, doing her bit between rounds.

TUESDAY 17 MAY 1938

Billie and the Artie Shaw Orchestra appear at Roseland-State Ballroom, Boston.
The orchestra do a 30 minute broadcast on WABC at midnight.

SATURDAY 21 MAY 1938

Billie and the Artie Shaw Orchestra appear at Roseland-State Ballroom, Boston.

TUESDAY 24 MAY 1938

Billie and the Artie Shaw Orchestra appear at Roseland-State Ballroom, Boston.
The orchestra do a 30 minute broadcast on WABC at midnight.

SATURDAY 28 MAY 1938

Billie and the Artie Shaw Orchestra appear at Roseland-State Ballroom, Boston.

TUESDAY 31 MAY 1938

Billie and the Artie Shaw Orchestra appear at Roseland-State Ballroom, Boston.
The orchestra do a 30 minute broadcast on WABC at midnight.

WED	1
THUR	2
FRI	3
SAT	4
SUN	5
MON	6
TUES	7
WED	8
THUR	9
FRI	10
SAT	11
SUN	12
MON	13
TUES	14
WED	15
THUR	16
FRI	17
SAT	18
SUN	19
MON	20
TUES	21
WED	22
THUR	23
FRI	24
SAT	25
SUN	26
MON	27
TUES	28
WED	29
THUR	30

SATURDAY 4 JUNE 1938
Billie and the Artie Shaw Orchestra appear at Roseland-State Ballroom, Boston.

TUESDAY 7 JUNE 1938
Billie and the Artie Shaw Orchestra appear at Roseland-State Ballroom, Boston.
The orchestra do a 30 minute broadcast on WABC starting at 11.30pm.

SATURDAY 11 JUNE 1938
Billie and the Artie Shaw Orchestra appear at Roseland-State Ballroom, Boston.

TUESDAY 14 JUNE 1938
Billie and the Artie Shaw Orchestra appear at Roseland-State Ballroom, Boston.
The orchestra do a 30 minute broadcast on WABC at midnight.

THURSDAY 23 JUNE 1938
Recording session as Billie Holiday and her Orchestra for Columbia in NYC. The session is produced by Bernie Hanighen.
The band is: CHARLIE SHAVERS (t), BUSTER BAILEY (cl), BEN WEBSTER (ts), CLAUDE THORNHILL (p), ALLAN REUSS (g), JOHN KIRBY (b), COZY COLE (d)
Havin' Myself A Time (2 takes) / *Says My Heart* (2 takes) / *I Wish I Had You* (2 takes) / *I'm Gonna Lock My Heart And Throw Away The Key* (2 takes)

SATURDAY 25 JUNE 1938
Billie and the Artie Shaw Orchestra appear at Philmont Country Club, Philadelphia, PA.

SUNDAY 26 JUNE 1938
Billie and the Artie Shaw Orchestra appear at Roton Point, South Norwalk, Connecticut.

TUESDAY 28 JUNE 1938
Billie and the Artie Shaw Orchestra appear at Johnson City, PA.

WEDNESDAY 29 JUNE 1938
Billie and the Artie Shaw Orchestra appear at Parkersberg, West Virginia.

THURSDAY 30 JUNE 1938
Billie and the Artie Shaw Orchestra appear at Charlestown, West Virginia.

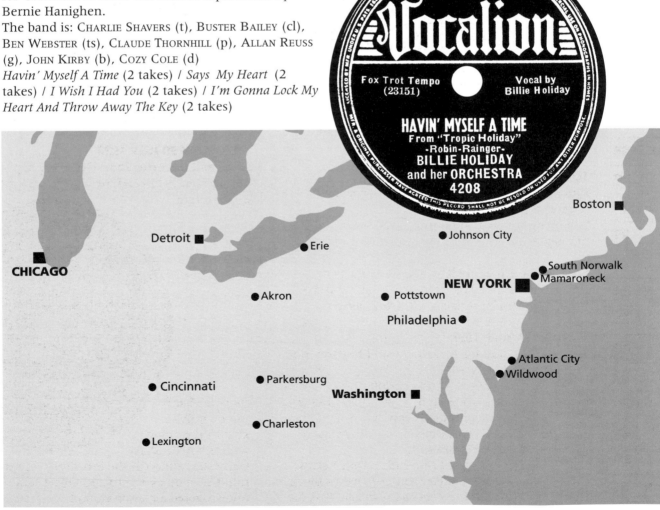

FRI	**1**
SAT	**2**
SUN	**3**
MON	**4**
TUES	**5**
WED	**6**
THUR	**7**
FRI	**8**
SAT	**9**
SUN	**10**
MON	**11**
TUES	**12**
WED	**13**
THUR	**14**
FRI	**15**
SAT	**16**
SUN	**17**
MON	**18**
TUES	**19**
WED	**20**
THUR	**21**
FRI	**22**
SAT	**23**
SUN	**24**
MON	**25**
TUES	**26**
WED	**27**
THUR	**28**
FRI	**29**
SAT	**30**
SUN	**31**

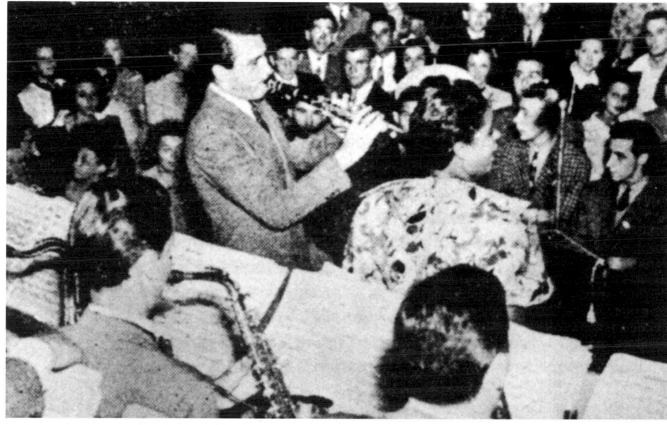

Billie with Artie Shaw and the Orchestra at the Million Dollar Pier, Atlantic City, New Jersey on Saturday 9th July.

SATURDAY 2 JULY 1938
Billie and the Artie Shaw Orchestra appear at the Sunnybrook Ballroom, Pottstown, PA.

TUESDAY 5 JULY 1938
Billie and the Artie Shaw Orchestra appear at Roseland-State Ballroom, Boston.
The orchestra do a 30 minute broadcast on WABC at midnight.

SATURDAY 9 JULY 1938
Billie and the Artie Shaw Orchestra appear at the Million Dollar Pier, Atlantic City, New Jersey.

SUNDAY 24 JULY 1938
Recording session for Artie Shaw and his Orchestra for Bluebird in New York.
ARTIE SHAW (cl), CHUCK PETERSON, JOHN BEST, CLAUDE BOWEN (t), GEORGE ARUS, TED VESELY, HARRY ROGERS (tb), LESLIE ROBINSON, HANK FREEMAN (as), RON PERRY, TONY PASTOR (ts), LESTER BURNESS (p), AL AVOLA (g), SID WEISS (b), CLIFF LEEMAN (d)
Begin The Beguine / Indian Love Call (v TONY PASTOR) / *Comin' On / Back Bay Shuffle / Any Old Time* (v BILLIE HOLIDAY) / *I Can't Believe That You're In Love With Me*

THURSDAY 28 JULY 1938
Billie and the Artie Shaw Orchestra appear at Summit Beach Park in Akron, Ohio. They draw 2,468 despite heavy rain.

SATURDAY 30 JULY 1938
Billie and the Artie Shaw Orchestra open at the Ocean Pier, Wildwood, New Jersey, for a one week engagement.

Any Old Time is Billie's only known recording with the Artie Shaw Orchestra, although she broadcast with them a number of times and there may be some undiscovered air shots around.

MON	1
TUES	2
WED	3
THUR	4
FRI	5
SAT	6
SUN	7
MON	8
TUES	9
WED	10
THUR	11
FRI	12
SAT	13
SUN	14
MON	15
TUES	16
WED	17
THUR	18
FRI	19
SAT	20
SUN	21
MON	22
TUES	23
WED	24
THUR	25
FRI	26
SAT	27
SUN	28
MON	29
TUES	30
WED	31

Chicago, August, 1938   **FEATURE NEWS**   DOWN

White Man's Jazz No Good for Holliday?

And Why Rate Phillips' Musical Miscarriages Over Teschmaker's Genius?

By Ted Locke

Boston, Mass.—It's a mystery to us why the true story of the Basie-Holliday split never came to light in print. The music mags all hinted that there was more to it than met the eye, but that was as far as they would carry it. Can it be that they were shielding John Hammond, who engineered the whole mephitic business! It really isn't any secret. Billie will talk, and with gestures. I imagine Basie will, if the Hammond hex can be lifted. At any rate, the affair should be made public property, even if it's only to show just how absurdly a dilettante critic can act when he allows his private quarrels to interfere with his artistic sensibilities.

It seems that Billie and Hammond had a few angry words, the result being that Billie received her notice. To save her own punctured pride, la Holliday immediately walked out, leaving Basie, who's a hell of a swell egg, deserving better breaks, holding the bag. The last time Billie was in New York, John got in touch with her and said he was sorry, but you see how it is . . . big critic . . . have to keep face . . . and all that sort of rot, you know. "I'm just a poor girl who lost her job," said Billie. It was left at that. Now everybody's happy . . . except Billie, the Count, Lester Young, and possibly John, who must by now realize what a damn lousy blow he has struck to the cause of good Jazz.

Artie Shaw finally

got a lot of rotten breaks, but the critics, at the crucial moment, when the logical successor to Pinetop needed plenty o~

FRIDAY 5 AUGUST 1938
Billie and the Artie Shaw Orchestra close at the Ocean Pier, Wildwood, New Jersey.

SATURDAY 6 AUGUST 1938
Billie and the Artie Shaw Orchestra appear at the Gateway Casino, Summersport, New Jersey.

SUNDAY 7 AUGUST 1938
Billie and the Artie Shaw Orchestra appear at Olcutt Beach (Mass or NY or PA).

SATURDAY 13 AUGUST 1938
Billie and the Artie Shaw Orchestra open at Eastwood Gardens, Detroit, for a 6-night engagement.

THURSDAY 18 AUGUST 1938
Billie and the Artie Shaw Orchestra close at Eastwood Gardens, Detroit.

FRIDAY 19 AUGUST 1938
Billie and the Artie Shaw Orchestra appear at Sandy Beach Park, Russell Point, Ohio.

SATURDAY 20 AUGUST 1938
Billie and the Artie Shaw Orchestra appear at Dunbar Cave, Clarkesville, Tennessee.

SUNDAY 21 AUGUST 1938
Billie and the Artie Shaw Orchestra appear at Coney Island, Cincinnati, Ohio.

MONDAY 22 AUGUST 1938
Billie and the Artie Shaw Orchestra appear at the Joyland Casino, Lexington, Kentucky.

TUESDAY 23 AUGUST 1938
Billie and the Artie Shaw Orchestra appear at Stonebrook Park, Stoneboro, Kentucky.

WEDNESDAY 24 AUGUST 1938
Billie and the Artie Shaw Orchestra appear at Hecia Park, Bellefonte, PA.

THURSDAY 25 AUGUST 1938
Billie and the Artie Shaw Orchestra appear at Summit Beach Park in Akron, Ohio.
Billboard reports:

Dateline Akron Ohio September 3rd; Art Shaw 'last Thursday' at Summit Beach Park Ballroom; new attendance record of 3,000 at 40c. Shaw topped his own draw of a month ago by 600.

FRIDAY 26 AUGUST 1938
Billie and the Artie Shaw Orchestra appear at the Eastern Show Club, Fordham Pavilion, Budd Lake, NJ.

SATURDAY 27 AUGUST 1938
Billie and the Artie Shaw Orchestra appear at the Beach Park Casino, Mamaroneck, New York.

SUNDAY 28 AUGUST 1938
Billie and the Artie Shaw Orchestra appear at Canadargo Park, Richfield Springs, New York.

MONDAY 29 AUGUST 1938
Billie and the Artie Shaw Orchestra appear at Waldamere Park, Erie, PA.

TUESDAY 30 AUGUST 1938
Billie and the Artie Shaw Orchestra appear at the Mapleview Ballroom, Washington.

WEDNESDAY 31 AUGUST 1938
Billie and the Artie Shaw Orchestra appear at the *Daily News* Harvest Moon Ball at Madison Square Garden in New York.

THUR	1
FRI	2
SAT	3
SUN	4
MON	5
TUES	6
WED	7
THUR	8
FRI	9
SAT	10
SUN	11
MON	12
TUES	13
WED	14
THUR	15
FRI	16
SAT	17
SUN	18
MON	19
TUES	20
WED	21
THUR	22
FRI	23
SAT	24
SUN	25
MON	26
TUES	27
WED	28
THUR	29
FRI	30

THURSDAY 8 SEPTEMBER 1938

Billie and the Artie Shaw Orchestra open at Eastwood Gardens in Detroit for a 4-night engagement.

SUNDAY 11 SEPTEMBER 1938

Billie and the Artie Shaw Orchestra close at Eastwood Gardens in Detroit.

THURSDAY 15 SEPTEMBER 1938

Recording session as Billie Holiday and her Orchestra for Vocalion/Columbia in New York.
BUCK CLAYTON (t), LESTER YOUNG (cl/ts), DICKIE WELLS (tb), MARGARET 'QUEENIE' JOHNSON (p), FREDDIE GREEN (g), WALTER PAGE (b), JO JONES (d)
The Very Thought Of You (2 takes) / *I Can't Get Started* (2 takes) / *I've Got A Date With A Dream* (2 takes) / *You Can't Be Mine*

FRIDAY 16 SEPTEMBER 1938

Billie and the Artie Shaw Orchestra appear in a band battle with Tommy Dorsey at the 105th Regiment Armory in New York City.

SUNDAY 18 SEPTEMBER 1938

Billie and the Artie Shaw Orchestra guest on the Magic Key radio show (NBC 2–3pm).
Nightmare / Indian Love Call / What Is This Thing Called Love? (BILLIE HOLIDAY)

TUESDAY 27 SEPTEMBER 1938

Billie is present at a recording session of the Kansas City Six in New York City. She coaches her lover, Freddie Green, as he takes the vocal on 'Them There Eyes'.
BUCK CLAYTON (trumpet), EDDIE DURHAM (trombone/electric guitar), LESTER YOUNG (clarinet/tenor sax), FREDDIE GREEN (guitar), WALTER PAGE (bass), JO JONES (drums)
'Way Down Yonder In New Orleans (2 takes) / *Countless Blues* (2 takes) / *Them There Eyes* (2 takes) / *I Want A Little Girl* (2 takes) / *Pagin' The Devil* (2 takes)

Artie Shaw Orchestra recording session for Bluebird in New York. Because of Billie's contract with Brunswick she is unable to take part and the vocals are by Helen Forrest.
Nightmare / Non-stop Flight / Yesterdays / What Is This Thing Called Love? / You're A Sweet Little Headache (vHF) / *I Have Eyes* (vHF)

FRIDAY 30 SEPTEMBER 1938

Billie and the Artie Shaw Orchestra begin a three-week residency at the Chase Hotel in St Louis. Helen Forrest joins the band and later recalls:

'I WAS SCARED TO DEATH. MY KNEES WERE SHAKING, I COULD HARDLY BOARD THE BUS FOR ST. LOUIS. BUT I GOT THERE. ARTIE EXPLAINED TO ME THAT BILLIE HOLIDAY WAS STILL WITH THE BAND BUT WAS GETTING READY TO GO OUT ON HER OWN. HE WAS WILLING TO TAKE ME ON EVEN BEFORE BILLIE LEFT. THAT WAS IN SEPTEMBER, 1938.'

SAT	1
SUN	2
MON	3
TUES	4
WED	5
THUR	6
FRI	7
SAT	8
SUN	9
MON	10
TUES	11
WED	12
THUR	13
FRI	14
SAT	15
SUN	16
MON	17
TUES	18
WED	19
THUR	20
FRI	21
SAT	22
SUN	23
MON	24
TUES	25
WED	26
THUR	27
FRI	28
SAT	29
SUN	30
MON	31

MONDAY 17 OCTOBER 1938

Billie and the Artie Shaw Orchestra travel to Chicago on their off-night to play a benefit for the Negro Christmas Basket Fund sponsored by the *Chicago Defender* at the Savoy Ballroom.
Billboard reports:

> '... Local Harlemites coughed up close to $3,500 last Monday eve to swing and sway to Artie Shaw when the ork took its night off from the Chase Hotel, St. Louis, to play at the Savoy Ballroom here' ... 'All attendance records were broken for the affair, the fifth, and Artie with his sepia songstress Billie Holiday had to work an extra half hour after pleading with the throng to go home.' ... 'only 4,500 tickets printed and all used up ...' 'Shaw worked a straight guarantee because it was a charity affair ...' ' ... broke Jimmy Dorsey attendance by far, who played gig last year' ... 'the crowd couldn't get enough of Shaw's jiving ... a surprise to Rockwell O'Keefe as Shaw is still not a name in this sector.'

c THURSDAY 20 OCTOBER 1938

Billie and the Artie Shaw Orchestra close at the Chase Hotel in St. Louis.

c SATURDAY 22 OCTOBER 1938

On the way back to New York after the Chase Hotel residency, Billie and the Shaw Orchestra play a prom one-nighter at the University of Indiana.

WEDNESDAY 26 OCTOBER 1938

Billie and the Artie Shaw Orchestra begin a residency at the Lincoln Hotel in New York. Soon after the opening, the hotel's owner and manager, Maria Kramer, tells Billie not to enter the Blue Room through the main entrance but to come through the kitchen with the rest of the band.

Billie later explains to Bill Chase of the *New York Amsterdam News*:

'Gee, it's funny, we were really a big hit all over the South and never ran into the color question until we opened at the Lincoln Hotel here in New York City. I was billed next to Artie himself, but was never allowed to visit the bar or the dining room, as did the other members of the band. Not only was I made to enter and leave the hotel through the kitchen but had to remain alone in a little dark room all evening until I was called on to do my numbers. And these numbers became fewer and fewer as time went on.'

Artie Shaw with Maria Kramer, owner and manager of the Lincoln Hotel in New York City.

MONDAY 31 OCTOBER 1938

Recording session with Teddy Wilson and his Orchestra for Brunswick in New York. John Hammond produces the session.
HARRY JAMES (t), EDGAR SAMPSON, BENNY CARTER (as), LESTER YOUNG, HERSCHEL EVANS (ts), BENNY MORTON (tb), TEDDY WILSON (p), AL CASEY (g), WALTER PAGE (b), JO JONES (d), BILLIE HOLIDAY (v)
Everybody's Laughin' / Here It Is Tomorrow Again

TUES	**1**
WED	**2**
THUR	**3**
FRI	**4**
SAT	**5**
SUN	**6**
MON	**7**
TUES	**8**
WED	**9**
THUR	**10**
FRI	**11**
SAT	**12**
SUN	**13**
MON	**14**
TUES	**15**
WED	**16**
THUR	**17**
FRI	**18**
SAT	**19**
SUN	**20**
MON	**21**
TUES	**22**
WED	**23**
THUR	**24**
FRI	**25**
SAT	**26**
SUN	**27**
MON	**28**
TUES	**29**
WED	**30**

WEDNESDAY 2 NOVEMBER 1938

Billie accompanies Artie Shaw to the Famous Door on 52nd Street for a farewell party for Count Basie.

THURSDAY 3 NOVEMBER 1938

The Artie Shaw Orchestra broadcasts from the Lincoln Hotel (WJZ 11.00–11.30pm). Billie is not a part of the broadcast, as Helen Forrest explains:

'... WE BOTH RECORDED <u>ANY OLD TIME</u> WITH ARTIE. ACTUALLY THAT WAS THE ONLY NUMBER SHE EVER RECORDED WITH HIM. AND SHE WAS NEVER ON HIS REMOTE BROADCASTS. A LOT OF PEOPLE INCLUDING HIS MANAGER, BOOKING AGENTS AND PRODUCERS PUT A LOT OF PRESSURE ON HIM NOT TO USE HER AND HE USED HER LESS AND LESS AS TIME WENT ON. HE HAD IT IN HIS MIND TO DO RIGHT BY HER, BUT HIS SKULL WAS CAVING IN FROM THE PRESSURE.'

WEDNESDAY 9 NOVEMBER 1938

Recording session with Teddy Wilson and his Orchestra for Brunswick in New York. John Hammond produces the session.
HARRY JAMES (t), EDGAR SAMPSON, BENNY CARTER (as), LESTER YOUNG, HERSCHEL EVANS (ts), BENNY MORTON (tb), TEDDY WILSON (p), AL CASEY (g), WALTER PAGE (b), JO JONES (d), BILLIE HOLIDAY (v)
Say It With A Kiss / April In My Heart (2 takes) / *I'll Never Fail You / They Say* (2 takes)

The Artie Shaw Orchestra, without Billie, broadcasts from the Lincoln Hotel (WEAF Midnight–12.30am).

THURSDAY 10 NOVEMBER 1938

The Artie Shaw Orchestra, without Billie, broadcasts from the Lincoln Hotel (WJZ 11.00–11.30pm).

WEDNESDAY 16 NOVEMBER 1938

The Artie Shaw Orchestra, without Billie, broadcasts from the Lincoln Hotel (WEAF Midnight–12.30am).

SUNDAY 20 NOVEMBER 1938

The Artie Shaw Orchestra, without Billie, starts Old Gold radio series with Robert Benchley and singer Dick Todd (WABC/CBS 10.00–10.30pm).

WEDNESDAY 23 NOVEMBER 1938

The Artie Shaw Orchestra, without Billie, broadcasts from the Lincoln Hotel (WEAF Midnight–12.30am).

THURSDAY 24 NOVEMBER 1938

The Artie Shaw Orchestra, without Billie, broadcasts from the Lincoln Hotel (WJZ 11.00–11.30pm).

SUNDAY 27 NOVEMBER 1938

The Artie Shaw Orchestra, without Billie, in second Old Gold radio show with Robert Benchley and singer Dick Todd (WABC/CBS 10.00–10.30pm).

MONDAY 28 NOVEMBER 1938

Recording session with Teddy Wilson and his Orchestra for Brunswick in New York. John Hammond produces the session.
BOBBY HACKETT (c), TOOTS MONDELLO, TED BUCKNER (as), CHU BERRY, BUD FREEMAN (ts), TRUMMY YOUNG (tb), TEDDY WILSON (p), AL CASEY (g), MILT HINTON (b), COZY COLE (d), BILLIE HOLIDAY (v)
You're So Desirable (2 takes) / *You're Gonna See A Lot Of Me* (2 takes) / *Hello My Darling* (2 takes) / *Let's Dream In The Moonlight* (2 takes)

WEDNESDAY 30 NOVEMBER 1938

The Artie Shaw Orchestra, without Billie, broadcasts from the Lincoln Hotel (WEAF Midnight–12.30am).

THUR	1
FRI	2
SAT	3
SUN	4
MON	5
TUES	6
WED	7
THUR	8
FRI	9
SAT	10
SUN	11
MON	12
TUES	13
WED	14
THUR	15
FRI	16
SAT	17
SUN	18
MON	19
TUES	20
WED	21
THUR	22
FRI	23
SAT	24
SUN	25
MON	26
TUES	27
WED	28
THUR	29
FRI	30
SAT	31

THURSDAY 1 DECEMBER 1938

The Artie Shaw Orchestra, without Billie, broadcasts from the Lincoln Hotel (WJZ 11.00–11.30pm).

SUNDAY 4 DECEMBER 1938

The Artie Shaw Orchestra, without Billie, in third Old Gold radio show with Robert Benchley and singer Dick Todd (WABC/CBS 10.00–10.30pm).

TUESDAY 6 DECEMBER 1938

The Artie Shaw Orchestra, without Billie, broadcasts from the Lincoln Hotel (WEAF Midnight–12.30am).

WEDNESDAY 7 DECEMBER 1938

The Artie Shaw Orchestra, without Billie, broadcasts from the Lincoln Hotel (WEAF Midnight–12.30am).

THURSDAY 8 DECEMBER 1938

The Artie Shaw Orchestra, without Billie, broadcasts from the Lincoln Hotel (WJZ 11.00–11.30pm).

c SATURDAY 10 DECEMBER

Billie leaves the Artie Shaw Orchestra.
Helen Forrest again:

THURSDAY 22 DECEMBER 1938

Café Society is scheduled to open, starring Billie Holiday, but is postponed due to a delay in obtaining a liquor licence.

FRIDAY 30 DECEMBER 1938

Café Society opens in Sheridan Square, Greenwich Village, New York. The club is owned by Barney Josephson and the entertainment is organised by John Hammond.
Billie is the star attraction. Also on the bill are the Frankie Newton Band, Big Joe Turner, and the Boogie Woogie Trio (Meade Lux Lewis, Albert Ammons, Pete Johnson). MC is comedian Jack Gilford. For the first few days, Billie is accompanied by Billy Kyle but he is soon replaced by Sonny White.

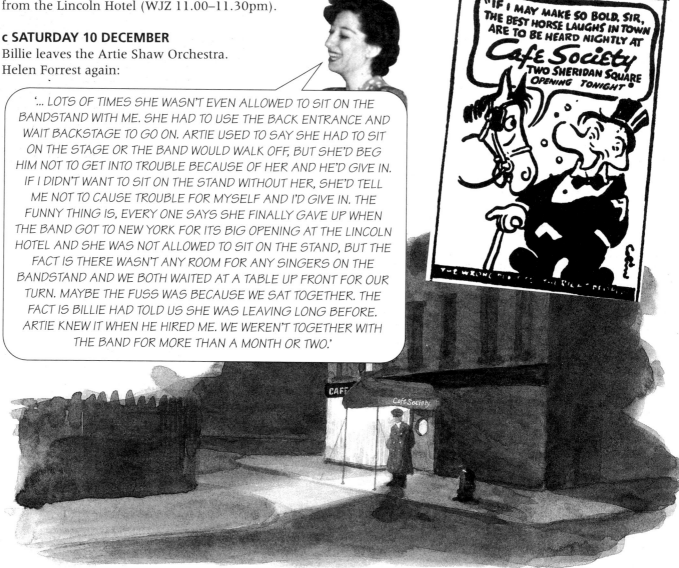

'... LOTS OF TIMES SHE WASN'T EVEN ALLOWED TO SIT ON THE BANDSTAND WITH ME. SHE HAD TO USE THE BACK ENTRANCE AND WAIT BACKSTAGE TO GO ON. ARTIE USED TO SAY SHE HAD TO SIT ON THE STAGE OR THE BAND WOULD WALK OFF, BUT SHE'D BEG HIM NOT TO GET INTO TROUBLE BECAUSE OF HER AND HE'D GIVE IN. IF I DIDN'T WANT TO SIT ON THE STAND WITHOUT HER, SHE'D TELL ME NOT TO CAUSE TROUBLE FOR MYSELF AND I'D GIVE IN. THE FUNNY THING IS, EVERY ONE SAYS SHE FINALLY GAVE UP WHEN THE BAND GOT TO NEW YORK FOR ITS BIG OPENING AT THE LINCOLN HOTEL AND SHE WAS NOT ALLOWED TO SIT ON THE STAND, BUT THE FACT IS THERE WASN'T ANY ROOM FOR ANY SINGERS ON THE BANDSTAND AND WE BOTH WAITED AT A TABLE UP FRONT FOR OUR TURN. MAYBE THE FUSS WAS BECAUSE WE SAT TOGETHER. THE FACT IS BILLIE HAD TOLD US SHE WAS LEAVING LONG BEFORE. ARTIE KNEW IT WHEN HE HIRED ME. WE WEREN'T TOGETHER WITH THE BAND FOR MORE THAN A MONTH OR TWO.'

SUN	**1**
MON	**2**
TUES	**3**
WED	**4**
THUR	**5**
FRI	**6**
SAT	**7**
SUN	**8**
MON	**9**
TUES	**10**
WED	**11**
THUR	**12**
FRI	**13**
SAT	**14**
SUN	**15**
MON	**16**
TUES	**17**
WED	**18**
THUR	**19**
FRI	**20**
SAT	**21**
SUN	**22**
MON	**23**
TUES	**24**
WED	**25**
THUR	**26**
FRI	**27**
SAT	**28**
SUN	**29**
MON	**30**
TUES	**31**

Throughout January, Billie is resident at Café Society, backed by the Frankie Newton Band.

TUESDAY 17 JANUARY 1939

Billie appears on the Camel Caravan Radio Show in New York.

Benny Goodman and his Orchestra are the stars : CY BAKER or IRVING GOODMAN, ZIGGY ELMAN, CHRIS GRIFFIN (t), RED BALLARD, VERNON BROWN (tb), BENNY GOODMAN (cl), NONI BERNARDI, HYMIE SCHERTZER (as), ARTHUR ROLLINI, JERRY JEROME (ts), JESS STACY (p), BEN HELLER (g), HARRY GOODMAN (b), BUDDY SCHUTZ (d).
BILLIE HOLIDAY (v), MARTHA TILTON (v), JOHNNY MERCER and LEO WATSON (v)
And The Angels Sing / I Cried For You (v BILLIE HOLIDAY) / *Jeepers Creepers* (v BILLIE HOLIDAY, MARTHA TILTON, JOHNNY MERCER, LEO WATSON) / *My Heart Belongs To Daddy* (v MARTHA TILTON) / *Hold Tight*

FRIDAY 20 JANUARY 1939

Recording session as Billie Holiday and her Orchestra for Vocalion/Columbia in New York. Bernie Hanighen is producer and the band is: CHARLIE SHAVERS (t), CHU BERRY (ts), TYREE GLENN (tb), SONNY WHITE (p), AL CASEY (g), JOHN WILLIAMS (b), COZY COLE (d), BILLIE HOLIDAY (v)
That's All I Ask Of You (2 takes) / *Dream of Life*

MONDAY 30 JANUARY 1939

Recording session with Teddy Wilson and his Orchestra for Brunswick in New York. John Hammond produces the session, but this is the last time he will be involved with a Billie Holiday recording.

ROY ELDRIDGE (t), ERNIE POWELL (cl/ts), BENNY CARTER (as), TEDDY WILSON (p), DANNY BARKER (g), MILT HINTON (b), COZY COLE (d), BILLIE HOLIDAY (v)
What Shall I Say? / It's Easy To Blame The Weather (2 takes) / *More Than You Know* (2 takes) / *Sugar*

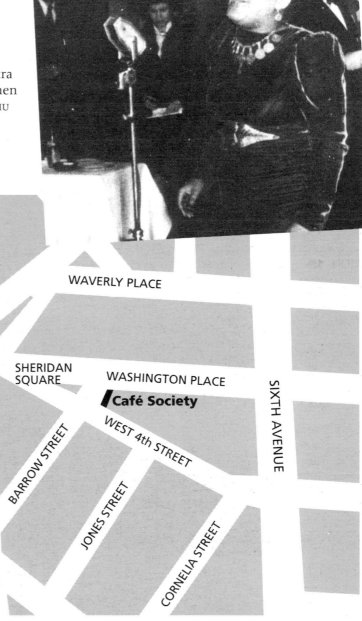

WED	1
THUR	2
FRI	3
SAT	4
SUN	5
MON	6
TUES	7
WED	8
THUR	9
FRI	10
SAT	11
SUN	12
MON	13
TUES	14
WED	15
THUR	16
FRI	17
SAT	18
SUN	19
MON	20
TUES	21
WED	22
THUR	23
FRI	24
SAT	25
SUN	26
MON	27
TUES	28

Throughout February, Billie is resident at Café Society, backed by the Frankie Newton Band.

FRIDAY 17 FEBRUARY 1939
Billie appears at the Friday Club, operated by Ernie Anderson and Paul Smith every Friday between 5 and 8pm at the Park Lane Hotel on Park Avenue. Eddie Condon was in charge of the music. Billie is backed by Joe Marsala, Pee Wee Russell, Bud Freeman, Hot Lips Page, Sterling Bose, Marty Marsala, Eddie Condon, Arthur Schutt, Morty Stuhlmaker and Zutty Singleton.

FRIDAY 24 FEBRUARY 1939
Billie appears at the Friday Club, between 5 and 8pm at the Park Lane Hotel on Park Avenue. Singer Lee Wiley is also on hand, along with Joe Marsala, Pee Wee Russell, Bud Freeman, Eddie Condon, Arthur Schutt, Morty Stuhlmaker and Zutty Singleton.

Billie at the Friday Club on 24 February. Joe Marsala is visible at the left.

WED	1
THUR	2
FRI	3
SAT	4
SUN	5
MON	6
TUES	7
WED	8
THUR	9
FRI	10
SAT	11
SUN	12
MON	13
TUES	14
WED	15
THUR	16
FRI	17
SAT	18
SUN	19
MON	20
TUES	21
WED	22
THUR	23
FRI	24
SAT	25
SUN	26
MON	27
TUES	28
WED	29
THUR	30
FRI	31

Throughout March, Billie is resident at Café Society, backed by the Frankie Newton Band.

TUESDAY 21 MARCH 1939
Recording session as Billie Holiday and her Orchestra for Vocalion in New York. Bernie Hanighen or Morty Palitz produce the session. HOT LIPS PAGE (t), TAB SMITH (ss/as), KENNETH HOLLON, STANLEY PAYNE (ts), KEN KERSEY (p), JIMMY McLIN (g), JOHN WILLIAMS (b), EDDIE DOUGHERTY (d), BILLIE HOLIDAY (v)
You're Too Lovely To Last (2 takes) / *Under A Blue Jungle Moon* (2 takes) / *Everything Happens For The Best* / *Why Did I Always Depend On You?* / *Long Gone Blues*

When Milt Gabler wants a blues for the recording session on 20 April, he and Billie sit down to write some blues verses and Gabler comes up with the phrase 'Fine and Mellow'.

A school teacher named Lewis Allen approaches Barney Josephson, the owner of Café Society, with a set of lyrics he has adapted from his poetry. It is set to music and Josephson suggests to Billie that she might sing it in the show. She agrees, and 'Strange Fruit' quickly becomes a big hit with the Café Society patrons. John Hammond refuses to record it for Columbia, but gives permission for Billie to record it with Milt Gabler on Commodore.

SAT	**1**
SUN	**2**
MON	**3**
TUES	**4**
WED	**5**
THUR	**6**
FRI	**7**
SAT	**8**
SUN	**9**
MON	**10**
TUES	**11**
WED	**12**
THUR	**13**
FRI	**14**
SAT	**15**
SUN	**16**
MON	**17**
TUES	**18**
WED	**19**
THUR	**20**
FRI	**21**
SAT	**22**
SUN	**23**
MON	**24**
TUES	**25**
WED	**26**
THUR	**27**
FRI	**28**
SAT	**29**
SUN	**30**

Throughout April, Billie is resident at Café Society, backed by the Frankie Newton Band.

Leonard Feather visits Café Society and reports in Melody Maker:
'Frankie Newton leads the regular band in this pleasant room which had modern decorations, and many brilliant murals to help the atmosphere. During the show the M.C. announced Billie Holiday who stood in a small jet of light, turned on her most wistful expression for the mike, and sang a number written specially for her, 'Strange Fruit', a grim and moving piece about lynching down South. Today she is recording this for a special Commodore Music Shop session.'

FRIDAY 7 APRIL 1939
Billie's 24th birthday

WEDNESDAY 19 APRIL 1939
Milt Gabler visits Billie at Café Society to get things set for the recording session next day. He wants a blues so he and Billie sit down to write some blues verses and Gabler comes up with the phrase 'Fine and Mellow'.

The Strange Fruit recording session. Right: Billie with Kenneth Hollon, Tab Smith, Stanley Payne and Sonny White. Below: Billie and Frankie Newton.

THURSDAY 20 APRIL 1939
Recording session for Milt Gabler's Commodore label at World Broadcasting Studio, 711 Fifth Avenue, New York City.
Billie is accompanied by the Café Society Band led by Frankie Newton.
FRANKIE NEWTON (t), TAB SMITH (ss/as), KENNETH HOLLON, STANLEY PAYNE (ts), SONNY WHITE (p), JIMMY McLIN (g), JOHN WILLIAMS (b), EDDIE DOUGHERTY (d), BILLIE HOLIDAY (v)
Strange Fruit (2 takes) / *Yesterdays* (2 takes) / *Fine And Mellow* / *I Gotta Right To Sing TheBlues* (2 takes)
Only Kenneth Hollon and the rhythm section accompany Billie on *Yesterdays*.

After the session Billie announces that she and pianist Sonny White are to marry.

MON	**1**
TUES	**2**
WED	**3**
THUR	**4**
FRI	**5**
SAT	**6**
SUN	**7**
MON	**8**
TUES	**9**
WED	**10**
THUR	**11**
FRI	**12**
SAT	**13**
SUN	**14**
MON	**15**
TUES	**16**
WED	**17**
THUR	**18**
FRI	**19**
SAT	**20**
SUN	**21**
MON	**22**
TUES	**23**
WED	**24**
THUR	**25**
FRI	**26**
SAT	**27**
SUN	**28**
MON	**29**
TUES	**30**
WED	**31**

Throughout May, Billie is resident at Café Society, backed by the Frankie Newton Band.

MONDAY 29 MAY 1939
Billie and Frankie Newton take a long break between sets at Café Society to appear at the National Swing Club of America's big concert at the Hippodrome. Billie is backed by Frankie Newton (trumpet), Charlie Barnet (tenor sax), Duke Ellington (piano), Sandy Block (bass) and Henry Adler (drums).

Below: Billie looking radiant as she performs for the Café Society crowd. And could that be humorist Sid Perelman sitting at ringside?

THUR	**1**
FRI	**2**
SAT	**3**
SUN	**4**
MON	**5**
TUES	**6**
WED	**7**
THUR	**8**
FRI	**9**
SAT	**10**
SUN	**11**
MON	**12**
TUES	**13**
WED	**14**
THUR	**15**
FRI	**16**
SAT	**17**
SUN	**18**
MON	**19**
TUES	**20**
WED	**21**
THUR	**22**
FRI	**23**
SAT	**24**
SUN	**25**
MON	**26**
TUES	**27**
WED	**28**
THUR	**29**
FRI	**30**

Throughout June, Billie is resident at Café Society, backed by the Frankie Newton Band.

Barney Josephson, the owner of Café Society, remembers the Billie Holiday of 1939, in a 1979 interview with Stanley Crouch:

> *BILLIE HOLIDAY WAS THIS KIND OF A GIRL, SHE DID WHAT SHE LIKED. IF A MAN SHE LIKED CAME UP, SHE'D GO WITH HIM; IF A WOMAN, THE SAME THING. IF SHE WAS HANDED A DRINK, SHE'D DRINK IT. **IF YOU HAD A STICK OF POT, SHE'D TAKE A CAB RIDE ON HER BREAK AND SMOKE IT.** IF YOU HAD SOMETHING STRONGER, SHE'D USE THAT. THAT WAS HER WAY. SHE DIDN'T APOLOGIZE FOR IT AND SHE DIDN'T FEEL ASHAMED. ALL SHE WANTED WAS TO HAVE FUN IN WHATEVER WAY IT STRUCK HER. SHE WAS SENSITIVE, SHE WAS PROUD. SHE COULD TELL A GOOD JOKE; SHE KNEW ALL THE WORDS TO USE IF YOU RUBBED HER THE WRONG WAY. **WHEN SHE TOLD YOU OFF, YOU WERE DAMN WELL TOLD – WHITE, BLACK, RICH, POOR.** SHE HAD A REAL ZEST FOR LIFE. AS A PERFORMER, SHE COULD MAKE YOU FALL IN LOVE, SHE COULD BREAK YOUR HEART. A LOT OF WHAT SHE DID ENDED UP BREAKING HER HEART. THAT WAS HER LIFE. THERE WAS NO OTHER PERSON ON THE FACE OF THIS EARTH WHO WAS LIKE HER. BILLIE HOLIDAY WAS A SINGLE EDITION.*

SAT	**1**
SUN	**2**
MON	**3**
TUES	**4**
WED	**5**
THUR	**6**
FRI	**7**
SAT	**8**
SUN	**9**
MON	**10**
TUES	**11**
WED	**12**
THUR	**13**
FRI	**14**
SAT	**15**
SUN	**16**
MON	**17**
TUES	**18**
WED	**19**
THUR	**20**
FRI	**21**
SAT	**22**
SUN	**23**
MON	**24**
TUES	**25**
WED	**26**
THUR	**27**
FRI	**28**
SAT	**29**
SUN	**30**
MON	**31**

Throughout July, Billie is resident at Café Society, backed by the Frankie Newton Band. The July issue of *Down Beat* reviews Billie's Commodore recordings:

—Charles Peterson Photo

Fine and Mellow is the name of the blues Billie Holiday sings in Milt Gabler's Commodore recording studios in Manhattan. Milt stands in the background, Sonny White is at the piano and the tenor is manned by Kenneth Hollon. Billie's four new Commodore sides are reviewed by Barrelhouse Dan below.

STRANGE FRUIT, FINE AND MELLOW, I GOTTA RIGHT TO SING THE BLUES and *YESTERDAYS*, all Commodore. Good and not so good.

Perhaps I expected too much of *Strange Fruit*, the ballyhooed Allan-Sacher tune which, via gory wordage and hardly any melody, expounds an anti-lynching campaign. At least I'm sure it's not for Billie, as for example, *Fine and Mellow* is. Accompanied by Sonny White, piano, and Frank Newton, trumpet, the latter is first-rate blues, convincingly sung. With a larger band, Billie clicks on *Gotta Right* and Jerome Kern's most melodious composition, *Yesterdays*. They are down her alley. But play all four at least three times before you say you didn't care for Billie. She's that subtle.

WEDNESDAY 5 JULY 1939

Recording session as Billie Holiday and her Orchestra for Vocalion/Columbia in New York. Bernie Hanighen or Morty Palitz produce. CHARLIE SHAVERS (t), TAB SMITH (ss/as), KENNETH HOLLON, STANLEY PAYNE (ts), SONNY WHITE (p), BERNARD ADDISON (g), JOHN WILLIAMS (b), EDDIE DOUGHERTY (d), BILLIE HOLIDAY (v)
Some Other Spring / Our Love Is Different / Them There Eyes / Swing, Brother, Swing

MONDAY 31 JULY 1939

Billie goes to the Famous Door on 52nd Street to hear Lester and the Basie Band. Coleman Hawkins arrives to hear Lester, having arrived back from Europe the same day. A party forms, including Billie, Ella Fitzgerald, Jimmie Lunceford, Charlie Shavers, Russell Procope, Coleman Hawkins, Buster Bailey and several others. At 4.30am they drive up to Harlem's 'Jimmie's Chicken Shack'.

TUES	1
WED	2
THUR	3
FRI	4
SAT	5
SUN	6
MON	7
TUES	8
WED	9
THUR	10
FRI	11
SAT	12
SUN	13
MON	14
TUES	15
WED	16
THUR	17
FRI	18
SAT	19
SUN	20
MON	21
TUES	22
WED	23
THUR	24
FRI	25
SAT	26
SUN	27
MON	28
TUES	29
WED	30
THUR	31

Early in August Billie accompanies Lester Young to a jam session at Puss Johnson's Tavern where Lester is involved in a cutting session with Coleman Hawkins, newly returned from Europe.

Billie closes at Café Society, possibly on Thursday 10 August.

FRIDAY 11 AUGUST 1939

Billie commences a week at the Apollo Theatre, Harlem. Also on the bill are Teddy Hill & his Band, The Boogie Woogie Trio, Big Joe Turner, Willie Bryant, Pigmeat Markham, Tip, Tap & Toe and The 16 Brownskin Dancing Beauties.

WEDNESDAY 16 AUGUST 1939

The Amateur Hour is broadcast from the Apollo via station WMCA.

THURSDAY 17 AUGUST 1939

Billie and the show closes at the Apollo.

AUGUST 1939

Billie attends a jam session at Burris Jenkins studio at W72nd and Riverside Drive. The session is put together by Ernie Anderson and Eddie Condon for *Life* magazine. Guest of honour is Harry Lim, and the roster of musicians includes Duke Ellington, Johnny Hodges, Cootie Williams, Rex Stewart, Juan Tizol, Cab Calloway, J. C. Higginbotham, Hot Lips Page, Cozy Cole, Dave Tough, Bud Freeman and many more.

WEDNESDAY 30 AUGUST 1939

Billie posts a letter to an English fan, Charles Saunders:

I received your letter and was glad to know I have a new friend and I have a plenty on new record on the market today in my own right and I hope to see you all soon. I am getting a manager now and I hope he send me there and when I get there I hope to make everyone like me and I expect to come very soon. Write again soon from B Holiday. Let me know if you want a picture.

Drummer Cozy Cole (left) jams with J.C.Higginbotham, Clyde Newcombe, Rex Stewart, Billie, Harry Lim, Eddie Condon, Max Kaminsky and Hot Lips Page.

SEPTEMBER 1939

FRI	1
SAT	2
SUN	3
MON	4
TUES	5
WED	6
THUR	7
FRI	8
SAT	9
SUN	10
MON	11
TUES	12
WED	13
THUR	14
FRI	15
SAT	16
SUN	17
MON	18
TUES	19
WED	20
THUR	21
FRI	22
SAT	23
SUN	24
MON	25
TUES	26
WED	27
THUR	28
FRI	29
SAT	30

Chicago, September, 1939

Bud Freeman, Billie Holiday To Open Chi's Off-Beat Club

Chicago — Bud Freeman, the great early-day Chicago tenor sax ace who left Goodman's and Dorsey's big bands to form his own little jam combination, will open with his jazz band at the Off-Beat Club here Sept. 15 along with Billie Holiday, rated by many to be the finest colored singer in the swing world.

Billie Holiday

Freeman, who won DOWN BEAT's popularity poll last winter, will bring Dave Tough, Max Kaminsky, Pee-Wee Russell, Eddie Condon, Dave Bowman and Clyde Newcomb with him. The band is making rec-

ords for RCA-Victor and is completing a run at Nick's in Greenwich Village, New York, this month.

The Off-Beat Club, which adjoins the famous Three Deuces, again will be managed by Carl Cons, managing editor of DOWN BEAT.

There's a chance that Ellington will come into the Sherman Christmas week, and it's definite that Tommy Dorsey's first long Chicago date starts Oct. 12 in the Empire room of the Palmer House. Added to this are Ella Fitzgerald's Sept. 18 opening at the Grand Terrace and a strong possibility that Charlie Barnet's gang will move down to the Hotel LaSalle October 1.

TUESDAY 5 SEPTEMBER 1939
Billie opens at Café Society opposite Stuff Smith's Band for 1 week.

MONDAY 11 SEPTEMBER 1939
Billie closes at Café Society. Later, she sits in with Count Basie at Monroe's Uptown House.

FRIDAY 15 SEPTEMBER 1939
Billie opens at the Off Beat Club in Chicago for a one-week engagement opposite Muggsy Spanier's Ragtimers. The club is downstairs at the Three Deuces and is partly owned by two *Down Beat* writers, Carl Conns and Glenn Burrs.

SATURDAY 23 SEPTEMBER 1939
Billie closes at the Off Beat in Chicago.

SUNDAY 24 SEPTEMBER 1939
Billie returns to Harlem to give a benefit concert for the Women's Welfare Club at Westchester County Center.

MONDAY 25 SEPTEMBER 1939
Billie returns to Chicago for another two weeks at the Off Beat Club, this time backed by Jimmy McPartland's Band: McPartland (cornet), Joe Rushton (clarinet), Joe Masek (tenor sax), Floyd Bean (piano), Pat Patterson (bass), Harry Jaeger (drums). *Down Beat* publishes a photograph of Frank Sinatra sitting in rapt attention at the club listening to Billie.

Left: Down Beat announces Billie's stint at the Off Beat Club. Bud Freeman didn't make it and Muggsy Spanier backs Billie for the first week. Below: Billie performing at the club in front of the Jimmy McPartland Band.

SUN	1
MON	2
TUES	3
WED	4
THUR	5
FRI	6
SAT	7
SUN	8
MON	9
TUES	10
WED	11
THUR	12
FRI	13
SAT	14
SUN	15
MON	16
TUES	17
WED	18
THUR	19
FRI	20
SAT	21
SUN	22
MON	23
TUES	24
WED	25
THUR	26
FRI	27
SAT	28
SUN	29
MON	30
TUES	31

Billie features quite heavily in the October editions of Down Beat.

The Pretty Teeth, the gardenia, pearls and two very good cats surround Billie Holiday in this shot snapped at the Off Beat Club. Dave Matthews, Harry James' alto man, grins over the head of Vido Musso, now in New York organizing a band.

Just Canned on blue-bird disks with the Bob Chester outfit, Kitty Lane, at ... was also just canne... the Chester com... of Dodie O'N... Teagarden ... did not sob in ... b...

'Les Young Wasn't Carved' -- Holiday

Chicago — Refuting statements made by members of Fats Waller's band and other colored musicians who were there, Billie Holiday last week branded reports that Coleman Hawkins "carved" Les Young in a tenor dual at Puss Johnson's tavern in Harlem as "unfair" to Les. "Young really cut the Hawk," said Billie, "and most everyone there who saw them tangle agreed on that."

Billie Holiday, McPartland Are Off-Beat Stars

Chicago—A highlight of the fall nitery season here last month was the reopening of the Off-Beat Club, managed by Carl Cons, which featured the singing of Billie Holiday and the ragtime music of Muggsy Spanier.

Spanier's band played the first week to record crowds, giving way Sept. 23 to Jimmy McPartland's band. McPartland, one of the famed trumpeters in the old Wolverines band, is set at the spot indefinitely.

Making her first appearance in Chicago since she sang at the Grand Terrace in 1935, Miss Holiday has attracted musicians and jazz lovers from throughout the Middle West. Cons' policy of making the Off-Beat a hangout for musicians made the spot one of the most succesful in town last winter. Judging from current crowds—who are flocking to hear Billie and McPartland's group—the Off-Beat will be even more successful this season.

SATURDAY 7 OCTOBER 1939
Billie closes at the Off Beat in Chicago.

TUESDAY 17 OCTOBER 1939
Billie opens at Café Society opposite Joe Marsala and Joe Sullivan Orchestras.

With Billie Holiday back from a short shift to Chicago's Off-Beat Club, m.c. Jack Gilford's excellent laugh routines and the bands of Joe Marsala and Joe Sullivan, Café Society, in Greenwich Village, starts off on a new stretch with tried pulling power. Gilford's in his 35th week at the head of the short floor show, which consists of himself, Miss Holiday and the two bands.

Miss Holiday clicks with several tunes, capped by the unusual 'Strange Fruit' tune. Her delivery is most effective on the rhythmic ballad type. Here she did a n.s.g. 'Travellin', an okay 'Back In Your Own Backyard' and the 'Fruit' number. Latter has an undefined appeal though it's basically a depressing piece. There's no compromise with Miss Holiday's stuff; either patrons like her very much or they don't care for her at all.

Two bands round out the show with jam sessions that show both to advantage

Throughout the summer Billie corresponds with a young English bass player, Jack Surridge. The onset of war in Europe brings the correspondence to an end.

WED	1
THUR	2
FRI	3
SAT	4
SUN	5
MON	6
TUES	7
WED	8
THUR	9
FRI	10
SAT	11
SUN	12
MON	13
TUES	14
WED	15
THUR	16
FRI	17
SAT	18
SUN	19
MON	20
TUES	21
WED	22
THUR	23
FRI	24
SAT	25
SUN	26
MON	27
TUES	28
WED	29
THUR	30

WEDNESDAY 1 NOVEMBER 1939

Down Beat publishes a long article on Billie by Dave Dexter Jr.

I'll Never Sing With A Dance Band Again–Holiday

You sit with Billie Holiday and watch her smoke cigarets chain fashion. The first thing that strikes you is her frankness.

"I'll never sing with a dance band again," she tells you. "Because it never works out right for me. They wonder why I left Count Basie, and why I left Artie Shaw. Well I'll tell you why – and I've never told this before.

"Basie had too many managers – too many guys behind the scenes who told everybody what to do. The Count and I got along fine. And the boys in the band were wonderful all the time. But it was this and that, all the time, and I got fed up with it. Basie didn't fire me; I gave him my notice.

Bad Kicks With Shaw

"Artie Shaw was a lot worse. I had known him a long time, when he was strictly from hunger around New York, long before he got a band. At first we worked together okay, then his managers started belly-aching. Pretty soon it got so

I would sing just two numbers a night. When I wasn't singing I had to stay backstage. Artie wouldn't let me sit out front with the band. Last year when we were at the Lincoln Hotel the hotel management told me I had to use the back door. That was all right. But I had to ride up and down in freight elevators, and every night Artie made me stay upstairs in a little room without a radio or anything all the time I wasn't downstairs with the band singing.

"Finally it got so I would stay up there, all by myself, reading everything I could get my hands on, from 10 o'clock to nearly 2 in the morning, going downstairs to sing just one or two numbers. Then one night when we had an airshot Artie said he couldn't let me sing. I always was given two shots on each program. The real trouble was this – Shaw wanted to sign me to a 5-year contract and when I refused, it burned him. He was jealous of the applause I got when I made one of my few appearances with the band each night."

MONDAY 6 NOVEMBER 1939

Billie closes at Café Society.

Billie is reported as appearing at Ernie's in Greenwich Village, but this is possibly in late November, after the theatre date in Washington.

FRIDAY 10 NOVEMBER 1939

Billie opens as headliner at the Howard Theatre, Washington for a one-week engagement. Also on the bill are Don Redman's Orchestra and the Three Jones Boys.

WEDNESDAY 15 NOVEMBER 1939

Down Beat publishes a letter from Artie Shaw refuting the allegations made by Billie in the previous issue (see above).

It also reports on the possibility of a role for Billie in the forthcoming Broadway production of Dorothy Baker's 'Young Man With A Horn':

Billie said the producer would give her a part if she could take off 15 pounds of weight during the period before rehearsals. But Billie expressed herself dubious, declaring she's satisfied with her own size at present.

THURSDAY 16 NOVEMBER 1939

Billie closes at the Howard Theatre, Washington.

Left: Another long letter from Billie to Jack Surridge. Although semi-literate, Billie always showed great dedication in replying to fan letters.

FRI	1	MON	1
SAT	2	TUES	2
SUN	3	WED	3
MON	4	THUR	4
TUES	5	FRI	5
WED	6	SAT	6
THUR	7	SUN	7
FRI	8	MON	8
SAT	9	TUES	9
SUN	10	WED	10
MON	11	THUR	11
TUES	12	FRI	12
WED	13	SAT	13
THUR	14	SUN	14
FRI	15	MON	15
SAT	16	TUES	16
SUN	17	WED	17
MON	18	THUR	18
TUES	19	FRI	19
WED	20	SAT	20
THUR	21	SUN	21
FRI	22	MON	22
SAT	23	TUES	23
SUN	24	WED	24
MON	25	THUR	25
TUES	26	FRI	26
WED	27	SAT	27
THUR	28	SUN	28
FRI	29	MON	29
SAT	30	TUES	30
SUN	31	WED	31

MID DECEMBER 1939
Billie at Kelly's Stable.

WEDNESDAY 13 DECEMBER 1939
Recording session as Billie Holiday and her Orchestra for Vocalion/Columbia in New York. BUCK CLAYTON, HARRY EDISON (t), EARLE WARREN (as), LESTER YOUNG (ts), JACK WASHINGTON (bs), JOE SULLIVAN (p), FREDDIE GREEN (g), WALTER PAGE (b), JO JONES (d), BILLIE HOLIDAY (v)
Night And Day (2 takes) / *The Man I Love* / *You're Just A No-Account* / *You're A Lucky Guy*

MONDAY 1 JANUARY 1940
Billie comes 3rd in the Annual Down Beat poll, behind Ella Fitzgerald and Mildred Bailey.

SUNDAY 21 JANUARY 1940
Billie attends a birthday party for Inez Cavanaugh at the Golden Gate Ballroom on W135th Street in Harlem with Lester Young, Count Basie, Sonny White and Clark Monroe.

A few days later she is beaten up on Seventh Avenue, close to her apartment at 286 W142nd Street. The beating is attributed to her boyfriend, Jimmy Monroe, brother of Clark.

Above: Billie with Sonny White and Lester Young at the Golden Gate Ballroom for Inez Cavanaugh's birthday party. Right: Billie takes her turn at the microphone for an impromptu song.

FEBRUARY **1940**

THUR	**1**
FRI	**2**
SAT	**3**
SUN	**4**
MON	**5**
TUES	**6**
WED	**7**
THUR	**8**
FRI	**9**
SAT	**10**
SUN	**11**
MON	**12**
TUES	**13**
WED	**14**
THUR	**15**
FRI	**16**
SAT	**17**
SUN	**18**
MON	**19**
TUES	**20**
WED	**21**
THUR	**22**
FRI	**23**
SAT	**24**
SUN	**25**
MON	**26**
TUES	**27**
WED	**28**
THUR	**29**

FEBRUARY to APRIL 1940
Billie at Ernie's, New York City. (dates unconfirmed)

THURSDAY 29 FEBRUARY 1940
Recording session as Billie Holiday and her Orchestra in New York.
ROY ELDRIDGE (t), JIMMY POWELL, CARL FRYE (as), KERMIT SCOTT (ts), SONNY WHITE (p), LAWRENCE LUCIE (g), JOHN WILLIAMS (b), HAROLD 'DOC' WEST (d), BILLIE HOLIDAY (v)
Ghost of Yesterday / Body and Soul / What Is This Going To Get Us? / Falling In Love Again (2 takes)

Billie at the 29 January recording session.
Below: With Billie are (l to r) Sonny White (piano), Roy Eldridge (trumpet), John Williams (bass), Harold West (drums), Carl Frye (alto sax), Jimmy Powell (alto sax), Lawrence Lucie (guitar) and Kermit Scott (tenor sax).

FRI	**1**	MON	**1**
SAT	**2**	TUES	**2**
SUN	**3**	WED	**3**
MON	**4**	THUR	**4**
TUES	**5**	FRI	**5**
WED	**6**	SAT	**6**
THUR	**7**	SUN	**7**
FRI	**8**	MON	**8**
SAT	**9**	TUES	**9**
SUN	**10**	WED	**10**
MON	**11**	THUR	**11**
TUES	**12**	FRI	**12**
WED	**13**	SAT	**13**
THUR	**14**	SUN	**14**
FRI	**15**	MON	**15**
SAT	**16**	TUES	**16**
SUN	**17**	WED	**17**
MON	**18**	THUR	**18**
TUES	**19**	FRI	**19**
WED	**20**	SAT	**20**
THUR	**21**	SUN	**21**
FRI	**22**	MON	**22**
SAT	**23**	TUES	**23**
SUN	**24**	WED	**24**
MON	**25**	THUR	**25**
TUES	**26**	FRI	**26**
WED	**27**	SAT	**27**
THUR	**28**	SUN	**28**
FRI	**29**	MON	**29**
SAT	**30**	TUES	**30**
SUN	**31**		

SUNDAY 10 MARCH 1940

Billie posts a letter to her English fan, Charles Saunders:

Dear Charles, I don't know whether I sent you a picture but I am sure I did but if I didn't let me know again please and the praise you gave Artie he deserved is because he treatened me. Still don't say he not a good musician because he is good one of the best and I bet he will come back bigger than ever. Now you know Charles everybody will take advantage of you if they can because you just got to watch everybody that all but it won't be a next time because I will watch out next time. Well Charles write me again soon
from B Holiday

SUNDAY 16 MARCH 1940

Billie is guest star at New York Crisis Committee's cocktail party at the Witoka Club in Harlem.

MONDAY 17 MARCH 1940

Billie opens at the Howard Theatre in Washington for a one-week engagement.

SATURDAY 22 MARCH 1940

Billie closes at the Howard Theatre.

MONDAY 25 MARCH 1940

Billie opens at the Hotel Sherman in Chicago for a one-month engagement, broadcasting nightly.

SUNDAY 7 APRIL 1940

Billie's 25th birthday

SATURDAY 20 APRIL 1940

Billie closes at the Hotel Sherman in Chicago.

THURSDAY 25 APRIL 1940

Billie opens at Kelly's Stable opposite Roy Eldridge and his Band. She stays for 18 weeks.

Roy says:

SHE SEEMED TO HAVE SUCH RAPPORT WITH THE PEOPLE. BY THEN I'D BEEN RECORDING WITH BILLIE FOR YEARS, AND I'D SEEN HER IN CLUBS WAY BEFORE THAT – BUT AT KELLY'S I SAW SHE WAS A STAR.

WED	**1**	SAT	**1**
THUR	**2**	SUN	**2**
FRI	**3**	MON	**3**
SAT	**4**	TUES	**4**
SUN	**5**	WED	**5**
MON	**6**	THUR	**6**
TUES	**7**	FRI	**7**
WED	**8**	SAT	**8**
THUR	**9**	SUN	**9**
FRI	**10**	MON	**10**
SAT	**11**	TUES	**11**
SUN	**12**	WED	**12**
MON	**13**	THUR	**13**
TUES	**14**	FRI	**14**
WED	**15**	SAT	**15**
THUR	**16**	SUN	**16**
FRI	**17**	MON	**17**
SAT	**18**	TUES	**18**
SUN	**19**	WED	**19**
MON	**20**	THUR	**20**
TUES	**21**	FRI	**21**
WED	**22**	SAT	**22**
THUR	**23**	SUN	**23**
FRI	**24**	MON	**24**
SAT	**25**	TUES	**25**
SUN	**26**	WED	**26**
MON	**27**	THUR	**27**
TUES	**28**	FRI	**28**
WED	**29**	SAT	**29**
THUR	**30**	SUN	**30**
FRI	**31**		

Throughout May, Billie is resident at Kelly's Stable opposite Roy Eldridge and his Band.

WEDNESDAY 1 MAY 1940

Billie appears on the WOR radio programme *Sheep and Goats* at 8pm, accompanied by Clarence Profit and his Trio.

THURSDAY 9 MAY 1940

Billie is asked to appear on John Kirby's radio show *Flow Gently, Sweet Rhythm*, but refuses to appear when she realises that Ella Fitzgerald is also a guest.

WEDNESDAY 29 MAY 1940

Billie appears at a Midnight Benefit concert in aid of the Harlem Children's Center at the Apollo Theatre. Among the many star performers are Abbott & Costello, Danny Kaye, Count Basie Orchestra, Andy Kirk Orchestra, John Kirby Orchestra, Roy Eldridge Orchestra, Charlie Barnet's Orchestra and the Clarence Profit Trio.

Throughout June, Billie is resident at Kelly's Stable opposite Roy Eldridge and his Band.

FRIDAY 7 JUNE 1940

Recording session as Billie Holiday and her Orchestra for Columbia in New York City. Bernie Hanighen or possibly Morty Palitz produce.
ROY ELDRIDGE (t), BILL BOWEN, JOE ELDRIDGE (as), KERMIT SCOTT, LESTER YOUNG (ts), TEDDY WILSON (p), FREDDIE GREEN (g), WALTER PAGE (b), J.C. HEARD (d), BILLIE HOLIDAY (v)
I'm Pulling Through / Tell Me More / Laughing at Life (2 takes) / *Time On My Hands*

Joe Glaser places an ad in *Down Beat* to announce Billie & Roy's 18th week at Kelly's Stable

Kelly's Stable, New York City

MON	**1**	THUR	**1**	SUN	**1**
TUES	**2**	FRI	**2**	MON	**2**
WED	**3**	SAT	**3**	TUES	**3**
THUR	**4**	SUN	**4**	WED	**4**
FRI	**5**	MON	**5**	THUR	**5**
SAT	**6**	TUES	**6**	FRI	**6**
SUN	**7**	WED	**7**	SAT	**7**
MON	**8**	THUR	**8**	SUN	**8**
TUES	**9**	FRI	**9**	MON	**9**
WED	**10**	SAT	**10**	TUES	**10**
THUR	**11**	SUN	**11**	WED	**11**
FRI	**12**	MON	**12**	THUR	**12**
SAT	**13**	TUES	**13**	FRI	**13**
SUN	**14**	WED	**14**	SAT	**14**
MON	**15**	THUR	**15**	SUN	**15**
TUES	**16**	FRI	**16**	MON	**16**
WED	**17**	SAT	**17**	TUES	**17**
THUR	**18**	SUN	**18**	WED	**18**
FRI	**19**	MON	**19**	THUR	**19**
SAT	**20**	TUES	**20**	FRI	**20**
SUN	**21**	WED	**21**	SAT	**21**
MON	**22**	THUR	**22**	SUN	**22**
TUES	**23**	FRI	**23**	MON	**23**
WED	**24**	SAT	**24**	TUES	**24**
THUR	**25**	SUN	**25**	WED	**25**
FRI	**26**	MON	**26**	THUR	**26**
SAT	**27**	TUES	**27**	FRI	**27**
SUN	**28**	WED	**28**	SAT	**28**
MON	**29**	THUR	**29**	SUN	**29**
TUES	**30**	FRI	**30**	MON	**30**
WED	**31**	SAT	**31**		

Throughout July and August, Billie is resident at Kelly's Stable opposite Roy Eldridge and his Band. Billie and Roy close at the Stable in September, Una Mae Carlisle comes in to replace them.

TUESDAY 9 JULY 1940
Billie is in the audience at Café Society when Teddy Wilson opens with his new band.

THURSDAY 12 SEPTEMBER 1940
Recording session as Billie Holiday with Teddy Wilson and his Orchestra for Columbia in New York City.
ROY ELDRIDGE (t), GEORGIE AULD, DON REDMAN (as), JIMMY HAMILTON, DON BYAS (ts), TEDDY WILSON (p), JOHN COLLINS (g), AL HALL (b), KENNY CLARKE (d), BILLIE HOLIDAY (v)
I'm All For You (2 takes) / *I Hear Music* (2 takes) / *The Same Old Story* (3 takes) / *Practice Makes Perfect* (4 takes)

FRIDAY 27 SEPTEMBER 1940
Billie opens at the Apollo Theatre for a one week engagement. Also on the bill are Roy Eldridge and his Band, The Cats and the Fiddle, and Butterbeans and Susie.
Opening night sees the gala premiere of the film 'Am I Guilty?', starring black actor Ralph Cooper.

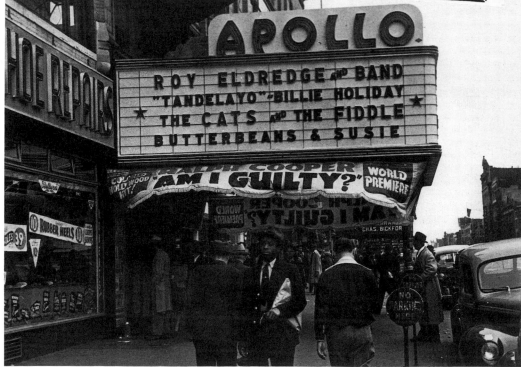

TUES	**1**	FRI	**1**
WED	**2**	SAT	**2**
THUR	**3**	SUN	**3**
FRI	**4**	MON	**4**
SAT	**5**	TUES	**5**
SUN	**6**	WED	**6**
MON	**7**	THUR	**7**
TUES	**8**	FRI	**8**
WED	**9**	SAT	**9**
THUR	**10**	SUN	**10**
FRI	**11**	MON	**11**
SAT	**12**	TUES	**12**
SUN	**13**	WED	**13**
MON	**14**	THUR	**14**
TUES	**15**	FRI	**15**
WED	**16**	SAT	**16**
THUR	**17**	SUN	**17**
FRI	**18**	MON	**18**
SAT	**19**	TUES	**19**
SUN	**20**	WED	**20**
MON	**21**	THUR	**21**
TUES	**22**	FRI	**22**
WED	**23**	SAT	**23**
THUR	**24**	SUN	**24**
FRI	**25**	MON	**25**
SAT	**26**	TUES	**26**
SUN	**27**	WED	**27**
MON	**28**	THUR	**28**
TUES	**29**	FRI	**29**
WED	**30**	SAT	**30**
THUR	**31**		

TUESDAY 1 OCTOBER 1940

Billie opens at Café Society Downtown with Art Tatum, Rosetta Tharpe and Joe Sullivan after her Apollo Theatre appearance. Barney Josephson is unhappy with her doubling at the Apollo and is ready to cancel her contract. He eventually agrees that she will finish her week at the Apollo and resume at Café Society on Friday.

Billie Takes A 'Holiday' At Opening

New York—Billie Holiday, whose temperament troubles have been the talk of the trade for years, was all set to open the new downtown Café Society show October 1. Came the opening night; Art Tatum, Sister Rosetta Tharpe and Joe Sullivan's new all-colored group made it a successful opening—but no Holiday. Billie failed to show up and manager Barney Josephson immediately decided to cancel her contract, declaring he could get along without her very well.

Teddy Wilson, denying that anything definite had been set with Benny Goodman, was ready to open with his small band at the uptown Café Society last week. "I spoke with Benny again," said Teddy, "and nothing was decided about whether I'd come back or on what terms. It's still quite possible that I'll be with him, but I'm keeping my own band together for the present." Plans are for him to work maybe another month with his band, then join Goodman for sure, it was learned.

WEDNESDAY 2 OCTOBER 1940

The Amateur Hour at the Apollo is broadcast on station WMCA.

THURSDAY 3 OCTOBER 1940

Billie closes at the Apollo

FRIDAY 4 OCTOBER 1940

Billie resumes her engagement at Café Society.

TUESDAY 8 OCTOBER 1940

Café Society Uptown opens at 128 E 58th Street.

TUESDAY 15 OCTOBER 1940

Recording session as Billie Holiday with Benny Carter and his All Star Orchestra for Columbia in New York City.

BILL COLEMAN (t), BENNY MORTON (tb), BENNY CARTER (cl/as), GEORGIE AULD (ts), SONNY WHITE (p), ULYSSES LIVINGSTON (g), WILSON MYERS (b), YANK PORTER (d), BILLIE HOLIDAY (v)

St Louis Blues (2 takes) / *Loveless Love* (2 takes)

This record session was part of a Leonard Feather/John Hammond tribute to W.C. Handy with Benny Carter and his All Star Orchestra. Eight tunes were planned for an album of four 78's, and two more tunes were recorded at this session featuring Joe Turner: *Joe Turner's Blues / BealeStreet Blues*.

The album was never completed.

Throughout November, Billie is resident at Café Society with Art Tatum, Sister Rosetta Tharpe and the Joe Sullivan Band. Billie is backed by Joe Sullivan until he leaves to go to the Famous Door. Art Tatum then accompanies her for the last few nights of her engagement.

SUNDAY 24 NOVEMBER 1940

Billie closes at Café Society. Art Tatum stays on, but the replacements include Ida Cox, Josh White and Red Allen's Band.

SUN	1	WED	1
MON	2	THUR	2
TUES	3	FRI	3
WED	4	SAT	4
THUR	5	SUN	5
FRI	6	MON	6
SAT	7	TUES	7
SUN	8	WED	8
MON	9	THUR	9
TUES	10	FRI	10
WED	11	SAT	11
THUR	12	SUN	12
FRI	13	MON	13
SAT	14	TUES	14
SUN	15	WED	15
MON	16	THUR	16
TUES	17	FRI	17
WED	18	SAT	18
THUR	19	SUN	19
FRI	20	MON	20
SAT	21	TUES	21
SUN	22	WED	22
MON	23	THUR	23
TUES	24	FRI	24
WED	25	SAT	25
THUR	26	SUN	26
FRI	27	MON	27
SAT	28	TUES	28
SUN	29	WED	29
MON	30	THUR	30
TUES	31	FRI	31

15 DECEMBER 1940

The new issue of *Down Beat* carries a Barrelhouse Dan review:

> ### BILLIE HOLIDAY
> ### *I Hear Music / I'm All For You*
> Okeh 5831
> Roy Eldridge's trumpet helps Billie, and there are very brief bits by Don Redman on alto, Georgie Auld and Teddy Wilson. Billie doesn't sing as well as she did three years ago and these tunes are pure crap – from the BMI books – but Holiday fans have no need to complain aside from those drawbacks.

THURSDAY 19 DECEMBER 1940

Billie takes part in a jam session which is broadcast via station WNEW.
HOT LIPS PAGE (t), CHARLIE BARNET (ss), COLEMAN HAWKINS, LESTER YOUNG (ts), TEDDY WILSON (p), unknown rhythm section, BILLIE HOLIDAY (v)
The Man I Love

After Christmas, Billie opens at the new Kelly's Stable, now located at 137 West 52nd Street. Coleman Hawkin's 7-piece Band with Hawkins (tenor sax), Sandy Williams (trombone), Peanuts Holland (trumpet), Eugene Fields (guitar), Clyde Hart (piano), George Duvivier (bass), J.C.Heard (drums) is also on the bill.

Throughout January Billie is resident at the new Kelly's Stable on 52nd Street with the Clarence Profit Trio and Coleman Hawkins' Band.

SUNDAY 26 JANUARY 1941

Billie takes part in a Milt Gabler Jam Session at Jimmy Ryan's Club on 52nd Street from 5 to 8pm. Also involved are HOT LIPS PAGE, HENRY RED ALLEN (t), PEE WEE RUSSELL, EDMOND HALL (cl), LESTER YOUNG (ts), J C HIGGINBOTHAM, BRAD GOWANS, GEORGE BRUNIES (tb), JOE SULLIVAN (p), EDDIE CONDON, JACK BLAND (g), BILL KING (b), ZUTTY SINGLETON (d).

Jimmy Ryan's ■■

■■ **Samoa Club**
■■ **Famous Door**
■■ **Three Deuces**

SIXTH AVENUE

52nd STREET

Kelly's Stable ■■
BILLIE HOLIDAY
COLEMAN HAWKINS

■■ **Hickory House**
JOE MARSALA
SPIRITS OF RHYTHM

SEVENTH AVENUE

JIMMY RYAN'S presents!
Milt Gabler's
SUNDAY SWING CLUB
JAM SESSIONS
every SUNDAY from 5 to 8 pm
featuring as usual the
most of the best Jazzmen.
COME EARLY!   COUVERT $1.00
———————————
WE'RE READY TO BLOW!
FOR RESERVATIONS
– PHONE EL5-9600
JIMMY RYAN'S
53 West 52nd ST., N.Y.

Kelly's Stable, New York City / Apollo Theatre, New York City

SAT	**1**
SUN	**2**
MON	**3**
TUES	**4**
WED	**5**
THUR	**6**
FRI	**7**
SAT	**8**
SUN	**9**
MON	**10**
TUES	**11**
WED	**12**
THUR	**13**
FRI	**14**
SAT	**15**
SUN	**16**
MON	**17**
TUES	**18**
WED	**19**
THUR	**20**
FRI	**21**
SAT	**22**
SUN	**23**
MON	**24**
TUES	**25**
WED	**26**
THUR	**27**
FRI	**28**

Throughout February Billie is resident at the new Kelly's Stable with the Clarence Profit Trio and Coleman Hawkins' Band.

FRIDAY 21 FEBRUARY 1941
Billie opens at the Apollo Theatre for a week in the musical comedy 'Up Harlem Way'. Also in the cast are Slim and Slam, Conway & Parks, Flournoy Miller and Nina Mae McKinney. Throughout the week, Billie doubles at Kelly's Stable on 52nd Street.

WEDNESDAY 26 FEBRUARY 1941
The Amateur Hour at the Apollo is broadcast via station WMCA.

THURSDAY 27 FEBRUARY 1941
Billie closes at the Apollo.

Coleman Hawkins leaves Kelly's Stable and is replaced by the Lester Young Band.

Below: Billie with Billy Eckstine

SAT	**1**
SUN	**2**
MON	**3**
TUES	**4**
WED	**5**
THUR	**6**
FRI	**7**
SAT	**8**
SUN	**9**
MON	**10**
TUES	**11**
WED	**12**
THUR	**13**
FRI	**14**
SAT	**15**
SUN	**16**
MON	**17**
TUES	**18**
WED	**19**
THUR	**20**
FRI	**21**
SAT	**22**
SUN	**23**
MON	**24**
TUES	**25**
WED	**26**
THUR	**27**
FRI	**28**
SAT	**29**
SUN	**30**
MON	**31**

Throughout March Billie is resident at the new Kelly's Stable with the Clarence Profit Trio and Lester Young's Sextet.

FRIDAY 21 MARCH 1941

Recording session as Billie Holiday with Eddie Heywood and his Orchestra for Columbia in New York City.

SHAD COLLINS (t), LESLIE JOHNAKINS, EDDIE BAREFIELD (as), LESTER YOUNG (ts), EDDIE HEYWOOD (p), JOHN COLLINS (g), TED STURGIS (b), KENNY CLARKE (d), BILLIE HOLIDAY (v)

Let's Do It (3 takes) / *Georgia On My Mind* (3 takes) / *Romance In The Dark* (6 takes) / *All Of Me* (3 takes)

The band included 3 members of Lester Young's Sextet which had just completed an engagement at Kelly's Stable.

Below: The Lester Young Band at Kelly's Stable with Harold 'Doc' West (drums), Nick Fenton (bass), Shad Collins (trumpet), Clyde Hart (piano), Lester Young (tenor sax) and John Collins (guitar)

TUES	1
WED	2
THUR	3
FRI	4
SAT	5
SUN	6
MON	7
TUES	8
WED	9
THUR	10
FRI	11
SAT	12
SUN	13
MON	14
TUES	15
WED	16
THUR	17
FRI	18
SAT	19
SUN	20
MON	21
TUES	22
WED	23
THUR	24
FRI	25
SAT	26
SUN	27
MON	28
TUES	29
WED	30

Throughout April Billie is resident at the new Kelly's Stable with the Clarence Profit Trio and.the Frankie Newton Band.

THURSDAY 3 APRIL 1941
Billie and the Louis Armstrong Orchestra open at Loew's State Theatre in Times Square, New York, for a one-week variety engagement. Also on the bill are Big Time Crip, The two Zephyrs and Sonny Woods.

Billie doubles at Kelly's Stable throughout the Loew's State engagement.

MONDAY 7 APRIL 1941
Billie's 26th birthday

WEDNESDAY 9 APRIL 1941
Billie and the Louis Armstrong Orchestra close at Loew's State Theatre in Times Square.

15 APRIL 1941
Down Beat carries a Dave Dexter review:

BILLIE HOLIDAY
St Louis Blues / Loveless Love   Okeh 6064
Time hasn't mellowed the voice of Billie. And even with a Benny Carter pickup group behind her, Billie's *St Louis Blues* and *Loveless Love* are not in the same class with the 1936–37 series of discs she made with Teddy Wilson. Billie's still one of the few fems who knows what she's doing, though, and Okeh 6064 is typical of her 1941 style. As such, it is recommended.

THUR	1
FRI	2
SAT	3
SUN	4
MON	5
TUES	6
WED	7
THUR	8
FRI	9
SAT	10
SUN	11
MON	12
TUES	13
WED	14
THUR	15
FRI	16
SAT	17
SUN	18
MON	19
TUES	20
WED	21
THUR	22
FRI	23
SAT	24
SUN	25
MON	26
TUES	27
WED	28
THUR	29
FRI	30
SAT	31

Throughout May Billie is resident at the new Kelly's Stable with the Clarence Profit Trio, Stuff Smith and the Hot Lips Page Band.

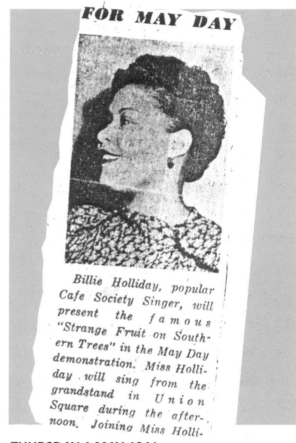

FOR MAY DAY

Billie Holliday, popular Cafe Society Singer, will present the famous "Strange Fruit on Southern Trees" in the May Day demonstration. Miss Holliday will sing from the grandstand in Union Square during the afternoon. Joining Miss Holli-

THURSDAY 1 MAY 1941
Billie performs at the May Day celebrations in Union Square. She sings 'Strange Fruit'.

FRIDAY 9 MAY 1941
Recording session as Billie Holiday with Eddie Heywood and his Orchestra for Columbia in New York City.
ROY ELDRIDGE (t), LESTER BOONE, JIMMY POWELL (as), ERNIE POWELL (ts),EDDIE HEYWOOD (p), PAUL CHAPMAN (g), GRACHAN MONCUR (b), HERBERT COWANS (d), BILLIE HOLIDAY (v)
I'm In A Low Down Groove / God Bless The Child (3 takes) / *Am I Blue?* (3 takes) / *Solitude*

15 MAY 1941
Down Beat carries a Dave Dexter review:

BILLIE HOLIDAY
Let's Do It / Georgia On My Mind   Okch 6134
Billie's attempts to carve Tony Pastor on the double-meaning *Let's Do It* lyrics fall short, but there's some swell Billie chanting anyway. She's even better on *Georgia On My Mind*, Okeh 6134, which gives little Eddie Heywood a chance to sport his ivory technique nicely. The pickup band behind her is weak on the whole.

SUN	1
MON	2
TUES	3
WED	4
THUR	5
FRI	6
SAT	7
SUN	8
MON	9
TUES	10
WED	11
THUR	12
FRI	13
SAT	14
SUN	15
MON	16
TUES	17
WED	18
THUR	19
FRI	20
SAT	21
SUN	22
MON	23
TUES	24
WED	25
THUR	26
FRI	27
SAT	28
SUN	29
MON	30

WEDNESDAY 4 JUNE 1941

Billie appears in 'Concert Swing', the last of a series of six 'Coffee' concerts organised by Louise Crane at the Museum of Modern Art. Also appearing are Zutty Singleton's Band, Hot Lips Page Band and Roy Eldridge

THURSDAY 12 JUNE 1941 (?)

Billie closes at Kelly's Stable.

FRIDAY 13 JUNE 1941

Billie opens at the Apollo Theatre for a one-week engagement in the revue 'Mr Washington Goes To Town' with Christopher Columbus & his Band, The Three Peters Sisters, Peg Leg Bates and Pigmeat Markham.

WEDNESDAY 18 JUNE 1941

The Amateur Hour at the Apollo is broadcast on station WMCA.

THURSDAY 19 JUNE 1941

Billie closes at the Apollo.

Billie spends the next three weeks hanging out with Jimmy Monroe at his brother Clark Monroe's Uptown House, 134th Street. She sits in regularly with the house band led by Floyd 'Horsecollar' Williams. On an unknown date in June Billie is recorded at the club by Jerry Newman. 'Horsecollar' plays alto sax with an unknown pianist and bassist.
I Cried For You / Fine And Mellow

Below: Billie and her mother, Sadie, together in a 52nd Street club, probably Kelly's Stable.

TUES	1
WED	2
THUR	3
FRI	4
SAT	5
SUN	6
MON	7
TUES	8
WED	9
THUR	10
FRI	11
SAT	12
SUN	13
MON	14
TUES	15
WED	16
THUR	17
FRI	18
SAT	19
SUN	20
MON	21
TUES	22
WED	23
THUR	24
FRI	25
SAT	26
SUN	27
MON	28
TUES	29
WED	30
THUR	31

1 JULY 1941

The new issue of *Down Beat* carries a Dave Dexter review:

> **BILLIE HOLIDAY**
> ***All Of Me / Romance In The Dark***
> Okeh 6214
> Again poor accompaniment hinders Billie Holiday, this time on her Okeh 6214 of *All Of Me* and *Romance In The Dark*. Piano stands out but the ensemble backgrounds are from Dixie and reveal lack of woodshedding before the date. Billie's terrific on *All Of Me*, though, and for 35 pennies it's a buy.

SATURDAY 12 JULY 1941

Billie opens at the Famous Door on 52nd Street with Babe Russin's group. Babe Russin (tenor sax) leads his brother Jackie Russin (piano), Barney Galbraith (guitar), Sid Jacobs (bass) and Hal Berman (drums).

FIFTH AVENUE

52nd STREET

(no21) **21 Club** ■

(no33)**Leon & Eddie's** ■

(no53) **Jimmy Ryan's** ■
(no57) **Tony's** ■

■ **Samoa Club** (no62)
■ **Famous Door** (no66)
■ **Three Deuces** (no72)

SIXTH AVENUE

FRI	**1**
SAT	**2**
SUN	**3**
MON	**4**
TUES	**5**
WED	**6**
THUR	**7**
FRI	**8**
SAT	**9**
SUN	**10**
MON	**11**
TUES	**12**
WED	**13**
THUR	**14**
FRI	**15**
SAT	**16**
SUN	**17**
MON	**18**
TUES	**19**
WED	**20**
THUR	**21**
FRI	**22**
SAT	**23**
SUN	**24**
MON	**25**
TUES	**26**
WED	**27**
THUR	**28**
FRI	**29**
SAT	**30**
SUN	**31**

THURSDAY 7 AUGUST 1941

Recording session as Billie Holiday accompanied by Teddy Wilson and his Orchestra for Columbia in New York City.

EMMETT BERRY (t), JIMMY HAMILTON (cl/ts), HYMIE SCHERTZER (as), BABE RUSSIN (ts), TEDDY WILSON (p), AL CASEY (g), JOHN WILLIAMS (b), J.C. HEARD (d), BILLIE HOLIDAY (v)

Jim (2 takes) / *I Cover The Waterfront* / *Love Me Or Leave Me* / *Gloomy Sunday* (3 takes)

FRIDAY 15 AUGUST 1941

Billie closes at the Famous Door on 52nd Street.

Down Beat carries a Dave Dexter record review:

BILLIE HOLIDAY
Solitude / God Bless The Child
Okeh
This department has long contended that Billie's chanting today is no match for the super-vocals she turned in with Teddy Wilson's pickup bands four and five years ago. And so it's with real relief that her *Solitude* measures up with anything she ever cut. Tempo is ideal, backgrounds elegant (piano especially) even though her mate side, *God Bless The Child* is so-so.

MONDAY 18 AUGUST 1941

Billie opens at the Howard Theatre in Washington for a one-week engagement.

SATURDAY 23 AUGUST 1941

Billie closes at the Howard Theatre in Washington. After the last show, Billie and Jimmy Monroe drive a hired car to Elkton, Maryland where they apply for a marriage licence

MONDAY 25 AUGUST 1941

Billie and Jimmy Monroe (30) are married in Elkton, Maryland.

They leave for Chicago where Billie makes some appearances with Lionel Hampton's new big band at the Hotel Sherman.

FRIDAY 29 AUGUST 1941

Billie opens at the Sherman Hotel in Chicago as a double attraction with the Lionel Hampton Band. The engagement is for 4 weeks.

Billie Holiday Elopes, Weds

New York—Billie Holiday completed a singing engagement Aug. 25 and a few hours later speeded to Elkton, Md., where she married Jimmy Monroe, 30-year-old former husband of Nina Mae McKinney.

It was the first marriage for Billie, whose sultry singing has long been acclaimed by musicians and hot fans. She gave her full name as Billie Eleanor Holiday and her age as 25.

Billie left for Chicago immediately after her elopement to appear with Lionel Hampton's new band at the Hotel Sherman, from where she'll go to Hollywood to appear as a solo act in a Hollywood revue.

Married in a surprise elopement three weeks ago was Billie Holiday, one of the greatest of all fem jazz singers. Billie married Jimmy Monroe Aug. 25 at Elkton, Md. She gave her age as 25, her real name as Billie Eleanor Holiday. Monroe is the ex-husband of Nina Mae McKinney. Billie began her spectacular career when her first records with Teddy Wilson appeared six years ago. Currently she is singing in the Panther room of Chicago's Hotel Sherman, featured in the show with Lionel Hampton's band. She goes to Hollywood next.

MON	**1**	WED	**1**
TUES	**2**	THUR	**2**
WED	**3**	FRI	**3**
THUR	**4**	SAT	**4**
FRI	**5**	SUN	**5**
SAT	**6**	MON	**6**
SUN	**7**	TUES	**7**
MON	**8**	WED	**8**
TUES	**9**	THUR	**9**
WED	**10**	FRI	**10**
THUR	**11**	SAT	**11**
FRI	**12**	SUN	**12**
SAT	**13**	MON	**13**
SUN	**14**	TUES	**14**
MON	**15**	WED	**15**
TUES	**16**	THUR	**16**
WED	**17**	FRI	**17**
THUR	**18**	SAT	**18**
FRI	**19**	SUN	**19**
SAT	**20**	MON	**20**
SUN	**21**	TUES	**21**
MON	**22**	WED	**22**
TUES	**23**	THUR	**23**
WED	**24**	FRI	**24**
THUR	**25**	SAT	**25**
FRI	**26**	SUN	**26**
SAT	**27**	MON	**27**
SUN	**28**	TUES	**28**
MON	**29**	WED	**29**
TUES	**30**	THUR	**30**
		FRI	**31**

THURSDAY 25 SEPTEMBER 1941

Billie closes at the Sherman Hotel in Chicago
From Chicago they move to California where
Billie is booked indefinitely into a new LA club
owned by Jerry Colonna – Café Society.

Billie Holliday Opens West Cafe Society

Los Angeles—A West Coast edition of New York's widely publicised Cafe Society debuted here Oct. 1. Featured attraction will be Billie Holiday, making her first West Coast appearance.

Band is a local crew headed by Al Golden, studio and radio trumpet player, taking a fling as band front. He's using a six-piece combo consisting of himself on trumpet, Les Barnett, piano; Cliff Oleson, sax; Julie Kinsler, sax; Johnny Cyr, drums; Al Woodbury, bass.

Headman of the West's Cafe Society is George (Red) McCullen, who also inaugurated Hollywood's Famous Door.

WEDNESDAY 1 OCTOBER 1941

Billie opens at Café Society in Los Angeles for
an extended engagement opposite the Al
Golden Band. Business is poor and the club
folds after a few weeks.

Down Beat carries a Dave Dexter record review:

> **BILLIE HOLIDAY**
> *Jim / Love Me Or Leave Me*
> Okeh 6369
> Everyone's cut *Jim* by now, but it is the newly-wedded Billie whose version, although late, tops 'em all, including Dinah Shore's more publicized disc. Here is singing with a soul, and distinctive. *Love Me Or Leave Me* also is first-rate singing, and the band behind her bats 100 per cent. Two bull's eyes on Okeh 6369.

TUESDAY 21 OCTOBER 1941

Café Society closes and Billie and Monroe are
broke. She returns east by train but Monroe
stays in LA.

Chicago, November 15, 1941

Billie Holiday Clicks on Coast

. I'm
band
play
Fan-
. Yet,
the
public
y art
tain-
the
f in-
play
y it.
pay-
share

tem-
want
y the
play.
isten-
Bo-
ay to
s. I'm
band

Hollywood—Billie Holiday has been wowing 'em out here, working the Cafe Society nitery and entertaining stars of the entertainment world. Here Billie (left) chats with Santo Pecora, the New Orleans trombonist; Gai Moran Shroff, the chirper, and her hubby Brodie Shroff, now playing hot trumpet with Freddy Slack's band. Shroff and Pecora only recently left Will Osborne. *Down Beat Pic.*

SAT	1
SUN	2
MON	3
TUES	4
WED	5
THUR	6
FRI	7
SAT	8
SUN	9
MON	10
TUES	11
WED	12
THUR	13
FRI	14
SAT	15
SUN	16
MON	17
TUES	18
WED	19
THUR	20
FRI	21
SAT	22
SUN	23
MON	24
TUES	25
WED	26
THUR	27
FRI	28
SAT	29
SUN	30

SATURDAY 8 NOVEMBER 1941
The *Chicago Defender* reports a possible movie role for Billie:

Billy Holliday To Sing Music By Duke Ellington In Picture

HOLLYWOOD, Calif.– Billy Holliday, famed New York chanteuse, currently appearing at Cafe Society here, was sure last week that she would be spotted in the forthcoming RKO Radio studio production featuring Louis Armstrong when the cameras begin to turn.

Miss Holliday is set to play the screen role of Bessie Smith, old time blues singer. The film panel will be based around the rise of Louis Armstrong, the King of the Trumpet, with adequate supporting scenes replica of the times.

Music for the highly interesting sepia movement in the screen story is being written by Duke Ellington, it was learned. Hazel Scott, another New York singer, currently appearing in Cafe Society in that city, will essay the role of wife of the noted trumpeter. Production on the picture is not slated until after the first of the year.

FRIDAY 28 NOVEMBER 1941
Billie appears as a special added attraction at the Apollo Theatre for a one-week engagement. Also on the bill are The Three Peters Sisters, Big Time Crip, Joyner & Foster and Lionel Hampton & his Band.

MON	1
TUES	2
WED	3
THUR	4
FRI	5
SAT	6
SUN	7
MON	8
TUES	9
WED	10
THUR	11
FRI	12
SAT	13
SUN	14
MON	15
TUES	16
WED	17
THUR	18
FRI	19
SAT	20
SUN	21
MON	22
TUES	23
WED	24
THUR	25
FRI	26
SAT	27
SUN	28
MON	29
TUES	30
WED	31

WEDNESDAY 3 DECEMBER 1941
The Amateur Hour at the Apollo is broadcast on station WMCA. Billie is accompanied by Lionel Hampton's Band.

THURSDAY 4 DECEMBER 1941
Billie closes at the Apollo.

THURSDAY 11 DECEMBER 1941
Billie opens at the Famous Door on 52nd Street, backed by the Benny Carter Band, which includes 24-yr-old Dizzy Gillespie. Clark Monroe is MC.

FRIDAY 12 DECEMBER 1941
Billie appears at the Star News 5th Annual Midnight Benefit at the Apollo Theatre in Harlem. Also on the bill are Count Basie and Gene Krupa.

MONDAY 15 DECEMBER 1941
Down Beat carries a Dave Dexter record review:

BILLIE HOLIDAY
I'm In A Low Down Groove / Gloomy Sunday
Okeh 6451
Roy Jacobs' *I'm In A Low Down Groove* is well suited to Billie's pipes, and the pickup band behind her is first rate. Many may enjoy the coupling, the mournful *Gloomy Sunday*, and while Holiday chirps it as it was never chirped before, the very mood of the song is disheartening. Billie, as always, does a grand job all the way.

THUR	**1**	SUN	**1**	SUN	**1**
FRI	**2**	MON	**2**	MON	**2**
SAT	**3**	TUES	**3**	TUES	**3**
SUN	**4**	WED	**4**	WED	**4**
MON	**5**	THUR	**5**	THUR	**5**
TUES	**6**	FRI	**6**	FRI	**6**
WED	**7**	SAT	**7**	SAT	**7**
THUR	**8**	SUN	**8**	SUN	**8**
FRI	**9**	MON	**9**	MON	**9**
SAT	**10**	TUES	**10**	TUES	**10**
SUN	**11**	WED	**11**	WED	**11**
MON	**12**	THUR	**12**	THUR	**12**
TUES	**13**	FRI	**13**	FRI	**13**
WED	**14**	SAT	**14**	SAT	**14**
THUR	**15**	SUN	**15**	SUN	**15**
FRI	**16**	MON	**16**	MON	**16**
SAT	**17**	TUES	**17**	TUES	**17**
SUN	**18**	WED	**18**	WED	**18**
MON	**19**	THUR	**19**	THUR	**19**
TUES	**20**	FRI	**20**	FRI	**20**
WED	**21**	SAT	**21**	SAT	**21**
THUR	**22**	SUN	**22**	SUN	**22**
FRI	**23**	MON	**23**	MON	**23**
SAT	**24**	TUES	**24**	TUES	**24**
SUN	**25**	WED	**25**	WED	**25**
MON	**26**	THUR	**26**	THUR	**26**
TUES	**27**	FRI	**27**	FRI	**27**
WED	**28**	SAT	**28**	SAT	**28**
THUR	**29**			SUN	**29**
FRI	**30**			MON	**30**
SAT	**31**			TUES	**31**

JANUARY 1942

Sometime in early January, Billie suddenly leaves the Famous Door to take a job in Montreal. Nobody knows why she suddenly takes off in the middle of a successful run, or the attraction of the Canadian job.

Following Montreal, Billie works at the Club Congo in Detroit where she is held over for a second week.

TUESDAY 10 FEBRUARY 1942

Recording session as Billie Holiday with Teddy Wilson and his Orchestra for Columbia in New York City.
EMMETT BERRY (t), JIMMY HAMILTON (cl/ts), HYMIE SCHERTZER (as), BABE RUSSIN (ts), TEDDY WILSON (p), GENE FIELDS (g), JOHN WILLIAMS (b), J.C. HEARD (d), BILLIE HOLIDAY (v)
Wherever You Are (2 takes) / *Mandy Is Two* (4 takes) / *It's A Sin To Tell A Lie* (4 takes) / *Until The Real Thing Comes Along* (2 takes)
This session is Billie's last for CBS. Her contract runs until the fall of 1943, but Columbia let it expire.

BILLIE HOLLIDAY HELD OVER AT CLUB CONGO

DETROIT, Mich. Mar. 12– Billie Holiday, the famous singer of torch songs, who invaded this city following a highly successful engagement in Canada, is being held over at the Club Congo, where she is proving a sensation.

WED	1
THUR	2
FRI	3
SAT	4
SUN	5
MON	6
TUES	7
WED	8
THUR	9
FRI	10
SAT	11
SUN	12
MON	13
TUES	14
WED	15
THUR	16
FRI	17
SAT	18
SUN	19
MON	20
TUES	21
WED	22
THUR	23
FRI	24
SAT	25
SUN	26
MON	27
TUES	28
WED	29
THUR	30

TUESDAY 7 APRIL 1942
Billie's 27th birthday

FRIDAY 10 APRIL 1942
Billie opens at the Apollo Theatre for a one-week engagement. Also on the bill are Pigmeat Markham, Moke & Poke, The Sons of the South, Al Guster and Benny Carter & his Band.

SATURDAY 11 APRIL 1942
Billie appears on the fourth Eddie Condon Jazz Concert at Town Hall in New York. The concert is at 5pm. Also on the bill are HOT LIPS PAGE, HENRY 'RED' ALLEN, COOTIE WILLIAMS (t), PEE WEE RUSSELL, ROD CLESS (cl), BUD FREEMAN (ts), SANDY WILLIAMS, BENNY MORTON (tb), JAMES P JOHNSON, DAVE BOWMAN (p), AL MORGAN (b), KANSAS FIELDS, ZUTTY SINGLETON, DAVE TOUGH (d)

WEDNESDAY 15 APRIL 1942
The Amateur Hour at the Apollo is broadcast on station WMCA. Billie is probably accompanied by Benny Carter & his Band.

THURSDAY 16 APRIL 1942
Billie closes at the Apollo.

Benny Carter Holiday Set For Joint Tour

New York—Benny Carter and his new 15-piece combination are playing this week at the Apollo theater in Harlem on the first leg of a series of theater dates which Benny will make jointly with Billie Holiday.

FRI	1
SAT	2
SUN	3
MON	4
TUES	5
WED	6
THUR	7
FRI	8
SAT	9
SUN	10
MON	11
TUES	12
WED	13
THUR	14
FRI	15
SAT	16
SUN	17
MON	18
TUES	19
WED	20
THUR	21
FRI	22
SAT	23
SUN	24
MON	25
TUES	26
WED	27
THUR	28
FRI	29
SAT	30
SUN	31

FRIDAY 1 MAY 1942
Billie opens at the Boogie Woogie Club in Cleveland for a two-week engagement accompanied by pianist Lannie Scott. The booking is for a month but poor business causes a cancellation after 2 weeks.

THURSDAY 14 MAY 1942
Billie closes at the Boogie Woogie Club.

Chicago, May 15, 1942

Clevelanders Get Kicks as Billie Sings

Cleveland—Two terrific weeks of some of the greatest jazz kicks we have had around here in ages was the result of Billie Holiday's opening of a new sepia spot in midtown. Also featured with her were the popular Cats and the Fiddle quartet.

Billie was set here for a month but was cancelled out to return to New York after two weks. Business was only fair at the spot, the Boogie Woogie club, which caters to a mixed trade but plenty of the local cats were there night after night to hear her. Brought in on piano to play for Billie was Cleveland's own particular pride and joy, Lannie Scott.

Billie learns that Jimmy Monroe has been arrested for drug-smuggling in Los Angeles and she travels immediately to the West Coast. She looks for work, and Lester Young persuades Billy Berg to add Billie to the cast at his Trouville Club, where the Lee & Lester Young Band are starring with Slim & Slam, Joe Turner and the Spirits of Rhythm.

MAY 1942
Billie opens at Billy Berg's Trouville Club in West Hollywood. The band is led by Lester Young and his brother Lee. Also in the band is pianist Jimmy Rowles who recalled: *'Lady was very feminine, good natured, salty, loving. She was young, and one of the most beautiful girls I had ever seen. She was nut brown, with hair dyed red, and she looked great. She was looked up to – one of the guys – no holding back with language, she loved dirty jokes like we do.'*

At the end of May Jimmy Monroe comes to trial and is sentenced to a year in jail.

MON	**1**	WED	**1**
TUES	**2**	THUR	**2**
WED	**3**	FRI	**3**
THUR	**4**	SAT	**4**
FRI	**5**	SUN	**5**
SAT	**6**	MON	**6**
SUN	**7**	TUES	**7**
MON	**8**	WED	**8**
TUES	**9**	THUR	**9**
WED	**10**	FRI	**10**
THUR	**11**	SAT	**11**
FRI	**12**	SUN	**12**
SAT	**13**	MON	**13**
SUN	**14**	TUES	**14**
MON	**15**	WED	**15**
TUES	**16**	THUR	**16**
WED	**17**	FRI	**17**
THUR	**18**	SAT	**18**
FRI	**19**	SUN	**19**
SAT	**20**	MON	**20**
SUN	**21**	TUES	**21**
MON	**22**	WED	**22**
TUES	**23**	THUR	**23**
WED	**24**	FRI	**24**
THUR	**25**	SAT	**25**
FRI	**26**	SUN	**26**
SAT	**27**	MON	**27**
SUN	**28**	TUES	**28**
MON	**29**	WED	**29**
TUES	**30**	THUR	**30**
		FRI	**31**

MONDAY 1 JUNE 1942

Billie and the band plus the Spirits of Rhythm broadcast from the club on station KHJ.
Lee & Lester Young Orchestra: 'RED' MACK MORRIS (t), LESTER YOUNG, BUMPS MYERS (ts), JIMMY ROWLES (p), LOUIS GONZALES (g), RED CALLENDER (b), LEE YOUNG (d), BILLIE HOLIDAY (v).
Spirits of Rhythm: LEO WATSON, WILBUR DANIELS, DOUGLAS DANIELS (v), EDDIE BEAL (p), TEDDY BUNN (g/v)
Broadway (band) / *I Hear Music* (Billie Holiday) / *Po-Go-Joe* (Spirits of Rhythm) / *Benny's Bugle* (band) / *Solitude* (Billie Holiday) / *Broadway* (band) / *Oh! Lady Be Good* (band)

During the stay at the Trouville Billie and Bumps Myers live together and, according to Jimmy Rowles, they got along well together. Billie also socialised with the stars who frequented the Trouville, like Martha Raye, John Garfield, Don Ameche, Bette Davis, Lana Turner, Merle Oberon and Orson Welles. She also meets Norman Granz.

She also meets up with Trummy Young who she had first met in 1937. Trummy said: *'Billie and I were in California together, both out of work. We were so poor we couldn't pay our room rent. I had this melody I used to play with Earl Hines' Band, something I made up, it never was arranged or copyrighted. I went to Jimmy Mundy who I'd worked with originally in Tommy Miles' Band in 1930, and got him to arrange the song – at the time he was working for Paul Whiteman. The tune didn't even have a title; one night Johnny Mercer and his wife heard the Paul Whiteman Band play the tune. Johnny's wife named it 'Trav'lin' Light', and Johnny wrote the lyrics!'*

FRIDAY 12 JUNE 1942

Billie records with the Paul Whiteman Orchestra for the new Capitol label in Los Angeles.
PAUL WHITEMAN (conductor), MONTY KELLY, LARRY NEILL, DON WADDILOVE (t), ALVY WEST, DANNY D'ANDREA (as), LENNY HARTMAN (ts), LESTER YOUNG (ts on 1st track only), SKIP LAYTON, TRUMMY YOUNG, MURRAY MCEACHERN (tb), unknown string section, BUDDY WEED (p), MIKE PINGITORE (g/bj), ARTIE SHAPIRO (b), WILLIE RODRIGUEZ (d), JIMMY MUNDY (arr)
Trav'lin' Light (Billie Holiday vocal) / *The Old Music Master* (JackTeagarden & Johnny Mercer vocal) / *I'm Old Fashioned* / *You Were Never Lovelier*

When Billie closes at the Trouville, she and Trummy Young ride the bus all the way back to New York.

> LET'S TELL YOU RIGHT NOW, WE'RE BROADCASTING FOR THE NEXT TWENTY-FIVE MINUTES FROM THE TROUVILLE ON BEVERLY BOULEVARD, ONE BLOCK EAST OF FAIRFAX, NO COVER, NO MINIMUM – RIGHT HERE IN HOLLYWOOD.'

Garrick Stagebar, Chicago

SAT	1	TUES	1
SUN	2	WED	2
MON	3	THUR	3
TUES	4	FRI	4
WED	5	SAT	5
THUR	6	SUN	6
FRI	7	MON	7
SAT	8	TUES	8
SUN	9	WED	9
MON	10	THUR	10
TUES	11	FRI	11
WED	12	SAT	12
THUR	13	SUN	13
FRI	14	MON	14
SAT	15	TUES	15
SUN	16	WED	16
MON	17	THUR	17
TUES	18	FRI	18
WED	19	SAT	19
THUR	20	SUN	20
FRI	21	MON	21
SAT	22	TUES	22
SUN	23	WED	23
MON	24	THUR	24
TUES	25	FRI	25
WED	26	SAT	26
THUR	27	SUN	27
FRI	28	MON	28
SAT	29	TUES	29
SUN	30	WED	30
MON	31		

SATURDAY 15 AUGUST 1942
Billie opens at Joe Sherman's Garrick Stagebar in Chicago opposite Henry 'Red' Allen and his Orchestra for a three-month stay. Opening night is a sell-out.

Throughout September Billie is resident at the Garrick Stagebar in Chicago.

MONDAY 21 SEPTEMBER 1942
Billie is present at the DuSable Lounge Monday Celebrity Night along with John Kirby's Band and the Red Allen Band.

Celebrity Night Is Feature At DuSable

The DuSable lounge, thanks to swingy music by Clarence Black and service that rates with the best is jumping nightly. For one thing, owners John Simmons, Harry Fields and Charlie Cobs are all smiles as their spot swings out with the celebrities. On Mondays the DuSable features its celebrity night with stars of the stage and screen present. Last week Billie Holliday, John Kirby's band, Red Allen's ork and many others attended.

Below: Billie sings at the Stagebar, backed by (l to r) Kenny Clarke (d), General Morgan (b), J. C. Higginbotham (tb), Red Allen (t)

THUR	1
FRI	2
SAT	3
SUN	4
MON	5
TUES	6
WED	7
THUR	8
FRI	9
SAT	10
SUN	11
MON	12
TUES	13
WED	14
THUR	15
FRI	16
SAT	17
SUN	18
MON	19
TUES	20
WED	21
THUR	22
FRI	23
SAT	24
SUN	25
MON	26
TUES	27
WED	28
THUR	29
FRI	30
SAT	31

Throughout October Billie is resident at the Garrick Stagebar in Chicago opposite Henry 'Red' Allen and his Orchestra.

Early in October Billie is on her way to work when the car in which she is travelling collides with an ambulance. Billie is nursing badly cut knees and is driven off to seek first-aid. However, she is apprehended by police and jailed for leaving the scene of an accident. Somehow it gets straightened out and Billie is able to appear on schedule at the Stagebar.

Down Beat carries the full story of the incident (below), as well as a review of the Henry 'Red' Allen Band (right).

BANDS DUG BY THE Beat

HENRY "RED" ALLEN
(Reviewed at the Garrick Stagebar, Chicago)

A six piece unit that can't miss with the amazing musicianship molded into their playing. Red, himself, the star of many bands from the time of his father's own brass band in New Orleans down to Lucky Millinder and now his own band, Red is stellar on trumpet. His ideas are superb and casual. There is no great fuss over his work, only cleanness, idea, and piercing tone.

J. C. Higginbotham plays trombone. That is an understatement in itself because if Jay merely plays a trombone then we have to think up a name for what the rest of the country's trombonists do on the instrument. Jay is head and shoulders above come one-come all of the rest. With apparently no mouthpiece pressure, Jay achieves power or delicacy, blast or bluff. His blues are excellent. His ideas on all things are wonderful and his ability to execute fast passages and difficult changes are unbelievable. So is he.

Don Stovall is the fair haired boy of the unit . . . coming over from a short stay with Cootie Williams and picked by Red from Fate Marable's Riverboat crew, so he says. Don's style is light and inspired. There is none of the heavy, impassioned playing that so many altoists and tenors try to play. Like Pete Brown, his stacatto style often could be confused for pizzicato violin in its extreme delicacy. He reminds us of Pete although his work varies from Pete's to some degree. Their styles, however, are comparable. Ideas are not.

The rhythm section is good with Benny Moten (no relation) and General Morgan on bass and piano, respectively, the standouts, and Kenny Clark playing steady drums. Morgan plays a full piano style with nice chords, no monotony, gentle and well worked treble, and steady rhythm. All in all, this is a topnotch crew. Please let them stay that way. No commerciality and yet a commercial appeal. Held over here, they should meet with the same reception everywhere.

4   DOWN BEAT

Billie Holiday Jailed in Light Comedy of Errors

Chicago—In a routine like Gangbusters with guns, screaming sirens, police cars and tough detectives, Billie Holiday was flung into jail but solidly two weeks ago following a slight misunderstanding between the car in which she was riding and an ambulance which met, antisocially, on a street corner in Chicago.

To straighten out the situation, if such a thing is possible, Billie was being driven to work at the Garrick Stagebar when the car in which she was riding collided with an ambulance. All parties participating in the crash got out and looked over the mess and waited for the inevitable police car, Billie meanwhile nursing a very bunged up pair of knees. Somehow, the inevitable police car was a bit less inevitable than usual, so when it didn't appear, it was decided that Billie should be taken somewhere for first aid. Her companion backed the car out of the fracas and proceeded on the way.

The Capture!

A few blocks later they heard sirens screaming behind them and a police car edged them into the curb. Two policemen, guns in hand, preparing to fight it out, plunged from the car, seized the culprits and, before you could sing the first eight bars of *Fine and Mellow*, had them at the nearest police station.

Police merely laughed at the excuse that Billie was being taken for first aid. "Get that," one of them said, "they run into an ambulance and then run off to find first aid. Some excuse!" So la Holiday was assigned to her room in the local bastile.

Joe Ain't Nowhere

Calls to manager Joe Sherman of the Stagebar brought more abuse upon Billie because Joe thought it was all a gag and kidded happily with Billie, assorted detectives and policemen, and the man at the desk before he finally realized that Billie actually was in the jug as specified. With the resounding cry of "You ain't nowhere" in the Holiday voice screaming through the phone, Joe hung up and hastened to bail.

First aid was obtained and Billie appeared as usual. She glared despicably at Sherman all evening and muttered when he chanced by, "Man, you just ain't nowhere." Joe was properly chastened.

SUN	**1**
MON	**2**
TUES	**3**
WED	**4**
THUR	**5**
FRI	**6**
SAT	**7**
SUN	**8**
MON	**9**
TUES	**10**
WED	**11**
THUR	**12**
FRI	**13**
SAT	**14**
SUN	**15**
MON	**16**
TUES	**17**
WED	**18**
THUR	**19**
FRI	**20**
SAT	**21**
SUN	**22**
MON	**23**
TUES	**24**
WED	**25**
THUR	**26**
FRI	**27**
SAT	**28**
SUN	**29**
MON	**30**

Throughout November Billie is resident at the Garrick Stagebar in Chicago opposite Henry 'Red' Allen and his Orchestra.

Billie is reportedly beefing with pianist Gladys Palmer at the Stagebar and threatening a walk out. *Down Beat* also reveals:

We nominate for the square of Randolph Street, Joe Sherman, manager of the Garrick Stagebar, the most righteous place in town. Proof: Joe hired Billie Holiday under the impression that she was a man.

The Holiday

Chicago—Here's a unique shot of Billie Holiday, who is continuing to lure hepsters to the Garrick with her sultry songs.

In late November, there is a fracas at the Stagebar when manager Joe Sherman punches Mel Draper, drummer with Jimmy Noone's Band which is appearing upstairs. The Union president pulls all coloured talent out of both rooms until a settlement is reached. Billie, though not covered by union restrictions, walks out in sympathy.

SATURDAY 28 NOVEMBER 1942
Billie appears at a Midnight Show to boost War Bonds at the Regal Theatre.

TUES	1
WED	2
THUR	3
FRI	4
SAT	5
SUN	6
MON	7
TUES	8
WED	9
THUR	10
FRI	11
SAT	12
SUN	13
MON	14
TUES	15
WED	16
THUR	17
FRI	18
SAT	19
SUN	20
MON	21
TUES	22
WED	23
THUR	24
FRI	25
SAT	26
SUN	27
MON	28
TUES	29
WED	30
THUR	31

Throughout most of December Billie is resident at the Garrick Stagebar in Chicago opposite Henry 'Red' Allen and his Orchestra.

In early December, drummer Kenny Clarke leaves the Red Allen Band to take his own group featuring Willy Nelson (t), Earl Hardy (tb), Ike Quebec (ts), Thelonious Monk (p), and Al Hall (b) into Kelly's Stable in NYC. He is replaced by Paul Barbarin.

c. THURSDAY 24 DECEMBER 1942
Billie closes at the Garrick Stagebar to be replaced by Louis Jordan and his Band.

FRIDAY 25 DECEMBER 1942
Billie opens a one-week engagement at the Regal Theatre in Chicago, opposite Lionel Hampton & his Band.

Red and Jay Amid the Palms

Chicago—Red Allen closes his eyes as he takes a soulful trumpet chorus at the Garrick Stagebar Down Beat room here where he and the band are currently in their fourth month. Included in the pic are Paul Barbarin, drums, Jay C. Higginbotham, trombone, Benny Moten, bass, Red, trumpet, Don Stovall, alto sax, and General Morgan, piano.

MONDAY 28 DECEMBER 1942
Billie and the Lionel Hampton Band are Guests of Honor at the Savoy Ballroom at a Miss Victory Dance.

THURSDAY 31 DECEMBER 1942
Billie and the Lionel Hampton Band close at the Regal Theatre.
Down Beat reports:

'Lady Day and Lionel Hampton's Band tore the roof off the Regal Theatre on New Year's Eve.'

FRI	**1**	MON	**1**
SAT	**2**	TUES	**2**
SUN	**3**	WED	**3**
MON	**4**	THUR	**4**
TUES	**5**	FRI	**5**
WED	**6**	SAT	**6**
THUR	**7**	SUN	**7**
FRI	**8**	MON	**8**
SAT	**9**	TUES	**9**
SUN	**10**	WED	**10**
MON	**11**	THUR	**11**
TUES	**12**	FRI	**12**
WED	**13**	SAT	**13**
THUR	**14**	SUN	**14**
FRI	**15**	MON	**15**
SAT	**16**	TUES	**16**
SUN	**17**	WED	**17**
MON	**18**	THUR	**18**
TUES	**19**	FRI	**19**
WED	**20**	SAT	**20**
THUR	**21**	SUN	**21**
FRI	**22**	MON	**22**
SAT	**23**	TUES	**23**
SUN	**24**	WED	**24**
MON	**25**	THUR	**25**
TUES	**26**	FRI	**26**
WED	**27**	SAT	**27**
THUR	**28**	SUN	**28**
FRI	**29**		
SAT	**30**		
SUN	**31**		

JANUARY 1943
Billie is 4th in the *Down Beat* poll behind Helen Forrest, Helen O'Connell and Anita O'Day.

15 JANUARY 1943
Down Beat reports:

Hampton Cracks Regal Record

Chicago—With seats filled and a constant overflow of cash customers standing along the walls of the Regal theater on Chicago's South Side, Lionel Hampton shattered the all time attendance record for the theater early this month.

Aided and abetted by Lady Day (Billie Holiday), Hamp drew over 20,000 people in his seven day stint. The consensus was that the young Hampton crew (with many new chairs replacing army draftees) was nothing sho...

Billie returns to New York and begins a run at Kelly's Stable with the bands of Coleman Hawkins and Henry 'Red' Allen.

SUNDAY 7 FEBRUARY 1943
Billie closes at Kelly's Stable.

In Los Angeles, Jimmy Monroe is released from jail to work with the Douglas aircraft plant . Billie suddenly leaves NYC and takes a train to Los Angeles to be near him. Perhaps she has notions of trying to re-establish her marriage. Leonard Feather is on the same train, and both say on arrival 'Here on vacations ...' Whatever hopes Billie may have for a reconciliation, it doesn't happen.

THURSDAY 25 FEBRUARY 1943
Billie opens at Club 331 in Los Angeles opposite Henry 'Red' Allen's Band.

MON	1	THUR	1	SAT	1
TUES	2	FRI	2	SUN	2
WED	3	SAT	3	MON	3
THUR	4	SUN	4	TUES	4
FRI	5	MON	5	WED	5
SAT	6	TUES	6	THUR	6
SUN	7	WED	7	FRI	7
MON	8	THUR	8	SAT	8
TUES	9	FRI	9	SUN	9
WED	10	SAT	10	MON	10
THUR	11	SUN	11	TUES	11
FRI	12	MON	12	WED	12
SAT	13	TUES	13	THUR	13
SUN	14	WED	14	FRI	14
MON	15	THUR	15	SAT	15
TUES	16	FRI	16	SUN	16
WED	17	SAT	17	MON	17
THUR	18	SUN	18	TUES	18
FRI	19	MON	19	WED	19
SAT	20	TUES	20	THUR	20
SUN	21	WED	21	FRI	21
MON	22	THUR	22	SAT	22
TUES	23	FRI	23	SUN	23
WED	24	SAT	24	MON	24
THUR	25	SUN	25	TUES	25
FRI	26	MON	26	WED	26
SAT	27	TUES	27	THUR	27
SUN	28	WED	28	FRI	28
MON	29	THUR	29	SAT	29
TUES	30	FRI	30	SUN	30
WED	31			MON	31

Throughout March and April Billie is resident at Club 331 in Los Angeles opposite Henry 'Red' Allen's Band.

WEDNESDAY 7 APRIL 1943
Billie's 28th birthday

MONDAY 26 APRIL 1943
Jubilee Program 22 broadcast?

EARLY MAY 1943
Billie closes at Club 331

FRIDAY 7 MAY 1943
Billie begins a one-week engagement at the Apollo Theatre. Also on the bill are Pops & Louie and Teddy Powell & his Band.

WEDNESDAY 12 MAY 1943
The Amateur Hour at the Apollo is broadcast on station WMCA

THURSDAY 13 MAY 1943
Billie closes at the Apollo.

SATURDAY 15 MAY 1943
Billie appears at the Hotel Capitol on 51st Street and 8th Avenue in New York City doing two shows, at 9pm and 2am.

TUES	1
WED	2
THUR	3
FRI	4
SAT	5
SUN	6
MON	7
TUES	8
WED	9
THUR	10
FRI	11
SAT	12
SUN	13
MON	14
TUES	15
WED	16
THUR	17
FRI	18
SAT	19
SUN	20
MON	21
TUES	22
WED	23
THUR	24
FRI	25
SAT	26
SUN	27
MON	28
TUES	29
WED	30

Throughout June Billie is resident at the Onyx Club, backed by the Cozy Cole Trio featuring Johnny Guarnieri (p) and Hank D'Amico (cl). All three members of the Cozy Cole Trio are moonlighting from their job with Raymond Scott's CBS studio orchestra.

Billie and Fine Trio at Onyx

New York—Billie Holiday opened at the *Onyx Club* on 52nd Street here three weeks ago with backing by the Cozy Cole trio which features Hank D'Amico on clarinet, Johnny Guarnieri on piano, and Cozy, of course, on drums.

Cozy Boys Not Prima Donnas

Trio Objected to Playing Behind Assorted Acts

New York—The alleged temperament of the Cozy Cole Trio at the Onyx on 52nd Street here, which drew comment from local columns wasn't prima donna stuff at all. The trio, made up of three top-ranking musicians, Cole, drums, Hank D'Amico, clary, and Johnny Guarnieri, piano, and brought into the spot purely on the strength of their superior musicianship, asked that they be excused from playing music behind the floor show acts.

The whole point of the booking was to get jazz music lovers to visit the spot and there seemed to be little point in having the three men waste their time playing *Over the Waves* while somebody hoofed it. The band suggested too that a solo piano would sound better behind Billie Holiday, also featured at the Onyx, than would the trio attempting to read arrangements in the dim light of a nitery.

Johnny Guarnieri has given his notice to CBS's Raymond Scott, in whose band he has been featured, but will continue doing free-lance radio work, doubling at the Onyx.

THUR	1
FRI	2
SAT	3
SUN	4
MON	5
TUES	6
WED	7
THUR	8
FRI	9
SAT	10
SUN	11
MON	12
TUES	13
WED	14
THUR	15
FRI	16
SAT	17
SUN	18
MON	19
TUES	20
WED	21
THUR	22
FRI	23
SAT	24
SUN	25
MON	26
TUES	27
WED	28
THUR	29
FRI	30
SAT	31

Throughout July Billie is resident at the Onyx with the Roy Eldridge Quintet.

SATURDAY 3 JULY 1943
Billie appears at the Manhattan Center, 34th Street at 8th Avenue, at 9pm prior to her first set at the Onyx.

THURSDAY 15 JULY 1943
Billie opens at the Loew's State Theatre on Broadway at Times Square for a one-week engagement. Also on the bill is Eddie South's Band. Billie is doubling at the Onyx.

WEDNESDAY 21 JULY 1943
Billie closes at the Loew's State Theatre.

Eddie and Billie Play Theater

New York—Violinist Eddie South with a seven-piece band opens at the Loew's State theater here July 15 with Billie Holiday featured as an extra attraction on the same bill. South will continue with a road tour aimed at theaters after his State date.

Another famous singer, Mildred Bailey, who has just concluded a record-breaking engagement at Cafe Society uptown, has a State booking which begins today with instrumental backing supplied by Van Alexander's new band.

SUN	**1**		WED	**1**
MON	**2**		THUR	**2**
TUES	**3**		FRI	**3**
WED	**4**		SAT	**4**
THUR	**5**		SUN	**5**
FRI	**6**		MON	**6**
SAT	**7**		TUES	**7**
SUN	**8**		WED	**8**
MON	**9**		THUR	**9**
TUES	**10**		FRI	**10**
WED	**11**		SAT	**11**
THUR	**12**		SUN	**12**
FRI	**13**		MON	**13**
SAT	**14**		TUES	**14**
SUN	**15**		WED	**15**
MON	**16**		THUR	**16**
TUES	**17**		FRI	**17**
WED	**18**		SAT	**18**
THUR	**19**		SUN	**19**
FRI	**20**		MON	**20**
SAT	**21**		TUES	**21**
SUN	**22**		WED	**22**
MON	**23**		THUR	**23**
TUES	**24**		FRI	**24**
WED	**25**		SAT	**25**
THUR	**26**		SUN	**26**
FRI	**27**		MON	**27**
SAT	**28**		TUES	**28**
SUN	**29**		WED	**29**
MON	**30**		THUR	**30**
TUES	**31**			

Throughout August and September Billie is resident at the Onyx with Roy Eldridge

15 AUGUST 1943

Down Beat, in an article headed 'Jazz Flows Again In Swing Lane: Several Spots Jump With Joy In 52nd Street', reviews Billie and Roy Eldridge:

'... **Billie is still not singing at her best, in our opinion, nor does she sing often enough, but Eldridge more than makes up for her by putting on a show every night that is sensational, as corny as that word may read. His horn is certainly as exciting a musical treat as you're apt to find in a lot of wandering all over Manhattan in search for the stuff hot. There's nothing lacking in Roy's work: taste, power, range, tone, ideas, all are on view and in large quantities.'**

In the last week of September *Life* magazine sponsors a jam session in the studio of photographer Gjon Mili at 6 E23rd Street. Many great jazz musicians are present including Duke Ellington, James P Johnson, Mary Lou Williams, Teddy Wilson, Sid Catlett, Jess Stacy, Eddie Condon and many more. The music is recorded for possible issue on V-disc but is never released. Billie 's photograph is published in a centre spread of the October 11 issue of *Life* magazine.

Several Spots Jump With Joy In 52nd Street

Hawkins, Eldridge, Holiday Contribute To Music Scene

New York — Our quarterly check-up on 52nd street and how it's treating jazz shows much improvement this time.

Coleman Hawkins, indisputably king of the tenor sax, has returned to Kelly's Stable and is in far better form than he was during his last visit. To make things even better, the Bean has varied his routine and stopped using innumerable choruses of *Body and Soul* under various other names. As a matter of fact, he has even changed his *Body and Soul* riffs themselves, and, on the night that we caught him, seemed to have recovered that old and wonderful feeling for ideas, coupled with the ultimate in breathy tone, that makes his jazz record...

FRI	**1**
SAT	**2**
SUN	**3**
MON	**4**
TUES	**5**
WED	**6**
THUR	**7**
FRI	**8**
SAT	**9**
SUN	**10**
MON	**11**
TUES	**12**
WED	**13**
THUR	**14**
FRI	**15**
SAT	**16**
SUN	**17**
MON	**18**
TUES	**19**
WED	**20**
THUR	**21**
FRI	**22**
SAT	**23**
SUN	**24**
MON	**25**
TUES	**26**
WED	**27**
THUR	**28**
FRI	**29**
SAT	**30**
SUN	**31**

Throughout October Billie is resident at the Onyx Club backed by the Al Casey Trio

THURSDAY 7 OCTOBER 1943

Billie and the entire Onyx Club show is scheduled to perform at a nearby USO Camp. It doesn't happen and the show's manager, Dick Campbell, in a letter to USO Camp Shows, explains:

> The show was cancelled at the last minute because the star, Billie Holiday, songstress, refused to ride a train to Camp Shanks and insisted upon a taxicab or bus. The Management of the Onyx Club, Cye Baron, had promised the show to Negro troops at Camp Shanks with Miss Holiday as star, the Toy Wilson Trio, Al Casey Trio and Ann Cornell, dancer, who though not working at Club Onyx had volunteered her services. It was agreed that the performers would leave the Onyx Club at 57 W. 52nd street at 5.00 p.m. on the date of the performance which was to have been Thursday, October 7. The Management insisted that the performers be back from camp and on the bandstand at 10.00 p.m.
>
> Realizing that there would be hardly enough time for the show to reach Camp Shanks from New York City, have dinner, and do an hour and quarter show, and at the same time be back at the Club Onyx at 10.00 o'clock, it was decided that it would be best to go by train and avoid what situations might develop from heavy traffic. The Management of Club Onyx was informed the night previous as well as on the date of the performance that it might be best to go by train rather than bus to make sure that the performers were back on their job at the proper time.
>
> There was not the slightest objection to this on the part of the Management. And there was not the slightest objection to this on the part of the Toy Wilson Trio, by the Al Caset Trio or Ann Cornell, singer. Not the slightest objection was made on the part of anyone until Miss Holiday rolled up in a taxicab with her manager, Cye Brown, forty-five minutes late and informed the USO Camp Show representative that she would not ride a train because it was too "wearing and tearing on her nerves." It was explained to her that she had been advertised in Camp Shanks as well as in the Press through our Public Relations Department, and that thousands of colored soldiers would be waiting to hear her. She remained adamant, and steadfastly refused to join the other members of the troupe, and go on the train. She then said that she would go in a taxicab. As this was impossible, the USO Camp Shows' representative then called the office and tried to arrange at the last minute for bus transportation.

SUNDAY 24 OCTOBER 1943

Billie appears at the Golden Gate Ballroom in Harlem for an All Star Victory Show in tribute to Benjamin J Davis Jr. Also on the bill are Freddi Washington, Paul Robeson, Mary Lou Williams and Coleman Hawkins.

MON	1	WED	1
TUES	2	THUR	2
WED	3	FRI	3
THUR	4	SAT	4
FRI	5	SUN	5
SAT	6	MON	6
SUN	7	TUES	7
MON	8	WED	8
TUES	9	THUR	9
WED	10	FRI	10
THUR	11	SAT	11
FRI	12	SUN	12
SAT	13	MON	13
SUN	14	TUES	14
MON	15	WED	15
TUES	16	THUR	16
WED	17	FRI	17
THUR	18	SAT	18
FRI	19	SUN	19
SAT	20	MON	20
SUN	21	TUES	21
MON	22	WED	22
TUES	23	THUR	23
WED	24	FRI	24
THUR	25	SAT	25
FRI	26	SUN	26
SAT	27	MON	27
SUN	28	TUES	28
MON	29	WED	29
TUES	30	THUR	30
		FRI	31

Throughout November Billie is resident at the Onyx Club backed by Pete Brown and his Band. Also on the bill is Dizzy Gillespie with the first bebop group to play on the Street. Dizzy's Quintet with Lester Young on tenor sax moved into the Onyx on 20th October.

The Dizzy Gillespie Quintet at the Onyx: Lester Young (ts), George Wallington (p), Oscar Pettiford (b), Max Roach (d) and Dizzy Gillespie (t).

Billie becomes involved with John Simmons, the bass player. He says that it is around this time that she begins using narcotics.

Early in December she closes at the Onyx Club where bebop is beginning to hold sway and Don Byas replaces Lester in the Dizzy Gillespie Quintet.

FRIDAY 17 DECEMBER 1943
Billie begins a one-week engagement at the Apollo Theatre. Also on the bill are The Harlem Highlanders, Eddie Rector and Teddy McRae & his Band.

WEDNESDAY 22 DECEMBER 1943
The Amateur Hour at the Apollo is broadcast on station WMCA

THURSDAY 23 DECEMBER 1943
Billie closes at the Apollo.

Billie begins a 4-week tour fronting the Teddy McRae Band.

SAT	**1**
SUN	**2**
MON	**3**
TUES	**4**
WED	**5**
THUR	**6**
FRI	**7**
SAT	**8**
SUN	**9**
MON	**10**
TUES	**11**
WED	**12**
THUR	**13**
FRI	**14**
SAT	**15**
SUN	**16**
MON	**17**
TUES	**18**
WED	**19**
THUR	**20**
FRI	**21**
SAT	**22**
SUN	**23**
MON	**24**
TUES	**25**
WED	**26**
THUR	**27**
FRI	**28**
SAT	**29**
SUN	**30**
MON	**31**

THURSDAY 13 JANUARY 1944
Billie opens at the Onyx Club on 52nd Street opposite the Al Casey Trio.

TUESDAY 18 JANUARY 1944
The *Esquire* magazine award-winners concert is held in New York's Metropolitan Opera House. Billie won the vocalist section with 23 votes, in front of Mildred Bailey (15) and Ella Fitzgerald (4).
This is Billie's first major concert appearance, and she becomes the first black woman to sing on the stage of the Metropolitan Opera House. Much of the concert is recorded.

SAT	**1**
SUN	**2**
MON	**3**
TUES	**4**
WED	**5**
THUR	**6**
FRI	**7**
SAT	**8**
SUN	**9**
MON	**10**
TUES	**11**
WED	**12**
THUR	**13**
FRI	**14**
SAT	**15**
SUN	**16**
MON	**17**
TUES	**18**
WED	**19**
THUR	**20**
FRI	**21**
SAT	**22**
SUN	**23**
MON	**24**
TUES	**25**
WED	**26**
THUR	**27**
FRI	**28**
SAT	**29**
SUN	**30**
MON	**31**

The concert begins at 8.30 with the All-Star Jam Band, introduced by Leonard Feather: ROY ELDRIDGE (t), BARNEY BIGARD (cl), COLEMAN HAWKINS (ts), JACK TEAGARDEN (tb), ART TATUM (p), AL CASEY (g), OSCAR PETTIFORD (b), SID CATLETT (d): *Esquire Blues /Mop Mop*
Billie joins the band for two numbers *Do Nothing Till You Hear From Me / Billie's Blues*
Louis Armstrong replaces Billie for two numbers with the band: *I Can't Give You Anything But Love / I Gotta Right To Sing The Blues* (v Jack Teagarden)
ART TATUM (p), OSCAR PETTIFORD (b), SID CATLETT (d): *Sweet Lorraine*
The All-Star Jam Band plus LOUIS ARMSTRONG (t) and RED NORVO (xylophone): *I Got Rhythm*
The All-Star Jam Band: *Blues*

At 9.30 the radio broadcast begins. Coca Cola's 'Victory Parade of Spotlight Bands' on NBC's Blue Network.
The All-Star Jam Band: *Esquire Bounce*
RED NORVO (vib), TEDDY WILSON (p), MILDRED BAILEY (v) added: *Rockin' Chair*

Opposite page: Billie on stage at the Metropolitan Opera House in front of the All Star Jam Band.
Below: Looking beautiful in a change of gown, Billie listens to Art Tatum, Sid Catlett and Oscar Pettiford.

The All-Star Jam Band plus Louis Armstrong (t/v): *Basin Street Blues*
Billie Holiday with the All-Star Jam Band: *I'll Get By*
BENNY GOODMAN (cl), JESS STACY (p), SID WEISS (b), MOREY FELD (d): *Rachel's Dream*
The All-Star Jam Band plus LIONEL HAMPTON (vib): *Tea For Two*
At this point (9.55pm) the radio broadcast ends.

The All-Star Jam Band plus LOUIS ARMSTRONG (t/v): *Back O' Town Blues / Muskrat Ramble / Buck Jumpin'* (Al Casey feature) */ Stompin' At The Savoy / For Bass Faces Only* (Oscar Pettiford feature)
COLEMAN HAWKINS (ts), ART TATUM (p), AL CASEY (g), OSCAR PETTIFORD (b), SID CATLETT (d): *My Ideal*
Barney Bigard replaces Coleman Hawkins with the rhythm section: *Rose Room*
TEDDY WILSON (solo piano): *I've Got A Feeling I'm Falling*
MILDRED BAILEY (v) joins TEDDY WILSON (p): *More Than You Know*
RED NORVO (vib) joins Mildred Bailey and Teddy Wilson: *Squeeze Me / Honeysuckle Rose*

The All-Star Jam Band plus LIONEL HAMPTON (vib): *Flyin' Home* (vibes feature) */ Flyin' Home* (drum feature)
Red Norvo (vib) joins the ensemble for the finale: *Jammin' The Blues / Star Spangled Banner*

TUES **1**	WED **1**	SAT **1**
WED **2**	THUR **2**	SUN **2**
THUR **3**	FRI **3**	MON **3**
FRI **4**	SAT **4**	TUES **4**
SAT **5**	SUN **5**	WED **5**
SUN **6**	MON **6**	THUR **6**
MON **7**	TUES **7**	FRI **7**
TUES **8**	WED **8**	SAT **8**
WED **9**	THUR **9**	SUN **9**
THUR **10**	FRI **10**	MON **10**
FRI **11**	SAT **11**	TUES **11**
SAT **12**	SUN **12**	WED **12**
SUN **13**	MON **13**	THUR **13**
MON **14**	TUES **14**	FRI **14**
TUES **15**	WED **15**	SAT **15**
WED **16**	THUR **16**	SUN **16**
THUR **17**	FRI **17**	MON **17**
FRI **18**	SAT **18**	TUES **18**
SAT **19**	SUN **19**	WED **19**
SUN **20**	MON **20**	THUR **20**
MON **21**	TUES **21**	FRI **21**
TUES **22**	WED **22**	SAT **22**
WED **23**	THUR **23**	SUN **23**
THUR **24**	FRI **24**	MON **24**
FRI **25**	SAT **25**	TUES **25**
SAT **26**	SUN **26**	WED **26**
SUN **27**	MON **27**	THUR **27**
MON **28**	TUES **28**	FRI **28**
TUES **29**	WED **29**	SAT **29**
	THUR **30**	SUN **30**
	FRI **31**	

Throughout February and March Billie is resident at the Onyx Club with the Al Casey Trio.

SATURDAY 25 MARCH 1944

Recording session as Billie Holiday accompanied by Eddie Heywood and his Orchestra for Commodore Records. The session takes place at WOR Recording Studios, 1440 Broadway, New York City and is produced by Milt Gabler. DOC CHEATHAM (t), LEM DAVIS (as), VIC DICKENSON (tb), EDDIE HEYWOOD (p), TEDDY WALTERS (g), JOHN SIMMONS (b), SID CATLETT (d), BILLIE HOLIDAY (v)
How Am I To Know (5 takes) / *My Old Flame* (4 takes) / *I'll Get By* (2 takes) / *I Cover The Waterfront* (4 takes)

SATURDAY 1 APRIL 1944

Recording session as Billie Holiday accompanied by Eddie Heywood and his Orchestra for Commodore Records. The session takes place at WOR Recording Studios, 1440 Broadway, New York City and is produced by Milt Gabler. DOC CHEATHAM (t), LEM DAVIS (as), VIC DICKENSON (tb), EDDIE HEYWOOD (p), JOHN SIMMONS (b), SID CATLETT (d), BILLIE HOLIDAY (v). Teddy Walters (g) didn't turn up for the session.
I'll Be Seeing You (4 takes) / *I'm Yours* (3 takes) / *Embraceable You* (3 takes) / *As Time Goes By* (2 takes)

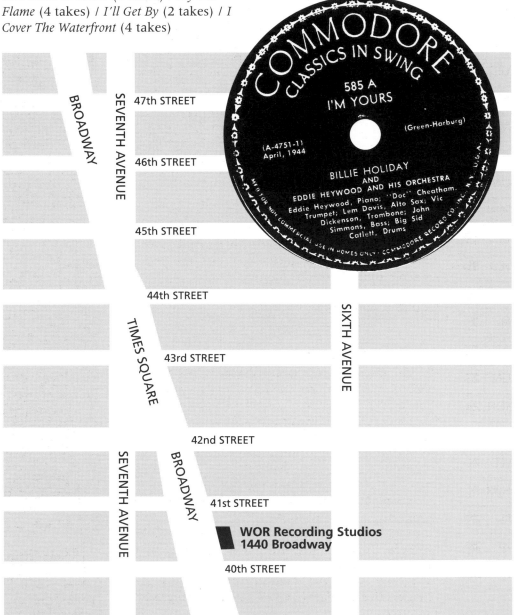

**WOR Recording Studios
1440 Broadway**

SAT	1
SUN	2
MON	3
TUES	4
WED	5
THUR	6
FRI	7
SAT	8
SUN	9
MON	10
TUES	11
WED	12
THUR	13
FRI	14
SAT	15
SUN	16
MON	17
TUES	18
WED	19
THUR	20
FRI	21
SAT	22
SUN	23
MON	24
TUES	25
WED	26
THUR	27
FRI	28
SAT	29
SUN	30

SUNDAY 2 APRIL 1944

Billie is advertised to appear in a 'Salute to Fats Waller' Concert at Carnegie Hall. Also on the bill are Count Basie & Orchestra, Teddy Wilson Band, Al Casey Trio, Hazel Scott, Hot Lips Page, Pee Wee Russell, Eddie Condon, Mary Lou Williams, Art Hodes and Sid Catlett.

Billie is not mentioned in reviews so it is possible she did not show up.

MONDAY 3 APRIL 1944

Billie is the guest star at Billy Eckstine's Monday Night Celebrity Party at the Yacht Club on 52nd Street. Joe Marsala and Lester Young are also there along with the resident Yacht Club band, the Dizzy Gillespie/Budd Johnson Quintet.

FRIDAY 7 APRIL 1944

Billie's 29th birthday

SATURDAY 8 APRIL 1944

Recording session as Billie Holiday accompanied by Eddie Heywood and his Orchestra for Commodore Records. The session takes place at WOR Recording Studios, 1440 Broadway, New York City and is produced by Milt Gabler.

FREDDIE WEBSTER (t), LEM DAVIS (as), VIC DICKENSON (tb), EDDIE HEYWOOD (p), TEDDY WALTERS (g), JOHN SIMMONS (b), SID CATLETT (d), BILLIE HOLIDAY (v)

She's Funny That Way (2 takes) / *Lover Come Back To Me* (2 takes)

For some reason the remainder of this session is with the Eddie Heywood Trio only, including remakes of the previous two titles.

She's Funny That Way (3 takes) / *Lover Come Back To Me* (2 takes) / *Billie's Blues* (3 takes) / *On The Sunny Side Of The Street*

Billie closes at the Onyx Club sometime around the time of this recording session.

THURSDAY 13 APRIL 1944

Billie opens a one-week engagement at Loew's State Theatre, New York City.

WEDNESDAY 19 APRIL 1944

Billie closes at Loew's State Theatre, New York City.

FRIDAY 21 APRIL 1944

Billie opens a one-week engagement at the Regal Theatre, Chicago as an added attraction on the bill to headliners Tiny Hill & his Orchestra.

THURSDAY 27 APRIL 1944

Billie closes at the Regal Theatre.

MON	1
TUES	2
WED	3
THUR	4
FRI	5
SAT	6
SUN	7
MON	8
TUES	9
WED	10
THUR	11
FRI	12
SAT	13
SUN	14
MON	15
TUES	16
WED	17
THUR	18
FRI	19
SAT	20
SUN	21
MON	22
TUES	23
WED	24
THUR	25
FRI	26
SAT	27
SUN	28
MON	29
TUES	30
WED	31

SUNDAY 7 MAY 1944

Billie appears at a 3pm show at the Golden Gate Auditorium, New York at a Celebration and Rally to end Jim Crow in NYC. Benjamin J Davis and Reverend Adam Clayton Powell are there as well as Billie, Count Basie, Teddy Wilson and Mary Lou Williams.

FRIDAY 19 MAY 1944

Billie opens a one-week engagement at the Apollo Theatre in Harlem opposite Noble Sissle and his Orchestra. Also on the bill are Billy Mitchell and Pinky Black.

WEDNESDAY 24 MAY 1944

During the Apollo Amateur Hour, Billie broadcasts over station WMCA accompanied by Noble Sissle's Orchestra.
Do Nothing Till You Hear From Me

THURSDAY 25 MAY 1944

Billie closes at the Apollo.

FRIDAY 26 MAY 1944

Billie opens at the Ruban Bleu on New York's East side. Also on the bill are Imogene Coca and Irwin Corey for the laughs, and harpist Daphne Hellman. Hellman is replaced at the end of the month by another harpist, La Villa Tullos.
During the first three weeks at the Ruban Bleu, Billie's dog, Rajah Ravoy (known as Gypsy), dies. Soon Billie has a replacement, a boxer called Mister.

FRIDAY 26 MAY 1944

Columnist Earl Wilson in the *NY Post*:

> **Frank Sinatra's** "tutor," according to rumors you hear along Swing St., was Billie Holiday, the terrific Negro gal swing singer. She's now at the Ruban Bleu and I asked her about this tale. "Listen, darling," she said, "I didn't teach Frank anything. I was at the Chicago Three Deuces and Frank was with Harry James.
>
> "So me like a dope, I didn't know, I went over there where he was and they wouldn't let me in. But Frank and the others saw me, so four of us, we just went out and had a ball. I told him he didn't phrase right. He should bend certain notes. He says, 'Lady, you aren't commercial.' But I told him certain notes at the end he could bend, and later he said I inspired him. Bending those notes – that's all I helped Frankie with."

THUR **1**
FRI **2**
SAT **3**
SUN **4**
MON **5**
TUES **6**
WED **7**
THUR **8**
FRI **9**
SAT **10**
SUN **11**
MON **12**
TUES **13**
WED **14**
THUR **15**
FRI **16**
SAT **17**
SUN **18**
MON **19**
TUES **20**
WED **21**
THUR **22**
FRI **23**
SAT **24**
SUN **25**
MON **26**
TUES **27**
WED **28**
THUR **29**
FRI **30**

Billie Holiday Opens At NYC Ruban Bleu

New York—Billie Holiday is singing currently at the Ruban Bleu club here. Originally set to return to the Onyx on 52nd Street, Billie surprised her local fans by opening at the swank east side spot. On the same bill at the Ruban is society deb Daphne Hellman, who plays boogie-woogie on the harp.

Billie's Back

New York—Billie Holiday, rated by many jazz lovers as the queen of them all, is back where she belongs (with exception of on the wax, of course) in an *intimate* spot, Le Ruban Bleu. Lady Day is at her best in an informal atmosphere.

MONDAY 19 JUNE 1944

Billie appears in the Negro Salute to the Fighting Jews of Europe at Town Hall in New York. Also on the bill are Teddy Wilson's Band, Mary Lou Williams, Josh White and many others.

NEGRO SALUTE
to the
Fighting Jews of Europe
at Town Hall, 123 West 43rd St.,
Monday, June 19, 8:30 P. M.
FEATURING
Muriel Smith   Mary Lou Williams
Aubrey Pankey   Billy Holliday
Teddy Wilson   Wilmas Gray
and Band   Josh White
Luther Saxon   Canada Lee
And Others
PRESENTATION Meyer Levin—
Doris Miller—SCROLLS
Tickets $1.20 to $3.30
Approved by Theatre Authority, Inc.
American Committee of Jewish
Writers, Artists and Scientists, Inc.
25 West 42nd Street, New York, N. Y.
Mail orders filled

SATURDAY 24 JUNE 1944

Billie closes at the Ruban Bleu when the club closes for the summer. After hours, Billie appears at the Golden Gate Ballroom for a Breakfast Dance and Jam Session. The dancing begins at midnight with Al Cooper's Savoy Sultans, followed by a jam session at 5am featuring Billie, Louise Metcalf, Ralph Cooper and others.

Starting At
MIDNIGHT
AL COOPER'S
Savoy Sultans
JAM SESSION
Starts at 5 A. M.
LOUISE METCALF
GUT BUCKET KING
RALPH COOPER
BILLIE HOLIDAY
AND OTHERS

GET SET FOR
MUSIC DIAL'S
1st ANNIVERSARY
BREAKFAST DANCE and
JAM·SESSION JUNE 24
Golden Gate Ballroom
Part of Proceeds to Benefit the NAACP and Riverdale Colored Orphan Home

SUNDAY 25 JUNE 1944

Billie appears on a radio broadcast 'New World A' Coming – The Story of Negro Music' via station WMCA. The programme, number 17 in the series, is narrated by Canada Lee and also features Josh White and the Hall Johnson Choir.

Billie, introduced as 'a blues singer', is accompanied by ROY ELDRIDGE, CHARLIE SHAVERS (t), EDMOND HALL (cl), BEN WEBSTER (ts), VIC DICKENSON, BENNY MORTON (tb), ART TATUM (p), SLAM STEWART (b), ARTHUR TRAPPIER (d)

Fine and Mellow / Royal Garden Blues (Billie out) / *All Of Me / I Got Rhythm* (Billie out)

THURSDAY 29 JUNE 1944

Billie opens a three-week engagement at the Grand Terrace, Chicago with the Darlings of Rhythm.

DINE AND DANCE

ANNOUNCING
THE GRAND OPENING
of the Greater

THREE SHOWS NIGHTLY

Air Conditioned Air Conditioned

Grand TERRACE Cafe
35th and South Parkway

SIX DAY CELEBRATION

JUNE 29, 30, JULY 1, 2, 3, 4
WITH
★ BILLIE HOLIDAY ★
AND VIVIAN TAYLOR'S
40 ARTISTS GRAND TERRACE CAFE REVUE 40 ARTISTS
TWO BITS OF RHYTHM — Two Sisters — Taps in Taps
ERNEST "BABY" SEALS — Harlem's Laugh-A-Minute Comedian
TINY MABERRY — A Ton of Personality and Swing
SHORTS DAVIS   ★ CHARLES CALLOWAY   ★ THE FOUR DANCING DEMONS
LEROY HILL   ★ JESSIE DAVIS   HENRY REYMO
SPORTY KID   ★ SCAT MAN   LONNIE JOHNSON, Shoe Dictator
                and Vivian Taylor's "THE BROWN SKIN GIRL"
★ TEN BRONZE BOMBSHELLS, Subordinating
with America's No. One All-Girl Orchestra
THE DARLINGS OF RHYTHM
14 Beauties — Spellbinding — 14 Beauties
★ JOAN LUNCEFORD and HELEN TABORN, featured vocalists
CLARENCE LOVE, Musical Director

ADMISSION $2.50 PER PERSON, ALL TAXES PAID

SAT	1
SUN	2
MON	3
TUES	4
WED	5
THUR	6
FRI	7
SAT	8
SUN	9
MON	10
TUES	11
WED	12
THUR	13
FRI	14
SAT	15
SUN	16
MON	17
TUES	18
WED	19
THUR	20
FRI	21
SAT	22
SUN	23
MON	24
TUES	25
WED	26
THUR	27
FRI	28
SAT	29
SUN	30
MON	31

Chicago, July 15, 1944

Billie Holiday, currently at the reopened Grand Terrace on the south side, will do a repeat at the Regal theater the week of July 21, sharing the bill with Noble Sissle and his orchestra, making the second appearance there for Billie in three months. Doubling from the Grand Terrace for six days, Billie closes that spot on July 26 when the Darlings of Rhythm vacate the bandstand for Snookum Russell and his band.

Woody Herman, who completed a successful engagement at the

THE NEW
Grand Terrace Cafe
PROUDLY PRESENTS
Chicago's GREATEST Floor Show
STARRING
BILLIE HOLIDAY
SWEETHEART OF SONG
FEATURING
BABY SEALS
A Laugh A Minute
LONNIE JOHNSON
Famous Blues Singer and His Guitar
INCLUDING A GREAT SUPPORTING CAST
OF 35 PEOPLE
Dine and Dance to the Rhythms of
THE DARLINGS OF RHYTHM
ALL GIRL ORCHESTRA
NO ADMISSION — NO COVER
3 Shows Nightly — 11 P.M., 1 A.M., 3 A.M.
• **ONLY THE BEST IN FOOD AND DRINKS** •
FOR RESERVATIONS
PHONE VICTORY 0577
CHARLES TAYLOR
Manager

FRIDAY 21 JULY 1944

Billie begins a one-week engagement at the Regal Theatre, Chicago with Noble Sissle and his Orchestra. Billie doubles at the Grand Terrace.

WEDNESDAY 26 JULY 1944

Billie closes at the Grand Terrace.

THURSDAY 27 JULY 1944

Billie closes at the Regal Theatre.

Billie does a screen test for Warner Brothers in Hollywood at the end of July.

Studios 'Find' Billie Holiday

New York — Billie Holiday, one of the few sepia beauties to be overlooked by the film industry so far, has finally been discovered by Warner Brothers and will head for the coast in late summer to make a picture. Her Hollywood trek follows three July weeks in Chicago, two at the Grand Terrace and one at the Regal. Successful cinema efforts of Lena Horne and Hazel Scott probably helped WB in making up their minds about Lady Day.

REGAL 47th-- South Parkway
PLUS SCREEN THRILLER!
Friday, July 21st ONE WEEK ONLY!
YEAR'S SMASH RED-HOT
★ **SIZZLE** ★
SHOW IN COOL COMFORT
ON STAGE — IN PERSON
NOBLE **BILLIE**
SISSLE AND HIS HOT HOT BAND **HOLIDAY** GOLDEN VOICED SWING SING STAR
"SIZZLE with SISSLE"
And A GIANT JIVE-FILLED REVUE
INCLUDING JOYNER and FOSTER
SURPRISE NOVELTY ACT
DOT and DELLAN'S FAMOUS BOXING FELINES!
DOORS OPEN 11 A.M.
— **COME EARLY** —
TAMPICO EDWARD G. ROBINSON

Following the screen test, Billie returns to New York for some urgent dental treatment, including extractions and new bridge-work.

TUES	1
WED	2
THUR	3
FRI	4
SAT	5
SUN	6
MON	7
TUES	8
WED	9
THUR	10
FRI	11
SAT	12
SUN	13
MON	14
TUES	15
WED	16
THUR	17
FRI	18
SAT	19
SUN	20
MON	21
TUES	22
WED	23
THUR	24
FRI	25
SAT	26
SUN	27
MON	28
TUES	29
WED	30
THUR	31

MONDAY 7 AUGUST 1944
Billie signs a recording contract with Decca.

FRIDAY 18 AUGUST 1944
Billie takes up residency at the Downbeat Club on 52nd Street with Red Norvo's Combo and a band led by Paul & Dud Bascomb. Down Beat's review says that Billie had lost weight

SATURDAY 19 AUGUST 1944
Billie makes an appearance at a Benefit Concert at the Lido Ballroom, NYC. Also on the bill is 61 year old Mamie Smith making her last appearance.

TUESDAY 29 AUGUST 1944
Billie writes to Greer Johnson to thank him for the things he is doing for her. The picture she refers to may be the recently taken portrait by Robin Carson (below).

Dear Greer:

I am sorry that our conversation was cut so short last night but you can understand those things I am sure.

I would like to thank you in advance for the many wonderful things that you are going to do for me and you will always find me ready to give you what ever assistance that I may.

I will have the picture for you Monday night and I shall be looking for you.

Cordially,
Billie Holiday

FRI	**1**	SUN	**1**
SAT	**2**	MON	**2**
SUN	**3**	TUES	**3**
MON	**4**	WED	**4**
TUES	**5**	THUR	**5**
WED	**6**	FRI	**6**
THUR	**7**	SAT	**7**
FRI	**8**	SUN	**8**
SAT	**9**	MON	**9**
SUN	**10**	TUES	**10**
MON	**11**	WED	**11**
TUES	**12**	THUR	**12**
WED	**13**	FRI	**13**
THUR	**14**	SAT	**14**
FRI	**15**	SUN	**15**
SAT	**16**	MON	**16**
SUN	**17**	TUES	**17**
MON	**18**	WED	**18**
TUES	**19**	THUR	**19**
WED	**20**	FRI	**20**
THUR	**21**	SAT	**21**
FRI	**22**	SUN	**22**
SAT	**23**	MON	**23**
SUN	**24**	TUES	**24**
MON	**25**	WED	**25**
TUES	**26**	THUR	**26**
WED	**27**	FRI	**27**
THUR	**28**	SAT	**28**
FRI	**29**	SUN	**29**
SAT	**30**	MON	**30**
		TUES	**31**

Throughout September and October Billie is resident at the Downbeat Club on 52nd Street. Milt Gabler, on his way to Jimmy Ryans, calls in at the Downbeat one night. Billie sings *Lover Man*, and he arranges for her to record it.

MONDAY 18 SEPTEMBER 1944
Coleman Hawkins replaces Sid Catlett at the Downbeat.

Billie Records With Holiday For Strings

New York—Singer Billie Holiday, currently at the Downbeat Club here, is set to wax a surprise date for Decca soon. Odd twist to the platter session will be the use of strings, oboes and French horns to provide Billie with a new-for-her background.

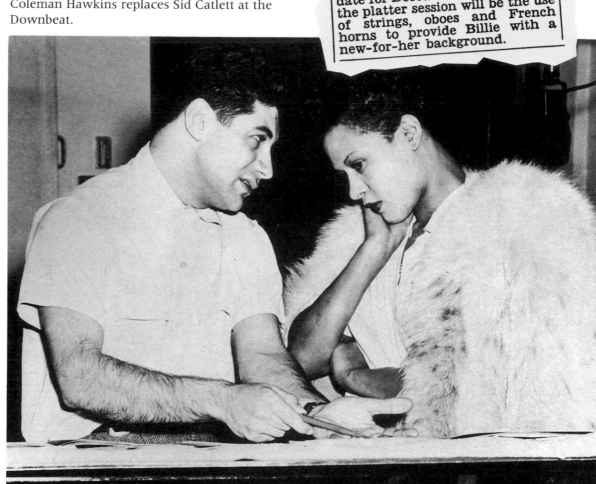

Toots Camarata and Billie at the 'Lover Man' recording session.

WEDNESDAY 4 OCTOBER 1944
Recording session (1pm–4pm) as Billie Holiday accompanied by Toots Camarata and his Orchestra for Decca at the Decca Studios, 50 W57th Street, New York City. Milt Gabler is the producer and he gives Billie the string section she has asked for.
TOOTS CAMARATA (cond/arr), RUSS CASE (t), HYMIE SCHERTZER, JACK CRESSY (as), LARRY BINYON, PAUL RICCI (ts), DAVE BOWMAN (p), CARL KRESS (g), HAIGH STEPHENS (b), JOHNNY BLOWERS (d), six strings, BILLIE HOLIDAY (v)
Lover Man / No More (2 takes)

SUNDAY 15 OCTOBER 1944
Down Beat carries a review by Jax:

BILLIE HOLIDAY
I'll Get By / I'll Be Seeing You
Commodore 553
Eddie Heywood arranged both sides, brought along Doc Cheatham and Vic Dickenson and Lem Davis from his own band to cut the stuff. John Simmons is on bass, Sid Catlett on drums. Teddy Walters gets a git on the first side. None of the others solo at all. Billie's as fine as ever, of course, one of the few fems worth an occasional rave today. *I'll Get By* is quite similar to her rendition with Teddy Wilson years back. *Seeing You* is taken at a drag tempo, sung more effectively than I had thought possible.

WED	1
THUR	2
FRI	3
SAT	4
SUN	5
MON	6
TUES	7
WED	8
THUR	9
FRI	10
SAT	11
SUN	12
MON	13
TUES	14
WED	15
THUR	16
FRI	17
SAT	18
SUN	19
MON	20
TUES	21
WED	22
THUR	23
FRI	24
SAT	25
SUN	26
MON	27
TUES	28
WED	29
THUR	30

WEDNESDAY 8 NOVEMBER 1944
Recording session (1pm–5pm) as Billie Holiday accompanied by Toots Camarata and his Orchestra for Decca in New York City. Milt Gabler is the producer.
TOOTS CAMARATA (cond/arr), RUSS CASE (t), HYMIE SCHERTZER, JACK CRESSY (as), LARRY BINYON, DAVE HARRIS (ts), DAVE BOWMAN (p), CARL KRESS (g), HAIGH STEPHENS (b), GEORGE WETTLING (d), six strings, BILLIE HOLIDAY (v)
That Ole Devil Called Love / Don't Explain / Big Stuff

FRIDAY 10 NOVEMBER 1944
Billie closes at the Downbeat.

Here's an interesting shot of the new, stream-lined Billie Holiday, taken while she was co-featured with the Red Norvo combo at the Down-beat club on 52nd Street in Gotham. *Photo by Red Wolfe*

After closing at the Downbeat, Billie travels to St Louis to open at the Plantation Club. Reports had seeped out of St Louis about the treatment of coloured performers at the Plantation, and Billie is apprehensive about opening there.

Under the headline

Billie Holiday And The "St. Louis Incident": Negro Performers Must Act Against Jim Crow

Don De Leighbur of the *New York Amsterdam News* reports:

From what I hear, Billie Holiday got along all right before her first show at the club. Between the first and second show, she was approached by a white man, a Mr. Joy, an old friend who once befriended her when she was in St. Louis back in 1938 with Artie Shaw's orchestra. As they tried to leave the club together, the owner is said to have rudely pointed out that Miss Holiday was not "allowed" to use the front door and "most certainly not with a white man". In the argument that took place, Joy was forcibly ejected, it was reported, but Billie followed him out. On her return for the second show, she was said to have been insulted again by the management and told she could forget the show.

Billie promptly "forgot" the show and is back in New York playing to capacity crowds at 52nd Street's Spotlite Club.

FRI	1
SAT	2
SUN	3
MON	4
TUES	5
WED	6
THUR	7
FRI	8
SAT	9
SUN	10
MON	11
TUES	12
WED	13
THUR	14
FRI	15
SAT	16
SUN	17
MON	18
TUES	19
WED	20
THUR	21
FRI	22
SAT	23
SUN	24
MON	25
TUES	26
WED	27
THUR	28
FRI	29
SAT	30
SUN	31

FRIDAY 1 DECEMBER 1944

Billie opens for a one-week engagement at the Apollo Theatre backed by Hot Lips Page and his Band. Also on the bill are Johnny Gardner, Rastus Murray and The Four Pin-Up Girls.

During this engagement, Billie hears that her husband, Jimmy Monroe, has been arrested again in Los Angeles for smuggling marijuana from Mexico.

WEDNESDAY 6 DECEMBER 1944

Billie and Hot Lips Page and His Orchestra broadcast from the Apollo via station WMCA.

I'll Be Seeing You

THURSDAY 7 DECEMBER 1944

Billie closes at the Apollo.

FRIDAY 8 DECEMBER 1944

Billie opens at the Spotlite Club, 56 W52nd Street (formerly the Famous Door) opposite the Oscar Pettiford Band, Tiny Grimes Quartet and Harry 'The Hipster' Gibson. In actual fact, Billie fails to show up on opening night, as her pianist Joe Springer recalls: **'She didn't even call the club. I don't know how she explained this to the management, but she told me "opening nights bug me something awful."'**

The manager of the Spotlite is Clark Monroe, Billie's brother-in-law and Billie plays to good audiences throughout the Christmas and New Year period into January 1945. She does three shows nightly, at 11pm, 1am and 3am. Billie is now seeing trumpet player Joe Guy.

MON	**1**
TUES	**2**
WED	**3**
THUR	**4**
FRI	**5**
SAT	**6**
SUN	**7**
MON	**8**
TUES	**9**
WED	**10**
THUR	**11**
FRI	**12**
SAT	**13**
SUN	**14**
MON	**15**
TUES	**16**
WED	**17**
THUR	**18**
FRI	**19**
SAT	**20**
SUN	**21**
MON	**22**
TUES	**23**
WED	**24**
THUR	**25**
FRI	**26**
SAT	**27**
SUN	**28**
MON	**29**
TUES	**30**
WED	**31**

JANUARY 1945

Billie wins the Metronome award for girl singers for the first time.

Down Beat announces: Billie Holiday is headlining at the Spotlite on 52nd Street. Lady Day's support at the Spotlite is the new Nat Jaffe-Charlie Shavers combo, featuring Don Byas, with frantic Harry Gibson and Tiny Grimes quartet also on hand.

MONDAY 8 JANUARY 1945

On her off night at the Spotlite, Billie appears at the Witoka Club, W145th Street, from 9pm to 3am with the Tiny Grimes Quartet.

SATURDAY 13 JANUARY 1945

Billie closes at the Spotlite and travels to Los Angeles to take part in Esquire magazine's second Annual Critics' Award Concert.

WEDNESDAY 17 JANUARY 1945

Billie takes part in the Esquire Second Annual Jazz Concert which is recorded from the stage of the Philharmonic Hall in Los Angeles.

The show is opened by Duke Ellington & his Orchestra: REX STEWART, TAFT JORDAN, SHELTON HEMPHILL, CAT ANDERSON (t), RAY NANCE (t/v), JOE NANTON, LAWRENCE BROWN, CLAUDE JONES (tb), JIMMY HAMILTON (cl/ts), JOHNNY HODGES (ss/as), OTTO HARDWICK (as), AL SEARS (ts), HARRY CARNEY (bs), DUKE ELLINGTON (p), FRED GUY (g), JUNIOR RAGLIN (b), HILLARD BROWN (d)

Blutopia / Air Conditioned Jungle / Frustration / Blue Cellophane / Suddenly It Jumped / Coloratura

Billie joins the Ellington Orchestra for one number *Lover Man*

The Ellington Orchestra then perform *It Don't Mean A Thing* with vocals from Ray Nance, Taft Jordan and Danny Kaye.

In the broadcast section of the show the Ellington Orchestra open with *Esquire Jump* before each award winner is presented to perform one number.

Willie Smith – *Tea For Two*
Anita O'Day – *Wish You Were Waiting For Me*
Billy Strayhorn – *Midriff*
Art Tatum – *The Man I Love / I Can't Give You AnythingBut Love*
Duke Ellington –*The Mood To Be Wooed*

Billie is then presented with her award for Best Female Vocalist of 1944 by Jerome Kern, and sings *I Cover The Waterfront*

Danny Kaye then presents Sid Catlett and Al Casey with the drum and guitar awards. They play *Honeysuckle Rose* accompanied by Duke Ellington (p) and Junior Raglin (b).

The broadcast section ends with a three-way jam session with Duke Ellington Orchestra playing *Things Ain't What They Used To Be* in Los Angeles, joined in a radio link by Louis Armstrong in New Orleans and Benny Goodman in New York.

Below: Billie and Duke Ellington at rehearsals for the Esquire Second Annual Jazz Concert in Los Angeles.

THUR	**1**
FRI	**2**
SAT	**3**
SUN	**4**
MON	**5**
TUES	**6**
WED	**7**
THUR	**8**
FRI	**9**
SAT	**10**
SUN	**11**
MON	**12**
TUES	**13**
WED	**14**
THUR	**15**
FRI	**16**
SAT	**17**
SUN	**18**
MON	**19**
TUES	**20**
WED	**21**
THUR	**22**
FRI	**23**
SAT	**24**
SUN	**25**
MON	**26**
TUES	**27**
WED	**28**

Early in February Billie does an unpublicised two-week stint at the New Plantation Club in Los Angeles.

MONDAY 12 FEBRUARY 1945

Billie appears in a Jazz at the Philharmonic Concert at the Philharmonic Hall in Los Angeles. Part of Billie's set is recorded: BILLIE HOLIDAY (vocal), HOWARD McGHEE (t), WILLIE SMITH (as), ILLINOIS JACQUET (ts), WARDELL GRAY and/or CHARLIE VENTURA (ts), probably MILT RASKIN (p), probably DAVE BARBOUR (g), CHARLIE MINGUS (b), DAVE COLEMAN (d):
Body And Soul / Strange Fruit (accompanied by piano only)

SUNDAY 18 FEBRUARY 1945

Billie appears in a Jazz at the Philharmonic Concert at the Philharmonic Hall in Los Angeles. Also on the bill are Peanuts Holland, Vic Dickenson, Coleman Hawkins Trio, Kid Ory's Band and the Gene Krupa Band. Joe Sullivan plays intermission piano accompanied by Zutty Singleton. Billie, accompanied by Eddie Heywood (p), Beverly Peer (b) and Gene Krupa (d) sings *Fine and Mellow* and *Squeeze Me*.

THURSDAY 22 FEBRUARY 1945

Billie's recording of *Lover Man* backed by *That Ole Devil Called Love* is released.

Below: Billie on stage at Philharmonic Hall, Los Angeles for a Jazz at the Philharmonic concert. Also visible are Coleman Hawkins (tenor sax), Joe Guy (trumpet), Willie Smith (alto sax), Illinois Jacquet (tenor sax), Howard McGhee (trumpet), Billy Hadnott (bass) and Gene Krupa (drums).

THUR	**1**	SUN	**1**
FRI	**2**	MON	**2**
SAT	**3**	TUES	**3**
SUN	**4**	WED	**4**
MON	**5**	THUR	**5**
TUES	**6**	FRI	**6**
WED	**7**	SAT	**7**
THUR	**8**	SUN	**8**
FRI	**9**	MON	**9**
SAT	**10**	TUES	**10**
SUN	**11**	WED	**11**
MON	**12**	THUR	**12**
TUES	**13**	FRI	**13**
WED	**14**	SAT	**14**
THUR	**15**	SUN	**15**
FRI	**16**	MON	**16**
SAT	**17**	TUES	**17**
SUN	**18**	WED	**18**
MON	**19**	THUR	**19**
TUES	**20**	FRI	**20**
WED	**21**	SAT	**21**
THUR	**22**	SUN	**22**
FRI	**23**	MON	**23**
SAT	**24**	TUES	**24**
SUN	**25**	WED	**25**
MON	**26**	THUR	**26**
TUES	**27**	FRI	**27**
WED	**28**	SAT	**28**
THUR	**29**	SUN	**29**
FRI	**30**	MON	**30**
SAT	**31**		

MARCH 1945

Billie is interviewed along with Duke Ellington and Ted Lewis on Al Jarvis' *Which is Which?* show on Radio KFWB.

MONDAY 5 MARCH 1945

Billie appears in a Jazz at the Philharmonic Concert at the Philharmonic Hall in Los Angeles. Also on the bill are Gene Krupa, Willie Smith and Illinois Jacquet.

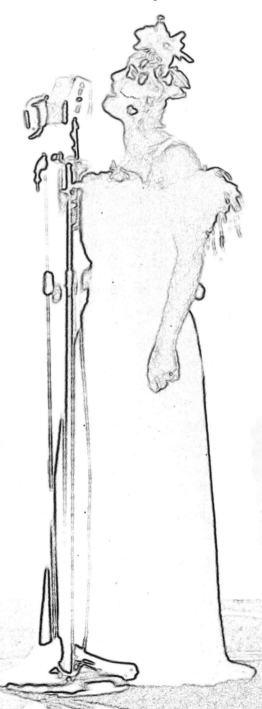

Sometime in March Billie opens at the Club Savoy in San Francisco where she settles in to a record-breaking 12-week run.

SUNDAY 1 APRIL 1945

Down Beat reviews Billie's latest record release:

Diggin' The Discs – Jax

BILLIE HOLIDAY
Lover Man / That Ole Devil Called Love
Decca 23391
Billie really sings these tunes for all they're worth, which unfortunately isn't very much. Toots supplies the background, such as it is. David and Sherman and Ramirez conspired together on the first. Allan Roberts and Doris Fisher, already represented this month by Jodie Man, bumped their heads together to produce the other. La Holiday alone can be commended here. The material is sad, and the orchestra far less than exciting.

SATURDAY 7 APRIL 1945

Billie's 30th birthday

After closing at the Club Savoy Billie returns to Los Angeles where she announces that she has obtained a divorce in Mexico and has married Joe Guy.

Soon she heads back to New York suffering from an enforced withdrawal from heroin.

Lady Day Marries

Los Angeles – Billie Holiday, before leaving here for the Downbeat Club in New York, caused commotion by news that she had secured a divorce in Mexico and had married Joe Guy, trumpet with Coleman Hawkins. Friends were puzzled by Billie's announcement as no one seems to know when Billie visited Mexico to secure the divorce. Couple left for New York with mystery still unsolved.

TUES	**1**
WED	**2**
THUR	**3**
FRI	**4**
SAT	**5**
SUN	**6**
MON	**7**
TUES	**8**
WED	**9**
THUR	**10**
FRI	**11**
SAT	**12**
SUN	**13**
MON	**14**
TUES	**15**
WED	**16**
THUR	**17**
FRI	**18**
SAT	**19**
SUN	**20**
MON	**21**
TUES	**22**
WED	**23**
THUR	**24**
FRI	**25**
SAT	**26**
SUN	**27**
MON	**28**
TUES	**29**
WED	**30**
THUR	**31**

TUESDAY 22 MAY 1945
Billie opens at the Downbeat Club on 52nd Street
sharing the bill with Sid Catlett's Band and the Al
Casey Trio.

BILLIE HOLIDAY

America's No. 1 Song Stylist—Winner Esquire Poll 1944-1945
After Concluding 12 Sensational Weeks
AT CLUB SAVOY, San Francisco
NOW IN 11th RECORD BREAKING WEEK AT
CLUB DOWNBEAT
New York
Assisted By

BIG SID CATLETT
Esquire's All-American Drummer Man
and His Sextet

AL CASEY
Esquire's All-American Guitarist
And His Trio

**Exclusive
DECCA
Recording Artist**

Latest Release
LOVER MAN
No. 23391

'Billie Holiday, the thrush, is breaking all 52nd Street records at the
Downbeat."—*Walter Winchell*

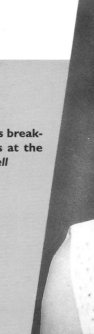

FRI	1		SUN	1
SAT	2		MON	2
SUN	3		TUES	3
MON	4		WED	4
TUES	5		THUR	5
WED	6		FRI	6
THUR	7		SAT	7
FRI	8		SUN	8
SAT	9		MON	9
SUN	10		TUES	10
MON	11		WED	11
TUES	12		THUR	12
WED	13		FRI	13
THUR	14		SAT	14
FRI	15		SUN	15
SAT	16		MON	16
SUN	17		TUES	17
MON	18		WED	18
TUES	19		THUR	19
WED	20		FRI	20
THUR	21		SAT	21
FRI	22		SUN	22
SAT	23		MON	23
SUN	24		TUES	24
MON	25		WED	25
TUES	26		THUR	26
WED	27		FRI	27
THUR	28		SAT	28
FRI	29		SUN	29
SAT	30		MON	30
			TUES	31

Throughout June, Billie is working at the Downbeat Club. Coleman Hawkin's Band replaces Sid Catlett.

NOW APPEARING NITELY

BILLIE **HOLIDAY**   COLEMAN **HAWKINS**

Al Casey Trio

CLUB DOWNBEAT

66 West 52nd Street, New York, N. Y.   EL. 5-8773

SATURDAY 9 JUNE 1945

Billie is scheduled to appear at an afternoon concert at Town Hall presented by Timme Rosenkrantz. Also on the bill are Mary Lou Williams & her All Girl Band, Teddy Wilson, Don Byas and Red Norvo. Milt Gabler records the concert for Commodore, and excerpts featuring Wilson, Byas and Norvo have been released. A *Down Beat* report of the concert suggests that Billie failed to show.

FRIDAY 15 JUNE 1945

Down Beat carries a review in **Jazz Jive by JAX:**

Commodore comes up with three new ten-inch discs, *I Cover the Waterfront* and *Lover Come Back To Me* by Billie Holiday on 559, *Eccentric* and *Guess Who's In Town* by Max Kaminsky on 560, *Struttin' With Some Barbecue* and *How Come You Do Me Like You Do* by George Wettling on 561.

Billie still sounds too affected to be very moving. The reverse, which Billie sings to the accompaniment of Heywood and Simmons and Catlett, can't compare with Mildred Bailey's version a few years back.

Hawk, Holiday Apple Holdovers; Tatum Due

NEW YORK–Coleman Hawkins, who opened the Downbeat Room on 52nd St. here Decoration Day, will hold over at the spot until early July, pulling out then for a date at Ciro's in Philly. The Hawk will be followed by Art Tatum, Benny Morton's Band and the Loumel Morgan Trio.

Billie Holiday, rumored earlier to have been taken ill en route here from the west coast, dispelled the gossips by being on hand for the opening at the Downbeat where she shares the billing with the Hawk.

WEDNESDAY 27 JUNE 1945

Billie is Guest of Honour at a Sports Dance for Williams Tavern Employees at the Audubon Ballroom, 160th Street and Broadway, New York City. Also appearing are Al Cooper's Savoy Sultans.

JULY 1945

Billie ceases working at the Downbeat and Joe Guy begins organising a 16-piece big band for touring.

Billie does some theatre dates with Don Redman's Band.

WED	**1**	SAT	**1**
THUR	**2**	SUN	**2**
FRI	**3**	MON	**3**
SAT	**4**	TUES	**4**
SUN	**5**	WED	**5**
MON	**6**	THUR	**6**
TUES	**7**	FRI	**7**
WED	**8**	SAT	**8**
THUR	**9**	SUN	**9**
FRI	**10**	MON	**10**
SAT	**11**	TUES	**11**
SUN	**12**	WED	**12**
MON	**13**	THUR	**13**
TUES	**14**	FRI	**14**
WED	**15**	SAT	**15**
THUR	**16**	SUN	**16**
FRI	**17**	MON	**17**
SAT	**18**	TUES	**18**
SUN	**19**	WED	**19**
MON	**20**	THUR	**20**
TUES	**21**	FRI	**21**
WED	**22**	SAT	**22**
THUR	**23**	SUN	**23**
FRI	**24**	MON	**24**
SAT	**25**	TUES	**25**
SUN	**26**	WED	**26**
MON	**27**	THUR	**27**
TUES	**28**	FRI	**28**
WED	**29**	SAT	**29**
THUR	**30**	SUN	**30**
FRI	**31**		

TUESDAY 14 AUGUST 1945

Recording session (1pm–5.45pm) as Billie Holiday accompanied by Bob Haggart and his Orchestra for Decca in New York. Milt Gabler is the producer.

JOE GUY (t), BILL STEGMEYER (as), HANK ROSS, ARMAND CAMGROS (ts), STANLEY WEBB (bs), MORRIS LEFTKOWITZ, FRANK SIEFIELD, GEORGE SWERNOFF, LEO KRUCZEK, CHARLES JAFFE (v), ARMAND KAPROFF (viola), SAMMY BENSKIN (p), TINY GRIMES (g), BOB HAGGART (b), SPECS POWELL (d), BILLIE HOLIDAY (vocal)

Don't Explain / Big Stuff / You Better Go Now / What Is This Thing Called Love?

FRIDAY 17 AUGUST 1945

Billie opens at the McKinley Theatre in Brooklyn for a one-week engagement backed by Don Redman and his Orchestra.

THURSDAY 23 AUGUST 1945

Billie and Don Redman close at the McKinley Theatre.

Pittsburgh Courier of 18 August 45 says the tour starts Sept 1 in Ohio.

Holiday Tours Midwest, South

NEW YORK—Billie Holiday, whose name has become a household word in New York and Hollywood, is down to give folk in the hinterland a taste of the art that has made her one of the biggest stars in the business. Holiday opens her tour in Ohio Sept. 1, accompanied by Joe Guy's swing outfit.

Affectionately known as Lady Day, Billie is one of Decca's money in the bank recorders and her latest platter, "Lover Man", has soared to the half-million mark in sales.

Proof of her ability shows in the fact that she invaded the Club Savoy in Frisco last year for two weeks and remained for six months. She has already put in nearly three months at the Downbeat Club in New York—her umpteenth engagement—and they want her to stay with a nice hike in salary. But Billie decided she wanted to see what the rest of the country was like, hence the tour of the Midwest and South.

Joe Guy formerly played with a number of name outfits and is an outstanding trumpet player. His new band is a hard-jumping unit which will threaten the big ten in a few months.

SATURDAY 1 SEPTEMBER 1945

The Billie/Joe Guy tour gets underway in Ohio.

TUESDAY 11 SEPTEMBER 1945

Billie and her band at Richmond, Virginia for a race prom at Skateland.

WEDNESDAY 12 SEPTEMBER 1945

Billie and her band at Bell's Hosiery Mill in Suffolk, Virginia.

THURSDAY 13 SEPTEMBER 1945

Billie and her band at the Auditorium in Columbia, South Carolina.

SUNDAY 23 SEPTEMBER 1945

Billie's mother, Sadie, suffers a stroke and is admitted to Wadsworth Hospital in Manhattan.

FRIDAY 28 SEPTEMBER 1945

Billie and her band open at the Howard Theatre, Washington for a one-week engagement.

MON	1
TUES	2
WED	3
THUR	4
FRI	5
SAT	6
SUN	7
MON	8
TUES	9
WED	10
THUR	11
FRI	12
SAT	13
SUN	14
MON	15
TUES	16
WED	17
THUR	18
FRI	19
SAT	20
SUN	21
MON	22
TUES	23
WED	24
THUR	25
FRI	26
SAT	27
SUN	28
MON	29
TUES	30
WED	31

THURSDAY 4 OCTOBER 1945
Billie and her band close at the Howard Theatre, Washington.

FRIDAY 5 OCTOBER 1945
Billie and her band open at the Royal Theatre, Baltimore for a one-week engagement.

SATURDAY 6 OCTOBER 1945
Billie's mother, Sadie, dies (aged 50) in the Wadsworth Hospital, Manhattan. Billie hears the news in Baltimore and returns to New York for the funeral. Billie's and Sadie's address is given as 1293 Union Avenue.

TUESDAY 9 OCTOBER 1945
Sadie's funeral is at 9am at St Charles Boromeo Church at 211 W141st Street in Harlem and the interrment is at St Raymond's Cemetery in the Bronx.

WEDNESDAY 10 OCTOBER 1945
Billie returns to Baltimore to finish the week at the Royal Theatre.

THURSDAY 11 OCTOBER 1945
Billie closes at the Royal Theatre.

SATURDAY 13 OCTOBER 1945
Billie returns to New York.

SUNDAY 14 OCTOBER 1945
Billie and her 16-piece Orchestra appear at Lincoln Square Center in New York.

TUESDAY 30 OCTOBER 1945
Billie opens at the Downbeat Club with the Sid Catlett Sextet and the Al Casey Trio. As Al Casey's pianist is unable to read Billie's arrangements, Joe Springer is hired as her accompanist.

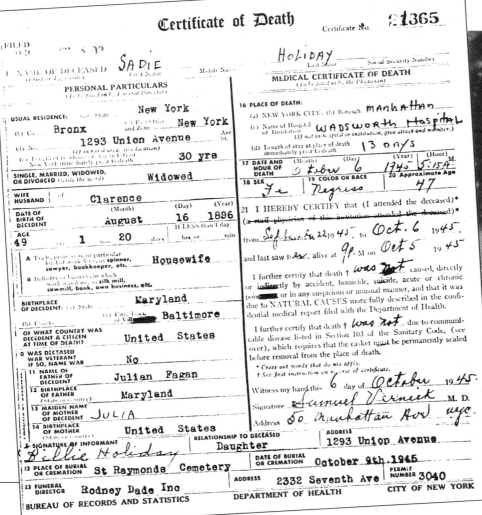

THUR	**1**	SAT	**1**
FRI	**2**	SUN	**2**
SAT	**3**	MON	**3**
SUN	**4**	TUES	**4**
MON	**5**	WED	**5**
TUES	**6**	THUR	**6**
WED	**7**	FRI	**7**
THUR	**8**	SAT	**8**
FRI	**9**	SUN	**9**
SAT	**10**	MON	**10**
SUN	**11**	TUES	**11**
MON	**12**	WED	**12**
TUES	**13**	THUR	**13**
WED	**14**	FRI	**14**
THUR	**15**	SAT	**15**
FRI	**16**	SUN	**16**
SAT	**17**	MON	**17**
SUN	**18**	TUES	**18**
MON	**19**	WED	**19**
TUES	**20**	THUR	**20**
WED	**21**	FRI	**21**
THUR	**22**	SAT	**22**
FRI	**23**	SUN	**23**
SAT	**24**	MON	**24**
SUN	**25**	TUES	**25**
MON	**26**	WED	**26**
TUES	**27**	THUR	**27**
WED	**28**	FRI	**28**
THUR	**29**	SAT	**29**
FRI	**30**	SUN	**30**
		MON	**31**

Throughout November Billie is resident at the Downbeat Club with the Sid Catlett Sextet and the Al Casey Trio.

SATURDAY 17 NOVEMBER 1945
Billie headlines at a dance at the Lincoln Square Center with Roy Eldridge and a 12-piece Orchestra.

52nd Street looks forlorn and empty when the clubs are shuttered following a police order charging that the clubs were rendexvous for persons engaging in the narcotics and marijuana traffic.

Throughout December Billie is resident at the Downbeat Club with the Sid Catlett Sextet and the Al Casey Trio.

Down Beat reports a crisis on 52nd Street:

> The Three Deuces, Spotlite, Downbeat and Onyx clubs, which were forced to pull out all talent last month on a police order charging that the clubs were rendezvous for persons engaging in the narcotics and marijuana traffic, became alive again after a lull of only a few nights.

SATURDAY 15 DECEMBER 1945
Billie appears on a radio broadcast from the Apollo Theatre via station WMCA. She is accompanied by Hot Lips Page and his Band.
Fine And Mellow / All Of Me
Billie's appearance is probably as a guest artist, because the bill at the Apollo for the week commencing 14 December is Hot Lips Page & his Band, Bishop & Palmer, O'Donnell & Blair and Duke Jenkins, with Louis Jordan & his Band being held over from the previous week.

JANUARY 1946

TUES	**1**
WED	**2**
THUR	**3**
FRI	**4**
SAT	**5**
SUN	**6**
MON	**7**
TUES	**8**
WED	**9**
THUR	**10**
FRI	**11**
SAT	**12**
SUN	**13**
MON	**14**
TUES	**15**
WED	**16**
THUR	**17**
FRI	**18**
SAT	**19**
SUN	**20**
MON	**21**
TUES	**22**
WED	**23**
THUR	**24**
FRI	**25**
SAT	**26**
SUN	**27**
MON	**28**
TUES	**29**
WED	**30**
THUR	**31**

Throughout January Billie is resident at the Downbeat Club with the Sid Catlett Sextet and the Al Casey Trio.

Billie is placed 2nd in the *Down Beat* poll behind Jo Stafford, but she wins the Metronome poll, in front of Anita O'Day.

TUESDAY 22 JANUARY 1946

Recording session (3–6pm) as Billie Holiday accompanied by Bill Stegmeyer and his Orchestra for Decca in New York City. Milt Gabler is the producer. GORDON 'CHRIS' GRIFFIN, JOE GUY (t), BILL STEGMEYER (as), HANK ROSS, BERNARD KAUFMAN, ARMAND CAMGROS (ts), JOE SPRINGER (p), TINY GRIMES (g), JOHN SIMMONS (b), SID CATLETT (d), plus 4 strings, BILLIE HOLIDAY (v)
Good Morning Heartache / No Good Man (2 takes) / *Big Stuff* (unissued)

Billie and Mister pop across the street to the Onyx Club to present J. C. Higginbotham with his Down Beat award for top trombonist of 1945. Red Allen looks on approvingly.

Leon & Eddie's

Jimmy Ryan's
RED McKENZIE
Onyx
RED ALLEN
JC HIGGINBOTHAM

52nd STREET

Spotlite
COLEMAN HAWKINS)
Samoa Club

Downbeat
BILLIE HOLIDAY
SID CATLETT
Three Deuces
SLAM STEWART
REX STEWART

SIXTH AVENUE

FRI	1
SAT	2
SUN	3
MON	4
TUES	5
WED	6
THUR	7
FRI	8
SAT	9
SUN	10
MON	11
TUES	12
WED	13
THUR	14
FRI	15
SAT	16
SUN	17
MON	18
TUES	19
WED	20
THUR	21
FRI	22
SAT	23
SUN	24
MON	25
TUES	26
WED	27
THUR	28

Throughout February Billie is resident at the Downbeat Club.

SATURDAY 2 FEBRUARY 1946
Billie appears at the Amsterdam News Annual Benefit at the Brooklyn Academy of Music. Also on the bill are Ella Fitzgerald, Dinah Washington, Billy Eckstine, The Ink Spots and Savannah Churchill.

WEDNESDAY 13 FEBRUARY 1946
Billie appears at a Concert at the Academy of Music, Philadelphia produced by Nat Segal. Also taking part are Dizzy Gillespie, Al Casey Trio, Buck Clayton, Bud Freeman, Joe Bushkin, John Simmons, Morey Feld and Lee Castle & his Band.
BILLIE HOLIDAY (v), JOE SPRINGER (p), AL CASEY (g), unknown drummer
He's Funny That Way / Lover Man / Fine And Mellow / Trav'lin' Light / Strange Fruit plus more

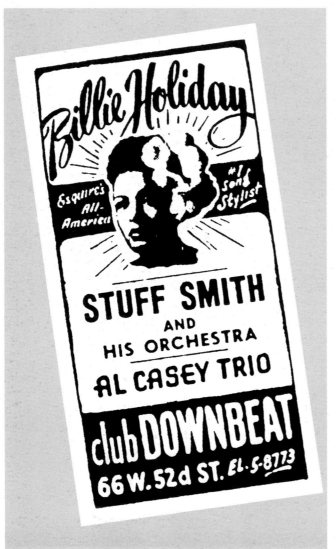

SATURDAY 16 FEBRUARY 1946
Billie appears at New York's Town Hall in her first solo concert. She is accompanied by JOE GUY (t), JOE SPRINGER (p), TINY GRIMES (g), LLOYD TROTMAN (b), EDDIE NICHOLSON (d).
During the 70 minute concert, Billie sings 18 songs including
All Of Me /Trav'lin' Light / You Better Go Now / My Old Flame / I Can't Get Started
Leonard Feather writes in the March issue of *Metronome*:

Lady Day was in wonderful voice; her dignified bearing and her wonderful poise helped to keep her large, quiet, intelligent audience enthralled.

Promoter Greer Johnson remembered:
'I had to get Billie up a full hour-and-a-half before, get her dressed, which wasn't easy, come downtown through the mob scene that had grown outside the Town Hall – and on the way down, Billie suddenly decided she wanted another dress, that she wanted to wear a second dress for the second half. I said that she didn't have to, that one doesn't at a recital. But she insisted, and we stopped at – I think it was W.R.Burnett... it wasn't a particularly elegant dress shop. Billie bought another dress... by the time we got to the hall I was hysterical, but she still went on on time. At intermission, Billie was elated, as she should have been. She was kicking up her heels and grabbing me, kissing people and carrying on. I was in her dressing room when the brother of one of the musicians came in to tell me that Billie's apartment had just been robbed. I said, for God's sake, don't tell her for another thirty-five or forty minutes. Her reputation was such that she would not show up for the first show, that she might make the second show possibly, and with luck she might make the third show – and I thought, seeing the way this was going, if anything happens now, it really would be pretty bad. So I asked him not to tell Billie because nothing more could be done, and to let her finish the concert. And she did.'

Billie Holiday Concert Makes Jazz History

New York—Billie Holiday's solo concert debut at Town Hall February 16 was an event to go down in jazz history. Unsurpassed in her own field as a great and individual song stylist, and long a favorite in jazz circles, the turnout for her first solo concert was way beyond expectations. With a crammed house, including several persons seated on the stage, close to a 1000 fans were turned away.

This concert, a startling success in every respect, should establish Miss Holiday in the top bracket and win for her the fame due her long before this. To those not too Holiday conscious and to her many fans, this performance was unexcelled and nothing short of magnificent.

Backed by a quintet lead by trumpeter Joe Guy, Miss Holiday did more than twenty selections ranging from Gershwin to her own original blues numbers. Difficult to name the most outstanding, her renditions of

BILLIE HOLIDAY

TOWN HALL · SATURDAY, FEBRUARY 16 · 5:30 p.m.

FRI **1**

SAT **2**

SUN **3**

MON **4**

TUES **5**

WED **6**

THUR **7**

FRI **8**

SAT **9**

SUN **10**

MON **11**

TUES **12**

WED **13**

THUR **14**

FRI **15**

SAT **16**

SUN **17**

MON **18**

TUES **19**

WED **20**

THUR **21**

FRI **22**

SAT **23**

SUN **24**

MON **25**

TUES **26**

WED **27**

THUR **28**

FRI **29**

SAT **30**

SUN **31**

Billie in her dressing room at the Downbeat with her boxer dog, Mister.

WEDNESDAY 6 MARCH 1946
Billie closes at the Downbeat where she is replaced by Art Tatum.

WEDNESDAY 13 MARCH 1946
Recording session (2–5.30pm) as Billie Holiday and her Orchestra for Decca in New York City. Milt Gabler is the producer
JOE GUY (t), JOE SPRINGER (p), TINY GRIMES (g), BILLY TAYLOR (b), KELLY MARTIN (d)
Big Stuff (2 takes)

Big Stuff is a difficult Leonard Bernstein composition for his ballet 'Fancy Free' which was premiered in April 1944. Billie is to make several attempts over the next two years at achieving a satisfactory rendition of the song.

MON	**1**	WED	**1**	
TUES	**2**	THUR	**2**	
WED	**3**	FRI	**3**	
THUR	**4**	SAT	**4**	
FRI	**5**	SUN	**5**	
SAT	**6**	MON	**6**	
SUN	**7**	TUES	**7**	
MON	**8**	WED	**8**	
TUES	**9**	THUR	**9**	
WED	**10**	FRI	**10**	
THUR	**11**	SAT	**11**	
FRI	**12**	SUN	**12**	
SAT	**13**	MON	**13**	
SUN	**14**	TUES	**14**	
MON	**15**	WED	**15**	
TUES	**16**	THUR	**16**	
WED	**17**	FRI	**17**	
THUR	**18**	SAT	**18**	
FRI	**19**	SUN	**19**	
SAT	**20**	MON	**20**	
SUN	**21**	TUES	**21**	
MON	**22**	WED	**22**	
TUES	**23**	THUR	**23**	
WED	**24**	FRI	**24**	
THUR	**25**	SAT	**25**	
FRI	**26**	SUN	**26**	
SAT	**27**	MON	**27**	
SUN	**28**	TUES	**28**	
MON	**29**	WED	**29**	
TUES	**30**	THUR	**30**	
		FRI	**31**	

THURSDAY 4 APRIL 1946

Billie appears at Carnegie Hall in a Concert of American Folk Music for the Russian Relief Programme with Joe Springer and the Al Casey Trio.

SUNDAY 7 APRIL 1946

Billie's 31st birthday.
In the evening, Billie appears at McKinley Gardens in Brooklyn.

TUESDAY 9 APRIL 1946

Recording session (2–5pm) as Billie Holiday accompanied by Billy Kyle and his Trio for Decca in New York City. Milt Gabler is the producer.
JOE GUY (t), BILLY KYLE (p), JIMMY SHIRLEY (g), THOMAS BARNEY (b), KENNY CLARKE (d)
Baby I Don't Cry Over You (2 takes) / *I'll Look Around* (2 takes)

Billie at the Apollo with Coleman Hawkins

SATURDAY 20 APRIL 1946

Billie appears at Carnegie Hall in a Concert of American Folk Music for the Russian Relief Programme. Also on the bill are the Hall Johnson Choir, Josh White, Woody Guthrie and Pete Seeger.

MONDAY 29 APRIL 1946

Billie appears in concert at Eaton Hall with Joe Springer and the Al Casey Trio.

Billie rehearsing at the Downbeat with her new backing band. Below l to r: Tiny Grimes (guitar), Joe Springer (piano).
The unseen members of the Tiny Grimes Trio are bassist Lloyd Trotman and drummer Eddie Nicholson.

MONDAY 27 MAY 1946

Billie appears at a JATP Concert at Carnegie Hall, New York. This is the first Monday night jazz bash in a series of Carnegie Hall Pop Concerts. Also on the bill are BUCK CLAYTON (t), COLEMAN HAWKINS, ILLINOIS JACQUET, LESTER YOUNG (ts), KEN KERSEY (p), JOHN COLLINS or TINY GRIMES (g), CURLEY RUSSELL (b), J.C. HEARD (d), BILLIE HOLIDAY (v except first four titles)
Philharmonic Blues / Oh! Lady Be Good / I Can't Get Started / Sweet Georgia Brown / I Cried For You / Fine And Mellow / He's Funny That Way

THURSDAY 30 MAY 1946

Billie opens at the Downbeat Club
Al Casey Trio moves to the Onyx and Billie's new backing group at the Downbeat is Joe Springer (p), Joe Guy (t), Tiny Grimes (g), Lloyd Trotman (b) and Eddie Nicholson (d).

SAT	**1**
SUN	**2**
MON	**3**
TUES	**4**
WED	**5**
THUR	**6**
FRI	**7**
SAT	**8**
SUN	**9**
MON	**10**
TUES	**11**
WED	**12**
THUR	**13**
FRI	**14**
SAT	**15**
SUN	**16**
MON	**17**
TUES	**18**
WED	**19**
THUR	**20**
FRI	**21**
SAT	**22**
SUN	**23**
MON	**24**
TUES	**25**
WED	**26**
THUR	**27**
FRI	**28**
SAT	**29**
SUN	**30**

Throughout June Billie is resident at the Downbeat Club with Tiny Grimes and his Trio and Trummy Young.

SUNDAY 2 JUNE 1946

Billie guest stars with JATP at the Apollo in New York.

MONDAY 3 JUNE 1946

Billie guest stars with JATP at Carnegie Hall in New York. Norman Granz allows her to use her own rhythm section plus JOE GUY (t) and LESTER YOUNG (ts)
The Man I Love / Gee Baby, Ain't I Good To You / All Of Me / Billie's Blues / He's Funny That Way / Them There Eyes

FRIDAY 6 JUNE 1946

Billie opens at the Apollo Theatre for a one-week engagement opposite Louis Armstrong and his Band. Also on the bill are The Two Zephyrs and Slim & Sweets. She doubles at the Downbeat Club.

WEDNESDAY 12 JUNE 1946

The Amateur Hour at the Apollo is broadcast on station WMCA

THURSDAY 13 JUNE 1946

Billie and Louis close at the Apollo.

Right: Harry Low, maitre d' at the Yank Sing on 51st Street, one of Billie's favourite restaurants.

New York—Very smooth imperturbable gentleman pictured above is Harry Low, who spends his time handling what most musicians consider life's second most important function: eating.

Handsome Harry is maitre d' at the town's best Chinese eating spot, Yank Sing on West 51 street, where around 3 a.m. any day you can catch a goodly as-

FRIDAY 14 JUNE 1946

Billie takes part in a Midnight Benefit Concert for the Riverdale Children's Association at the RKO Hamilton Theatre at 146th and Broadway. This is the World premiere of Louis Jordan's movie 'Beware'. Appearing in the stage show are Louis Jordan's Band, Billie Holiday, Canada Lee, Thelma Carpenter, Dave Miller Trio, Bob Howard and the combined Café Society Uptown / Café Society Downtown show.

MONDAY 17 JUNE 1946

Billie appears at a JATP Concert at Carnegie Hall, New York. This is the last of the Monday night jazz bashes in the series of Carnegie Hall Pop Concerts. Also on the bill are Buck Clayton, Dizzy Gillespie, Trummy Young, Illinois Jacquet, Lester Young, Allen Eager, Chubby Jackson, Slam Stewart and J.C. Heard. 'Smash crowd success was tenor saxist Illinois Jacquet, whose driving jazz and high note forensics had the balconies rocking. Right with him as an audience-pleaser was Billie Holiday, who did a quartet of songs in the show's second act.'

MON	**1**	THUR	**1**
TUES	**2**	FRI	**2**
WED	**3**	SAT	**3**
THUR	**4**	SUN	**4**
FRI	**5**	MON	**5**
SAT	**6**	TUES	**6**
SUN	**7**	WED	**7**
MON	**8**	THUR	**8**
TUES	**9**	FRI	**9**
WED	**10**	SAT	**10**
THUR	**11**	SUN	**11**
FRI	**12**	MON	**12**
SAT	**13**	TUES	**13**
SUN	**14**	WED	**14**
MON	**15**	THUR	**15**
TUES	**16**	FRI	**16**
WED	**17**	SAT	**17**
THUR	**18**	SUN	**18**
FRI	**19**	MON	**19**
SAT	**20**	TUES	**20**
SUN	**21**	WED	**21**
MON	**22**	THUR	**22**
TUES	**23**	FRI	**23**
WED	**24**	SAT	**24**
THUR	**25**	SUN	**25**
FRI	**26**	MON	**26**
SAT	**27**	TUES	**27**
SUN	**28**	WED	**28**
MON	**29**	THUR	**29**
TUES	**30**	FRI	**30**
WED	**31**	SAT	**31**

Throughout July and August, Billie is resident at the Downbeat Club with Tiny Grimes and his Trio and Trummy Young.'

1 JULY 1946

Down Beat reports: 'Joe Guy scuffling with wife Billie Holiday, with the Downbeat Club refusing him entrance – next night they were eating together amicably at Yank Sing.'

Down Beat also reviews Billie's latest release:s:

BILLIE HOLIDAY
*** *What Is This Thing Called Love*
*** *Don't Explain*
Billie has sung better than on *Love* – both her tone and her phrasing have been surer. But it's still far better than the mill-run stuff you usually hear. Whoever the lead alto man on the date is, he's fine – reeds really blend. The beat is good, but the strings sound a little uneasy about the whole thing. Saxes could have been heard to better advantage too. *Explain* is credited to Billie and Art Herzog, the tale of the guy who can get away with murder. Billie sings it as though she means it. (*Decca 23565*)

BILLIE HOLIDAY
*** *She's Funny That Way*
** *How Am I To Know*
Way is supported by the Eddie Heywood Trio, *Know* by Eddie's band. There has been better Billie, especially on *Know*, whose tempo drags even too much for Billie to keep moving effectively. (*Commodore 569*)

FRIDAY 16 AUGUST 1946
Billie appears at the Isaac Woodward Benefit Show at Lewisohn Stadium, 137th Street and Convent Avenue, New York City.

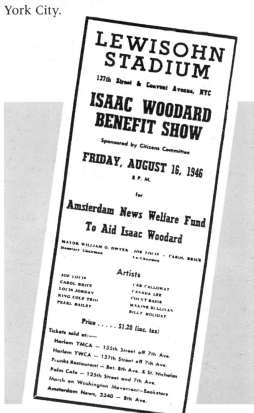

SUN	1
MON	2
TUES	3
WED	4
THUR	5
FRI	6
SAT	7
SUN	8
MON	9
TUES	10
WED	11
THUR	12
FRI	13
SAT	14
SUN	15
MON	16
TUES	17
WED	18
THUR	19
FRI	20
SAT	21
SUN	22
MON	23
TUES	24
WED	25
THUR	26
FRI	27
SAT	28
SUN	29
MON	30

Early in September, Billie closes at the Downbeat Club and heads for Hollywood for pre-recording and filming for the movie 'New Orleans'.

WEDNESDAY 11 SEPTEMBER 1946
Filming begins for the movie in the Hal Roach Studios, Culver City, Los Angeles. Recording and filming work takes Billie well into October. The track with Louis Armstrong and his Orchestra is probably recorded on Tuesday 8 October.

PRE-PRODUCTION RECORDING

BILLIE HOLIDAY (v), CHARLIE BEAL (p)
Do You Know What It Means To Miss New Orleans?

Billie Holiday with Louis Armstrong and his Band:
LOUIS ARMSTRONG (t/v), BARNEY BIGARD (cl), KID ORY (tb), CHARLIE BEAL (p), BUD SCOTT (g), RED CALLENDER (b), ZUTTY SINGLETON (d), BILLIE HOLIDAY (v)
Do You Know What It Means To Miss New Orleans?

Billie Holiday with Louis Armstrong and his Band:
LOUIS ARMSTRONG (t/v), BARNEY BIGARD (cl), KID ORY (tb), CHARLIE BEAL (p), BUD SCOTT (g), RED CALLENDER (b), ZUTTY SINGLETON (d), BILLIE HOLIDAY (v)
Farewell to Storyville

Billie Holiday with Louis Armstrong and his Orchestra: LOUIS ARMSTRONG, ROBERT BUTLER, LOUIS GRAY, FATS FORD, ED MULLINS (t), RUSSELL MOORE, WADDET WILLIAMS, NAT ALLEN, JAMES WHITNEY (tb), DON HILL, AMOS GORDON (as), JOE GARLAND, JOHN SPARROW (ts), LUCKY THOMPSON (bs), EARL MASON (p), ELMER WARNER (g), ARVELL SHAW (b), EDMUND McCONNEY (d), BILLIE HOLIDAY (v)
The Blues Are Brewin'

Below: Billie singing 'The Blues Are Brewin' at the conclusion of the movie. Opposite page (top): with Louis Armstrong (bottom): with Louis and Barney Bigard.

TUES	**1**
WED	**2**
THUR	**3**
FRI	**4**
SAT	**5**
SUN	**6**
MON	**7**
TUES	**8**
WED	**9**
THUR	**10**
FRI	**11**
SAT	**12**
SUN	**13**
MON	**14**
TUES	**15**
WED	**16**
THUR	**17**
FRI	**18**
SAT	**19**
SUN	**20**
MON	**21**
TUES	**22**
WED	**23**
THUR	**24**
FRI	**25**
SAT	**26**
SUN	**27**
MON	**28**
TUES	**29**
WED	**30**
THUR	**31**

FILM SOUND TRACK
Hal Roach Studios, Culver City, Los Angeles

Billie Holiday with Louis Armstrong and his Band:
LOUIS ARMSTRONG (t/v), BARNEY BIGARD (cl), KID ORY (tb), CHARLIE BEAL (p), BUD SCOTT (g), RED CALLENDER (b), ZUTTY SINGLETON (d), BILLIE HOLIDAY (v)
Do You Know What It Means To Miss New Orleans? / Farewell To Storyville

Billie Holiday with Louis Armstrong and his Orchestra: LOUIS ARMSTRONG, ROBERT BUTLER, LOUIS GRAY, FATS FORD, ED MULLINS (t), RUSSELL MOORE, WADDET WILLIAMS, NAT ALLEN, JAMES WHITNEY (tb), DON HILL, AMOS GORDON (as), JOE GARLAND, JOHN SPARROW (ts), LUCKY THOMPSON (bs), EARL MASON (p), ELMER WARNER (g), ARVELL SHAW (b), EDMUND McCONNEY (d), BILLIE HOLIDAY (v)
The Blues Are Brewin'

MONDAY 7 OCTOBER 1946
Billie appears at a JATP Concert at the Shrine Auditorium in Los Angeles.
HOWARD McGHEE (t), ILLINOIS JACQUET (ts), TRUMMY YOUNG (tb), KEN KERSEY (p), BARNEY KESSEL (g), CHARLIE DRAYTON (b), JACKIE MILLS (d), BILLIE HOLIDAY (v)
Travelin' Light / He's Funny That Way

At the conclusion of filming for *New Orleans* Billie travels back to New York.

FRI	1
SAT	2
SUN	3
MON	4
TUES	5
WED	6
THUR	7
FRI	8
SAT	9
SUN	10
MON	11
TUES	12
WED	13
THUR	14
FRI	15
SAT	16
SUN	17
MON	18
TUES	19
WED	20
THUR	21
FRI	22
SAT	23
SUN	24
MON	25
TUES	26
WED	27
THUR	28
FRI	29
SAT	30

TUESDAY 12 NOVEMBER 1946

Billie opens at the Downbeat Club on 52nd Street. Eddie Heywood has been starring at the club on the strength of his hit record 'Begin the Beguine', but he refuses to back Billie unless his name goes on the sign outside. At the last minute, Bobby Tucker (23) is drafted as her accompanist and later said:

'I was scared that first time, yes. There was no bass, no drums, just me; and I wasn't dressed. But for the next four or five weeks I played for her at the Downbeat, and I felt like I was stealing her money. Wherever I put the tune, she found the groove and made it happen. She could swing in the hardest tempo and float on top of it like it was made for her; when I put it slow, she sang it slow – but the most beautiful slow you ever heard.

To her fans, Lady could do no wrong; but Lady was getting very unreliable. First off, we never did a show before midnight. I would take my train out of Morristown, the tube out of Hoboken, the D train out of 34th Street and walk into the Downbeat every night at exactly twenty-eight minutes to ten. The show was supposed to go on between 9.30 and ten, but what's wrong? Where's Lady? They're knocking on her door, and she's saying, 'Just a minute, just a minute.' For two and a half hours.'

SUNDAY 17 NOVEMBER 1946

Art Tatum replaces Eddie Heywood's Band at the Downbeat.

SUN	1
MON	2
TUES	3
WED	4
THUR	5
FRI	6
SAT	7
SUN	8
MON	9
TUES	10
WED	11
THUR	12
FRI	13
SAT	14
SUN	15
MON	16
TUES	17
WED	18
THUR	19
FRI	20
SAT	21
SUN	22
MON	23
TUES	24
WED	25
THUR	26
FRI	27
SAT	28
SUN	29
MON	30
TUES	31

SATURDAY 14 DECEMBER 1946

Billie and Bobby Tucker appear at a JATP Benefit Concert for Sydenham Hospital at Carnegie Hall. Also on the bill are The King Cole Trio, Lionel Hampton, Charlie Shavers, Pete Johnson, Coleman Hawkins, Illinois Jacquet, Buck Clayton and Teddy Wilson.

MONDAY 16 DECEMBER 1946

Billie appears at a Double Benefit Concert, for Disabled Veterans and for Sydenham Hospital at the Renaissance Casino. Also featured are Billy Daniels, Al Casey Trio, Josh White and Thelma Carpenter.

Right: Billie and Art Tatum at the Downbeat Club.

SATURDAY 21 DECEMBER 1946

Billie appears at a Benefit Concert for Sydenham Hospital at Carnegie Hall.

FRIDAY 27 DECEMBER 1946

Recording session (2.30–6.10pm) as Billie Holiday accompanied by John Simmons and his Orchestra for Decca in New York City. Milt Gabler is the producer.
ROSTELLE REESE (t), LEM DAVIS (as), BOB DORSEY (ts), BOBBY TUCKER (p), JOHN SIMMONS (b), DENZIL BEST (d), BILLIE HOLIDAY (v)
The Blues Are Brewin' / Guilty (3 takes) / *Careless Love* (unissued)

WED	1
THUR	2
FRI	3
SAT	4
SUN	5
MONR	6
TUES	7
WEDT	8
THUR	9
FRI	10
SAT	11
SUN	12
MON	13
TUES	14
WED	15
THUR	16
FRI	17
SAT	18
SUN	19
MON	20
TUES	21
WED	22
THUR	23
FRI	24
SAT	25
SUN	26
MON	27
TUES	28
WED	29
THUR	30
FRI	31

Throughout January Billie is resident at the Downbeat Club with Art Tatum.

Billie and Teddy Wilson receive their Esquire awards from Arthur Godfrey on his CBS radio show.

MONDAY 13 JANUARY 1947

Billie appears on *Arthur Godfrey Time*, a 30-minute radio show via CBS in New York. Also on the show is Teddy Wilson.

Billie is interviewed by Arthur Godfrey prior to singing *The Man I Love* accompanied by Bobby Tucker at the piano.

WEDNESDAY 15 JANUARY 1947

Under the headline **Jazz Blows Final Breath on 52nd Street**, *Down Beat* reports that Kelly's Stable and the Spotlite – which for the last month has been called the Famous Door – have both switched from jazz to strip shows. It also reports :

> Across the street at the Downbeat club, Billie Holiday and Art Tatum may find contract problems forcing one of them out shortly after the first of the year, possibly Tatum, who may move down the street to the Three Deuces. Ruby Breadbar, club mentor, has been eyeing a package that will include Red Allen, Mary Lou Williams, June Richmond and a Tiny Grimes unit to follow la Holiday and Tatum.

SATURDAY 18 JANUARY 1947

Billie appears at Brooklyn's 13th Regiment Armory with the Jimmie Lunceford and Luis Russell Bands.

SATURDAY 25 JANUARY 1947

Billie appears on *Saturday Night Surprise Party*, a new radio show on station WNEW, New York, 8.35–9pm. Also on the show are Red Norvo and Charlie Shavers. The MC is Art Ford.

Billie May Have To Take Cut

New York — Fifty-second street's Downbeat club is negotiating for a 10-week contract with Billie Holiday at a 20 percent reduction, it was learned here at press time.

SAT	1
SUN	2
MON	3
TUES	4
WED	5
THUR	6
FRI	7
SAT	8
SUN	9
MON	10
TUES	11
WED	12
THUR	13
FRI	14
SAT	15
SUN	16
MON	17
TUES	18
WED	19
THUR	20
FRI	21
SAT	22
SUN	23
MON	24
TUES	25
WED	26
THUR	27
FRI	28

Throughout February Billie is resident at the Downbeat Club with Art Tatum. *Down Beat* reports that they have both had their salaries cut because of poor business.

SATURDAY 8 FEBRUARY 1947

Billie appears as a surprise guest star at Louis Armstrong's Carnegie Hall Concert.
LOUIS ARMSTRONG (t/v), BOBBY TUCKER (p), ELMER WARNER (g), ARVELL SHAW (b), SID CATLETT (d), BILLIE HOLIDAY (v)
Do You Know What It Means To Miss New Orleans?
BILLIE HOLIDAY (v), BOBBY TUCKER (p) *Don't Explain*

Louis Armstrong, Billie and Leonard Feather backstage at Carnegie Hall.

Michael Levin reviews the concert for Down Beat:

"Didn't he play wonderfully!", quoth a member of the audience, one Dizzy Gillespie, which about sums up the reaction to the Louis Armstrong concert here at Carnegie Hall.

Louis, supported by Ed Hall's six piece band, and his own large group for the last quarter of the show, turned out 25 pieces of jazz to lusty applause from NY critics and a three-quarters house.

Earl Hines, ballyhooed as supporting Louis in the second or Chicago section of the concert was tied up in Nashville, Tenn., by bad weather and an unco-operative promoter and failed to show. Billie Holiday was brought on at the concert's close to fill the star-gap, joining Louis in *New Orleans* and her own *Don't Explain*. Audience liked her singing, but with the show running close to the 7:30 p.m. deadline as it was, the added number prevented Louis from getting a due measure of applause from a crowd there to hear him, not Miss Holiday.

WEDNESDAY 12 FEBRUARY 1947

Down Beat reviews Billie's latest release:

BILLIE HOLIDAY
*** *Good Morning Heartache*
** *No Good Man*
A couple of Irene Higginbotham tunes, of which *Morning* is the better. Billie's ideas are a shade too candy-cute these days. play some of her sides with the Wilson pickup bands and you'll mark the difference. (*Decca 23676*)

THURSDAY 13 FEBRUARY 1947

Recording session (2–5.10pm) as Billie Holiday accompanied by Bob Haggart and his Orchestra for Decca in New York City.
BILLY BUTTERFIELD (t), BILL STEGMEYER (cl/as), TOOTS MONDELLO, AL KLINK (as), HANK ROSS, ARTIE DRELINGER (ts), BOBBY TUCKER (p), DANNY PERRY (g), BOB HAGGART (b), BUNNY SHAWKER (d), BILLIE HOLIDAY (v)
Deep Song / There Is No Greater Love / Easy Living / Solitude (2 takes)

Bobby Tucker remembers the session:
She was living on La Salle Street [125th Street just off LaSalle Street in Harlem] and I couldn't get her downtown. The band's been there since 12 o'clock, and they're ready to pack up but the company's taken the place till 3, so they sit there ... So we walk in at 20 minutes after 2 and she goes to the ladies' room. And she came in at 20 minutes to 3 and we were done at 10 minutes to 3. And those are the records you hear now.

SUNDAY 23 FEBRUARY 1947

Billie appears at the Bronx Merry Makers Matinee Dance (4–9pm) at The Celebrity Club, 35 E125th Street. Also appearing are Frances Hill, Shorty Ward & Little Curty with music by Sol Moore and his Orchestra.

SAT 1
SUN 2
MON 3
TUES 4
WED 5
THUR 6
FRI 7
SAT 8
SUN 9
MON 10
TUES 11
WED 12
THUR 13
FRI 14
SAT 15
SUN 16
MON 17
TUES 18
WED 19
THUR 20
FRI 21
SAT 22
SUN 23
MON 24
TUES 25
WED 26
THUR 27
FRI 28
SAT 29
SUN 30
MON 31

SUNDAY 2 MARCH 1947
Billie appears at a matinee concert (2pm) at Symphony Hall, Boston with Sy Oliver and his Orchestra.

MONDAY 3 MARCH 1947
Billie stars at a Blue Monday Jam Session at Smalls Paradise in Harlem.

SATURDAY 15 MARCH 1947
Billie takes part in the 1947 Poll Winners Midnight Concert at Carnegie Hall. Also taking part are Count Basie, Walter Page, Jo Jones, Cootie Williams, Dizzy Gillespie, Lionel Hampton & his Orchestra, Louis Armstrong, Ella Fitzgerald and Earl Bostic.

Billie Holiday Gets Check-Up

New York—Famed chanter Billie Holiday for the last couple weeks has been confined to a local hospital for a general check-up.

Downbeat club on 52nd Street where she had been featured remains closed. Spot will reopen soon, according to operator Ruby Breadbar.

SATURDAY 22 MARCH 1947
Billie closes at the Downbeat when Rudy Breadbar, manager of the Downbeat Club, decides to cut his losses and closes the club for the summer.

The enforced closure of the Downbeat leaves Billie temporarily unemployed. Manager Joe Glaser takes advantage of the unscheduled rest and insists that Billie tries to break her drug habit. Billie enters a New York clinic, the Park West Hospital in midtown New York, for a $2000 3-week cold-turkey cure.
Bobby Tucker said:
She wasn't taking a cure. They had glucose to clean out her system, they had great big bottles of that stuff – jugs – it's like purifying the system and those kind of things don't work, all it does is make her like a virgin when she comes out. I remember visiting her in hospital; in fact there were only three people that could visit her and they were Louis Armstrong, Joe Glaser and me. And it ended up that she was getting stuff from the nurse.

TUES	1
WED	2
THUR	3
FRI	4
SAT	5
SUN	6
MON	7
TUES	8
WED	9
THUR	10
FRI	11
SAT	12
SUN	13
MON	14
TUES	15
WED	16
THUR	17
FRI	18
SAT	19
SUN	20
MON	21
TUES	22
WED	23
THUR	24
FRI	25
SAT	26
SUN	27
MON	28
TUES	29
WED	30

MONDAY 7 APRIL 1947
Billie's 32nd birthday

TUESDAY 15 APRIL 1947
Billie holds a photo shoot at the hospital.

WEDNESDAY 16 APRIL 1947
Billie leaves the hospital to recuperate at the home of Bobby Tucker's mother on Cleveland Avenue in Morristown, New Jersey.

SATURDAY 26 APRIL 1947
Billie appears in a Midnight Variety Concert at Town Hall with Bobby Hackett and his Band. 'New Orleans' is premiered at the Saenger Theatre in New Orleans. Neither Billie nor Louis Armstrong appear.

SUNDAY 27 APRIL 1947
Billie opens at Colosimo's New Theatre Restaurant, 22nd Street at Wabash, Chicago. Also on the bill are Red Allen & J. C. Higginbotham and their Orchestra, The Two Zephyrs and Cindy & Windy. Four shows nightly, starting at 9.30pm.

Below: Billie recuperating from her 'cure' at Park West Hospital.

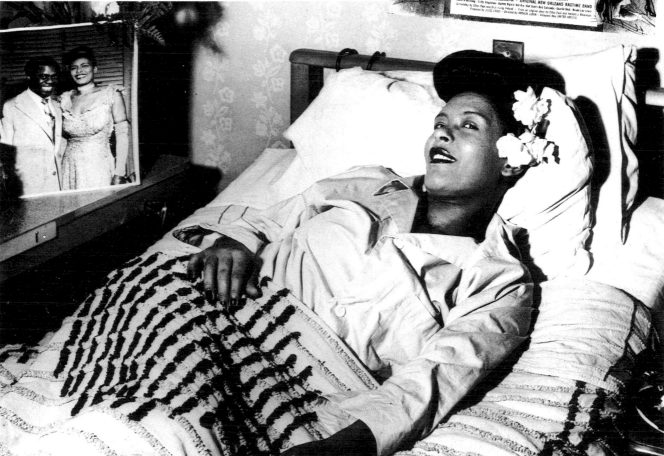

THUR	**1**
FRI	**2**
SAT	**3**
SUN	**4**
MON	**5**
TUES	**6**
WED	**7**
THUR	**8**
FRI	**9**
SAT	**10**
SUN	**11**
MON	**12**
TUES	**13**
WED	**14**
THUR	**15**
FRI	**16**
SAT	**17**
SUN	**18**
MON	**19**
TUES	**20**
WED	**21**
THUR	**22**
FRI	**23**
SAT	**24**
SUN	**25**
MON	**26**
TUES	**27**
WED	**28**
THUR	**29**
FRI	**30**
SAT	**31**

LAST THREE DAYS!!
FRIDAY - SATURDAY - SUNDAY
To See and Hear That' Master Mistress of Song

IN PERSON!
THE INCOMPARABLE

BILLIE HOLIDAY
Esquire's Gold Medal Award Winner
for Three Straight Years
DECCA RECORDING ARTIST
and Star of the new Samuel Goldwynn
picture "New Orleans"

WITH THE SPARKLING RHYTHMS OF
RED ALLEN ★ J. C. HIGGINBOTHAM
THEIR R.C.A. VICTOR RECORDING ORCHESTRA
TWO ZEPHYRS - CINDY and WINDY and the Southside's Gayest Floor Show

NO MINIMUM or COVER (Except on Weekends)

"Where the Southside Meets the Loop"
COLOSIMO'S NEW THEATRE RESTAURANT
22nd Street at Wabash — CALumet 7200

FOUR SHOWS NIGHTLY
First at 9:30 P.M.

SUNDAY 4 MAY 1947
Billie closes at Colosimo's.

MONDAY 5 MAY 1947
Billie is guest of honour at Ann Hughes' Monte Carlos Café, 6320 Cottage Grove, Chicago.

MONDAY 12 MAY 1947
Billie opens at the Earle Theatre in Philadelphia for a one-week engagement with Louis Armstrong and his Big Band. Billie, Joe Guy, Bobby Tucker and road manager Jimmy Ascendio check into the Attucks Hotel, 801 South 15th Street, Philadelphia.

FRIDAY 16 MAY 1947
Billie closes at the Earle Theatre. After removing her make-up in the dressing room her driver takes her back to her hotel to collect her luggage. The hotel was being raided by narcotics agents and the driver speeds away, colliding with a car, with the police shooting at them. Billie makes it back to New York.

SATURDAY 17 MAY 1947
Billie opens at the Onyx Club, now called Club 18.

MONDAY 19 MAY 1947
At 5am Billie is arrested at the Hotel Marden, 142 W44th Street. She is taken by police to Room 32 of the Grampion Hotel on St Nicholas Avenue in Harlem where they arrest Joe Guy. At 10am they are both questioned at the Federal Bureau of Narcotics at 90 Church Street, New York City. Billie is released on a bail of $1000, but Joe Guy is held.

In the evening, Billie performs at Club 18.

WEDNESDAY 21 MAY 1947
Down Beat carries a Charles Emge review of *New Orleans*. He writes:

> Billie Holiday, as a singer, was handicapped by the material given her to sing. As an actress, in her role as a maid (the official credit list insults her by listing her as playing "herself") she does well enough but she'll hear plenty from the Negro press for accepting such a role.

SATURDAY 24 MAY 1947
During intermission at Club 18 Billie and Bobby Tucker are whisked by car to Carnegie Hall to make a surprise appearance on a JATP Concert.
You Better Go Now / You're Driving Me Crazy /There Is No Greater Love / I Cover The Waterfront

After the show they resume at Club 18.

TUESDAY 27 MAY 1947
Billie telephones Assistant US Attorney Joseph Hildenberger and says she wants to get the court case over as soon as possible. Arrangements are made to begin the trial the same morning. Billie arrives an hour late and the trial is postponed until 4pm. She is charged with violation of Section 174 of the US Narcotics Act: 'That she did receive,conceal and facilitate the transportation and concealment of drugs.' Billie is without representation and addresses the judge herself, pleading guilty, saying that she is broke and willing to enter a state hospital to be cured of her addiction. However, the judge sentences her to a year and a day in the Federal Reformatory for Women at Alderson, West Virginia.

A few hours after being sentenced Billie begins the train journey to Alderson in the custody of two white matrons. To prevent withdrawal symptoms on the train journey, Billie is given a shot of heroin.

WEDNESDAY 28 MAY 1947
Billie enters the Federal Reformatory for Women at Alderson, West Virginia at 9.30am.

'Don't Blame Show Biz!'—Billie

Daily Press Taking Usual Rap At Trade With Holiday Case

By MICHAEL LEVIN

BULLETIN—At press time, Billie Holiday was released on $1,000 bail by U.S. Commissioner Norman J. Griffith, in Philadelphia to return for further hearing today, June 4. The *Beat* learned from an unimpeachable source that in all probability charges would not be pressed against her, she would be allowed to finish out her present run at the Club 18, NYC, and other work presently contracted, and then would probably go to Lexington, Ky., for medical treatment of some months' duration.

New York—"When you're writing, straighten them out about my people. Tell 'em maybe I made my mistake but that show people aren't all like that. Whatever I did wrong, nobody else but me was to blame—and show people aren't wrong."

Billie Holiday said

New York—In the wake of the news stories on the Billie Holiday affair came the usual yellow reporting by some of the Broadway press. N.Y. *Daily News* columnist Danton Walker topped them all with a crack at the top of his column: "Federal agents will be cracking down on other musicians on the same drug charges that snared Billie Holiday."

This is what working newspapermen call a "blind item" and, unlike columnists, avoid like poison. The *Beat* has run them very infrequently, usually as a trade joke. Certainly no reputable writer would pound out damaging tripe of this kind and expect anything other than Walker's reputation in the trade.

This paper is as well acquainted with the music business as Danton Walker. We know of very few musicians who are heroin

DOWN BEAT

CHICAGO, JUNE 4, 1947
(Copyright 1947, Down Beat Publishing Co.)

VOL. 14—No. 12

McGhee Nabbed On Tea Charge

Hollywood — Howard McGhee, be-bop trumpet man, was arrested on a marijuana possession charge in the current L. A. campaign against weed, and, it seems, music figures.

McGhee, who was arrested with his wife, Dorothy, and a friend, W. L. Jones, and then released on bail after being booked, was particularly vehement about the incident.

"My wife and I have been continually subject to persecution here because she is white. This is the result of that persecution.

"The police officers entered our house without a warrant and treated us all roughly. One of them pulled something out from under a chair cushion and said it was a marijuana cigarette. Whatever it was, I never saw it before."

McGhee had planned to go to New York to join the Norman Granz unit, had delayed his departure due to a foot infection contracted by his wife.

Judy Starr Divorces

Chicago—Former radio singer Judy Starr was granted a divorce from Mait-

'Walk Out On Raeburn? I'm N

Hollywood—
What do they
Stillman Pond
ing his report

Cafe

Holiday Pleads Guilty, Gets A Year And Day

New York—Billie Holiday, previously scheduled for June 3 hearing on narcotics possession charges in Philadelphia federal court, was sentenced on May 27 to a year and a day in the federal reformatory for women at Alderson, W. Va.

Pleading guilty and with no attorney representing her, Billie sobbed as she told federal Judge J. Cullen Ganey that she was broke and wanted to be sent to a hospital for a cure.

Reason for her earlier sentencing caused some comment here, especially since Judge Ganey indicated dissatisfaction with the way Miss Holiday observed her parole to manager Joe Glaser. He also told her she must cooperate with federal agents in their efforts to track down drug supply sources.

Granting satisfactory progress medically, Miss Holiday will be eligible for parole in about eight months. However a felony conviction of 366 days will make it extremely difficult for her to work here, as police regulations forbid issuance of a cafe working card to anyone convicted of a felony.

During the course of the case, Assistant U. S. Attorney Joseph Hildenberger stated that Miss Holiday was the victim of "the worst type of parasite you can imagine. They followed her around and charging her $100 for dosages of narcotics costing $5."

Left: Billie, Bobby Tucker (centre) and road manager Jimmy Ascendio await charges in the District Court in Philadelphia. Bobby Tucker was released without charge.

Billie's admission documents reveal her to be 5ft 5ins tall, weighing 172lbs and of large build. Her age is erroneously given as 28 (she is, in fact, 32) and her address as 142 W44th Street, New York City (the Marden Hotel). She has just $6.34 in her possession.

Re Billie's education: Rates best in language and vocabulary, poor in factual knowledge. Has done singing and housework. Quit school to go to work. Seems inconsistent in her reasoning.

D. C. Form No. 61 a

Judgment and Commitment

District Court of the United States
EASTERN DISTRICT OF PENNSYLVANIA

8407

United States		No. 14234	Criminal¹ Informati
v.		in One	counts for violation
BILLIE HOLIDAY		of U.S.C., Title 21 U.S.C.A.	
		Secs. 174	

On this **27th** day of **May** , 19**47**, came the United States Attorney, and the defendant **Billie Holiday** appearing in proper person, and having been asked by the Court whether she desired counsel appointed, replied she did not and,

The defendant having ... **Guilty** of the offense charged ..., to wit: **Receiving, conceal-** ... **been imported,**

UNITED STATES DEPARTMENT OF JUSTICE
PENAL AND CORRECTIONAL INSTITUTION.

Federal Reformatory for Women

Alderson, West Va.
(Location)

Received 5-28-47

From USDC - E. Pa.

Crime Narc: Receive & conceal drugs

Sentence: 1 yrs mos 1 days

Date of sentence 5-27-47

Sentence begins 5-27-47

Sentence expires 5-27-48

Good time sentence expires 3-16-48

Date of birth 4-7-19 Occupation Singer

Birthplace Md. Nationality Am.

Age 28 Comp. Brown

Eyes Brown

has anything to say why judgment cause to the contrary being shown or

guilty of said offenses, is hereby com- representative for imprisonment for the

Record Form No. 7
July, 1936

...rs and marks Needle scars on

NAME	NUMBER

(Please furr...

LEAVE THIS SPACE BLANK

...me HOLIDAY, Billie

...s nee Holiday, Monroe Class.

8407-W Color Negro Sex Female Ref.

RIGHT HAND

1. Thumb	2. Index Finger	3. Middle Finger	4. Ring Finger	5. Little Finger

LEFT HAND

6. Thumb	7. Index Finger	8. Middle Finger	9. Ring Finger	10. Little Finger

Note Amputations

...ssified ...arched Assembled
...ex Card Verified
Answered

Prisoner's Signature
Billie Holiday

Four Fingers Taken Simultaneously

L. Thumb	R. Thumb

Four Fingers Taken Simultaneously
Right Hand

...t Hand

The cold turkey cure begins immediately and the first 19 days are pure hell for Billie. After four weeks, Billie is set to work, picking vegetables, tending pigs and washing dishes. She is allowed no visitors during her imprisonment and only three letters per day.

In September, Billie is taken back to the court in Philadelphia to appear as a witness at Joe Guy's trial. She tells the court that the drugs found in their apartment were for her use and nothing to do with Guy. Largely because of her testimony, Joe Guy is found 'Not Guilty'.

In New York, Norman Granz organises a benefit concert for Billie at Carnegie Hall featuring the Nat King Cole Trio and the JATP package. The concert is set for 29 November, but Billie's manager Joe Glaser announces to the press that the concert is unauthorised, and that Billie neither wants nor needs a concert. In the ensuing row, Nat King Cole is forced to withdraw because of contractual difficulties, and the bad publicity results in a meagre net profit of $514. Joe Glaser refuses to accept the money on Billie's behalf and Granz gives the money to charity.

Parole Form No. 18
January, 1937

THE UNITED STATES BOARD OF PAROLE
WASHINGTON, D.C.

Certificate of Conditional Release

Know All Men by these Presents:

It having been made to appear to the United States Board of Parole that _____ **Billie HOLIDAY** _____, Register No. **8407-W**, a prisoner in the **Federal Reformatory for Women Alderson, West Virginia** _____, now being entitled to **72 Days** deduction from the term of his sentence, based on commutation for good conduct as provided by Section 1 of the act of June 21, 1902, Section 2 of the Act of February 26, 1929, and Section 8 of the Act of May 27, 1930, and Amendments thereto, is about to be released in accordance with said Act on the date as determined by the Warden or Superintendent of the said institution, and

WHEREAS, Section 4 of the Act of June 29, 1932, provides that such prisoner shall, upon release, be treated as if released on parole and shall be subject to all provisions of the law relating to the parole of United States prisoners until the expiration of the maximum term or terms specified in his sentence,

Now, THEREFORE, the United States Board of Parole, in accordance with said statute, has decided that the CONDITIONS AS SET FORTH ON THE REVERSE SIDE OF THIS BLANK shall be the conditions under which the said prisoner shall be released, and furthermore, said prisoner shall be subject to such conditions until **May 27, 1948** which date will be the expiration of the maximum term or terms specified in his sentence, and

BE IT ALSO KNOWN, that this Certificate of Conditional Release does not in any way lessen the obligation of the prisoner to satisfy for payment of fine if such is part of his sentence.

BE IT ALSO KNOWN, that this Certificate of Conditional Release shall not prevent the delivery of the prisoner to authorities of the Federal Government or of any State otherwise entitled to his custody.

Given under the hand and the seal of the said United States Board of Parole this **1st**

day of **March**, Nineteen hundred **Forty-Eight**.

UNITED STATES BOARD OF PAROLE:

Daniel M. Lyons
Fred S. Rogers
D. J. Monkiewics

ARTHUR D. WOOD, Chairman
T. WEBBER WILSON, Member
ERNEST P. BAILY, Member

By _Walter X. Mundin_
Parole Executive

UNITED STATES BOARD OF PAROLE:
The above-named prisoner was released on this **16th** day of **March**, 194**8**

Helen Hironimus
Warden or Superintendent

MON	1
TUES	2
WED	3
THUR	4
FRI	5
SAT	6
SUN	7
MON	8
TUES	9
WED	10
THUR	11
FRI	12
SAT	13
SUN	14
MON	15
TUES	16
WED	17
THUR	18
FRI	19
SAT	20
SUN	21
MON	22
TUES	23
WED	24
THUR	25
FRI	26
SAT	27
SUN	28
MON	29
TUES	30
WED	31

TUESDAY 16 MARCH 1948

Billie is released on parole until 27 May. She has a slight tumour on her cheek which will need a minor operation to remove. She travels by train from Alderson, West Virginia to Bobby Tucker's mother's house in Morristown, New Jersey arriving there on Wednesday morning at 9am. She rehearses with Bobby for her welcome home concert at Carnegie Hall. Billie also decides to appoint a new manager. Ed Fishman had telephoned her regularly at Alderson with plans for her future and she agrees to sign up with him.

FRIDAY 26 MARCH 1948

Billie arrives in Manhattan and checks into a hotel on W47th Street.

Ernie Anderson is the promoter of Billie's Carnegie Hall concert: *'When she arrived in Manhattan she wanted to be in a hotel in midtown. She asked for a hotel on Dream Street, West 47th Street, so called because of all the drug busts. I put her in there and I got the impression that she was clean and was going to stay off drugs, that she was trying to stay away from Harlem and drugpushers and ex-husbands, who sometimes provided drugs to keep her in line. She did ask for comic books; I went out to a news-stand and bought her a huge stack. She was terribly grateful...*
Meanwhile at Carnegie Hall the box office was going crazy. The five Heck brothers who ran the box office said it was an enormous draw. The senior Heck said we could sell more concerts by Billie that night. He even asked, 'Why not? She could do another concert at 2 a.m. and another at 5 a.m. ...' He seriously proposed this but I wouldn't hear of it...
Well, the gross we racked up set a new house record for Carnegie Hall. Moreover, I later discovered the Heck brothers had made a private killing on seats sold that weren't ever on the floor plan. A few years later they were all arrested for a similar scam.

Billie Ducats Like Hotcakes

New York—Tickets for the Billie Holiday concert at Carnegie Hall, March 27, will be at a premium by the time this issue hits the streets, if pre-press time indications mean anything. Promoter Ernie Anderson reports the advance demand is comparable to that of the recent Stan Kenton Carnegie Hall bash. Anderson's Chubby Jackson concert, incidentally, was postponed from its original date, February 28.

SATURDAY 27 MARCH 1948

Billie performs two concerts at Carnegie Hall, each consisting of 30 numbers. She is accompanied by BOBBY TUCKER (p), REMO PALMIERI (g), JOHN LEVY (b), DENZIL BEST (d)

Jack Egan of *Down Beat* magazine is at the midnight show and writes:

Billie Back: Sans Verbiage, Plus Lbs.

Three thousand ardently enthusiastic fans packed Carnegie Hall to extra capacity and welcomed Billie Holiday back to the world of music as she gave a two-hour midnight performance, Saturday, March 27.

Introduced by disc jock Fred Robbins, Lady Day made her entrance to one of the most thunderous ovations ever given a performer in this or any other concert hall. Billie beamed, said nary a word, but went right into one of her top hits, *I Cover The Waterfront*. That headed the procession of 21 tunes which made up her program, which in turn was followed by six encores.

While noisy with its applause, on the whole the audience was well behaved, its concentrated attention attesting to the sincerity of its tribute to a great artist. Toward the end of the second half there were a few yells from an upper tier box in left field and spotted calls from the orchestra floor, similar to those heard from the congregation at a revival meeting, but the over-enthusiastic bellowers were quickly brought back to earth by the protests of more reserved members of the assemblage.

Billie was accompanied by a quartet of popular musicians: Bobby Tucker on piano; Denzil Best, drums; John Levy, bass, and Remo Palmieri, guitar. All instrumental work was confined to accompaniment, however, there being no "band" numbers. It was Billie's show from start to finish.

After 15 minutes, Billie took a quarter-hour intermission, during which time she changed from a black to blue gown, came back fresh as a newborn and went into her own composition, *Don't Explain* and six other numbers. The encores followed and, if the audience had had its way, Billie still would be out there. They just wouldn't let her go.

Aside from a few words of thanks before starting the second half of the recital, Billie confined all vocal efforts to singing. Whether or not her voice is quite as perfect as it was a year ago didn't matter a whit to the 3,000 disciples who crowded every nook and cranny of the stage and house of the high and mighty Carnegie. Lady Day did put on a little weight, maybe 15 or 20 pounds, but on her it looked good. She wore well that evening in all departments.

Heaviest receptions were given *All Of Me*, the blues hit *My Man Don't Love Me* and *Solitude*, though no tune was received with anything so cool as mere hot reaction. Torrid better describes it and even that is inadequate.

Lady Day is back, bigger than ever – and we don't mean those extra pounds.

The concert is an enormous success and Anderson says: *'So I booked the hall for a second concert three weeks later, and that sold out on announcement. This time Billie broke her own Carnegie Hall record.'*

MON	**1**
TUES	**2**
WED	**3**
THUR	**4**
FRI	**5**
SAT	**6**
SUN	**7**
MON	**8**
TUES	**9**
WED	**10**
THUR	**11**
FRI	**12**
SAT	**13**
SUN	**14**
MON	**15**
TUES	**16**
WED	**17**
THUR	**18**
FRI	**19**
SAT	**20**
SUN	**21**
MON	**22**
TUES	**23**
WED	**24**
THUR	**25**
FRI	**26**
SAT	**27**
SUN	**28**
MON	**29**
TUES	**30**
WED	**31**

SUNDAY 28 MARCH 1948

Carl Van Vechten writes to his friend, the painter Karl Priebe, about Billie's Carnegie Hall concert:

Well Billie is a really gone girl. She weighs considerably more. Prison fare must be good ... They not only sat, they stood, hundreds of 'em ... Then Fred Robbins introduced her, all in black, a little black lace here and there, the skirt slit at the front showed her legs when she moved. White gloves long with no fingers, just caught around the thumbs. Her hair in a twisted and unbraided coronet on top her head. White gardenias ... She was nervous and perspiring freely, but her first tones were reassuring and rewarded with a whoop. There was no set programme. She turned to the pianist and announced her numbers sotto voce ... Some Other Spring, All Of Me, Billie's Blues, No Greater Love, Travellin' Light, No More, You're Driving Me Crazy, She's Funny That Way: you know, you're hep. All with that seesaw motion of the arms, fingers always turned in, that swanlike twitching of the thighs, that tortured posture of the head, those inquiring wondering eyes, a little frightened at first and then as the applause increased they became grateful. The voice the same, in and out between tones, unbearably poignant, that blue voice.

THUR	**1**
FRI	**2**
SAT	**3**
SUN	**4**
MON	**5**
TUES	**6**
WED	**7**
THUR	**8**
FRI	**9**
SAT	**10**
SUN	**11**
MON	**12**
TUES	**13**
WED	**14**
THUR	**15**
FRI	**16**
SAT	**17**
SUN	**18**
MON	**19**
TUES	**20**
WED	**21**
THUR	**22**
FRI	**23**
SAT	**24**
SUN	**25**
MON	**26**
TUES	**27**
WED	**28**
THUR	**29**
FRI	**30**

WEDNESDAY 7 APRIL 1948
Billie's 33rd birthday

SATURDAY 17 APRIL 1948
Billie's second concert at Carnegie Hall breaks her
own Carnegie Hall box-office record. Billie is limping
with a badly sprained ankle.
Ernie Anderson says afterwards: *I don't honestly know
whether Billie was back on the stuff for this second show. I
rather think she was. But it was not too long afterwards
that she was certainly back on it.*

TUESDAY 27 APRIL 1948
Billie opens on Broadway at the Mansfield Theatre in
Holiday on Broadway. Also in the show are Bob Wyatt
& Billy Taylor (an organ-piano duo), Cozy Cole and
the Slam Stewart Trio. Billie is accompanied by the
Bobby Tucker Quartet. The show folds after five days.
During the week, Billie splits with Ed Fishman and
signs with Joe Glaser.

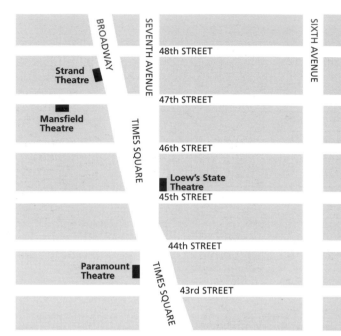

Billie Nixes Ed For Joe

New York—In a dispute
settled via a confab at the
American Guild of Variety
Artists' office, Billie Holiday
discharged Ed Fishman as her
personal manager and put her
business affairs in the hands of
Joe Glaser and his Associated
booking outfit.

Fishman was appointed sole
manager of the singer by her
when she was released from the
government institution in mid-
March. However, an exclusive
agency contract with Glaser's

ABC had been on file with
AGVA and, while Billie had sent
a letter discharging the Glaser
forces, this matter was left in
the air since she had not followed regulation procedure in
terminating the deal.

In the AGVA meeting several
days ago, Billie made void that
letter and asked that her deal
with Fishman be abrogated. She
also asked for an accounting
from Fishman of finances since
her release. This was forthcoming at press time.

THUR **1**
FRI **2**
SAT **3**
SUN **4**
MON **5**
TUES **6**
WED **7**
THUR **8**
FRI **9**
SAT **10**
SUN **11**
MON **12**
TUES **13**
WED **14**
THUR **15**
FRI **16**
SAT **17**
SUN **18**
MON **19**
TUES **20**
WED **21**
THUR **22**
FRI **23**
SAT **24**
SUN **25**
MON **26**
TUES **27**
WED **28**
THUR **29**
FRI **30**

Mansfield Theatre

FIRE NOTICE: The exit indicated by a red light and sign nearest to the seat you occupy is the shortest route to the street. In the event of fire please do not run—WALK TO THAT EXIT.

Frank J. Quayle,
FIRE COMMISSIONER

Thoughtless persons annoy patrons and distract actors and endanger the safety of others by lighting matches during the performance. Lighting of matches in theatres during the performances or at intermissions violates a city ordinance and renders the offender liable to a summons.

THE · PLAYBILL · A · WEEKLY · PUBLICATION · OF · PLAYBILL · INCORPORATED

Beginning Tuesday, April 27, 1948

Matinees Saturday and Sunday

AL WILDE

presents

HOLIDAY ON BROADWAY

starring

BILLIE HOLIDAY

SLAM STEWART   COZY COLE   BOBBY TUCKER

WYATT and TAYLOR

PART I.

WYATT and TAYLOR

Piano and Organ

SAT   **1**

SUN   **2**

MON   **3**

TUES   **4**

WED   **5**

THUR   **6**

FRI   **7**

SAT   **8**

SUN   **9**

MON **10**

TUES **11**

WED **12**

THUR **13**

FRI **14**

SAT **15**

SUN **16**

MON **17**

TUES **18**

WED **19**

THUR **20**

FRI **21**

SAT **22**

SUN **23**

MON **24**

TUES **25**

WED **26**

THUR **27**

FRI **28**

SAT **29**

SUN **30**

MON **31**

SATURDAY 1 MAY 1948

Holiday on Broadway closes.
Producer Al Wilde has plans to present the show in other cities, but nothing materialises.
John H. Levy, manager of the Ebony Club at 1678 Broadway persuades Billie that she can work at the Ebony, despite not having a New York cabaret card, without problems with the NY police and she begins a 4-week engagement.

FRIDAY 7 MAY 1948

Billie opens at the Ebony Club for a 4-week engagement. Bobby Tucker is on piano and Ted Sturgis is on bass.

Soon after starting work at the Ebony Billie begins an affair with John Levy. Levy initially spends money on Billie, renting her an expensive apartment in Queens, buying her a mink coat and a pea-green Cadillac. Soon, however, he is controlling her and her finances, and Billie has to ask him for pocket money.

Dan Burley reviews the opening in the *New York Amsterdam News*:

The Prodigal Daughter:-
Billie Holiday Triumphs In Her Broadway Debut At Club Ebony

BY DAN BURLEY

Rain had cascaded on the pavements all day. It finally dwindled reluctantly down to a persistent drizzle and hung around like a spring cold to bug people and make them wish they were in a long trance until the sun came out again. There were those up and down Broadway Friday night who cussed in Broadway cusswords the fleeting taxicabs that flitted past them, ignoring yelps, whistles and waving hands. The sidewalks were but sparsely inhabited as people sought shelter and made plans to stay home that night. But in front of Club Ebony there was a line that steadily augmented itself to the place where a minor traffic jam took place as people milled and mobbed the narrow doorway trying to get to the gaily bedecked cellar to hear Billie Holiday in her Broadway nightclub debut.

SAT	**1**
SUN	**2**
MON	**3**
TUES	**4**
WED	**5**
THUR	**6**
FRI	**7**
SAT	**8**
SUN	**9**
MON	**10**
TUES	**11**
WED	**12**
THUR	**13**
FRI	**14**
SAT	**15**
SUN	**16**
MON	**17**
TUES	**18**
WED	**19**
THUR	**20**
FRI	**21**
SAT	**22**
SUN	**23**
MON	**24**
TUES	**25**
WED	**26**
THUR	**27**
FRI	**28**
SAT	**29**
SUN	**30**
MON	**31**

The May 12 issue of *Variety* reviews Billie's opening at Club Ebony:

The Billie Holiday opening at the Club Ebony, Friday (7) gives further support to the contention that there's nothing wrong with the café business that a solid attraction won't cure. The sepia singer, who's making her first café appearance since her enforced temporary retirement from showbusiness a year ago, gave the Club Ebony its strongest business in the history of the spot.

Miss Holiday of late has been making frequent appearances around New York, having in the space of a little more than a month made two successful appearances at Carnegie Hall, and played a variety revue at the Mansfield theatre, which didn't pan out too well. Now that she's back in the nitery field, it seems there are a considerable number of spenders who prefer her in these surroundings. Miss Holiday has lost none of her potency in this field. Her smoothly underplayed and stylized renditions take on greater potency in cafés than in any of the other fields she played. It's in this element that she finds a highly appreciative audience.

Miss Holiday's stint included only six numbers for two encores and several bows. Her best is the provocative "Strange Fruit," a plaintive and spine-chilling description of the southern landscape. Others in her repertoire are "My Man," "I Cover The Waterfront" and tunes she's been identified with for sometime. She stopped the show here.

Rest of the layout includes vets on the sepia circuit including Dynamite Jefferson, who lifts tremendous weights with his choppers; Apus & Estrellita, with a weak comedy and song routine, and the Smith Kids' calyypsos which are charmingly projected. Production includes six-girl line in a series of torrid routines in the best Cotton Club tradition, and Rosebud, whose sinuous writhings in the production numbers generate excitement.

While Billie is visited at the Ebony by Sarah Vaughan and Mr & Mrs Billy Eckstine (bottom), the May issue of Metronome features Billie in the Hall of Fame section.

billie holiday, looking as beautiful and sounding as wonderful as ever, returned to the jazz world on March 27 in a concert at New York's Carnegie Hall. To the enthusiastic ovation of an audience that overflowed onto Carnegie's huge stage, Lady Day came back in a blaze of glory, singing all her familiar songs in the highly stylized Holiday fashion, to the accompaniment of a rhythm section. Billie has long been one of America's top jazz singers, making some of her most famous records with equally famous pianist Teddy Wilson, proving the most consistent drawing card 52nd St. has ever known, winning many polls every year. Welcome home, Billie!

METRONOME

hall of *Fame.*

SAT	**1**
SUN	**2**
MON	**3**
TUES	**4**
WED	**5**
THUR	**6**
FRI	**7**
SAT	**8**
SUN	**9**
MON	**10**
TUES	**11**
WED	**12**
THUR	**13**
FRI	**14**
SAT	**15**
SUN	**16**
MON	**17**
TUES	**18**
WED	**19**
THUR	**20**
FRI	**21**
SAT	**22**
SUN	**23**
MON	**24**
TUES	**25**
WED	**26**
THUR	**27**
FRI	**28**
SAT	**29**
SUN	**30**
MON	**31**

SATURDAY 15 MAY 1948
The One-Nite Stand series of Midnight concerts at Carnegie Hall, conducted by Ernie Anderson and Fred Robbins, ends with Count Basie Orchestra Plus Guests. Woody Herman sings an ad-lib blues, Billie Holiday sings two songs and Jimmy Rushing does 10 minutes of blues. Hot Lips Page, Buck Clayton and Leo Parker sit in on the final number. During the Saturday afternoon rehearsal, Earle Warren collapses with pleurisy and is rushed to hospital.

FRIDAY 21 MAY 1948
Billie headlines a benefit concert for Sydenham Hospital at the Renaissance Casino in Harlem.

TUESDAY 25 MAY 1948
Billie joins in the 70th birthday celebrations for Bill 'Bojangles' Robinson at the Ebony Club.

THURSDAY 27 MAY 1948
Billie closes at the Ebony Club.

SATURDAY 29 MAY 1948
New York Amsterdam News columnist Dan Burley writes:
Yep. Billie Holiday has sung her way into the heart of that co-bossman at Club Ebony.

Right: Billie dances with Bill 'Bojangles"Robinson at his 70th birthday party. Below: 'Bojangles' presents his dancing shoes to the owners of Club Ebony. L to r: Al Martin, John Levy, Dicky Wells, Bill Robinson.

TUES	1
WED	2
THUR	3
FRI	4
SAT	5
SUN	6
MON	7
TUES	8
WED	9
THUR	10
FRI	11
SAT	12
SUN	13
MON	14
TUES	15
WED	16
THUR	17
FRI	18
SAT	19
SUN	20
MON	21
TUES	22
WED	23
THUR	24
FRI	25
SAT	26
SUN	27
MON	28
TUES	29
WED	30

TUESDAY 1 JUNE 1948
Billie opens at Frank Palumbo's in Philadelphia for a one-week engagement.

SUNDAY 6 JUNE 1948
Billie closes at Frank Palumbo's

MONDAY 7 JUNE 1948
Billie is Leonard Feather's guest on his WHN radio show *Jazz at its Best* as he spins some of her rarest recordings and tells the story of her career from the day she cut her first record with Benny Goodman in 1933.

MONDAY 14 JUNE 1948
Billie opens at the Blue Note in Chicago for a 3-week engagement opposite the Jimmy McPartland Band with Marian McPartland (p), Bud Freeman (ts), Ben Carlton (b), Chick Evans (d).

Below: Billie is pictured with Jimmy McPartland and at the microphone during her Blue Note engagement.

Holiday Holds Chicagoans In Palm Of Hand

BY CHARLES A. DAVIS

You're down in the Blue Note leaning casually on the bar talking in the crowd through a soft blue haze. Here and there the red dot of a cigaret winks and fades. A clarinet wails and a staccato trumpet gives out with the music of Dixieland. You're waiting for Billie. Everybody is.

It has been better than a year since you last heard her at Colosimo's. There's been tragedy and bad days for her since she was last your way. You wonder how she looks, how she feels, and if she's still as great as ever.

Then she comes out, tall, buxom, and at ease, two familiar gardenias in her hair. The first questions are answered. She mounts the bandstand behind Bobby Tucker, her pianist, and Joe Johnson, her bassist.

'Miss Billie Holiday'

Someone is talking "...Miss Billie Holiday, America's greatest singer of songs..."

Then she starts. Slow, soft tones slip into your ears, cling, make you set down your glass and drop your cigaret. "It's that old devil love again ... rain in my heart ... rocks in my bed ..."

This is it. Billie is back. Billie is O.K. And she sounds greater than ever.

THUR	**1**
FRI	**2**
SAT	**3**
SUN	**4**
MON	**5**
TUES	**6**
WED	**7**
THUR	**8**
FRI	**9**
SAT	**10**
SUN	**11**
MON	**12**
TUES	**13**
WED	**14**
THUR	**15**
FRI	**16**
SAT	**17**
SUN	**18**
MON	**19**
TUES	**20**
WED	**21**
THUR	**22**
FRI	**23**
SAT	**24**
SUN	**25**
MON	**26**
TUES	**27**
WED	**28**
THUR	**29**
FRI	**30**
SAT	**31**

SUNDAY 4 JULY 1948

Billie closes at the Blue Note in Chicago.

Either just before, or just after, the Blue Note, Billie does a week at Club Tia Juana in Cleveland. During the course of the week, Billie and Bobby Tucker attend an award ceremony at the Majestic Theatre where Lionel Hampton and his Orchestra and Wynonie Harris are appearing. The ceremony is broadcast and Billie is featured in one number: BILLIE HOLIDAY (v), BEN KYNARD (cl), BOBBY TUCKER (p), CHARLIE MINGUS (b), EARL WALKER (d) plus full band at end of number: *I Cover The Waterfront*

FRIDAY 16 JULY 1948

Billie opens at the Strand Theatre on Broadway with Count Basie and his Orchestra, Stump & Stumpy, and The Two Zephyrs. The movie presentation is *Key Largo* starring Humphrey Bogart. They play 5 shows a day, 7 days a week, for the next six weeks.

Barry Ulanov writes about the show in the October issue of *Metronome*:

> For six weeks in the worst heat of July and August, Billie acknowledged the applause of audiences at the Strand Theatre in New York, the largest audiences that New York theatre had seen in years. The movie, *Key Largo*, pulled in a large part of the audiences; Count Basie was some draw; but there have been big movies before and Count Basie has appeared at New York theatres before. As very few singers in our time, as no uncompromising jazz singer in our time, Billie is a box office attraction. She has her own explanation.
>
> "They come to see me get all fouled up. They're just waiting for that moment. Just waiting. But they're not going to get it. I'm not going to get all fouled up. I'm not! I'm not..."

THUR	**1**
FRI	**2**
SAT	**3**
SUN	**4**
MON	**5**
TUES	**6**
WED	**7**
THUR	**8**
FRI	**9**
SAT	**10**
SUN	**11**
MON	**12**
TUES	**13**
WED	**14**
THUR	**15**
FRI	**16**
SAT	**17**
SUN	**18**
MON	**19**
TUES	**20**
WED	**21**
THUR	**22**
FRI	**23**
SAT	**24**
SUN	**25**
MON	**26**
TUES	**27**
WED	**28**
THUR	**29**
HUR	**30**
HUR	**31**

WEDNESDAY 28 JULY 1948

Billie is taken to task in the *Down Beat* editorial:

Chicago July 28, 1948

That 'Third Chance' Doesn't Exist, Billie

"I guess Down Beat is going to chew me to shreds like the papers are doing"—Billie Holiday (June 4, 1947, p. 6). We didn't, Billie . . . at a time when yellow journalism got yellower in decrying the "horrible" morals of musicians in general, because you asked for, and took, the rap for a mistake in judgment. Not a word from us, save in your defense, while members of the fourth estate muck-raked the marijuana situation and music within an inch of libel.

Naught but praise from the Beat when you came back . . . a little more stout, a lot healthier . . . when you "thanked God" for the second chance. Only praise in our minds for handling yourself as you have, singing as you still do . . . up to a point. Familiar with your background (you may recall the influence of one of this staff in setting up your first break . . . singling at New York's Cotton Club in 1935), we realize the road was rough, the pitfalls now self-evident, but we aren't sufficiently adept seers to figure out how the "third chance" you're aiming for is going to happen.

You, Miss Holiday, are knifing a lot of people who worship your singing, trill your praise to the sky, and pay a buck for colored water so that you can continue to draw that $2,200 weekly. This sudden affinity for Courvoisier, this rude up-stage attitude, this indefinite quality . . . "will she be late to-night, or will she show at all" . . . is nowhere.

Your refusal to go on without gardenias in your hair is understandable . . . a trademark is essential. We condone your "hesitancy" in performing on opening night at the Chicago club where your accompanying trio was late . . . arranged backgrounds and familiar musicians are essential to a good performance. But we don't subscribe to your liquid formula for success, nor to the amount, nor to the obvious effect, brought to our attention by spectators both in the trade and non-professional.

Too long evidently, we, and other publications, have automatically conceded our heroes to be simon-pure, over-looked their faults, minimized their failures. Today, business can't afford black eyes. Tribulations like your conviction last year, multiplied, force music and musicians to fight twice as hard for decent recognition, polite handling, and living wages. The crowds aren't parting with drink money for the privilege of watching a performer gradually cultivate a glow.

Though music is at bat again with two substantial strikes, it still has a third coming. About that "third chance" for you. . . . we don't know.

FRIDAY 30 JULY 1948

Billie is guest of honour on *Turn Back The Turntable*, the first in a proposed new series of 30-minute radio quiz programmes on Station WMBC about records of yesteryear. Also taking part are Lionel Ricco, Bob Sherry, Jack Meltzer, Robert Wile and Bill Grauer (editor of *Record Changer* magazine).

Opposite page: Billie and the Count Basie Orchestra on stage at the Strand Theatre on Broadway. Below: Basie and Billie at the microphone with Bobby Tucker at the piano.

SUN	1	WED	1
MON	2	THUR	2
TUES	3	FRI	3
WED	4	SAT	4
THUR	5	SUN	5
FRI	6	MON	6
SAT	7	TUES	7
SUN	8	WED	8
MON	9	THUR	9
TUES	10	FRI	10
WED	11	SAT	11
THUR	12	SUN	12
FRI	13	MON	13
SAT	14	TUES	14
SUN	15	WED	15
MON	16	THUR	16
TUES	17	FRI	17
WED	18	SAT	18
THUR	19	SUN	19
FRI	20	MON	20
SAT	21	TUES	21
SUN	22	WED	22
MON	23	THUR	23
TUES	24	FRI	24
WED	25	SAT	25
THUR	26	SUN	26
FRI	27	MON	27
SAT	28	TUES	28
SUN	29	WED	29
MON	30	THUR	30
TUES	31		

WEDNESDAY 25 AUGUST 1948
Billie guests on NBC's *Swingtime at the Savoy*.

THURSDAY 26 AUGUST 1948
Billie and Basie close at the Strand Theater.

TUESDAY 31 AUGUST 1948
Billie opens at the Club Astoria, Baltimore for a one-week engagement.

SUNDAY 5 SEPTEMBER 1948
Billie closes at the Club Astoria, Baltimore.

FRIDAY 10 SEPTEMBER 1948
Billie opens at the Club Bali, Washington for a one-week engagement backed by Bobby Tucker and local musicians Benny Fonsville (bass) and Al Dunn (drums).

THURSDAY 16 SEPTEMBER 1948
Billie closes at the Club Bali, Washington.

FRIDAY 17 SEPTEMBER 1948
Billie back at the Ebony Club with Buster Harding's Orchestra when it reopens after a summer break. Esy Morales' Orchestra is on hand for Latin American dancing.

Below: Billie at the Club Bali, Washington with Al Dunn (drums), Bobby Tucker (piano) and Benny Fonsville (bass).

FRI **1**
SAT **2**
SUN **3**
MON **4**
TUES **5**
WED **6**
THUR **7**
FRI **8**
SAT **9**
SUN **10**
MON **11**
TUES **12**
WED **13**
THUR **14**
FRI **15**
SAT **16**
SUN **17**
MON **18**
TUES **19**
WED **20**
THUR **21**
FRI **22**
SAT **23**
SUN **24**
MON **25**
TUES **26**
WED **27**
THUR **28**
FRI **29**
SAT **30**
SUN **31**

OCTOBER 1948

Billie appears on the cover of *Metronome* and is featured in an article by editor Barry Ulanov, entitled *Day or night, a great lady.*

FRIDAY 15 OCTOBER 1948

Billie opens at the Apollo Theatre for a one-week engagement backed by Buster Harding's Orchestra. Also on the bill are Jimmie Smith, Dynamite Jefferson, Princess de Paur & Toulae and Apus, Estrellita & George.

WEDNESDAY 20 OCTOBER 1948

Amateur Hour at the Apollo is broadcast via station WMCA.

THURSDAY 21 OCTOBER 1948

Billie closes at the Apollo.

FRIDAY 22 OCTOBER 1948

Billie is scheduled to record for Decca at 2p.m. but doesn't turn up.

SATURDAY 23 OCTOBER 1948

Billie closes at Club Ebony in New York.

MONDAY 25 OCTOBER 1948

Billie opens a 3-week engagement at the Silhouette Club in Chicago opposite the Jimmy McPartland Band. Her salary is $2,850 a week plus a percentage of bar takings.

Billie is accompanied by BOBBY TUCKER (p), JOHN LEVY (b) and DODO ANDERSON (d). The engagement is not a happy one. Billie has a heavy cold on opening night, and for most of the engagement sings only four songs per set.

Pat Harris of *Down Beat* :

> Billie didn't seem interested in singing. Her presentation was so mechanically stylised as to seem almost a mimic's mockery of what she had done before.

TUESDAY 26 OCTOBER 1948

Isabelle Marks, of Decca Records, writes to Billie:
Due to your having failed to appear for the recording session scheduled for you and at which you agreed to perform on Friday, October 22, 1948 at 2p.m. we will find it necessary to charge the cost of all expenses involved to your royalty account.

SATURDAY 30 OCTOBER 1948

Billie and John Levy are guests of Jimmy the Fixer at a New Orleans Gumbo Dinner prior to her appearance at the Silhouette Club.

MON	1
TUES	2
WED	3
THUR	4
FRI	5
SAT	6
SUN	7
MON	8
TUES	9
WED	10
THUR	11
FRI	12
SAT	13
SUN	14
MON	15
TUES	16
WED	17
THUR	18
FRI	19
SAT	20
SUN	21
MON	22
TUES	23
WED	24
THUR	25
FRI	26
SAT	27
SUN	28
MON	29
TUES	30

SUNDAY 14 NOVEMBER 1948
Billie closes at the Silhouette Club in Chicago.

Probably during the Silhouette Club engagement, Billie appears at the first of Chicago DJ Al Benson's Civic Opera House concerts. Also on the bill at the sell-out concert are Gene Ammons, Tom Archia, Charlie Ventura (appearing at the Blue Note), Benny Green, Ed Shaughnessy, Miles Davis, Allen Eager, Fats Navarro, Max Roach, Dolores Bell and Jackie Paris.

TENTH ANNIVERSARY OF CAFE SOCIETY
During the week 14 to 22 November Barney Josephson presents a special '10th Anniversary Week'. The regular show features Pearl Primus, Jack Gilford and the Golden Gate Quartet. A number of special guests appear during the week including Billie Holiday.

MONDAY 22 NOVEMBER 1948
Billie is in Milwaukee for a concert with Miles Davis, Fats Navarro, Max Roach, Gene Ammons and Jackie Paris.

MONDAY 29 NOVEMBER 1948
Billie opens a one-week engagement at Ciro's in Philadelphia. Billie is accompanied by BOBBY TUCKER (p), JOHN LEVY (b) and PHIL HAVER (d)
It is during this engagement that Billie first unveils her $10,000 silver blue mink coat.

WED	1
THUR	2
FRI	3
SAT	4
SUN	5
MON	6
TUES	7
WED	8
THUR	9
FRI	10
SAT	11
SUN	12
MON	13
TUES	14
WED	15
THUR	16
FRI	17
SAT	18
SUN	19
MON	20
TUES	21
WED	22
THUR	23
FRI	24
SAT	25
SUN	26
MON	27
TUES	28
WED	29
THUR	30
FRI	31

SUNDAY 5 DECEMBER 1948
Billie closes at Ciro's.

FRIDAY 10 DECEMBER 1948
Recording session (3–7.15pm) for Decca in New York City, produced by Milt Gabler.
BILLIE HOLIDAY (vocal), BOBBY TUCKER (p), JOHN LEVY (b), DENZIL BEST (d), MUNDELL LOWE (g), THE STARDUSTERS (vocal group)
Weep No More / Girls Were Made To Take Care Of Boys / I Loves You Porgy / My Man (2 takes)
The studio call is for 2pm but Billie arrives an hour late, forcing the date into overtime.
Bobby Tucker:

WE GOT THERE VERY LATE. SHE WAS INDISPOSED MOST OF THAT DATE. THOSE WERE ONE-TAKE THINGS; THE ORCHESTRA HAD BEEN THOROUGHLY REHEARSED READY FOR HER.

Billie Set For Two Weeks At Billy Berg's

Philadelphia — Billie Holiday, who closed a week's engagement at Ciro's here recently, was to have two weeks at Billy Berg's in Hollywood around Christmas time, sandwiched between a west coast tour and a European jaunt. The overseas trip reportedly will include appearances in England, France, and Belgium and will start about January 1. The singer will take her trio, pianist Bobby Tucker, bassist John Levy, and new drummer Phil Haver, with her.

Norvo Septet Due To Back Holiday

Hollywood—The Red Norvo combo was set at press time to back Billie Holiday when the latter opened at Billy Berg's, December 15.
With vibist Norvo will be Herbie Stewart, alto; Neal Hefti, trumpet; Herbie Harper, trombone; Blinky Gerner, drums; Iggy Shevak, bass, and Jimmy Rowles, piano.

WEDNESDAY 15 DECEMBER 1948
Billie opens at Billy Berg's in Hollywood with BOBBY TUCKER (p) and the Red Norvo Combo with HERBIE STEWARD (as), NEAL HEFTI (t), HERBIE HARPER (tb), JIMMY ROWLES (p), IGGY SHEVAK (b) and BLINKIE GARNER (d)

At some point during the Billy Berg engagement, the show is recorded (unknown to Bobby Tucker or Jimmy Rowles) and transmitted later in the year on Gene Norman's Just Jazz radio show.
BILLIE HOLIDAY (vocal), RED NORVO (v), NEAL HEFTI (t), HERBIE STEWARD (cl/as), HERBIE HARPER (tb), JIMMY ROWLES or BOBBY TUCKER (p), IGGY SHEVAK (b), BLINKIE GARNER (d)
My Man / Miss Brown To You / Lover Man / I Wonder Where Our Love Has Gone? / Them There Eyes / I Love My Man / You Ain't Gonna Bother Me No More / Good Morning Heartache / You're Driving Me Crazy / Maybe You'll Be There

FRIDAY 31 DECEMBER 1948
On New Year's Eve, Billy Berg's is packed for the last night of Billie's engagement. Billie is jostled after her first set and a fight ensues. John Levy stabs a guest and is arrested. He is later released on bail of $2,500.

Jimmy Rowles remembers:
It was New Year's Eve, about a minute to twelve. I was playing with Red Norvo, Neal Hefti, Herbie Steward – about a six-piece band, playing the alternative set from hers – and the place was packed hand over fist. So where the piano was on the right side of the stage, there's a curtain there closing off the kitchen, and Lady spent a lot of time in there with this peg-legged cat, he's the chef, and Red Norvo's saying, 'Any minute now, Auld Lang Syne.' And John Levy – Al Capone – he was out there countin' the bread because he wants his taste, and he goes in the kitchen, and all of a sudden I hear this terrifyin' noise and this cursing and screaming, and she's throwing plates and tearing the kitchen apart and it's a big rumpus. Shit, that bitch is at it again. Redesign the club tonight. And from behind the curtain comes this ofay cat I've never seen before, and he's got a white shirt on, no tie, and in this hand he's got a basket of biscuits and he's got a twelve-inch butcher's knife buried in his left shoulder just above his heart, and the blood is gushing out and his eyes are glazed and he's coming at me: he's in shock and he's two feet from me and he's gah-gah-gah, and I look at this cat and I say 'Holy Christ!' and I went right under the piano backwards clear across the stage, and the bass player looks up and says 'Jesus!' and the next thing you know we were all over in the corner. And the police came. And we went on the next night, and we finished the engagement. But I never thought I'd see anything like that.

SAT	**1**
SUN	**2**
MON	**3**
TUES	**4**
WED	**5**
THUR	**6**
FRI	**7**
SAT	**8**
SUN	**9**
MON	**10**
TUES	**11**
WED	**12**
THUR	**13**
FRI	**14**
SAT	**15**
SUN	**16**
MON	**17**
TUES	**18**
WED	**19**
THUR	**20**
FRI	**21**
SAT	**22**
SUN	**23**
MON	**24**
TUES	**25**
WED	**26**
THUR	**27**
FRI	**28**
SAT	**29**
SUN	**30**
MON	**31**

SUNDAY 2 JANUARY 1949

Billie plays a concert in Seattle, Washington. 15-yr-old Quincy Jones is playing trumpet in the band.

MONDAY 3 JANUARY 1949

Billie surrenders to the police when a warrant for her arrest is issued. She is charged on three counts of assault with a deadly weapon and freed on bail of $2,500. The preliminary hearing is set for 13 January 1949.

TUESDAY 4 JANUARY 1949

Billie opens at the Palomar Supper Club in Vancouver for a one-week engagement.

SATURDAY 8 JANUARY 1949

Billie is interviewed for the radio programme, 'The Curfew Club' on Radio KQW, Los Angeles. The long interview is interspersed with recordings from Billie's JATP concert at Carnegie Hall on 3 June 1946.

SUNDAY 9 JANUARY 1949

Billie closes at the Palomar Supper Club in Vancouver.

THURSDAY 13 JANUARY 1949

The charges against Billie relating to the affray at Billy Berg's are dropped, but continued against Levy who is released on $2,500 bond.

Billie opens at Joe Tenner's Café Society Uptown on Fillimore Street in San Francisco for a four-week engagement. Crowds flock to see Billie following the publicity of the fracas at Berg's.

Billie, Berg's Sued In Melee

Hollywood — A $15,000 damage suit has been filed against singer Billie Holiday and Billy Berg, the result of an alleged New Year's morning brawl in Berg's Vine street club.

The complaint, brought by Marie Epstein, charged that Miss Holiday "threw a dish that struck her (Miss Epstein) on the foot, cutting her severely."

Following the affray, Miss Holiday and her manager, John Levy, faced three counts of assault with a deadly weapon, but charges were dropped later against Miss Holiday.

Charges were continued against Levy, released on $2,500 bond, who allegedly drove a knife into the shoulder of one of the participants in the melee that took place in the kitchen of the club.

Shortly thereafter, Miss Holiday left town for an engagement in San Francisco.

SATURDAY 22 JANUARY 1949

Narcotics agents raid Billie's hotel on Taylor Street. A quantity of opium is found and Billie and John Levy are both charged but later released on $500 bail each. The Federal Narcotics Agency superintendent Colonel George H. White remembered the arrest:

One Saturday morning, at any rate, I got together a couple of police officers – in those days search warrants were required in federal court but not in state court, so if we found anything it would have gone to state court because we didn't have warrants – and I found out somewhere that they were staying at the Mark Twain in the Tenderloin district, and went down there and asked the desk clerk what room they were in, and went up and knocked on the door ... 'Just a minute, just a minute' ... finally we kicked it open. It doesn't matter who makes the arrest; I made it, and we took them into state court.

Apparently Levy had gathered up the paraphernalia and a small quantity of opium and told her to get rid of it. She was up against the door in the other room – I think she slammed the door and I opened it – and she ran into the bathroom of the other room to try to flush the stuff down the toilet, though the smoking paraphernalia was such that I don't think it would have readily flushed; there was an improvised pipe with a little glass bottle, and a little lamp of some kind, and a little bit of opium ... We both reached the bathroom at the same time, and she tried to throw the stuff into the open toilet and sort of fell into the bathtub, without hurting herself.

Café Society is packed for the evening show, and for the rest of the engagement.

Billie, Levy Arrested On Opium Count

San Francisco—Curiosity seekers jam-packed Cafe Society Uptown here to see Billie Holiday following her arrest January 22 on charges of possession of "a small quantity of opium and an opium pipe."

John Levy, Billie's manager, was arrested with the singer. Both were released on $500 bail with a preliminary hearing set for January 24.

Enter Singer's Room

Members of the San Francisco police special services detail and Col. George White, district supervisor of the federal narcotics bureau here, entered the singer's room at the Mark Twain hotel here early in the afternoon and claim to have found the drug and the pipe.

Both Billie and her manager deny any knowledge of either the pipe or the opium. Col. White did not make the arrest but allowed local authorities to make the charge.

A postponement of the hearing was made to February 2.

Billie didn't miss a show on account of the affair. Crowds, quite sympathetic, greeted her the night following her arrest.

Return, Arrested

Levy had been in Los Angeles and had returned to San Francisco at noon the day of the arrest. Billie met him at the station, and the pair was arrested shortly after returning to the hotel. Both Billie and Levy claim the singer was not at the hotel the previous evening at all and that the room had been loaned to a friend known only as "Mandy."

Billie's engagement at the night spot ended February 9.

TUES	**1**	TUES	**1**
WED	**2**	WED	**2**
THUR	**3**	THUR	**3**
FRI	**4**	FRI	**4**
SAT	**5**	SAT	**5**
SUN	**6**	SUN	**6**
MON	**7**	MON	**7**
TUES	**8**	TUES	**8**
WED	**9**	WED	**9**
THUR	**10**	THUR	**10**
FRI	**11**	FRI	**11**
SAT	**12**	SAT	**12**
SUN	**13**	SUN	**13**
MON	**14**	MON	**14**
TUES	**15**	TUES	**15**
WED	**16**	WED	**16**
THUR	**17**	THUR	**17**
FRI	**18**	FRI	**18**
SAT	**19**	SAT	**19**
SUN	**20**	SUN	**20**
MON	**21**	MON	**21**
TUES	**22**	TUES	**22**
WED	**23**	WED	**23**
THUR	**24**	THUR	**24**
FRI	**25**	FRI	**25**
SAT	**26**	SAT	**26**
SUN	**27**	SUN	**27**
MON	**28**	MON	**28**
		TUES	**29**
		WED	**30**
		THUR	**31**

WEDNESDAY 2 FEBRUARY 1949
Billie and Levy appear at a preliminary hearing with their lawyer, Jake Ehrlich (*above*).

FRIDAY 11 FEBRUARY 1949
Billie is indicted by a grand jury; the case against Levy is dropped and he leaves California immediately to avoid being subpoena'ed as a witness. Billie pleads not guilty and her lawyer, Jake Ehrlich, tells her that the only way to beat the rap is to take the test. In order to give her time for detoxification he gets the case deferred, pointing out that Billie would suffer serious financial loss if she could not fulfil her contracted engagements. The trial is set for 14th March. Billie's doctor, Dr Herbert B. Henderson is convinced Billie is not addicted to hard drugs and sets out to prove her innocence. He arranges for her to be admitted to Belmont Sanatorium and drives her there himself. On the way they stop at Mountain View where Billie buys herself a tiny chihuahua dog. Billie stays at Belmont for two weeks where it is established that there is no trace of opium in her body.

TUESDAY 22 FEBRUARY 1949
Billie closes at Café Society Uptown.

Billie decides to go ahead with her scheduled tour of Northern California accompanied by Red Norvo's combo which includes young bassist, Charlie Mingus. They play one-nighters at the Civic Auditorium, Portland and in Oakland but the tour flops and after a bad night in Bakersfield, Billie quits.

FRIDAY 11 MARCH 1949
Billie appears at the Shrine Auditorium in Los Angeles with Duke Ellington

SUNDAY 13 MARCH 1949
Billie does a one-nighter at the Pershing Ballroom in Chicago with Claude McLin and his Orchestra.

MONDAY 14 MARCH 1949
Billie's trial is adjourned until 15th April.

FRIDAY 18 MARCH 1949
Billie opens at Club Bali in Washington for a three-week engagement.

The Royal Roost makes Billie a substantial offer (rumoured at $3000 a week) providing she can get Police Department clearance. Billie makes a formal appeal against the cabaret card ruling but is turned down.

THURSDAY 31 MARCH 1949
San Francisco Chronicle reports:

Billie Holiday Denied N.Y. Permit

NEW YORK, March 31–(AP)–Billie Holiday, Negro blues singer, today was denied a Supreme Court order to compel police to give her a cabaret employees identification card. Without such a card she is unable to appear as a night club entertainer.

Supreme Court Justice Aaron J. Levy rejected her petition. Assistant corporation counsel Leonard E. Katlin said that Miss Holiday had three convictions against her. And that she was free now in $500 bail pending trial of a narcotics charge in San Francisco.

FRI **1**

SAT **2**

SUN **3**

MON **4**

TUES **5**

WED **6**

THUR **7**

FRI **8**

SAT **9**

SUN **10**

MON **11**

TUES **12**

WED **13**

THUR **14**

FRI **15**

SAT **16**

SUN **17**

MON **18**

TUES **19**

WED **20**

THUR **21**

FRI **22**

SAT **23**

SUN **24**

MON **25**

TUES **26**

WED **27**

THUR **28**

FRI **29**

SAT **30**

FRI	1
SAT	2
SUN	3
MON	4
TUES	5
WED	6
THUR	7
FRI	8
SAT	9
SUN	10
MON	11
TUES	12
WED	13
THUR	14
FRI	15
SAT	16
SUN	17
MON	18
TUES	19
WED	20
THUR	21
FRI	22
SAT	23
SUN	24
MON	25
TUES	26
WED	27
THUR	28
FRI	29
SAT	30

THURSDAY 7 APRIL 1949

Billie's 34th birthday.

Billie closes at Club Bali after three record-breaking weeks.

The *Baltimore Afro-American* later reports:

A Day in the Life of Lady Day; 'Twas Her Birthday

by ALICE A DUNNIGAN

WASHINGTON—The zing zest and zip which the zealous Billie Holiday demonstrated last Thursday night as she zoomed to the zenith of her three record-breaking weeks at Club Bali here astounded her well-wishers and confounded her severest critics.

The final curtain of this performance was rung down with a birthday celebration in honor of "the-charm-of-the-day" called Billie Holiday with scores of radio, stage and concert artists participating in the grand finale, before she left for Baltimore to open at Club Astoria.

Taken by Surprise

With a look of surprise in her eyes and joy in her voice as she noted fellow-entertainers, press representatives assembled around a special table to do her honor on her 30th [sic] birthday, the singing star remarked "and I just expected to celebrate my birthday by seeing Washington."

The siren song-bird had spent a portion of the day on what she had hoped would be a quiet sight-seeing tour but as she stood in Lincoln's Memorial before the great statue of Honest Abe, flash bulbs began to go off, and the blithesome Billie found herself the target of flash-guns from photographers of *Holiday* magazine.

Admired Reflection Pool

One of the things she enjoyed most on her sight-seeing tour, she said was the reflection pool which bears the reflection of both the Lincoln Memorial and the Washington Monument. She went through the capitol but was too late for the White House and the monument and visited both Freedmen's and the Walter Reed Hospitals, where she entertained patients.

FRIDAY 8 APRIL 1949

Billie opens at Club Astoria in Baltimore probably for the weekend only.

THURSDAY 14 APRIL 1949

Billie attends the opening night of Bop City, a new nightclub, on Broadway. Artie Shaw and Ella Fitzgerald are the opening attractions.

FRIDAY 15 APRIL 1949

Billie's trial is adjourned until 12 May. She is scheduled to open at the Music Bowl in Chicago, but it has folded.

FRIDAY 22 APRIL 1949

Billie opens at the Paradise Theatre in Detroit for a one-week engagement.

THURSDAY 28 APRIL 1949

Billie closes at the Paradise Theatre in Detroit.

FRIDAY 29 APRIL 1949

Billie opens at the Continental Club in Milwaukee for a weekend engagement.

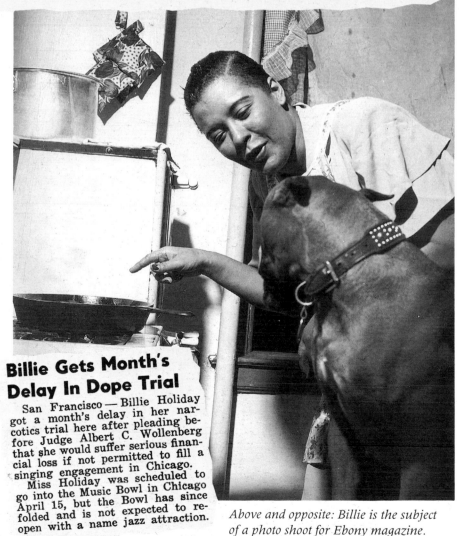

Billie Gets Month's Delay In Dope Trial

San Francisco — Billie Holiday got a month's delay in her narcotics trial here after pleading before Judge Albert C. Wollenberg that she would suffer serious financial loss if not permitted to fill a singing engagement in Chicago.

Miss Holiday was scheduled to go into the Music Bowl in Chicago April 15, but the Bowl has since folded and is not expected to re-open with a name jazz attraction.

Above and opposite: Billie is the subject of a photo shoot for Ebony magazine.

MAY 1949

SUN	1
MON	2
TUES	3
WED	4
THUR	5
FRI	6
SAT	7
SUN	8
MON	9
TUES	10
WED	11
THUR	12
FRI	13
SAT	14
SUN	15
MON	16
TUES	17
WED	18
THUR	19
FRI	20
SAT	21
SUN	22
MON	23
TUES	24
WED	25
THUR	26
FRI	27
SAT	28
SUN	29
MON	30
TUES	31

SUNDAY 1 MAY 1949
Billie closes at the Continental Club in Milwaukee.

Bobby Tucker quits as Billie's accompanist:

I came in from Milwaukee, and I told them I was not going to make it any more. I was building my house, on the road, things were going wrong with the contract, so I told them I gotta look out for my house, and he says okay. He's in New York; he told her to go to Chicago, he'd meet her there. Our last night in Milwaukee, she said, 'Don't get lost. We've got a dinner date tomorrow night.' I said, 'Not me. I got a reservation on that 2 o'clock plane.' She says, 'You're gonna leave me here?' I said, 'No, just go make your reservation.' She said, 'I can't go, 'cause my daddy told me to meet him in Chicago.' I said, 'I gotta take the bread to him.' I was handling the money if he wasn't there. We were on a percentage plus a guarantee, and I gotta bring him the bread. And he'd hold the bread for a week before he'd pay me, all that nasty kind of stuff.

I couldn't take it any more. I really liked her and I couldn't stand the way he was treating her. If she asked him for fifty dollars, he'd knock her down. He said, 'Don't ask me for money in public.' He'd knock her down literally – with his fist in her face, in her stomach, anywhere.

He'd once told me piano players are a dime a dozen. Well, he went to Chicago; she said, 'Where's Bobby?' He says, 'He's not going to make it.' And she hit the ceiling; she screamed bloody murder. He called me up and he said, 'I guess we were a little hasty, and she doesn't want you to leave.' I said, 'Look, I explained it to you ...' and he went into his gangster bag. He said, 'I'm sending the bread to you, a plane – I'll have some guys – you'll never play the piano again!' I wrote her a letter and she wrote me back that she understood.

I got a letter from Joe Glaser telling me she wanted me to come back. She knew how I felt about John. Glaser guaranteed that John wasn't in the picture any more; but every night I heard that I'd had a long distance call from Washington, and it turns out to be John Levy. He finally got on to me and he said, 'Hey buddy, believe me she's straight, and I told her if she stayed straight I'd get you back.' In his mind, the reason I left was because she's a junkie. I said, 'John, I can't leave; I'm working for Billy Eckstine now.' He says, 'I don't care how much you're making; we'll double it.' He told me piano players are a dime a dozen, and he doesn't even know what my salary is, and I'm a musical director now. I just said 'Later' and hung up.

WEDNESDAY 11 MAY 1949
Billie opens at the Tivoli Theater in San Francisco for a one-week engagement.

THURSDAY 12 MAY 1949
Billie's trial is adjourned until 19 May.

TUESDAY 17 MAY 1949
Billie closes at the Tivoli Theater in San Francisco. Pele Edises reports in the *San Francisco Chronicle*:

Billie Holliday's back in town, winding up her week as star of the Tivoli's pocket-size stage show. It added up to fine and mellow entertainment, with the emphasis on quality rather than quantity.

Large and luscious in a dazzling white beaded gown, Lady Day delivered half a dozen popular songs and one fine slow blues in the casual, drowsy style that has made her an Esquire Jazz Award winner year after year.

THURSDAY 19 MAY 1949
Billie's trial is adjourned until 31 May.

MONDAY 23 MAY 1949
S F Chronicle columnist Herb Caen observes:

Blues dept: Billie Holiday, the torchanteuse, is singing these nights with more than lumps in her throat; she has lumps elsewhere, too, after being beaten pretty brutally one night last week. She knows some lovely people ...

TUESDAY 31 MAY 1949
Billie attends her opium possession trial in San Francisco. She arrives sporting a black eye. The first day is given over to selection of the jury. The trial lasts three days.

WED	1
THUR	2
FRI	3
SAT	4
SUN	5
MON	6
TUES	7
WED	8
THUR	9
FRI	10
SAT	11
SUN	12
MON	13
TUES	14
WED	15
THUR	16
FRI	17
SAT	18
SUN	19
MON	20
TUES	21
WED	22
THUR	23
FRI	24
SAT	25
SUN	26
MON	27
TUES	28
WED	29
THUR	30

THURSDAY 2 JUNE 1949

The second day of the trial and Billie undergoes the test.

FRIDAY 3 JUNE 1949

The third day of the trial. Billie is found 'Not Guilty' and acquitted.

WEDNESDAY 8 JUNE 1949

Joe Glaser writes to Bobby Tucker on Billie's behalf. He claims that John Levy is no longer involved and requests that Bobby rejoins Billie. Bobby is not impressed, happy as musical director for Billy Eckstine.

WEDNESDAY 15 JUNE 1949

Billie opens as headliner of the show at Fox's Million Dollar Theatre in Los Angeles.

WEDNESDAY 22 JUNE 1949

Billie closes at the Million Dollar Theatre in Los Angeles.

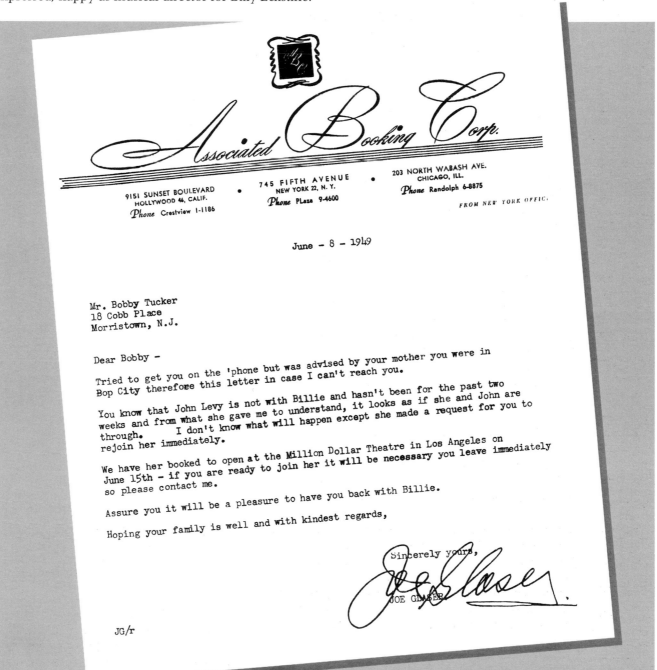

FRI	1
SAT	2
SUN	3
MON	4
TUES	5
WED	6
THUR	7
FRI	8
SAT	9
SUN	10
MON	11
TUES	12
WED	13
THUR	14
FRI	15
SAT	16
SUN	17
MON	18
TUES	19
WED	20
THUR	21
FRI	22
SAT	23
SUN	24
MON	25
TUES	26
WED	27
THUR	28
FRI	29
SAT	30
SUN	31

FRIDAY 1 JULY 1949

Down Beat reviews Billie's latest release:

BILLIE HOLIDAY
** *Porgy*
** *My Man*

Porgy is a lovely tune, too seldom done, from the Gershwin *Porgy and Bess* score. Billie completely misses the grace and meaning of the song in her over-exaggerated phrasing and too lush pauses (only Holiday can make a pause lush). There is a limit to the distortion to which you can subject a good song for purposes of your own interpretation and this is it. It might as well be faced: what was a great singing style has lapsed into over-ornate sloppiness. (*Decca 24638*)

FRIDAY 29 JULY 1949

Billie plays a Mid-Nite Concert at the Corpus Christi Auditorium, Chicago.

Broke, Alone, Billie Goes Back To Work

San Francisco—Broke and alone after her manager, John Levy, left her to face the trial here at which she was acquitted, Billie Holiday decided to go back to work. Other than that, her plans were indefinite. But despite the fact the jury said they believed Billie had been framed by Levy, she said:

"If he was to walk in the room this minute I'd melt. He's my man and I love him."

The three-day trial seemed to prove to the jury that a package of opium had been planted on Billie just before narcotics men raided her apartment.

My Aching Back

Billie came to the trial with a black eye she said Levy gave her the night he left. "You should see my back," she added. "And he even took my silver blue mink coat —18 grand worth of coat. He said he was going to give it to his sister to take care of for me. I got nothing now and I'm scared."

Billie's version of what happened went like this: "I turned all my life over to John. He took all my money. I never had any money. We were supposed to get married. On January 22, John came back from Los Angeles. We had been arguing about money."

While Levy was unpacking his suitcase the telephone rang. Im-

Billie Cabaret Card Appeal Turned Down

New York—Billie Holiday may have made her last New York night club appearance. Her attempt to get a court order which would force the police department to give her a cabaret employe identification card was turned down this month.

Billie had to cancel out of the Royal Roost last month when she was refused a cabaret license.

Justice Aaron J. Levy, in turning down her appeal, said the police department "deserves commendation" for refusing to give her a card.

MON **1**
TUES **2**
WED **3**
THUR **4**
FRI **5**
SAT **6**
SUN **7**
MON **8**
TUES **9**
WED **10**
THUR **11**
FRI **12**
SAT **13**
SUN **14**
MON **15**
TUES **16**
WED **17**
THUR **18**
FRI **19**
SAT **20**
SUN **21**
MON **22**
TUES **23**
WED **24**
THUR **25**
FRI **26**
SAT **27**
SUN **28**
MON **29**
TUES **30**
WED **31**

THURSDAY 4 AUGUST 1949

Billie is scheduled to open at Bop City in New York with Count Basie and his Orchestra, but the cabaret card card situation is not resolved and she is unable to appear.

Horace Henderson becomes her pianist.

WEDNESDAY 17 AUGUST 1949

Record session (2–5.30pm) accompanied by Buster Harding and his Orchestra for Decca in New York City. Milt Gabler is the producer.

BILLIE HOLIDAY (vocal), BUSTER HARDING (conductor), EMMETT BERRY, JIMMY NOTTINGHAM, BUCK CLAYTON (t), DICKIE WELLS, GEORGE MATTHEWS (tb), RUDY POWELL, GEORGE DORSEY (as), LESTER YOUNG, JOE THOMAS (ts), SOL MOORE (bs), HORACE HENDERSON (p), MUNDELL LOWE (g), GEORGE DUVIVIER (b), SHADOW WILSON (d)

Tain't Nobody's Business If I Do (2 takes) / *Baby Get Lost*

FRIDAY 19 AUGUST 1949

Billie opens at the Apollo Theatre for a one-week engagement. Also on the bill are Machito and his Orchestra, The Three Berry Brothers, The Angel and Pigmeat Markham.

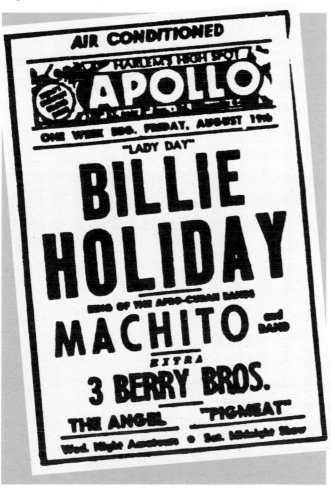

WEDNESDAY 24 AUGUST 1949

The Amateur Hour at the Apollo is broadcast via station WMCA.

THURSDAY 25 AUGUST 1949

Billie closes at the Apollo.

SATURDAY 27 AUGUST 1949

Billie is featured in the NBC TV broadcast *The Eddie Condon Floor Show* from 9.30 to 10 pm.

Eddie Condon Band – BOBBY HACKETT (c), PEE WEE RUSSELL (cl), CUTTY CUTSHALL (tb), JOE BUSHKIN (p), EDDIE CONDON (bj), JACK LESBERG (b), GEORGE WETTLING (d) plus guest SIDNEY BECHET (ss):

One Hour Tonight / MEDLEY: *Mandy Make Up Your Mind* (Pee Wee Russell), *I Love A Piano* (Joe Bushkin), *Soft Lights And Sweet Music* (Bobby Hackett), *I Know That You Know* (Sidney Bechet), *I Want A Little Girl* (Cutty Cutshall), *The Man I Love* (Jack Lesberg) / *I Got Rhythm*

BILLIE HOLIDAY (vocal), ORAN 'HOT LIPS' PAGE (t), HORACE HENDERSON (p), JACK LESBERG (b), GEORGE WETTLING (d)

Reminiscin' with Billie / *Keeps On A'Rainin'* / *Lover Man*

Part Two features the Condon Band plus guests LOUIS ARMSTRONG (t/vocal), JACK TEAGARDEN (tb) and EARL HINES (p):

We Called It Music / *Chinatown, My Chinatown* / *Someday* / *Three Little Bears* / *Anniversary Blues* (featuring Hot Lips Page (t/vocal)

Billie is often cited as appearing on the Art Ford TV Show on this date, but during her interview with Art Ford she mentions that she has just recorded two Bessie Smith songs (see 8 September entry), which makes Saturday 10 September a more likely date.

MONDAY 29 AUGUST 1949

Recording session accompanied by Sy Oliver and his Orchestra for Decca in New York City. The session is produced by Milt Gabler.

BILLIE HOLIDAY (vocal), SY OLIVER (conductor), BERNIE PRIVIN, DICK VANCE, TONY FASO (t), HENDERSON CHAMBERS, MORTY BULLMAN (t), EDDIE BAREFIELD (cl/bs), JOHNNY MINCE, GEORGE DORSEY (as), BUDD JOHNSON, FREDDIE WILLIAMS (ts), HORACE HENDERSON (p), EVERETT BARKSDALE (g), GEORGE DUVIVIER (b), COZY COLE (d)

Keeps On A Rainin' / *Them There Eyes*

THUR	**1**
FRI	**2**
SAT	**3**
SUN	**4**
MON	**5**
TUES	**6**
WED	**7**
THUR	**8**
FRI	**9**
SAT	**10**
SUN	**11**
MON	**12**
TUES	**13**
WED	**14**
THUR	**15**
FRI	**16**
SAT	**17**
SUN	**18**
MON	**19**
TUES	**20**
WED	**21**
THUR	**22**
FRI	**23**
SAT	**24**
SUN	**25**
MON	**26**
TUES	**27**
WED	**28**
THUR	**29**
FRI	**30**

SATURDAY 3 SEPTEMBER 1949

Billie is again featured as a guest on the NBC TV broadcast *The Eddie Condon Floor Show* from 9.30 to 10 pm.

Eddie Condon Band – WILD BILL DAVISON (t), PEANUTS HUCKO (cl), ERNIE CACERES (bs), CUTTY CUTSHALL (tb), JOE BUSHKIN (p), EDDIE CONDON (g), JACK LESBERG (b), GEORGE WETTLING (d)
Walking My Baby Back Home
BILLIE HOLIDAY joins the band, with HORACE HENDERSON on piano, to sing three numbers:
Fine And Mellow / I Loves You Porgy / Them There Eyes
Eddie Condon Band:
Running Wild
The Eddie Condon Band is joined by guests LOUIS ARMSTRONG (t/vocal), JACK TEAGARDEN (tb) and EARL HINES (p):
These Foolish Things / Swing That Music / Heebie Jeebies / Aunt Hagar's Blues / Farewell To Storyville / Rockin' Chair
Eddie Condon Band plus BILLIE HOLIDAY:
I Love My Man
Eddie Condon Band:
Ole Miss

THURSDAY 8 SEPTEMBER 1949

Recording session (6–9.30pm) accompanied by Sy Oliver and his Orchestra for Decca in New York City. The session is produced by Milt Gabler.
BILLIE HOLIDAY (vocal), SY OLIVER (conductor), BUCK CLAYTON, SHAD COLLINS, BOB WILLIAMS (t), HENDERSON CHAMBERS, GEORGE STEVENSON (tb), PETER CLARK, GEORGE DORSEY (as), BUDD JOHNSON, FREDDIE WILLIAMS (ts), DAVE McRAE (bs), HORACE HENDERSON (p), EVERETT BARKSDALE (g), JOE BENJAMIN (b), WALLACE BISHOP (d)
Do Your Duty / Gimme A Pigfoot And A Bottle Of Beer
These two tracks plus *Keeps On Rainin'* from the 29 August session appear to be the only recordings of Bessie Smith tunes from the planned album.

SATURDAY 10 SEPTEMBER 1949

Billie appears on the Art Ford TV Show in New York City. Billie is interviewed by Art Ford, during which she mentions she has just recorded 2 tunes for an album of 8 Bessie Smith songs, and sings 4 numbers with HOT LIPS PAGE (t), HORACE HENDERSON (p) and a rhythm section.
Them There Eyes / Detour Ahead / I Cover The Waterfront / All Of Me

Right: Billie and Louis Armstrong at the recording session for 'You Can't Lose A Broken Heart' and 'My Sweet Hunk O' Trash' on 30 September. Louis' use of an expletive during 'My Sweet Hunk O Trash' causes the record to be withdrawn and the offending word over-dubbed.

FRIDAY 16 SEPTEMBER 1949

Billie flies into Baltimore as a last-minute replacement for headliner Charles Brown at the Royal Theater. Also starring is Dizzy Gillespie and his Orchestra with Joe Carroll and Tiny Irvin. A local Baltimore newspaper reports:

Billie Holiday, the famed torch singer, is making an unscheduled (torchy) appearance this week here at the Royal Theater.

Miss Holiday, who just closed an engagement at Harlem's Apollo Theater, has top billing as added attraction with the Dizzy Gillespie Band, following a run-out by Charles ("Trouble Blues") Brown which left the Friday opening without a feature attraction.

Miss Holiday, contacted in New York (after Brown had allegedly feigned illness, packed up and left before curtain time), flew down with her manager John Levy arriving in time for the third show on Friday, and has been playing to capacity audiences since.

The rest of the stage attractions, in addition to Gillespie, include Joe Carroll and Tiny Irvin, vocalists, Lewis and White, comedy team, and the veteran dancer, Derby Wilson.

The Royal management turned in a piece of fast work in the replacement. Before Miss Holiday arrived here, all advertisements featuring Brown had to be blacked-out by her name with local radio stations making periodic announcements. Miss Holiday, herself, was featured in a special broadcast from Club Casino at 5 o'clock.

THURSDAY 22 SEPTEMBER 1949

Billie closes at the Royal Theatre, Baltimore.

FRIDAY 30 SEPTEMBER 1949

Recording session (2–5.30pm) with Louis Armstrong accompanied by Sy Oliver and his Orchestra for Decca in New York City. The session is produced by Milt Gabler.
BILLIE HOLIDAY, LOUIS ARMSTRONG (vocal), SY OLIVER (cond), BERNIE PRIVIN (t), JOHNNY MINCE, SID COOPER (as), ARTIE DRELINGER, PAT NIZZA (ts), BILLY KYLE (p), EVERETT BARKSDALE (g), JOE BENJAMIN (b), JIMMY CRAWFORD (d)
You Can't Lose A Broken Heart / My Sweet Hunk O' Trash
BILLIE HOLIDAY (vocal): *Now Or Never*

SAT	**1**
SUN	**2**
MON	**3**
TUES	**4**
WED	**5**
THUR	**6**
FRI	**7**
SAT	**8**
SUN	**9**
MON	**10**
TUES	**11**
WED	**12**
THUR	**13**
FRI	**14**
SAT	**15**
SUN	**16**
MON	**17**
TUES	**18**
WED	**19**
THUR	**20**
FRI	**21**
SAT	**22**
SUN	**23**
MON	**24**
TUES	**25**
WED	**26**
THUR	**27**
FRI	**28**
SAT	**29**
SUN	**30**
MON	**31**

Billie scheduled to appear at Bop City in NYC, but is unable to do so without her cabaret card.

In the first week of October, Billie attends the private viewing of an exhibition of paintings by Karl Priebe at the Perls Gallery, 32 E58th Street, New York City. Karl Priebe, a friend of Carl Van Vechten, specialised in African subjects.

During early October, Billie is reported doing a one-nighter in the Boston area with Horace Henderson, and then a week in Washington.

WEDNESDAY 19 OCTOBER 1949

Recording session (2–4.45pm) accompanied by Gordon Jenkins and his Orchestra for Decca in New York City. The session is produced by Milt Gabler. BILLIE HOLIDAY (vocal), GORDON JENKINS (cond), BOBBY HACKETT (c), MILT YANER (cl/as), JOHN FULTON (fl/cl/ts), BERNIE LEIGHTON (p), TONY MOTTOLA (g), JACK LESBERG (b), BUNNY SHAWKER (d), plus five strings
You're My Thrill / Crazy He Calls Me / Please Tell Me Now / Somebody's On My Mind

The *New York Amsterdam News* reports that Billie flew into La Guardia from Washington on the morning of the session, and rushed direct to the Decca studios.

FRIDAY 21 OCTOBER 1949

Down Beat reviews Billie's latest release:

> **BILLIE HOLIDAY**
> ** *Baby, Get Lost*
> ** *Ain't Nobody's Business If I Do*
> *Lost* is blues sung by Billie with a big band, both of which lack finesse. *Business* will of course be interpreted by everyone in light of recent events in Billie's private life. It is, however, bad singing for Holiday. (*Decca 24638*)

The cabaret card problem also prevents Billie opening at Café Society in New York as planned, so Billie hits the road. By the end of October she is in Detroit at the Flame Show Bar, backed by the Snooky Young Band

While at the Flame Show Bar, Billie meets up with Chuck Peterson, a trumpet player in the pit band at the Fox Theatre. Peterson had worked with Billie in the Artie Shaw Band and they arrange to meet for a drink at the Old Colony Bar. When they arrive with two white girls, they are refused service. In the ensuing fracas, Peterson is badly beaten up. The incident makes the front page of the *New York Amsterdam News*.

Slug Billie Holiday's Escort In Bar

Horace Henderson is disturbed by the incident and quits as Billie's accompanist at the end of the engagement. He is replaced by Carl Mark.

TUES	**1**	THUR	**1**
WED	**2**	FRI	**2**
THUR	**3**	SAT	**3**
FRI	**4**	SUN	**4**
SAT	**5**	MON	**5**
SUN	**6**	TUES	**6**
MON	**7**	WED	**7**
TUES	**8**	THUR	**8**
WED	**9**	FRI	**9**
THUR	**10**	SAT	**10**
FRI	**11**	SUN	**11**
SAT	**12**	MON	**12**
SUN	**13**	TUES	**13**
MON	**14**	WED	**14**
TUES	**15**	THUR	**15**
WED	**16**	FRI	**16**
THUR	**17**	SAT	**17**
FRI	**18**	SUN	**18**
SAT	**19**	MON	**19**
SUN	**20**	TUES	**20**
MON	**21**	WED	**21**
TUES	**22**	THUR	**22**
WED	**23**	FRI	**23**
THUR	**24**	SAT	**24**
FRI	**25**	SUN	**25**
SAT	**26**	MON	**26**
SUN	**27**	TUES	**27**
MON	**28**	WED	**28**
TUES	**29**	THUR	**29**
WED	**30**	FRI	**30**
		SAT	**31**

FRIDAY 18 NOVEMBER 1949

Down Beat reviews Billie's latest release:

BILLIE HOLIDAY
*** *It's A Sin To Tell A Lie*
** *Wherever You Are*
These are two unreleased sides from the last session Billie made for Columbia on Feb. 10, 1942. Solos are by Emmett Berry, trumpet, and Babe Russin, tenor, in a little band led by Teddy Wilson. Billie herself sounds much better than she has on some of her over-phrased dragged-out recent disks. (*Harmony 1075*)

Plan Tour For Billie

Chicago—Plans for a touring concert troupe involving blues shouter Joe Turner, singer Billie Holiday, and pianist-singer Ivory Joe Hunter, were being made at presstime by Joe Glaser's Associated Booking corporation. Office was waiting for Billie's okay before setting dates and getting together a band to be led by Hunter.

MONDAY 12 DECEMBER 1949

Billie opens at the Blue Note in Chicago for a one month engagement accompanied by Herbie Fields' Band.

Frank Holzfeind, the Blue Note owner, says:

> BILLIE HOLIDAY CAME TO THE BLUE NOTE THOROUGHLY PLASTERED WITH EVERY STIGMA AND ACCUSATION IN THE BOOKS, SO MUCH SO, THAT I DOUBTED MY REASON FOR SIGNING HER IN THE FIRST PLACE. THAT FIRST NIGHT I JUST KNEW SHE WOULDN'T SHOW UP.

But Billie does show up and after two weeks has broken all previous attendance records at the club.

The Blue Note engagement is reviewed in the 13 January issue of *Down Beat*:

HOLIDAY, FIELDS
Blue Note, Chicago

Chicago – The loop Blue Note, with Herbie Fields and Billie Holiday set for four weeks, until Charlie Shavers' combo opens Jan. 2, has found itself a good holiday show. Not the greatest, for neither Billie nor Herbie do quite all they are capable of doing musically, but it's a well-balanced and entertaining program.

Billie, for whom the Blue Note date is reportedly a rather crucial engagement, is singing well, and, unlike her more recent Chicago appearances, apparently interested in the songs she's using and their effect on her listeners. The effect is gratifyingly intent, with the house at hushed attention throughout Billie's sets.

Sleek, Comfortable

Looking sleek, relaxed, and comfortable, Billie sang the same way, on such new numbers as Where Are You?, Ain't Nobody's Business If I Do, and her own Now, Baby, Or Never, in addition to such standards as Porgy, Man I Love, and Strange Fruit. Despite it being nobody's business, numbers on the order of the first three are almost embarrassingly pertinent in their associations, which might be one reason for Billie's singing them with such intensity. Her accompanist, Carl Mark, aids with a more than competent and selfless job.

Fields' band, with Doug Mettome, trumpet; Frank Rosolino, trombone; Joe Gatto, piano; Tiny Kahn, drums; Rudy Cafaro, guitar, and Max Bennett, bass, sounded a great deal better than it did at their last local date.

SUN	1
MON	2
TUES	3
WED	4
THUR	5
FRI	6
SAT	7
SUN	8
MON	9
TUES	10
WED	11
THUR	12
FRI	13
SAT	14
SUN	15
MON	16
TUES	17
WED	18
THUR	19
FRI	20
SAT	21
SUN	22
MON	23
TUES	24
WED	25
THUR	26
FRI	27
SAT	28
SUN	29
MON	30
TUES	31

SUNDAY 8 JANUARY 1950
Billie closes at the Blue Note in Chicago

FRIDAY 13 JANUARY 1950
Billie opens at the Regal Theatre in Chicago for a one-week engagement opposite the Jay Burkhart Band. The 18-piece Burkhart Band (including Miles Davis, Leo Parker and Wardell Gray) substitute for Charlie Ventura who cancels because of illness.

THURSDAY 19 JANUARY 1950
Billie closes at the Regal Theatre in Chicago

FRIDAY 20 JANUARY 1950
Billie opens at Club Riviera in St Louis for a one-week engagement with the Earl Bostic Band.

THURSDAY 26 JANUARY 1950
Billie closes at Club Riviera in St Louis.

Billie, CV On Tour

Chicago — First date of a tour for Billie Holiday and Charlie Ventura's band, as a package, will be a week at the Regal theater here starting Jan. 13. The Ventura unit will be augmented for the Regal date, but will go back to its regular size when the package moves into the Riviera in St. Louis for eight days, starting Jan. 21. Midwest one-niters, through Associated Booking corporation, will follow.

ST. LOUIS—After completing a capacity week here at the Club Riviera, "Showpiece of the 'Show-Me'" metropolis on the banks of the "Ole Man" Mississippi river, Billie Holiday, America's Number One song stylist, left for California.

Just before her departure via TWA plane for San Francisco, "Lady Day" expressed delight in returning to St. Louis again, her first engagement in four years, meeting and greeting old friends and new, who still rave over her musical styling of "Lover Man" etc.

During her engagement at Club Riviera, Miss Holiday was happily surprised to note in her audience the presence of her good friend and pal, Tallulah Bankhead, noted stage star, currently appearing here in "Private Lives" at the American Theater, and Maurice Rocco, also currently at the Chase Hotel. She was fondly reminiscent of her appearance here, singing with Artie Shaw and his orchestra, not so long ago.

While on the West Coast, Miss Holiday will make appearances in Los Angeles, San Jose, Portland, Seattle, Vancouver etc. before returning to Bop City in New York, early spring.

WED	1
THUR	2
FRI	3
SAT	4
SUN	5
MON	6
TUES	7
WED	8
THUR	9
FRI	10
SAT	11
SUN	12
MON	13
TUES	14
WED	15
THUR	16
FRI	17
SAT	18
SUN	19
MON	20
TUES	21
WED	22
THUR	23
FRI	24
SAT	25
SUN	26
MON	27
TUES	28

SATURDAY 11 FEBRUARY 1950

Billie opens at the New Orleans Swing Club in San Francisco for a two-week engagement with accompanist Carl Mark. Record breaking business coincides with the hearing of 2 Superior Court cases against Billie. She discovers that John Levy has left her owing money everywhere.

SUNDAY 12 FEBRUARY 1950

After her show at the New Orleans Swing Club, Billie flies to Los Angeles for a court appearance on Monday morning.

MONDAY 13 FEBRUARY 1950

Billie discovers that the court is closed to honour Lincoln's birthday, and flies back to San Francisco. Between sets at the New Orleans Swing Club, Billie attends Billy Eckstine's opening at Ciro's. She joins in an impromptu show with Stan Kenton, Nat King Cole, George Shearing and Denzil Best.

Ralph J. Gleason in *Down Beat*:

> Mr B jam-packed Ciro's and kept the cash register tinkling happily all night. He also attracted all the talent in the area that night and assembled an impromptu show that couldn't be bought by any club. Stan Kenton, Nat Cole, Billie Holiday, Jack Costanza, George Shearing, Denzil Best, John Levy, and a host of others all appeared to pay their respects to Billy and to, so help me, perform. It was quite a tribute to the *real* Voice and those who were there will never forget it.

TUESDAY 14 FEBRUARY 1950

Billie flies to Los Angeles for her court appearance, but arrives too late and immediately flies back to San Francisco for the evening appearance at the New Orleans Swing Club.

A *San Francisco Chronicle* columnist attends:

> ... TO THE NEW ORLEANS SWING CLUB on Post to find feelings high for the moment. Louis Landry, the prop., being wroth with Billie Holiday, his singer, Miss Holiday not having appeared although it was 10 p.m. And Mr. Landry declaring he would not have her late, that he had promised a show at 9:30 and thereafter, that he had hired special help and that he was paying Miss Holiday $2500 weekly and more and that he would roast her ears as soon as possible. Miss Holiday then appearing, bore a small dog called Chicuita and swept through the turmoil. Mr. Landry going to her dressing room to reprimand her. But back in a few minutes to confess he could not be harsh with such a jewel of a singer, she having said, "Sugar, I promise I won't be late again," and Landry's defenses crumbling. Then Dame Holiday singing in such a way to charm the listeners, among them the fine pianist J.B. (Boodie) Johnson and Saunders King, he the master of ceremonies. Johnson, when the music was done, confided he sees no sense in be-bop music, which he made a pledge to avoid.

WEDNESDAY 15 FEBRUARY 1950

Wednesday is Billie's off-night at the New Orleans Swing Club, so she flies to Los Angeles and stays overnight.

THURSDAY 16 FEBRUARY 1950

Billie finally makes her court appearance in Los Angeles as the *LA Times* explains:

Lawsuit Makes Billie Holiday Air Commuter

Billie Holiday, Negro blues singer, has been commuting by plane between her San Francisco night-club engagement and a $75,000 breach of contract suit before Superior Judge Frank G. Swain here.

This she disclosed yesterday on her appearance in the suit filed against her by Ed Fishman, who claims she owes him $3272.10 for his expenses in her behalf when she was in New York in 1948.

Judge Swain held that Fishman was not entitled to $75,000 in commissions he might have received as Miss Holiday's manager, as he had no California license for the position. However, the court ruled that Fishman had the right to present his story of expenditures.

Back and Forth

Miss Holiday said she had flown here Sunday night after her show, in order to appear in court Monday. Monday was a court holiday, Lincoln's birthday. She flew back Monday to sing in San Francisco, then flew down Tuesday, but arrived too late to testify, so returned north to sing, then to Los Angeles again ... too late.

Wednesday nights she does not sing in San Francisco, she said, so remained over and arrived in court – on time.

"The pilot – I've had the same one on most of the trips – asked me if it would not be cheaper for me to buy my own plane," Miss Holiday said.

WED	1
THUR	2
FRI	3
SAT	4
SUN	5
MON	6
TUES	7
WED	8
THUR	9
FRI	10
SAT	11
SUN	12
MON	13
TUES	14
WED	15
THUR	16
FRI	17
SAT	18
SUN	19
MON	20
TUES	21
WED	22
THUR	23
FRI	24
SAT	25
SUN	26
MON	27
TUES	28
WED	29
THUR	30
FRI	31

FRIDAY 3 MARCH 1950

Billie closes at the New Orleans Swing Club after being held over for a third week.

SATURDAY 4 MARCH 1950

Billie is back in court in San Francisco. The next day's issue of the *San Francisco Chronicle* explains:

Billie Holiday Told to Pay
Blues Singer Ordered to Honor Two Notes

Songstress Billie Holiday was singing the blues again yesterday to the tune of $3,750.

The entertainer now appearing at the New Orleans Swing Club was ordered to pay up on two promissory notes for that sum by Superior Judge Preston Devine.

The notes are made out to Attorney J. W. Ehrlich and cover court costs for the trial last summer in which she was acquitted of a narcotics possession charge.

Ehrlich explained that Miss Holiday "wants to pay" but that her money is currently tied up in New York by her manager, John Levy, 41.

WEDNESDAY 8 MARCH 1950

Recording session (3–6pm) for Decca at their Hollywood studio at 5505 Melrose Avenue in Los Angeles.

BILLIE HOLIDAY (vocal), DENT ECKLES (fl/ts), CHARLES LAVERE (p), BOB BAIN (g), LOU BUTTERMAN (b), NICK FATOOL (d), DAVID FRISCINA, JOSEPH QUADRI (violin), MAURICE PERLMUTTER (viola), KURT REHER (cello), GORDON JENKINS SINGERS
God Bless The Child / This Is Heaven To Me

THURSDAY 23 MARCH 1950

Billie arrives in New York.

FRIDAY 24 MARCH 1950

Billie opens at the Strand Theatre on Broadway, accompanied by Carl Mark, for a two-week engagement. Also on the bill are Count Basie's All Stars (including Buddy De Franco and Georgie Auld), The Chocolateers and The Will Mastin Trio featuring Sammy Davis Jr.

Variety reviews the show:

Current bill has potent marquee strength, particularly for jazzophiles, and should give the theatre a good two weeks, if packed houses the last two shows opening day are a criterion. Show is fast, entertaining, and filled with high-caliber talent, only fault lying in the pacing which lumps jump, dance and comedy numbers in the first 40 minutes, leaving Billie Holiday's blues and ballads spotted at the end. Billing could obviously have it no other way, but it still makes for uneven routining.

Miss Holiday, looking exceptionally well in a white gown and under soft pin-spot lighting, does her accustomed superior job of jazz warbling. "Lover Man," "Crazy He Calls Me," "All Of Me" and other blues items, plus a couple of up-tempo numbers, reveal once more this singer's distinctive, subtle way with a lyric. Especially hep crowd at the show caught couldn't get enough of her.

SAT	1	MON	1
SUN	2	TUES	2
MON	3	WED	3
TUES	4	THUR	4
WED	5	FRI	5
THUR	6	SAT	6
FRI	7	SUN	7
SAT	8	MON	8
SUN	9	TUES	9
MON	10	WED	10
TUES	11	THUR	11
WED	12	FRI	12
THUR	13	SAT	13
FRI	14	SUN	14
SAT	15	MON	15
SUN	16	TUES	16
MON	17	WED	17
TUES	18	THUR	18
WED	19	FRI	19
THUR	20	SAT	20
FRI	21	SUN	21
SAT	22	MON	22
SUN	23	TUES	23
MON	24	WED	24
TUES	25	THUR	25
WED	26	FRI	26
THUR	27	SAT	27
FRI	28	SUN	28
SAT	29	MON	29
SUN	30	TUES	30
		WED	31

THURSDAY 6 APRIL 1950

Billie closes at the Strand Theatre.

Metronome reviews the Strand show:

> **billie holiday** made one of her all too infrequent New York appearances at the Strand last month, and how there can be any quibbling as to whether or not she's still Lady Day is a mystery not only to me but I'm sure to her enthusiastic audience as well. Even with the dubious backing of the Basie group and more specifically of an accompanist who shall be nameless, Billie was every inch the Lady throughout every bar of *Fine and Mellow*, *Billie's Blues*, *Them There Eyes*, *Crazy, He Calls Me* and other Holiday standards. On only one or two of her songs did one of the jazzmen present step out and blow behind her. On most of them the band played a pallid approximation of the tunes' familiar arrangements. At all times they blew too loud, nearly engulfing the Holiday voice, but unruffled and statuesque, beautiful in a new and becoming short hairdo, Billie's every note, every inflection, every movement spelled out her very special brand of sensuous vocal magic.

FRIDAY 7 APRIL 1950

Billie's 35th birthday.

FRIDAY 14 APRIL 1950

Billie opens at the Earle Theatre in Philadelphia for a one-week engagement. Also on the bill are the George Shearing Quintet, Roger Ray, The Satisfiers, Adrian & Charlie and Frankie Jule's House Orchestra.
Billie is not at her best:

> A potentially great show was badly marred by the slipshoddy performance of a name act at the Earle Friday night. Billie Holiday was the offender, and at the show caught the singer was scarcely intelligible. The Earle management was incensed at the poor showing made by the star, who was in the closing spot; and stated categorically after the show that the singer would never play the house again.
>
> For the sake of the record, "Lady Day" tried woefully to sing some of her more artistic familiars, such as "Crazy, He Calls Me," "Lover Man" and "God Bless the Child." She was away off, however, and lost the audience after the first number when they began to walk out on her. It was doubly unfortunate for the vocalist, since M-G-M records had invited about every disk jockey in the area for the last show, in order to have them on hand for a still later reception and party for George Shearing's Quintet.

THURSDAY 20 APRIL 1950

Billie closes at the Earle Theatre in Philadelphia

FRIDAY 5 MAY 1950

Down Beat reviews Billie's latest release:

> **BILLIE HOLIDAY**
> *** *Somebody's On My Mind*
> *** *Please Tell Me Now*
> *Mind* has a curious start: Dixie brass followed by Billie and strings. It's like the old Shaw experiment of the small seven-piece jazz band playing against a full string section. Billie sings better than she has on recent discs here — less dragging, less milking of phrases. Rhythm is awfully chuggy though, holds the whole record down. (*Decca 24857*)

Two Judgments Tap Billie's Till

Hollywood—Ed Fishman, whose personal manager's breach-of-contract suit for $75,000 against Billie Holiday was denied in a California superior court ruling here recently, came out of the legal doings with a judgment against the singer for $2,145.

Judge Frank Swain held that Fishman's contract with the singer was invalid because he did not hold a California agent's license. He did, however, award judgment for a sum of money Fishman said he had advanced.

About the time Billie was winding up her court business with Fishman, another superior court judgment against her was awarded Marian Epstein for $1,540 worth of injuries said to have been received from Billie during a New Year's Eve fracas at Billy Berg's now-dark nitery a couple of years ago.

FRIDAY 19 MAY 1950

Billie opens at the Apollo Theatre in Harlem for a one-week engagement. Also on the bill are Noro Morales and his Band, Peg Leg Bates, Pigmeat Markham, and the Wallace Brothers.

WEDNESDAY 24 MAY 1950

The Amateur Hour at the Apollo is broadcast over station WMCA. Billie is accompanied by the Noro Morales Band and sings: *You're My Thrill*

THURSDAY 25 MAY 1950

Billie closes at the Apollo Theatre.

SUNDAY 28 MAY 1950

Billie sings in concert at the Brooklyn Academy of Music with the Edward Boatner A Capella Choir:
God Bless The Child / Strange Fruit.
For her jazz repertoire she is accompanied by MILES DAVIS (t), BENNIE GREEN (tb), CARL MARK (p), MUNDELL LOWE (g), PERCY HEATH (b) and ART BLAKEY (d).

THUR	1
FRI	2
SAT	3
SUN	4
MON	5
TUES	6
WED	7
THUR	8
FRI	9
SAT	10
SUN	11
MON	12
TUES	13
WED	14
THUR	15
FRI	16
SAT	17
SUN	18
MON	19
TUES	20
WED	21
THUR	22
FRI	23
SAT	24
SUN	25
MON	26
TUES	27
WED	28
THUR	29
FRI	30

FRIDAY 16 JUNE 1950

Down Beat reviews Billie's latest release:

> **BILLIE HOLIDAY**
> ******** *God Bless The Child*
> ******* *Am I Blue?*
> This re-release of a side Billie made 10 years ago should pretty well settle the argument of what has happened to her singing. Listen to the Decca version she made a short time ago: note the lagging phrasing, the over-exaggeration of ideas. Then check this side, backed by the Savoy Sultans with Roy Eldridge on trumpet. Argument should cease at that point. (Columbia 38792)

In late June Billie goes on tour with a big band led by Gerald Wilson. The 4-week tour of one-nighters is scheduled to wind through the southern states ending in New Orleans on 23 July. John Levy promises to act as guarantor for the musicians' wages.

SUNDAY 25 JUNE 1950

Billie and the Gerald Wilson big band appear at the New Dance Pavilion, Carr's Beach, Maryland.

MONDAY 26 JUNE 1950

Billie and the Gerald Wilson big band appear at the Pier Ballroom, Ocean City, Maryland.

TUESDAY 27 JUNE 1950

Billie and the Gerald Wilson big band appear at the Mosque Ballroom in Richmond, Virginia.

WEDNESDAY 28 JUNE 1950

Billie and the Gerald Wilson big band appear in Salisbury, Maryland.

THURSDAY 29 JUNE 1950

Billie and the Gerald Wilson big band appear at the Highway Boxing Arena in Newport News, Virginia.

FRIDAY 30 JUNE 1950

Billie and the Gerald Wilson big band appear in Petersburg, Virginia.

Down Beat reviews Billie's latest release:

> **BILLIE HOLIDAY**
> ******* *Now Or Never*
> ******* *Gimme A Pigfoot and a Bottle Of Beer*
> Billie does something unusual for her these days on *Never*: she sings an up-tempo blues. Nothing novel, but good blues. Flipover is equally unusual: it's meant for a humorous side. (Decca 24947)

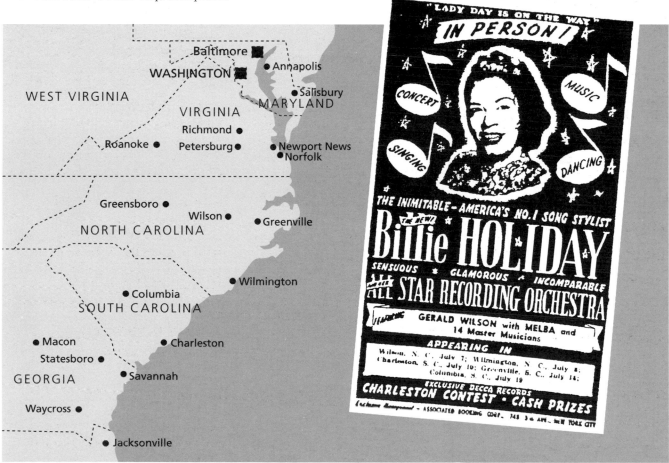

SAT	**1**
SUN	**2**
MON	**3**
TUES	**4**
WED	**5**
THUR	**6**
FRI	**7**
SAT	**8**
SUN	**9**
MON	**10**
TUES	**11**
WED	**12**
THUR	**13**
FRI	**14**
SAT	**15**
SUN	**16**
MON	**17**
TUES	**18**
WED	**19**
THUR	**20**
FRI	**21**
SAT	**22**
SUN	**23**
MON	**24**
TUES	**25**
WED	**26**
THUR	**27**
FRI	**28**
SAT	**29**
SUN	**30**
MON	**31**

MONDAY 3 JULY 1950
Billie and the Gerald Wilson big band appear in Roanoke, Virginia.

TUESDAY 4 JULY 1950
Billie and the Gerald Wilson big band appear at the Municipal Auditorium in Norfolk, Virginia.

FRIDAY 7 JULY 1950
Billie and the Gerald Wilson big band are scheduled to appear in Wilson, North Carolina.

SATURDAY 8 JULY 1950
Billie and the Gerald Wilson big band are scheduled to appear in Wilmington, North Carolina.

MONDAY 10 JULY 1950
Billie and the Gerald Wilson big band are scheduled to appear in Charleston, South Carolina.

TUESDAY 11 JULY 1950
Billie and the Gerald Wilson big band are scheduled to appear in Savannah, Georgia.

WEDNESDAY 12 JULY 1950
Billie and the Gerald Wilson big band are scheduled to appear in Macon, Georgia.

THURSDAY 13 JULY 1950
Billie and the Gerald Wilson big band are scheduled to appear in Statesboro, Georgia.

FRIDAY 14 JULY 1950
Billie and the Gerald Wilson big band are scheduled to appear in Greenville, South Carolina.

SATURDAY 15 JULY 1950
Billie and the Gerald Wilson big band are scheduled to appear in Columbia, South Carolina.

TUESDAY 18 JULY 1950
Billie and the Gerald Wilson big band are scheduled to appear in Jacksonville, Florida.

WEDNESDAY 19 JULY 1950
Billie and the Gerald Wilson big band are scheduled to appear in Waycross, Georgia.

SUNDAY 23 JULY 1950
Billie and the Gerald Wilson big band are scheduled to appear in New Orleans, Louisiana.

At some point during this brief series of one-nighters, Billie and the band are stranded, probably in Norfolk, Virginia.

Billie blames John Levy:
'He walked out and left me and my goddam band stranded in the Deep South without a dime.'

Billie writes to her friend, Maely Bartholomew, from the Prince George Hotel in Norfolk, Virginia:

Hi Mailey Honey
I know you will be surprised hearing from me and from me and from this Godforsaken country. Well Mr John Levy has lived up to every thing that you said he would He wont give me a fucking penny to come home with and I have to wait until he gets ready for me to eat. I have wrote to Joe asking him for money to come to New York with. When I insisted he pay me the other night for my work he beat me in the head with a bottle. I now have five stitches so baby if you receive this please look for me any day girl
My love to Freddie
Will wire you before I get there
Billie Holiday

Somehow Billie makes it back to New York, where she prepares for her trip to the west coast.

TUES	**1**	FRI	**1**
WED	**2**	SAT	**2**
THUR	**3**	SUN	**3**
FRI	**4**	MON	**4**
SAT	**5**	TUES	**5**
SUN	**6**	WED	**6**
MON	**7**	THUR	**7**
TUES	**8**	FRI	**8**
WED	**9**	SAT	**9**
THUR	**10**	SUN	**10**
FRI	**11**	MON	**11**
SAT	**12**	TUES	**12**
SUN	**13**	WED	**13**
MON	**14**	THUR	**14**
TUES	**15**	FRI	**15**
WED	**16**	SAT	**16**
THUR	**17**	SUN	**17**
FRI	**18**	MON	**18**
SAT	**19**	TUES	**19**
SUN	**20**	WED	**20**
MON	**21**	THUR	**21**
TUES	**22**	FRI	**22**
WED	**23**	SAT	**23**
THUR	**24**	SUN	**24**
FRI	**25**	MON	**25**
SAT	**26**	TUES	**26**
SUN	**27**	WED	**27**
MON	**28**	THUR	**28**
TUES	**29**	FRI	**29**
WED	**30**	SAT	**30**
THUR	**31**		

SATURDAY 19 AUGUST 1950

Billie spends the week 19–25 August at Universal Studios in Hollywood working on a musical movie short featuring the Count Basie Sextet, Billie Holiday and Sugar Chile Robinson. Billie sings two numbers in the film accompanied by the Count Basie Sextet: BILLIE HOLIDAY (vocal), CLARK TERRY (t), BUDDY DE FRANCO (cl), WARDELL GRAY (ts), COUNT BASIE (p), FREDDIE GREEN (g), JIMMY LEWIS (b), GUS JOHNSON (d)
God Bless The Child / Now Baby Or Never

FRIDAY 15 SEPTEMBER 1950

Billie opens at the Oasis Bar in Los Angeles for a two-week engagement accompanied by Lee Young and his Band, MAXWELL DAVIS (ts), PARR JONES (t), DUDLEY BROOKS (p), BILLY HADNOTT (b) and LEE YOUNG (d).

MONDAY 25 SEPTEMBER 1950

Billie features in a transcription, possibly a broadcast from the Oasis, with an unidentified big band.
You Gotta Show Me /Crazy He Calls Me

THURSDAY 28 SEPTEMBER 1950

Billie closes at the Oasis Bar in Los Angeles. Around this time, Billie breaks with John Levy, and Maely Bartholomew helps with her bookings and general administration.

Above: Billie in the movie short with (l to r) Gus Johnson, Count Basie, Jimmy Lewis, Marshall Royal (not on the soundtrack), Clark Terry and Wardell Gray.

FRIDAY 29 SEPTEMBER 1950

Billie is due to open at Louis Landry's New Orleans Swing Club in San Francisco, but after Landry's narcotics conviction on 28th September, she switches to Shirley Corlett's Long Bar, a rival San Francisco Club.

Landry Gets Prison Term

San Francisco — Louis Landry, operator of the New Orleans Swing club who was found guilty on a narcotics charge by jury trial early in September, was sentenced Sept. 28 "for the term prescribed by ... by Superior Judge H. J. ...
... offense was illegal ... of narcotics. The charge ... term in San Quentin of ... to six years. In sen... e judge brushed aside ... ecommendation of clem... se attorney Leslie Gil... ask for a new trial but ... ce of appeal. Landry ... l on $5,000 bail. ... , two contracts which ... had for the Swing club ... d. Billie Holiday was ... or the Longbar, whose ... y Corlett, was brought ... andry trial as an ... Landry with the in... he was behind Lan... ies. A two-week con... uis Armstrong was ... and the probability ... roup would not play ... ll this fall.

Frisco Op Guilty On Dope Charge

San Francisco — Louis Landry, 43-year-old operator of the New Orleans Swing club, Fillmore section night spot, was convicted on a charge of narcotics possession here Sept. 14. He will be sentenced Oct. 4.

Landry was arrested last May when a raiding party, led by Col. George White, federal narcotics chief here, burst into the Swing club in a pre-dawn raid. At the trial, arresting officers testified that Landry met them with a drawn gun, claimed he thought they were robbers. In a subsequent search of the premises, the agents found 58 grains of heroin cached away.

SUN	**1**	WED	**1**	FRI	**1**
MON	**2**	THUR	**2**	SAT	**2**
TUES	**3**	FRI	**3**	SUN	**3**
WED	**4**	SAT	**4**	MON	**4**
THUR	**5**	SUN	**5**	TUES	**5**
FRI	**6**	MON	**6**	WED	**6**
SAT	**7**	TUES	**7**	THUR	**7**
SUN	**8**	WED	**8**	FRI	**8**
MON	**9**	THUR	**9**	SAT	**9**
TUES	**10**	FRI	**10**	SUN	**10**
WED	**11**	SAT	**11**	MON	**11**
THUR	**12**	SUN	**12**	TUES	**12**
FRI	**13**	MON	**13**	WED	**13**
SAT	**14**	TUES	**14**	THUR	**14**
SUN	**15**	WED	**15**	FRI	**15**
MON	**16**	THUR	**16**	SAT	**16**
TUES	**17**	FRI	**17**	SUN	**17**
WED	**18**	SAT	**18**	MON	**18**
THUR	**19**	SUN	**19**	TUES	**19**
FRI	**20**	MON	**20**	WED	**20**
SAT	**21**	TUES	**21**	THUR	**21**
SUN	**22**	WED	**22**	FRI	**22**
MON	**23**	THUR	**23**	SAT	**23**
TUES	**24**	FRI	**24**	SUN	**24**
WED	**25**	SAT	**25**	MON	**25**
THUR	**26**	SUN	**26**	TUES	**26**
FRI	**27**	MON	**27**	WED	**27**
SAT	**28**	TUES	**28**	THUR	**28**
SUN	**29**	WED	**29**	FRI	**29**
MON	**30**	THUR	**30**	SAT	**30**
TUES	**31**			SUN	**31**

TUESDAY 3 OCTOBER 1950

Billie opens at Shirley Corlett's Long Bar in San Francisco.

SUNDAY 8 OCTOBER 1950

Billie misses a show and, after a dispute with Shirley Corlett, storms out of the club.

FRIDAY 6 OCTOBER 1950

Down Beat reviews Billie's latest release:

> **BILLIE HOLIDAY**
> *** *Them There Eyes*
> ** *Keeps On Rainin'*
> Billie sings *Eyes* at a raucous tempo, backed by Sy Oliver's big, swingin' band. You might be interested in listening to the Columbia of the same tune she made in 1939. She leaned less on the band, her phrases had more force and drive. At least on the current platter Billie is out of the groove of ultra-slow, dragging tempos which she has affected too often lately. (*Decca 27145*)

TUESDAY 17 OCTOBER 1950

Billie's chauffeur, Amos Cottrell, is arrested at Geary and Scott streets while standing beside Billie's blue Lincoln convertible. 2 packets of heroin are discovered in his pockets. The car is impounded.

FRIDAY 22 DECEMBER 1950

Billie opens at the Hi Note club in Chicago for a two-week engagement, accompanied by pianist Jack Russin. Miles Davis Group is also on the bill. The club is packed for every show and Billie's behaviour is exemplary.
Hi Note Manager Mort Denenberg says: *'She's a wonderful person, very easy to get along with, goes on stand on time. I couldn't ask for more.'*

FOR A LIMITED ENGAGEMENT
OPENING FRI., DEC. 22
Billie **HOLIDAY**
HI·NOTE
450 N. CLARK
For Res. Call SUperior 7-9978
MAKE YOUR NEW YEAR'S RESERVATION NOW!

Billie In Hassel In Frisco Again

San Francisco—This town is no romantic place to Billie Holiday. It's nothing but trouble town. Lady Day had one long running beef with Long bar owner Shirley Corlett over everything, including missed shows; her blue Lincoln was impounded by local authorities when the law picked up her chauffeur, Cotrell Amos, with heroin in his possession; attorney Jake Ehrlich wanted his loot from Billie's famous narcotic trial here last year, and she found her booking was a bone of contention between Corlett and Louis Landry, recently convicted on a dope charge, who was trying to keep her contract for his New Orleans Swing club.

A couple of non-narcotics squad cops brought in Amos and charged him with possessing and transporting narcotics. The latter charge was the basis for impounding Billie's new car. Amos was charged with having two small packages of heroin in the car.

Attorney Ehrlich successfully defended the singer last year during her widely-publicized narcotics trial here.

The trouble between Landry and Corlett grew out of the former's recent trial, in which he inferred that Corlett was "out to get him." Landry originally had the contract for Billie's date here and she had appeared twice before at his club. In an effort to keep the contract and prevent her appearing at the rival Longbar, Landry threatened legal action. Result was a relatively-unpublicized opening for Billie.

MON **1**	THUR **1**	THUR **1**
TUES **2**	FRI **2**	FRI **2**
WED **3**	SAT **3**	SAT **3**
THUR **4**	SUN **4**	SUN **4**
FRI **5**	MON **5**	MON **5**
SAT **6**	TUES **6**	TUES **6**
SUN **7**	WED **7**	WED **7**
MON **8**	THUR **8**	THUR **8**
TUES **9**	FRI **9**	FRI **9**
WED **10**	SAT **10**	SAT **10**
THUR **11**	SUN **11**	SUN **11**
FRI **12**	MON **12**	MON **12**
SAT **13**	TUES **13**	TUES **13**
SUN **14**	WED **14**	WED **14**
MON **15**	THUR **15**	THUR **15**
TUES **16**	FRI **16**	FRI **16**
WED **17**	SAT **17**	SAT **17**
THUR **18**	SUN **18**	SUN **18**
FRI **19**	MON **19**	MON **19**
SAT **20**	TUES **20**	TUES **20**
SUN **21**	WED **21**	WED **21**
MON **22**	THUR **22**	THUR **22**
TUES **23**	FRI **23**	FRI **23**
WED **24**	SAT **24**	SAT **24**
THUR **25**	SUN **25**	SUN **25**
FRI **26**	MON **26**	MON **26**
SAT **27**	TUES **27**	TUES **27**
SUN **28**	WED **28**	WED **28**
MON **29**		THUR **29**
TUES **30**		FRI **30**
WED **31**		SAT **31**

CHICAGO BAND BRIEFS

Hi-Note Inaugurates New Policy: Brings In Holiday

By JACK TRACY

Chicago—In an abrupt and surprising mov times at least, the Hi-Note sliced off half of thei tables into the cavity, and brought in Billie H by a Miles Davis-fronted group. All this after m omy-style bookings caused rival ops to say the club was foolish—it wouldn't work.

So Billie packed the joint nightly. And although the management had nothing definite set to follow Lady after her Jan. 7 closing, a succession of similar talent was promised. Miles was schedul stay on, however.

Billie was looking better than in her las here about a year ag

sound) were Ollie brothers Swope (making up the t and bassist Mert Count Basie's o up again at the

Last 3 Nights
CLOSING JAN. 7
Billie HOLIDAY
HI-NOTE
450 N. Clark
For Reser. Call Superior 7-5478

SUNDAY 7 JANUARY 1951
Billie closes at the Hi Note club in Chicago.

THURSDAY 8 FEBRUARY 1951
Billie opens at the Rendezvous club in Philadelphia opposite Lester Young's Band.

MONDAY 12 FEBRUARY 1951
Billie closes at the Rendezvous club in Philadelphia.

MARCH 1951
Decca do not renew Billie's recording contract and she signs for Aladdin.

Aladdin Inks Billie Holiday

New York—Billie Holiday, who hasn't recorded for a year, has been signed by Aladdin records. She'll wax a minimum of 12 sides a year, possibly will be backed by some of the label's other artists—Charles Brown, Amos Milburn, or Floyd Dixon.

Decca is building a west coast singer, Kitty White, to take over Billie's spot on the label.

Chiquitorooney

New York—Its usually bourbon and Clorox, but this time the unwitting prop for Slim Gaillard's fooling happened to be Chiquita, Billie Holiday's Chihuahua. Tiny Chiquita seems to take Slim's youtish capering in her stride. Billie brought her pet to Birdland one evening, and both enjoyed Slim's show.

During the week of 8–14 March, Billie goes to Birdland to hear Slim Gaillard, who is photographed with Billie's chihuahua.

Return engagement at the Rendezvous Club in Philadelphia.
The *Philadelphia Inquirer* reviews her show: *[Billie] is splendid as always with her fascinating combination of the sultry and the sad, her rich and feverish intonations and her warm clear phrasing.*

Billie meets Louis McKay while in Detroit at the Club Juana. She had known Louis in Harlem in the thirties and within 2 weeks he becomes her manager and personal advisor.

SUN	**1**	TUES	**1**
MON	**2**	WED	**2**
TUES	**3**	THUR	**3**
WED	**4**	FRI	**4**
THUR	**5**	SAT	**5**
FRI	**6**	SUN	**6**
SAT	**7**	MON	**7**
SUN	**8**	TUES	**8**
MON	**9**	WED	**9**
TUES	**10**	THUR	**10**
WED	**11**	FRI	**11**
THUR	**12**	SAT	**12**
FRI	**13**	SUN	**13**
SAT	**14**	MON	**14**
SUN	**15**	TUES	**15**
MON	**16**	WED	**16**
TUES	**17**	THUR	**17**
WED	**18**	FRI	**18**
THUR	**19**	SAT	**19**
FRI	**20**	SUN	**20**
SAT	**21**	MON	**21**
SUN	**22**	TUES	**22**
MON	**23**	WED	**23**
TUES	**24**	THUR	**24**
WED	**25**	FRI	**25**
THUR	**26**	SAT	**26**
FRI	**27**	SUN	**27**
SAT	**28**	MON	**28**
SUN	**29**	TUES	**29**
MON	**30**	WED	**30**
		THUR	**31**

SATURDAY 7 APRIL 1951

Billie's 36th birthday

FRIDAY 20 APRIL 1951

Down Beat reviews Billie's latest album release:

> **BILLIE HOLIDAY**
> **Time On My Hands / Laughin' At Life / It's A Sin To Tell A Lie / Swing, Brother, Swing / Loveless Love / Without Your Love / Tell Me More / Mandy Is Two**
> An LP of Holiday reissues that spot her with Lester Young, Roy Eldridge, Teddy Wilson, Georgie Auld, and many others. You've already read thousands of tributes to Billie, this won't be another. Suffice it to say that this item is a must. (**Columbia CL 6163.**)

FRIDAY 27 APRIL 1951

Billie opens with Hot Lips Page for a 3-night weekend engagement at the New Holiday Inn in Newark, New Jersey.

SUNDAY 29 APRIL 1951

Recording session for Aladdin in New York City.
BILLIE HOLIDAY (vocal), UNKNOWN (ts/bs), CARL DRINKARD (p), TINY GRIMES (g), UNKNOWN (bass), UNKNOWN (d)
Be Fair To Me / Rocky Mountain Blues / Blue Turning Gray Over You / Detour Ahead
On 'Rocky Mountain Blues' Carl Drinkard is replaced by the pianist from Tiny Grimes' group.

In the evening Billie finishes her 3-might stint with Hot Lips Page at the New Holiday Inn in Newark.

FRIDAY 25 MAY 1951

Billie opens a two and a half week engagement at the Hi Note Club in Chicago.

IN PERSON BILLY HOLIDAY
and
HOT LIPS PAGE'S BAND and REVUE
3 nights only: Fri,. Sat,. & Sun,. April 27, 28 and 29th
NEW HOLIDAY INN
149 Market Street Newark N. J.
3 SHOWS NIGHTLY — 10–11:30 p. m and I a. m.
Plus Nightly Broadcasting Over Station WHBI
Come and Take Part in the Broadcast which starts at 12:30 a. m.

FRI	1	SUN	1
SAT	2	MON	2
SUN	3	TUES	3
MON	4	WED	4
TUES	5	THUR	5
WED	6	FRI	6
THUR	7	SAT	7
FRI	8	SUN	8
SAT	9	MON	9
SUN	10	TUES	10
MON	11	WED	11
TUES	12	THUR	12
WED	13	FRI	13
THUR	14	SAT	14
FRI	15	SUN	15
SAT	16	MON	16
SUN	17	TUES	17
MON	18	WED	18
TUES	19	THUR	19
WED	20	FRI	20
THUR	21	SAT	21
FRI	22	SUN	22
SAT	23	MON	23
SUN	24	TUES	24
MON	25	WED	25
TUES	26	THUR	26
WED	27	FRI	27
THUR	28	SAT	28
FRI	29	SUN	29
SAT	30	MON	30
		TUES	31

SUNDAY 10 JUNE 1951

Billie closes at the Hi Note Club in Chicago.

FRIDAY 15 JUNE 1951

Billie opens a two-week engagement at the Stage Door in Milwaukee.

THURSDAY 28 JUNE 1951

Billie closes at the Stage Door in Milwaukee.

FRIDAY 29 JUNE 1951 probably

Billie opens a two-week engagement at the Club Juana in Detroit. Maely Bartholomew negotiates a $100 advance for Billie.

THURSDAY 12 JULY 1951

Billie closes at the Club Juana in Detroit.

FRIDAY 20 JULY 1951

Billie opens at the Apollo Theatre in Harlem for a one-week engagement, accompanied by Bobby Tucker (piano) and the Paul Williams Band. Also on the bill are Buck & Bubbles, Joe Chisholm, Rae & Rae and Maxie & Millie.

WEDNESDAY 25 JULY 1951

Amateur Hour at the Apollo is broadcast via station WMCA.

THURSDAY 26 JULY 1951

Billie closes at the Apollo.

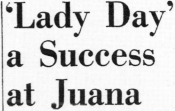

'Lady Day' a Success at Juana

Not since Billie Holiday appeared in a Detroit date engagement several months ago has the serious jazz fan had an opportunity to enter a crowded club and gain primary enjoyment from the featured star rather than a bore at the next table.

And that is what happened at the Club Juana this week as the almost flawless Lady Day captured the microphone and silenced the throng with musical Holidayisms.

She sang "I Cover the Waterfront", "Lover Man", "Strange Fruit"—all with the mellifluous, sensitive and soulful nuances and phrasings that have made the singer from Baltimore one of the greatest influences in the history of music.

Supporting Billie Holiday were Emile Jones, singing master of ceremonies; Ramsey and Payne, leopard-coated comedy duo, Darlene O'Day, shapely interpretative dancer, and Leamon Bolar and his Lemon Drops.

WED	**1**	SAT	**1**
THUR	**2**	SUN	**2**
FRI	**3**	MON	**3**
SAT	**4**	TUES	**4**
SUN	**5**	WED	**5**
MON	**6**	THUR	**6**
TUES	**7**	FRI	**7**
WED	**8**	SAT	**8**
THUR	**9**	SUN	**9**
FRI	**10**	MON	**10**
SAT	**11**	TUES	**11**
SUN	**12**	WED	**12**
MON	**13**	THUR	**13**
TUES	**14**	FRI	**14**
WED	**15**	SAT	**15**
THUR	**16**	SUN	**16**
FRI	**17**	MON	**17**
SAT	**18**	TUES	**18**
SUN	**19**	WED	**19**
MON	**20**	THUR	**20**
TUES	**21**	FRI	**21**
WED	**22**	SAT	**22**
THUR	**23**	SUN	**23**
FRI	**24**	MON	**24**
SAT	**25**	TUES	**25**
SUN	**26**	WED	**26**
MON	**27**	THUR	**27**
TUES	**28**	FRI	**28**
WED	**29**	SAT	**29**
THUR	**30**	SUN	**30**
FRI	**31**		

FRIDAY 24 AUGUST 1951

Down Beat reviews Billie's latest record release:

> **BILLIE HOLIDAY**
> *** *Rocky Mountain Blues*
> *** *Blue Turning Gray Over You*
> The second of Billie's Aladdin discs to reach us, this is not an auspicious one. *Blues* is a rigidly standard shoutin' blues, which hardly seems suited to Lady Day. Tiny Grimes, whose sextet backs Billie, twangs the universal blues chords on his guitar. The Fats Waller–Andy Razaf classic suffers from a lack of interest, or conviction, or both, by all concerned. It is depressingly lifeless. (*Aladdin 3102.*)

FRIDAY 31 AUGUST 1951

Billie opens at the Regal Theatre in Chicago with Herbie Fields and his Orchestra for a one-week engagement.

THURSDAY 6 SEPTEMBER 1951

Billie closes at the Regal Theatre in Chicago.

SATURDAY 8 SEPTEMBER 1951

Billie guests at the Club Tally Ho Lounge in Chicago.

TUESDAY 11 SEPTEMBER 1951

Billie opens at the Band Box in Chicago. *Down Beat* reports:

> Billie Holiday looked very sleek and lovely in her Band Box appearance and was singing well.

MONDAY 17 SEPTEMBER 1951

Billie closes at the Band Box.

Following the Band Box engagement, Billie plays some theatre dates with Herbie Fields and his Band.

MON	**1**
TUES	**2**
WED	**3**
THUR	**4**
FRI	**5**
SAT	**6**
SUN	**7**
MON	**8**
TUES	**9**
WED	**10**
THUR	**11**
FRI	**12**
SAT	**13**
SUN	**14**
MON	**15**
TUES	**16**
WED	**17**
THUR	**18**
FRI	**19**
SAT	**20**
SUN	**21**
MON	**22**
TUES	**23**
WED	**24**
THUR	**25**
FRI	**26**
SAT	**27**
SUN	**28**
MON	**29**
TUES	**30**
WED	**31**

MONDAY 29 OCTOBER 1951

Billie opens a one-week engagement at George Wein's Storyville Club in the Copley Square Hotel, Boston, sharing the bill with the Stan Getz Quintet. *Bandstand USA* is broadcast from the club on opening night.

STAN GETZ (ts), AL HAIG (p), JIMMY RANEY (g), TEDDY KOTICK (b), TINY KAHN (d), NAT HENTOFF (announcer)
Hershey Bar / Sweetie Pie / Wild Root

BILLIE HOLIDAY (vocal), BUSTER HARDING (p), JOHN FIELDS (b), MARQUIS FOSTER (d), NAT HENTOFF (announcer)
He's Funny That Way / Billie's Blues

STAN GETZ QUINTET:
Body And Soul / Thou Swell / How High The Moon

Down Beat reports:

A new Lady Day calmly conquered the jazz-oriented citizenry of Boston in the course of a rewardingly successful week. Billie Holiday, singing better than anyone here had heard her in the last few years, demonstrated a new sense of responsibility and co-operativeness. As a result she made every set on time and even volunteered an extra set some nights for the WMEX wire from the club.

Some of the broadcasts made during the week have found their way onto record:

BILLIE HOLIDAY (vocal), BUSTER HARDING (p), JOHN FIELDS (b), MARQUIS FOSTER (d), STAN GETZ (ts)
Tain't Nobody's Business If I Do / You're Driving Me Crazy / Lover Come Back To Me

BILLIE HOLIDAY (vocal), BUSTER HARDING (p), JOHN FIELDS (b), MARQUIS FOSTER (d)
Billie's Blues / Lover Man / Them There Eyes / My Man / I Cover The Waterfront / Crazy He Calls Me / Lover Come Back To Me / Detour Ahead / Strange Fruit / Tain't Nobody's Business If I Do / All Of Me / I Loves You Porgy / Miss Brown To You

Stan Getz remembered:

66 I MARVELLED HOW STRONG SHE WAS FOR A PERSON WHO HAD TAKEN SO MANY KNOCKS FROM LIFE, AND AT HER HONESTY AS AN ARTIST. WHEN I HAD THE OPPORTUNITY TO WORK WITH HER I FOUND HER TO BE NOTHING BUT SWEET AND GENTLE. **99**

THUR	1	SAT	1
FRI	2	SUN	2
SAT	3	MON	3
SUN	4	TUES	4
MON	5	WED	5
TUES	6	THUR	6
WED	7	FRI	7
THUR	8	SAT	8
FRI	9	SUN	9
SAT	10	MON	10
SUN	11	TUES	11
MON	12	WED	12
TUES	13	THUR	13
WED	14	FRI	14
THUR	15	SAT	15
FRI	16	SUN	16
SAT	17	MON	17
SUN	18	TUES	18
MON	19	WED	19
TUES	20	THUR	20
WED	21	FRI	21
THUR	22	SAT	22
FRI	23	SUN	23
SAT	24	MON	24
SUN	25	TUES	25
MON	26	WED	26
TUES	27	THUR	27
WED	28	FRI	28
THUR	29	SAT	29
FRI	30	SUN	30
		MON	31

Basie, Holiday, Gillespie Head New Concert Unit

New York—A new concert package with a barrage of names rivalling the Ellington-Vaughan-Cole unit has been cooked up by Willard Alexander.

The unit, which will be known as "Carnival of Jazz," features Count Basie's full orchestra, Dizzy Gillespie's combo, Billie Holiday, and Buddy Rich.

All these attractions will appear today (Nov. 16) at the Philadelphia Academy of Music, and will do a second concert on Sunday in Buffalo.

After th...
break up ...
fill previou...
ever, Alexa...
the "Carniv...
late Decemb...

SUNDAY 4 NOVEMBER 1951
Billie closes at the Storyville Club in Boston. Frankie Newton sits in with Billie.

FRIDAY 16 NOVEMBER 1951
Billie appears in a 'Carnival of Jazz' concert package at Philadelphia Academy of Music. Also featured are Count Basie and his newly reformed Orchestra, Dizzy Gillespie's Combo and Buddy Rich.

SUNDAY 18 NOVEMBER 1951
Billie and the 'Carnival of Jazz' package appear in concert in Buffalo, NY.

FRIDAY 21 DECEMBER 1951
Billie returns to the Club Juana in Detroit for a two-week engagement.
She meets Louis McKay's family and says:
His mother, she's eighty years old, and she had this dog and she loved this dog so much, and ... the dog died, and they buried the dog and he preached ... we were walking down the street and somebody says "Hey Preach ..." That's when I found out [that Louis had been a preacher].

TUES	1	FRI	1
WED	2	SAT	2
THUR	3	SUN	3
FRI	4	MON	4
SAT	5	TUES	5
SUN	6	WED	6
MON	7	THUR	7
TUES	8	FRI	8
WED	9	SAT	9
THUR	10	SUN	10
FRI	11	MON	11
SAT	12	TUES	12
SUN	13	WED	13
MON	14	THUR	14
TUES	15	FRI	15
WED	16	SAT	16
THUR	17	SUN	17
FRI	18	MON	18
SAT	19	TUES	19
SUN	20	WED	20
MON	21	THUR	21
TUES	22	FRI	22
WED	23	SAT	23
THUR	24	SUN	24
FRI	25	MON	25
SAT	26	TUES	26
SUN	27	WED	27
MON	28	THUR	28
TUES	29	FRI	29
WED	30		
THUR	31		

A New Day

Billie Holiday, Now Remarried, Finds Happiness, A New Sense Of Security

By NAT HENTOFF

Boston—A new Lady Day calmly conquered the jazz-oriented citizenry of Boston in the course of a rewardingly successful week at Storyville recently. Billie Holiday, singing better than any one here had heard her in the last few years, demonstrated as well a new sense of responsibility and cooperativeness.

As a result, she made every set —on time — and even volunteered an extra set some nights for the WMEX wire from the club.

Due to Husband

A large part of Billie's new sense of security and consequent ease is due to her husband and advisor, Louis McKay. In fact, Billie's personal life has become so ordered that she is thinking now of retiring in two or three years because "I just want to be a housewife and take care of Mr. McKay."

Musically, Billie is happy at the invaluable support she receives from arranger-accompanist Buster Harding, whose originals have been included in the books of Basie, Shaw, Goodman, Herman, Calloway, and other bands.

"Buster," says Billie, "not only plays for me, writes for me—he feels the way I feel. Some nights I'm tired, or I don't feel too good, and I don't want the tempo too fast; he knows, and sets exactly the right tempo and mood."

Pleased

Billie is also pleased at the imminent prospect of working in New York again, now that her difficulties in obtaining a license there have been evolved. Then there's the prospect of the Basie-Gillespie-Holiday concert tour, mentioned in a previous issue of the *Beat*.

Lady Day received added kicks in Boston at working opposite the Stan Getz quintet and occasionally singing with the band—kicks which were entirely reciprocal. On questioning, she expressed great admiration for the work of Getz and other modern men "who swing."

Billie added, "for me, music, if you can't pat your foot to it or hum it, it's not music. And that you can do with Stan. Though not with some of the too-modern modernists I've heard."

This brought about a discussion of her own style and its relation to that of a man she admires the

Billie Bemuses In Boston Bistro

Bushkin 4 To Embers

New York—Joe Bushkin, whose combo was the Embers' first attraction when the club opened last spring, returned there Dec. 13 with a new group.

Personnel for the opening night comprised Charlie Mingus on bass, Jo Jones, drums, and Jonah Jones, trumpet.

Bushkin planned to vary the personnel of the quartet, using various guest instrumentalists from night to night.

most, Pres Young. "I always try to sing like a horn—a trumpet or a tenor sax, and I think Lester is just the opposite. He likes to play like a voice.

"Of her contemporaries," I like Ella and Sarah, but I really go for Jo Stafford. I've been listening to her for six or seven years. She sounds like an instrument."

As for bands, Ellington is still for Billie "The world's greatest," though she has musical eyes for Kenton, Herman, and "my pet, Count Basie." Getting back to herself, Billie avowed that her earliest idols were Bessie Smith and Louis.

A discophile then asked which of her records she was especially pleased with. "Very few. *Gloomy Sunday, Fine and Mellow, No More.* But really, I don't like my records. ...an always find some fault. I

THURSDAY 3 JANUARY 1952

Billie closes at the Club Juana in Detroit.

Following the Club Juana engagement Billie sets up temporary headquarters in California.

Down Beat says:

> One of the reasons so many wires were pulled to get Billie Holiday back to San Francisco, is that she still owes Jake Ehrlich loot for beating that dope rap a few years back.

WEDNESDAY 6 FEBRUARY 1952

Billie opens at the Clayton Club in Sacramento for a one-week engagement.

TUESDAY 12 FEBRUARY 1952

Billie closes at the Clayton Club in Sacramento.

WEDNESDAY 13 FEBRUARY 1952

Billie opens at the Say When Club in San Francisco for a four-week engagement.
Down Beat reports:

> Billie Holiday's stint at the Say When drew capacity crowds, with lines out on Bush Street in front of the joint night after night. Singer sported a black eye for a time, but she's still a "new" Billie.

SAT	1
SUN	2
MON	3
TUES	4
WED	5
THUR	6
FRI	7
SAT	8
SUN	9
MON	10
TUES	11
WED	12
THUR	13
FRI	14
SAT	15
SUN	16
MON	17
TUES	18
WED	19
THUR	20
FRI	21
SAT	22
SUN	23
MON	24
TUES	25
WED	26
THUR	27
FRI	28
SAT	29
SUN	30
MON	31

SUNDAY 16 MARCH 1952
Billie closes at the Say When Club in San Francisco.

MONDAY 17 MARCH 1952
Billie is involved in an auto accident near Fort Ord on her way to entertain servicemen at Fort Ord Hospital.
AP wire: Although she was tossed out of a rolling automobile and suffered cuts and bruises, blues singer Billie Holiday gave a scheduled performance Monday to 300 servicemen at Fort Ord Hospital.
The car in which she was riding blew a tire near Fort Ord and overturned three times. Billie, her husband Louis McKay, and another companion all escaped serious injury.

TUESDAY 18 MARCH 1952
Billie opens at the Tiffany Club in Los Angeles for a two-week engagement backed by Wardell Gray's Group which includes Hampton Hawes (piano) and Chico Hamilton (drums).

SATURDAY 29 MARCH 1952
A newspaper reports:

Billie Holiday opened last week at the Tiffany Club for a 2-week engagement, still suffering from severe bruises suffered in an auto accident near Monterey. En route to Fort Ord hospital to entertain veterans, her car blew a tyre and turned over three times. She was unconscious, performed for veterans and later in the evening appeared at Delmonte Gardens.

Appearing Nitely
BILLIE HOLIDAY

★ TIFFANY ★
★ CLUB ★
3260 W. 8 St.
DU 2-5206
FREE PARKING

TUES	**1**	THUR	**1**	SUN	**1**
WED	**2**	FRI	**2**	MON	**2**
THUR	**3**	SAT	**3**	TUES	**3**
FRI	**4**	SUN	**4**	WED	**4**
SAT	**5**	MON	**5**	THUR	**5**
SUN	**6**	TUES	**6**	FRI	**6**
MON	**7**	WED	**7**	SAT	**7**
TUES	**8**	THUR	**8**	SUN	**8**
WED	**9**	FRI	**9**	MON	**9**
THUR	**10**	SAT	**10**	TUES	**10**
FRI	**11**	SUN	**11**	WED	**11**
SAT	**12**	MON	**12**	THUR	**12**
SUN	**13**	TUES	**13**	FRI	**13**
MON	**14**	WED	**14**	SAT	**14**
TUES	**15**	THUR	**15**	SUN	**15**
WED	**16**	FRI	**16**	MON	**16**
THUR	**17**	SAT	**17**	TUES	**17**
FRI	**18**	SUN	**18**	WED	**18**
SAT	**19**	MON	**19**	THUR	**19**
SUN	**20**	TUES	**20**	FRI	**20**
MON	**21**	WED	**21**	SAT	**21**
TUES	**22**	THUR	**22**	SUN	**22**
WED	**23**	FRI	**23**	MON	**23**
THUR	**24**	SAT	**24**	TUES	**24**
FRI	**25**	SUN	**25**	WED	**25**
SAT	**26**	MON	**26**	THUR	**26**
SUN	**27**	TUES	**27**	FRI	**27**
MON	**28**	WED	**28**	SAT	**28**
TUES	**29**	THUR	**29**	SUN	**29**
WED	**30**	FRI	**30**	MON	**30**
		SAT	**31**		

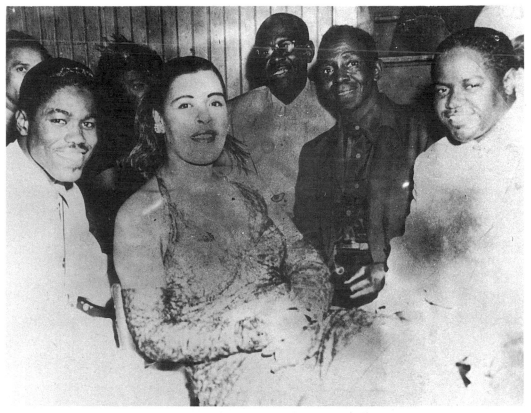

Billie relaxing in Los Angeles during a visit to Billy Berg's Waldorf Cellar in the company of the Simon Brothers, Maurice and Simon.

MONDAY 7 APRIL 1952
Billie's 37th birthday

A bench warrant is issued by LA Superior Court Commissioner Shepherd, charging Billie with contempt for failure to appear in Debtor's Court to explain why she had not paid $1040 on a judgement against her. The judgement was awarded Mrs Marian E. Donovan in 1949 following a New Year's Day altercation in which she said Billie had thrown a dish which cut her foot.

Billie closes her engagement at the Tiffany Club in Los Angeles.

After 21 APRIL 1952
Billie makes her recording debut for Norman Granz and Mercury Records at the Radio Recorders studio in Los Angeles. Norman Granz produces the session.
BILLIE HOLIDAY (vocal), CHARLIE SHAVERS (t), FLIP PHILLIPS (ts), OSCAR PETERSON (p), BARNEY KESSEL (g), RAY BROWN (b), ALVIN STOLLER (d)
East Of The Sun / Blue Moon / You Go To My Head /You Turned The Tables On Me / Easy To Love / These Foolish Things / I Only Have Eyes For You / Solitude

A second recording session for Norman Granz and Mercury Records follows a few days later.
BILLIE HOLIDAY (vocal), CHARLIE SHAVERS (t), FLIP PHILLIPS (ts), OSCAR PETERSON (p), BARNEY KESSEL (g), RAY BROWN (b), ALVIN STOLLER (d)
Everything I Have Is Yours / Love For Sale (Billie & Oscar Peterson only) / *Moonglow / Tenderly / If The Moon Turns Green / Remember / Autumn In New York* (2 takes)

From Los Angeles, Billie moves on to Honolulu for an extended club engagement.

TUES	**1**	FRI	**1**
WED	**2**	SAT	**2**
THUR	**3**	SUN	**3**
FRI	**4**	MON	**4**
SAT	**5**	TUES	**5**
SUN	**6**	WED	**6**
MON	**7**	THUR	**7**
TUES	**8**	FRI	**8**
WED	**9**	SAT	**9**
THUR	**10**	SUN	**10**
FRI	**11**	MON	**11**
SAT	**12**	TUES	**12**
SUN	**13**	WED	**13**
MON	**14**	THUR	**14**
TUES	**15**	FRI	**15**
WED	**16**	SAT	**16**
THUR	**17**	SUN	**17**
FRI	**18**	MON	**18**
SAT	**19**	TUES	**19**
SUN	**20**	WED	**20**
MON	**21**	THUR	**21**
TUES	**22**	FRI	**22**
WED	**23**	SAT	**23**
THUR	**24**	SUN	**24**
FRI	**25**	MON	**25**
SAT	**26**	TUES	**26**
SUN	**27**	WED	**27**
MON	**28**	THUR	**28**
TUES	**29**	FRI	**29**
WED	**30**	SAT	**30**
THUR	**31**	SUN	**31**

Billie tries again to win back her cabaret card:

> Billie Holiday, in New York from Honolulu to get an okay on work here. You remember, she's been banned many years now from singing wherever liquor is sold. There's hope that her newest appeal will win out.

THURSDAY 24 JULY 1952

Billie goes to Birdland for the opening of Count Basie's new big band. Lester Young and his group are also on the bill at Birdland, and Lester is featured in a battle with Basie's new tenor star, Paul Quinichette. The battle is billed as 'Pres versus Vice Pres'.

Billie visits Lester Young at Birdland where his Quintet share the stand with Count Basie's Orchestra.

SUNDAY 27 JULY 1952

Recording session as Billie Holiday and her Lads of Joy for Mercury in New York City. Norman Granz produces the session.
BILLIE HOLIDAY (vocal), JOE NEWMAN (t), PAUL QUINICHETTE (ts), OSCAR PETERSON (p/org), FREDDIE GREEN (g), RAY BROWN (b), GUS JOHNSON (d)
My Man / Lover Come Back To Me / Stormy Weather / Yesterdays / He's Funny That Way / I Can't Face The Music

FRIDAY 22 AUGUST 1952

Billie opens at Weekes in Atlantic City for a one-week engagement.

WEDNESDAY 27 AUGUST 1952

The new issue of *Down Beat* reports that Billie is set for a 30 day tour of Britain starting October 12, probably followed by other Continental dates.

Basie, Haymes, Billie Holiday Set For Europe

By Leonard Feather

New York–Call it emigration or exportation, invasion or penetration; whichever way you look at it, the big foreign push in the music business is on!

Completely halted during the war years and heavily impeded by currency and transportation difficulties, American bands, instrumentalists and singers are flocking across the Atlantic in unprecedented numbers. Where before the war the international dealings were limited mainly to jazz names and a few top pop stars, today there are almost as many pop artists as jazz musicians receiving and accepting lucrative offers from everywhere this side of the Iron Curtain.

Records Helped

The increased potency of American records and songs has been a vital factor in expanding this market. A typical case was the big hit registered last month by Guy Mitchell at the London Palladium, where the headliner nowadays is almost always an American. Mitchell's records had preceded him and created the same enthusiasm as in his native land.

Biggest news of the past month was the visit to New York of British impresario Maurice Kinn, who made fabulous offers to a slew of U.S. names, most of whom accepted.

One result is that Billie Holiday, long a top favorite of British jazz fans, has been set for her first Transatlantic tour. She will do 30 days of concerts in Great Britain, starting Oct. 12, probably followed by Continental dates.

THURSDAY 28 AUGUST 1952

Billie closes at Weekes in Atlantic City.

FRIDAY 29 AUGUST 1952

Billie opens at Storyville in Boston for a two-week engagement.

MON	1	WED	1
TUES	2	THUR	2
WED	3	FRI	3
THUR	4	SAT	4
FRI	5	SUN	5
SAT	6	MON	6
SUN	7	TUES	7
MON	8	WED	8
TUES	9	THUR	9
WED	10	FRI	10
THUR	11	SAT	11
FRI	12	SUN	12
SAT	13	MON	13
SUN	14	TUES	14
MON	15	WED	15
TUES	16	THUR	16
WED	17	FRI	17
THUR	18	SAT	18
FRI	19	SUN	19
SAT	20	MON	20
SUN	21	TUES	21
MON	22	WED	22
TUES	23	THUR	23
WED	24	FRI	24
THUR	25	SAT	25
FRI	26	SUN	26
SAT	27	MON	27
SUN	28	TUES	28
MON	29	WED	29
TUES	30	THUR	30
		FRI	31

Nat Hentoff reviews the Storyville engagement in *Down Beat*:

> Lady Day seems to have chronic opening night jitters. Billie was less than perfect musically, besides being hampered by a rather disorganized rhythm section.
>
> A widely read Boston columnist caught the show, and his column the next day was hardly a eulogy. It was actually a puzzled essay, as he tried to explain to himself and his readers why Billie was so highly regarded by other sources.
>
> **Rapid Recovery**
>
> The next night, and all succeeding nights, Billie was superb and, at the Sunday afternoon session, provided this listener with a major musical experience. But the columnist had not returned, and both he and those of his listeners who had not found out for themselves will long associate Billie with inadequacy.

MONDAY 8 SEPTEMBER 1952

Billie and Sarah Vaughan appear as guests at the Welcome Home Party for Clarence Robinson & his Tropical Revue at Connie's 5-Star Musical Bar, 2283 7th Avenue at 134th Street in Harlem.

THURSDAY 11 SEPTEMBER 1952

Billie closes at Storyville.

SATURDAY 13 SEPTEMBER 1952

Billie is a surprise guest on the Jazz at the Philharmonic concert at Carnegie Hall in New York City. The package stars Ella Fitzgerald, Flip Phillips, Lester Young, Buddy Rich, Charlie Shavers, Roy Eldridge, Benny Carter, Gene Krupa and the Oscar Peterson Trio.

Down Beat says:

> Biggest letdown of the night was a surprise guest Granz had saved especially for the New York crowd, Billie Holiday. In her first appearance in New York in several years, Billie sang half-heartedly, nervously.

Early OCTOBER 1952

Billie's scheduled tour of Britain is cancelled due to the tax problems of Dick Haymes who was to share the billing with Billie.

SUNDAY 19 OCTOBER 1952

Billie stars in a 3pm concert '100 Years of American Music' at the Civic Opera House in Chicago.

SAT	**1**
SUN	**2**
MON	**3**
TUES	**4**
WED	**5**
THUR	**6**
FRI	**7**
SAT	**8**
SUN	**9**
MON	**10**
TUES	**11**
WED	**12**
THUR	**13**
FRI	**14**
SAT	**15**
SUN	**16**
MON	**17**
TUES	**18**
WED	**19**
THUR	**20**
FRI	**21**
SAT	**22**
SUN	**23**
MON	**24**
TUES	**25**
WED	**26**
THUR	**27**
FRI	**28**
SAT	**29**
SUN	**30**

FRIDAY 14 NOVEMBER 1952

Billie appears at Carnegie Hall in New York City in 'Duke Ellington's 25th Anniversary in the Music Business'. Also on the bill are Duke Ellington & his Orchestra, Stan Getz Quintet, Ahmad Jamal Trio, Charlie Parker with Strings, and Dizzy Gillespie.
At the first house at 8.15pm:
BILLIE HOLIDAY (vocal), JIMMY HAMILTON (cl), RAY NANCE (vln), BUSTER HARDING (p), JOHN FIELDS (b), MARQUIS FOSTER (d)
Lover Man / My Man / Miss Brown To You / Easy Living / What A Little Moonlight Can Do / Tenderly / Strange Fruit / Fine And Mellow
At the second house at 11.45pm:
BILLIE HOLIDAY (vocal), JIMMY HAMILTON (cl), RAY NANCE (vln), BUSTER HARDING (p), JOHN FIELDS (b), MARQUIS FOSTER (d)
Lover Come Back To Me / I Cover The Waterfront / What A Little Moonlight Can Do / My Man / Fine And Mellow
The concert is a great success for Billie and she sings *Fine And Mellow* as an encore at both concerts.

Bill Coss reviews the concert in *Metronome*:

> Lady Day finished the concert for me. Looking more handsome than ever, more humble and considerably fresher, Billie began with *I Cover the Waterfront* with Jimmy Hamilton's clarinet and Ray Nance's violin as pleasant supports. Her voice was perhaps a little harder, a bit more tired – fitting more perfectly now the description once offered, that her voice was like the taste of copper pennies – but she sang with such authority, taste and attack. *Lover Come Back to Me* was even better though considerably harsher. Her *Porgy* was as emotion-packed as a song can be; *What A Little Moonlight Can Do* was beautifully phrased and swung; *My Man* was too choppy and obviously styled, but the projection here, as in the other tunes, was masterful; *Fine and Mellow* was a friendly, happy encore, so unlike the *Strange Fruit* that so often used to serve that function. Perhaps this is an indication of the new Holiday. Certainly it was a real holiday for me.

SATURDAY 15 NOVEMBER 1952

Billie attends the Billy Eckstine, Count Basie, George Shearing concert at Carnegie Hall in New York City.

Backstage at Carnegie Hall, Tony Scott, Billie and Charlie Parker get acquainted with a shy young fan.

MON	**1**
TUES	**2**
WED	**3**
THUR	**4**
FRI	**5**
SAT	**6**
SUN	**7**
MON	**8**
TUES	**9**
WED	**10**
THUR	**11**
FRI	**12**
SAT	**13**
SUN	**14**
MON	**15**
TUES	**16**
WED	**17**
THUR	**18**
FRI	**19**
SAT	**20**
SUN	**21**
MON	**22**
TUES	**23**
WED	**24**
THUR	**25**
FRI	**26**
SAT	**27**
SUN	**28**
MON	**29**
TUES	**30**
WED	**31**

Billie signs autographs for her fans outside the Apollo.

FRIDAY 5 DECEMBER 1952

Billie opens at the Apollo Theatre in Harlem for a one-week engagement. Also on the bill are Johnny Hodges and his Band, The Checkers, Salt & Pepper, Lady Terry, Spo-De-O-Dee & Co.

WEDNESDAY 10 DECEMBER 1952

Amateur Hour from the Apollo is broadcast via station WMCA.

BILLIE HOLIDAY (vocal), TONY SCOTT (cl), BUSTER HARDING (p) plus members of the Johnny Hodges Band.

Tenderly / My Man

THURSDAY 11 DECEMBER 1952

Billie closes at the Apollo Theatre.

FRIDAY 12 DECEMBER 1952

Billie appears at the *New York Amsterdam News* 15th Annual Midnight Benefit Show at the Apollo Theatre. Also on the bill are the Ink Spots, Eartha Kitt, Slim Gaillard, George Shearing Quintet, Hot Lips Page and the Arnett Cobb Band.

THUR	**1**	SUN	**1**	SUN	**1**
FRI	**2**	MON	**2**	MON	**2**
SAT	**3**	TUES	**3**	TUES	**3**
SUN	**4**	WED	**4**	WED	**4**
MON	**5**	THUR	**5**	THUR	**5**
TUES	**6**	FRI	**6**	FRI	**6**
WED	**7**	SAT	**7**	SAT	**7**
THUR	**8**	SUN	**8**	SUN	**8**
FRI	**9**	MON	**9**	MON	**9**
SAT	**10**	TUES	**10**	TUES	**10**
SUN	**11**	WED	**11**	WED	**11**
MON	**12**	THUR	**12**	THUR	**12**
TUES	**13**	FRI	**13**	FRI	**13**
WED	**14**	SAT	**14**	SAT	**14**
THUR	**15**	SUN	**15**	SUN	**15**
FRI	**16**	MON	**16**	MON	**16**
SAT	**17**	TUES	**17**	TUES	**17**
SUN	**18**	WED	**18**	WED	**18**
MON	**19**	THUR	**19**	THUR	**19**
TUES	**20**	FRI	**20**	FRI	**20**
WED	**21**	SAT	**21**	SAT	**21**
THUR	**22**	SUN	**22**	SUN	**22**
FRI	**23**	MON	**23**	MON	**23**
SAT	**24**	TUES	**24**	TUES	**24**
SUN	**25**	WED	**25**	WED	**25**
MON	**26**	THUR	**26**	THUR	**26**
TUES	**27**	FRI	**27**	FRI	**27**
WED	**28**	SAT	**28**	SAT	**28**
THUR	**29**			SUN	**29**
FRI	**30**			MON	**30**
SAT	**31**			TUES	**31**

Because of the Cabaret Card situation, Billie cannot play clubs in New York and is forced to travel the country.

WEDNESDAY 11 FEBRUARY 1953
Billie opens at the Say When Club in San Francisco for an extended four-week engagement.

TUESDAY 17 FEBRUARY 1953

Billie Holiday Sued on Contract

S.W. "Shirley" Corlett, Fillmore Street night club figure, filed suit in San Francisco superior court yesterday for $30,229.89 damages against Billie Holiday, night club singer, for breach of contract.
The complaint alleges she failed to complete the last ten days of a contract in 1950.

The *San Francisco Chronicle* of Friday 26 February reports:

TALK OF THE TOWN: Billie Holiday's current San Francisco engagement hasn't been much of a holiday. First the singer was sued by Shirley Corlett, former owner of the padlocked Longbar Club, and now she's asked Nate Cohn to file a $60,000 counter suit. "If she loses," quipped Nate, "debts will take a Holiday."

TUESDAY 10 MARCH 1953
Billie closes at the Say When Club in San Francisco.

WED	**1**	FRI	**1**	MON	**1**
THUR	**2**	SAT	**2**	TUES	**2**
FRI	**3**	SUN	**3**	WED	**3**
SAT	**4**	MON	**4**	THUR	**4**
SUN	**5**	TUES	**5**	FRI	**5**
MON	**6**	WED	**6**	SAT	**6**
TUES	**7**	THUR	**7**	SUN	**7**
WED	**8**	FRI	**8**	MON	**8**
THUR	**9**	SAT	**9**	TUES	**9**
FRI	**10**	SUN	**10**	WED	**10**
SAT	**11**	MON	**11**	THUR	**11**
SUN	**12**	TUES	**12**	FRI	**12**
MON	**13**	WED	**13**	SAT	**13**
TUES	**14**	THUR	**14**	SUN	**14**
WED	**15**	FRI	**15**	MON	**15**
THUR	**16**	SAT	**16**	TUES	**16**
FRI	**17**	SUN	**17**	WED	**17**
SAT	**18**	MON	**18**	THUR	**18**
SUN	**19**	TUES	**19**	FRI	**19**
MON	**20**	WED	**20**	SAT	**20**
TUES	**21**	THUR	**21**	SUN	**21**
WED	**22**	FRI	**22**	MON	**22**
THUR	**23**	SAT	**23**	TUES	**23**
FRI	**24**	SUN	**24**	WED	**24**
SAT	**25**	MON	**25**	THUR	**25**
SUN	**26**	TUES	**26**	FRI	**26**
MON	**27**	WED	**27**	SAT	**27**
TUES	**28**	THUR	**28**	SUN	**28**
WED	**29**	FRI	**29**	MON	**29**
THUR	**30**	SAT	**30**	TUES	**30**
		SUN	**31**		

TUESDAY 7 APRIL 1953
Billie's 38th birthday.

WEDNESDAY 22 APRIL 1953
Down Beat reviews Billie's latest record release:

> **BILLIE HOLIDAY**
> *** *Lover, Come Back To Me*
> **** *Yesterdays*
> Billie cut both these tunes before, for Commodore, in 1939 and 1944, respectively. There are so many great tunes she *hasn't* recorded that we feel she should stop inviting comparisons. *Lover* is noteworthy for a full chorus of great Peterson piano. *Yesterdays* pulls off a coup by offering Peterson's first Hammond organ side. He plays it discreetly, offering a fine background for Billie's wonderful mood. The easing into double-time is accomplished effectively, with Quinichette quietly offering aid. (*Mercury 89037.*)

MONDAY 18 MAY 1953
Billie opens at the Hi-Hat in Boston for a one-week engagement.
Popular singer Johnnie Ray opens the same night at Blinstrub's and he rushes crosstown to the Hi-Hat to hear Billie. He says: *'I think Billie has contributed more to jazz singing than anyone else in our generation. I've certainly learned a lot from her, and I always hear her whenever I can.'*

SUNDAY 24 MAY 1953
Billie closes at the Hi-Hat in Boston, where, according to *Down Beat*, she had sung brilliantly to large crowds.

Dan Morgenstern: *'The Hi-Hat was the first time I saw Billie in person, she was playing opposite Flip Phillips. There were three sets and we stayed for all three. Billie noticed us after the second set and came over to join us. She was very sweet and in terrific form in 1953. I think it is nonsense to suggest she was in steep decline throughout the fifties; there were some performances that maybe were not so hot, but here she was in wonderful form and no other problems as far as I could see.'*

FRIDAY 29 MAY 1953
Billie opens at the Beaucoup, a new jazz club at 5068 Broadway, in Chicago for a three-week engagement.

THURSDAY 18 JUNE 1953
Billie closes at the Beaucoup in Chicago.

WED	1	SAT	1	TUES	1
THUR	2	SUN	2	WED	2
FRI	3	MON	3	THUR	3
SAT	4	TUES	4	FRI	4
SUN	5	WED	5	SAT	5
MON	6	THUR	6	SUN	6
TUES	7	FRI	7	MON	7
WED	8	SAT	8	TUES	8
THUR	9	SUN	9	WED	9
FRI	10	MON	10	THUR	10
SAT	11	TUES	11	FRI	11
SUN	12	WED	12	SAT	12
MON	13	THUR	13	SUN	13
TUES	14	FRI	14	MON	14
WED	15	SAT	15	TUES	15
THUR	16	SUN	16	WED	16
FRI	17	MON	17	THUR	17
SAT	18	TUES	18	FRI	18
SUN	19	WED	19	SAT	19
MON	20	THUR	20	SUN	20
TUES	21	FRI	21	MON	21
WED	22	SAT	22	TUES	22
THUR	23	SUN	23	WED	23
FRI	24	MON	24	THUR	24
SAT	25	TUES	25	FRI	25
SUN	26	WED	26	SAT	26
MON	27	THUR	27	SUN	27
TUES	28	FRI	28	MON	28
WED	29	SAT	29	TUES	29
THUR	30	SUN	30	WED	30
FRI	31	MON	31		

JULY 1953
Billie appears at the Blue Note Club in Chicago

THURSDAY 13 AUGUST 1953
Billie's face is badly swollen from an abscessed tooth. She is due to open at the Apollo Theatre next day with Duke Ellington.

FRIDAY 14 AUGUST 1953
Joe Glaser sends for Annie Ross as a replacement for Billie.
Annie Ross:

> I GOT A CALL EARLY THAT MORNING FROM JOE GLASER. I HAD JUST SIGNED WITH HIM AND HE SAID I WAS TO STAND IN FOR BILLIE HOLIDAY. I WAS SCARED OUT OF MY WITS; NUMBER ONE IT WAS THE APOLLO AND NUMBER TWO, I WAS REPLACING MY IDOL BILLIE HOLIDAY. DUKE ELLINGTON TOOK ME BY THE HAND TO MEET HER. SHE ASKED IF I NEEDED A GOWN, A PIANO PLAYER AND SO ON. SHE WAS TRULY LOVELY TO ME. THE TIME CAME FOR ME TO SING; IT'S A TOUGH AUDIENCE AT THE APOLLO. THERE WERE LOTS OF HOLLERS AND HOOTS WHEN I WALKED OUT BUT I WAS SINGING ADVANCED STUFF LIKE "TWISTED" AND "FARMER'S MARKET" AND THAT SAVED MY BACON. WHEN I CAME OFF SHE GAVE ME A BIG HUG AND WE BOTH STARTED TO CRY; DUKE SAID, "C'MON, YOU TWO LOVELY LADIES, COME OUT AND TAKE A BOW," AND THAT'S HOW I FIRST GOT TO KNOW BILLIE HOLIDAY.

Annie fills in for the first show, but Billie is back for the second show and finishes the week.

WEDNESDAY 19 AUGUST 1953
Amateur Night at the Apollo.

THURSDAY 20 AUGUST 1953
Billie closes at the Apollo.

GALA RE-OPENING SHOW
HARLEM'S HIGH SPOT
APOLLO
One WEEK Beg. FRI., August 14th
DUKE ELLINGTON AND HIS BAND WITH
CAT ANDERSON · RAY NANCE · JUAN TIZOL · JIMMY GRISSOM · BRITT WOODMAN · HARRY CARNEY
BILLIE HOLIDAY
MARGIE McGLORY MIMIC · MOKE and POKE
Reserved Seats Now On Sale For
WED. NIGHT BROADCAST - SAT. Midnight Show

SATURDAY 26 SEPTEMBER 1953
Billie appears at Carnegie Hall on a bill that features Stan Kenton and his Orchestra, Dizzy Gillespie and Bud Powell.

Down Beat reports:

> Billie was in good voice and very charmingly gowned.

The *NY Age* columnist, Alan MacMillan:

> This reporter was very happy to have been present at Carnegie Hall concert when Stan Kenton, Billie Holiday and Dizzy Gillespie drew a capacity audience. Kenton's crew of 10 brass, five reeds and four rhythm is a powerful combination, but Lady Day stole the show. She was her old self again and was in good voice. She begged off after nine songs.
>
> ...Following the Stan Kenton–Billie Holiday concert at Carnegie Hall we went with Lady Day and her husband-manager, Louis McKay, to hear Dinah Washington at the Birdland Jazz Emporium, having a helluva good time and enjoying the joyous atmosphere.
>
> On the following night, which was Sunday, we had a party for Billie Holiday at Wells Music bar, as a sort of celebration to her success, and it turned out to be one of the nicest parties we have ever given.

SUNDAY 27 SEPTEMBER 1953
Billie attends a party in her honour at Wells Music Bar, given by the NY Age.

THUR	1	SUN	1	TUES	1
FRI	2	MON	2	WED	2
SAT	3	TUES	3	THUR	3
SUN	4	WED	4	FRI	4
MON	5	THUR	5	SAT	5
TUES	6	FRI	6	SUN	6
WED	7	SAT	7	MON	7
THUR	8	SUN	8	TUES	8
FRI	9	MON	9	WED	9
SAT	10	TUES	10	THUR	10
SUN	11	WED	11	FRI	11
MON	12	THUR	12	SAT	12
TUES	13	FRI	13	SUN	13
WED	14	SAT	14	MON	14
THUR	15	SUN	15	TUES	15
FRI	16	MON	16	WED	16
SAT	17	TUES	17	THUR	17
SUN	18	WED	18	FRI	18
MON	19	THUR	19	SAT	19
TUES	20	FRI	20	SUN	20
WED	21	SAT	21	MON	21
THUR	22	SUN	22	TUES	22
FRI	23	MON	23	WED	23
SAT	24	TUES	24	THUR	24
SUN	25	WED	25	FRI	25
MON	26	THUR	26	SAT	26
TUES	27	FRI	27	SUN	27
WED	28	SAT	28	MON	28
THUR	29	SUN	29	TUES	29
FRI	30	MON	30	WED	30
SAT	31			THUR	31

TUESDAY 6 OCTOBER 1953

Billie opens at the Storyville Club in Boston for one-week. Some airchecks exist from the engagement.

BILLIE HOLIDAY (vocal), CARL DRINKARD (p), JIMMY WOODE (b), PETER LITTMAN (d), GEORGE WEIN (announcer)

I Cover The Waterfront / Too Marvellous For Words / I Loves You Porgy / Them There Eyes / Willow Weep For Me / I Only Have Eyes For You / You Go To My Head

The *Boston Guardian* reports:

> She had the house rocking despite that abscessed jaw.

MONDAY 12 OCTOBER 1953

Billie closes at Storyville.

TUESDAY 13 OCTOBER 1953

Billie has a dental operation to fix her abscessed jaw.

FRIDAY 16 OCTOBER 1953

Billie appears as featured guest on George Jessel's TV show *Comeback*, screened on the ABC Television Network from New York City from 9.30 to 10pm. George Jessel introduces the show, *Tonight's comeback story is a little different from others we have presented, for this artist's real comeback was made five years ago after she had paid the penalty for falling victim to one of society's most dread diseases – the use of narcotics. And in a sense she has been coming back with every song she sings.*

Also taking part are Artie Shaw, Pods Hollingsworth, Arthur Herzog, Louis Armstrong, Count Basie, Mae Barnes and Leonard Feather, their comments interspersed with excerpts from Billie's recordings. Billie sings *God Bless The Child* with Carl Drinkard's Trio.

WEDNESDAY 2 DECEMBER 1953

Joe Glaser signs contracts with Swedish promoter Nils Hellstrom for an All-Star Jazz Show starring Billie to tour Europe starting 7 January 1954. The show is named Jazz Club USA after Leonard Feather's Voice of America radio programme.

FRIDAY 4 DECEMBER 1953

Billie opens at Joe Tenner's Down Beat Club on Market Street in San Francisco, after a 3-day drive from New York

TUESDAY 15 DECEMBER 1953

Billie's pianist, Carl Drinkard, is arrested. A hearing is set for Wednesday 23 December.

THURSDAY 24 DECEMBER 1953

Billie opens at the Tiffany Club in Los Angeles for a two-week engagement.

WEDNESDAY 30 DECEMBER 1953

Down Beat announces a European tour for Billie. The magazine also reviews her latest record release:

> **BILLIE HOLIDAY**
> ***** *My Man*
> ***** *He's Funny That Way*
> I should admit that my admiration for Lady Day's singing is probably beyond the bounds of reason. I'm aware of the comparisons that are often made between the various Holiday stages from *Your Mother's Son-in-Law* to the latest Clef—with partisans for each era. I'm sorry, I dig them all. Less subjectively, mention should be made of the subtle accompaniment she receives. Joe Newman on both sides sounds like her shadow (listen closely to *Funny*) and Paul Quinichette is almost equally intuitive. (**Clef 89089**)

Billie To Make European Tour

New York — Contracts were signed here last month for *Down Beat* writer Leonard Feather to take a jazz package starring Billie Holiday on a four-week tour of Europe.

Completing the lineup will be the Red Norvo Trio, the Buddy DeFranco Quartet, the Beryl Booker trio, and Carl Drinkard, Billie's pianist.

Show will be billed as *Jazz Club U. S. A.* after the similarly-named series of broadcasts which Feather has been airing since 1950 for the Voice of America.

This will be Billie's first overseas trip. A tour last year was canceled when Dick Haymes, who had been booked jointly with her, was unable to leave the country because of tax difficulties.

The unit will play its first date Jan. 11 in Stockholm and will proceed to concerts in other Swedish cities and in Norway, Denmark, Germany, Belgium, Holland, and France.

FRI	1
SAT	2
SUN	3
MON	4
TUES	5
WED	6
THUR	7
FRI	8
SAT	9
SUN	10
MON	11
TUES	12
WED	13
THUR	14
FRI	15
SAT	16
SUN	17
MON	18
TUES	19
WED	20
THUR	21
FRI	22
SAT	23
SUN	24
MON	25
TUES	26
WED	27
THUR	28
FRI	29
SAT	30
SUN	31

Above: Louis and Billie arrive in Stockholm.
Right: Billie onstage at the Stockholm concert.

WEDNESDAY 6 JANUARY 1954
Billie closes at the Tiffany Club in Los Angeles.

SUNDAY 10 JANUARY 1954
Billie and the other members of the Jazz Club USA troupe (Red Norvo, Buddy De Franco, Beryl Booker, Carl Drinkard, Sonny Clark, Red Mitchell, Elaine Leighton and Leonard Feather) board a plane at Idlewild Airport, bound for Stockholm. They fly to Scotland and then to Copenhagen.

MONDAY 11 JANUARY 1954
The plane is grounded in Copenhagen by snow and the troupe have to take a boat to Malmo and a train to Stockholm. The troupe arrive in Stockholm, exhausted and with no time for rehearsal. The opening concert is, not surprisingly, rather disappointing. A row ensues over who is to play bass and drums behind Billie. Eventually Red Mitchell and Elaine Leighton agree to back her. Guitarist Jimmy Raney is missing. He had travelled over earlier on the Ile de France but had been taken ill in London.

TUESDAY 12 JANUARY 1954
Jazz Club USA play a second concert in Stockholm. Billie is interviewed for a radio programme by Olle Helander.

WEDNESDAY 13 JANUARY 1954
Jazz Club USA play in Uppsala, Sweden.

THURSDAY 14 JANUARY 1954
Jazz Club USA play in Örebro, Sweden.

FRIDAY 15 JANUARY 1954
Jazz Club USA play in Gothenburg, Sweden.

SATURDAY 16 JANUARY 1954
Jazz Club USA play in Oslo, Norway.

SUNDAY 17 JANUARY 1954
Jazz Club USA play in Malmo, Sweden.

MONDAY 18 JANUARY 1954
Jazz Club USA play in Copenhagen, Denmark.

FRI	**1**
SAT	**2**
SUN	**3**
MON	**4**
TUES	**5**
WED	**6**
THUR	**7**
FRI	**8**
SAT	**9**
SUN	**10**
MON	**11**
TUES	**12**
WED	**13**
THUR	**14**
FRI	**15**
SAT	**16**
SUN	**17**
MON	**18**
TUES	**19**
WED	**20**
THUR	**21**
FRI	**22**
SAT	**23**
SUN	**24**
MON	**25**
TUES	**26**
WED	**27**
THUR	**28**
FRI	**29**
SAT	**30**
SUN	**31**

TUESDAY 19 JANUARY 1954
Jazz Club USA play in Hamburg, Germany.

WEDNESDAY 20 JANUARY 1954
Jazz Club USA play in Berlin, Germany.

THURSDAY 21 JANUARY 1954
Jazz Club USA play in Dusseldorf, Germany.

FRIDAY 22 JANUARY 1954
Jazz Club USA play in Cologne, Germany. The concert is broadcast.
Red Norvo Trio: RED NORVO (vib), JIMMY RANEY (g), RED MITCHELL (b)
Move / Tenderly
Buddy De Franco Quartet: BUDDY DE FRANCO (cl), SONNY CLARK (p), RED MITCHELL (b), BOB WHITE (d)
I'll Remember April / Sweet Georgia Brown
BILLIE HOLIDAY (vocal), CARL DRINKARD (p), RED MITCHELL (b), ELAINE LEIGHTON (d), LEONARD FEATHER (mc)
Billie's Blues / What A Little Moonlight Can Do
BUDDY DE FRANCO (cl), RED NORVO (vib), JIMMY RANEY (g) added
Lover Come Back To Me

SATURDAY 23 JANUARY 1954
Jazz Club USA play in Amsterdam, Holland. Leonard Feather reports on the tour in the *Melody Maker*:

We're in good shape now ... but it took weeks of headaches to reach this stage. Lady Day is looking and singing better than she has in years. She has been bringing out songs like "Strange Fruit", "Don't Explain", "My Man", and "Porgy", and it's a thrill to hear this unique voice back at the pinnacle of its form.

SUNDAY 24 JANUARY 1954
Jazz Club USA play in the Palais Des Beaux-Arts, 20 Rue Royale, Brussels, Belgium. The concert is recorded.
BILLIE HOLIDAY (vocal), CARL DRINKARD (p), RED MITCHELL (b), ELAINE LEIGHTON (d), LEONARD FEATHER (mc)
He's Funny That Way / All Of Me / My Man / Them There Eyes / Don't Explain / I Cried For You / Fine And Mellow / What A Little Moonlight Can Do

MONDAY 25 JANUARY 1954
Jazz Club USA play in Frankfurt, Germany. Billie and Leonard Feather miss the bus from Brussels to Frankfurt and have to take a plane.

TUESDAY 26 JANUARY 1954
Jazz Club USA play at US Army Camp Baumholder in Germany.

WEDNESDAY 27 JANUARY 1954
Jazz Club USA play in Munich, Germany.

THURSDAY 28 JANUARY 1954
Jazz Club USA play in Stuttgart, Germany.

FRIDAY 29 JANUARY 1954
Jazz Club USA play in Nuremberg, Germany.

SATURDAY 30 JANUARY 1954
Jazz Club USA have a rest day.

SUNDAY 31 JANUARY 1954
Jazz Club USA play in The Hague, Holland.

MON	**1**
TUES	**2**
WED	**3**
THUR	**4**
FRI	**5**
SAT	**6**
SUN	**7**
MON	**8**
TUES	**9**
WED	**10**
THUR	**11**
FRI	**12**
SAT	**13**
SUN	**14**
MON	**15**
TUES	**16**
WED	**17**
THUR	**18**
FRI	**19**
SAT	**20**
SUN	**21**
MON	**22**
TUES	**23**
WED	**24**
THUR	**25**
FRI	**26**
SAT	**27**
SUN	**28**

MONDAY 1 FEBRUARY 1954

Jazz Club USA play in Paris.

Billie meets up again with Annie Ross, who recalls the time: *'She looked fantastic, wearing a red ski suit, a red hat and her blue mink coat. We set off down the Champs Elysées to do the shopping, but en route Billie decided it would be a good idea to visit all the bars. At that time she was drinking Pernod with a brandy floater. I was well and truly drunk by the end of the marathon but Lady seemed to be absolutely sober. She changed her plans and said she'd like to buy some jewellery; we entered this magnificent store and Billie began looking at tray after tray of brooches and trinkets, but in the end she said she wouldn't be buying anything and out we came. When we settled in the next bar, I started talking about some of the nice things that we had seen. Lady fished her hand in and out of her coat and showed me two gold medallions and a St. Christopher, she said "Thought I'd pick up a little something for my daddy." She had pocketed them right in front of my eyes and the eyes of the assistant – she had money enough in her wallet to pay for them a dozen times over, it was just that she really got a big kick out of lifting something from a very high class establishment.'*

Billie also meets up with Mary Lou Williams in Paris who introduces Billie to Beryl Bryden. Billie visits the Metro Club where Beryl is working. Later, Billie, Mary Lou, Beryl and friends visit the Pied de Cochon restaurant. Billie is dressed in plaid trousers, an expensive sweater and elegant high heels.

TUESDAY 2 FEBRUARY 1954

Jazz Club USA play in Geneva, Switzerland.

WEDNESDAY 3 FEBRUARY 1954

Jazz Club USA play in Zurich, Switzerland.

THURSDAY 4 FEBRUARY 1954

Jazz Club USA's final concert of the tour at the Mustermesse in Basel, Switzerland is recorded.
BILLIE HOLIDAY (vocal), CARL DRINKARD (p), RED MITCHELL (b), ELAINE LEIGHTON (d), LEONARD FEATHER (mc)
Blue Moon / All Of Me / My Man / Them There Eyes / I Cried For You / What A Little Moonlight Can Do / I Cover The Waterfront
BILLIE HOLIDAY (vocal), BUDDY DE FRANCO (cl), RED NORVO (vib), SONNY CLARK (p), BERYL BOOKER (2nd piano solo on *Billie's Blues*), JIMMY RANEY (guitar), RED MITCHELL (b), ELAINE LEIGHTON (d), LEONARD FEATHER (mc)
Billie's Blues / Lover Come Back To Me

FRIDAY 5 FEBRUARY 1954

Billie returns to Paris and sings at the Mars Club where pianist Art Simmons is celebrating his birthday.

SATURDAY 6 FEBRUARY 1954

Billie sings at the Ringside Club. Louis McKay busies himself taking photographs.

SUNDAY 7 FEBRUARY 1954

Beryl Bryden rings Billie in the afternoon to invite her to the Metro Club. Billie compliments Beryl on her singing of *Young Woman's Blues*.

MONDAY 8 FEBRUARY 1954

Billie, with Louis McKay and Carl Drinkard arrive at Heathrow Airport, London on the midday flight from Paris. Max Jones is there to meet her.

Below: Billie at Heathrow Airport with her pianist Carl Drinkard (left) and dancer Taps Miller.

MON	**1**
TUES	**2**
WED	**3**
THUR	**4**
FRI	**5**
SAT	**6**
SUN	**7**
MON	**8**
TUES	**9**
WED	**10**
THUR	**11**
FRI	**12**
SAT	**13**
SUN	**14**
MON	**15**
TUES	**16**
WED	**17**
THUR	**18**
FRI	**19**
SAT	**20**
SUN	**21**
MON	**22**
TUES	**23**
WED	**24**
THUR	**25**
FRI	**26**
SAT	**27**
SUN	**28**

Early in the afternoon there is a press reception at the Piccadilly Hotel, where Billie is staying. The press harp on about dope and such, and Billie is rescued by Max Jones who pointedly asks questions about her music. In the evening, Max and Betty Jones return to the hotel at Billie's invitation with a record player and a pile of Billie's recordings. They spend a happy evening playing music and gossiping.

TUESDAY 9 FEBRUARY 1954

Billie attends the Jazz Record Retailers' Annual Dinner with Max and Betty Jones.

WEDNESDAY 10 FEBRUARY 1954

Down Beat reviews Billie's latest album release:

BILLIE HOLIDAY
Stormy Weather / Lover Come Back To Me / My Man / He's Funny That Way / Yesterdays / Tenderly / I Can't Face The Music / Remember
Rating: *****
All have been issued previously on 78. Like Mr. Granz says "... the time spent here with Billie is what you make it, because there is every possible mood in this album ... Billie is accompanied by Joe Newman, Paul Quinichette, Flip Phillips, Charlie Shavers, Oscar Peterson, Ray Brown, Barney Kessel, J.C. Heard, and Alvin Stoller, and they complement her with an affinity and admiration which is saved only for the great." And for this Holiday-struck listener, there is no one greater. **(Clef LP MGC-144)**

THURSDAY 11 FEBRUARY 1954

Billie tours the London drinking clubs with Max and Betty Jones. First to the Studio Club in Swallow Street where Billie enjoys the piano playing of Alan Clare. Later they move on to the Stork Club where she sings two or three songs with resident pianist Denny Termer.

FRIDAY 12 FEBRUARY 1954

Billie's opening concert is at the Free Trade Hall in Manchester.
BILLIE HOLIDAY (vocal), CARL DRINKARD (p), DON RENDELL, TOMMY WHITTLE, RONNIE ROSS (saxes), DICKIE HAWDON (t), TONY KINSEY (d)
Billie's Blues / All Of Me / Porgy / I Cried For You / Them There Eyes / Blue Moon / My Man / I Only Have Eyes For You / Strange Fruit

SATURDAY 13 FEBRUARY 1954

At midday Billie leaves for Nottingham, where she is to do two shows at the Astoria Ballroom. After a 5 o'clock rehearsal, Billie does two sets of five songs, at 9pm and 10.45pm. She is accompanied by CARL DRINKARD (p), DON SANFORD (g), JIMMY LUKE (b), KEN PYNE (d)
Afterwards, Max & Betty Jones offer Billie and McKay a lift back to their London hotel. The car breaks down repeatedly and they arrive at the Piccadilly Hotel at 5.30am.

Below: Billie enjoying herself in London with new friends, Max and Betty Jones (left) and an unknown dog.

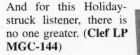

MON **1**
TUES **2**
WED **3**
THUR **4**
FRI **5**
SAT **6**
SUN **7**
MON **8**
TUES **9**
WED **10**
THUR **11**
FRI **12**
SAT **13**
SUN **14**
MON **15**
TUES **16**
WED **17**
THUR **18**
FRI **19**
SAT **20**
SUN **21**
MON **22**
TUES **23**
WED **24**
THUR **25**
FRI **26**
SAT **27**
SUN **28**

SUNDAY 14 FEBRUARY 1954

In the afternoon, Billie rehearses with Jack Parnell's Band for the evening concert at the Royal Albert Hall. Jack Parnell remembered:

> WHEN I WALKED INTO THE REHEARSALS, SHE REALLY LOOKED LIKE A SACK OF OLD CLOTHES SITTING ON A CHAIR. BUT BY THE END OF THE CONCERT IN THE EVENING SHE LOOKED LIKE A GIRL OF EIGHTEEN, IT WAS QUITE UNCANNY! BUT I'M AFRAID THERE WAS AN AWFUL LOT OF JUNK PUSHED IN THERE. SHE WAS VERY FRIENDLY, DOWN TO EARTH, BUT TREMENDOUS SWINGS AND CHANGES OF MOOD. THE ONLY TROUBLE WAS THAT HER AND HER PIANIST GOT SO OUT OF IT WE FOUND IT VERY DIFFICULT TO DO WHAT WE HAD REHEARSED; CERTAINLY SHE WAS QUITE A DIFFERENT PERSON TO THE ONE EARLIER IN THE DAY. BUT TERRIFIC, THERE'S NO DOUBT ABOUT THAT!

Above: Billie and Betty Jones backstage at the Albert Hall.

After the show Billie appears at the Flamingo Club in Wardour Street. Singer Marie Bryant organises an after-hours party at her flat in Victoria, but Billie doesn't turn up.

MONDAY 17 FEBRUARY 1954

Billie and Louis fly to Paris with some friends.

TUESDAY 16 FEBRUARY 1954

Beryl Bryden, back in Paris, hears that Billie is to appear at the Metro Club, but Billie doesn't show.

THURSDAY 18 FEBRUARY 1954

Back in England, Billie goes to a party at a private house with Max & Betty Jones and Beryl Bryden. Afterwards the party moves on to the Studio Club and then to the Stork Club. Louis McKay is again busy with his camera.

FRIDAY 19 FEBRUARY 1954

At 2pm Beryl Bryden visits Billie at the Piccadilly Hotel to help her pack. Billie and Louis take an evening flight back to New York.

At the evening concert at the Royal Albert Hall, Billie sings 15 songs accompanied by Carl Drinkard (p), Kenny Napper (b) and Phil Seamen (d):
I Cover The Waterfront / Them There Eyes / My Man / Blue Moon / I Loves You Porgy / All Of Me / Fine And Mellow / I Only Have Eyes For You / Willow Weep For Me / Too Marvellous For Words / Lover Man / What A Little Moonlight Can Do / Billie's Blues / I Cried For You / Strange Fruit

THE NEW MUSICAL EXPRESS

Friday, February 19, 1954

BILLIE HOLIDAY SINGS "BILLIE'S BLUES" AT THE ALBERT HALL—Special action photos by NME cameraman Harry Hammond.

" Some men like me short and snappy . . ."

" Others like me when I'm happy . . ."

" Some like to call me 'honey' . . ."

" Others think I've got money . . ."

" Some say, 'Billie, baby, you're built for speed !' . . ."

" Put all that together, makes me everything a good man can need !"

THE INCOMPARABLE BILLIE HOLIDAY
Sunday's Royal Albert Hall Concert, reviewed
by MIKE BUTCHER

AS you can well imagine, we of the NME are feeling pleased with ourselves this week ! It was through our initiative that the incomparable Billie Holiday sang in London, on Gerry Mulligan's "Young Blood" that stayed close to the Kenton version and was none the worse for that !

Nothing of great importance happened when Jo Hunter (trumpet) and Max Minshull . . .

A Little Moonlight Can Do." "Lover Man," "Them There Eyes," "I Only Have Eyes For You," "All Of Me."

And on a higher spot among so many highspots there was Miss Holiday's glorious, unique interpretation of George Gershwin's "Porgy."

She sang her own, groovy "Fine And Mellow" and "Billie's Blues," and to cap it all, she told the cruel, bitter lynching song-story of "Strange Fruit," a challenge to humanity which cannot leave any right-thinking man or woman unaffected.

The crowd hung on to her every syllable, to every nuance of Billie's indescribably moving voice. She went to leave the stage three times, but of course, they would not let her go.

In short, Miss Holiday made an impression which will remain in the minds of her London listeners for years to come. Yet in one important respect Billie's Albert Hall con . . . than her . . .

sounded great, and left Billie tremendously impressed.

In London, however, it was impossible for her to use the same group, and the Jack Parnell contingent, which was given the job of backing her had been forced by touring commitments to squeeze the preparatory runs-through into the space of about 100 minutes.

Manchester

Naturally, they seemed somewhat at sea some of the time. Especially in Billie's up-tempo songs, when the tempos lurched a bit . . .

At the Flamingo jazz club, where Miss Holiday sang in a suffocating atmosphere after her Albert Hall presentation, she had Stokes and Kinsey with her again, so all was well.

But please don't think we're being severely critical of Jack's boys. They did their best—and a very good best, too, some of the time—but the odds were against them.

It now merely remains for us to . . . that Michael Black, making . . .

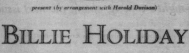

"NEW MUSICAL EXPRESS" LTD.

present (by arrangement with Harold Davison)

BILLIE HOLIDAY

AND

JACK PARNELL & HIS ORCHESTRA
Royal Albert Hall — Sunday, Feb. 14, 1954

Right: Billie enthralls her British audience at Soho's Flamingo Club, after the successful concert at the Royal Albert Hall.

MON	1	THUR	1	SAT	1
TUES	2	FRI	2	SUN	2
WED	3	SAT	3	MON	3
THUR	4	SUN	4	TUES	4
FRI	5	MON	5	WED	5
SAT	6	TUES	6	THUR	6
SUN	7	WED	7	FRI	7
MON	8	THUR	8	SAT	8
TUES	9	FRI	9	SUN	9
WED	10	SAT	10	MON	10
THUR	11	SUN	11	TUES	11
FRI	12	MON	12	WED	12
SAT	13	TUES	13	THUR	13
SUN	14	WED	14	FRI	14
MON	15	THUR	15	SAT	15
TUES	16	FRI	16	SUN	16
WED	17	SAT	17	MON	17
THUR	18	SUN	18	TUES	18
FRI	19	MON	19	WED	19
SAT	20	TUES	20	THUR	20
SUN	21	WED	21	FRI	21
MON	22	THUR	22	SAT	22
TUES	23	FRI	23	SUN	23
WED	24	SAT	24	MON	24
THUR	25	SUN	25	TUES	25
FRI	26	MON	26	WED	26
SAT	27	TUES	27	THUR	27
SUN	28	WED	28	FRI	28
MON	29	THUR	29	SAT	29
TUES	30	FRI	30	SUN	30
WED	31			MON	31

MONDAY 1 MARCH 1954
Billie opens at the Hi-Hat Club in Boston.

SUNDAY 7 MARCH 1954
Billie broadcasts from the Hi-Hat Club in Boston.
BILLIE HOLIDAY (vocal), CARL DRINKARD (p), JIMMY WOODE (b), MARQUIS FOSTER (d), SYMPHONY SID TORIN (mc)
Blue Moon / All Of Me / Tenderly / Them There Eyes / Willow Weep For Me

THURSDAY 25 MARCH 1954
Billie opens at the Club Trinidad in Washington for an eleven day engagement.

SUNDAY 4 APRIL 1954
Billie closes at the Club Trinidad in Washington.

WEDNESDAY 7 APRIL 1954
Billie's 39th birthday

FRIDAY 9 APRIL 1954
Billie appears at Carnegie Hall in New York City in a Charity Lighthouse Concert for the New York Association for the Blind. The concert is organised by Neil Reiser and produced by John Hammond. Also taking part are Gerry Mulligan Quartet, Gene Krupa Trio, Mel Powell, Urbie Green, Buck Clayton, Jerry Vale, Ruby Braff, Tony Scott, Buddy Tate, Jo Jones, Erroll Garner Trio and many others.

WEDNESDAY 14 APRIL 1954
Recording session as Billie Holiday and her Band for Verve at the Fine Sound Studios in New York City. Norman Granz produces the session.
BILLIE HOLIDAY (vocal), CHARLIE SHAVERS (t), OSCAR PETERSON (p), HERB ELLIS (g), RAY BROWN (b), ED SHAUGHNESSY (d)
How Deep Is The Ocean? / What A Little Moonlight Can Do / I Cried For You

The session lasts from 1.00pm to 4pm when Norman Granz cuts it off after only three tracks. Oscar Peterson recalled:
I can't remember what Billie was drinking that day, but she was in bad shape.

WEDNESDAY 5 MAY 1954
Down Beat reviews Billie's latest record release:

> **BILLIE HOLIDAY**
> ***** *If The Moon Turns Green*
> ***** *Autumn in New York*
> Billie is backed by Flip, Shavers, Peterson, Brown, Kessel, and Stoller on the first, and principally Oscar on the second (there's also Ray and what may be brushes). Shaver's solo opening to *Green* is beautifully effective. Both tunes are superior songcraft and they couldn't hope for a more musically penetrating interpreter than Billie when she's in this form. Her *Autumn* is an especially rare listening experience with subtly understanding accompaniment by Oscar. (**Clef 89108**)

WEDNESDAY 19 MAY 1954
Down Beat reports that Billie is being set for a tour of Alaska.

TUES	1	THUR	1
WED	2	FRI	2
THUR	3	SAT	3
FRI	4	SUN	4
SAT	5	MON	5
SUN	6	TUES	6
MON	7	WED	7
TUES	8	THUR	8
WED	9	FRI	9
THUR	10	SAT	10
FRI	11	SUN	11
SAT	12	MON	12
SUN	13	TUES	13
MON	14	WED	14
TUES	15	THUR	15
WED	16	FRI	16
THUR	17	SAT	17
FRI	18	SUN	18
SAT	19	MON	19
SUN	20	TUES	20
MON	21	WED	21
TUES	22	THUR	22
WED	23	FRI	23
THUR	24	SAT	24
FRI	25	SUN	25
SAT	26	MON	26
SUN	27	TUES	27
MON	28	WED	28
TUES	29	THUR	29
WED	30	FRI	30
		SAT	31

WEDNESDAY 2 JUNE 1954

Billie is in the audience at Minton's Playhouse in Harlem. Bill Coleman, concluding a ten-day visit to New York with a tour of the clubs in the company of Oscar Pettiford, recalls the night in his book *Trumpet Story*:

But the surprise of the night was to see Billie sitting among the clientele at Minton's that night. I'd always dug Lady Day from the first time I'd heard her, so it pleased me to hear her once more, in person.

Feud Is Over

Newport, R. I. — The long feud between Billie Holiday and Lester Young ended during the Newport Jazz festival when Lady Day was joined halfway through her set by the Pres.

Billie's early recording scenes were trying to be recreated by having Teddy Wilson on piano and Lester on tenor. The Pres balked because of the feud that started five years ago. Gerry Mulligan lugged his baritone on to the stage and provided some picturesque clusters of sound behind Lady Day. This was enough for Lester.

He shuffled onstage and once again was a part of a Billie presentation. They later embraced in the dressing room, and the feud was over.

Billie at the first Newport Jazz Festival with Teddy Wilson (right), and with Teddy, Dizzy Gillespie and Gerry Mulligan (below).

SUNDAY 18 JULY 1954

Billie is featured on the final night of the Inaugural Newport Jazz Festival at Newport, Rhode Island. The final night of the festival is mc'ed by Stan Kenton and features:

1 A tribute to Count Basie by Basie sidemen
2 Oscar Peterson Trio
3 Johnny Smith with the Oscar Peterson Trio
4 Dizzy Gillespie
5 George Shearing Quintet
6 Gil Melle Quartet
7 Teddy Wilson Group
8 Lennie Tristano and Lee Konitz
9 BILLIE HOLIDAY (vocal), BUCK CLAYTON (t), LESTER YOUNG (ts), GERRY MULLIGAN (bs), VIC DICKENSON (tb), TEDDY WILSON (p), MILT HINTON (b), JO JONES (d)
10 Gene Krupa Trio

Billie's appearance is described in *Down Beat* as

The climax of the concert, it was the most relaxed and subtly compelling performance in many years.

SUN	**1**
MON	**2**
TUES	**3**
WED	**4**
THUR	**5**
FRI	**6**
SAT	**7**
SUN	**8**
MON	**9**
TUES	**10**
WED	**11**
THUR	**12**
FRI	**13**
SAT	**14**
SUN	**15**
MON	**16**
TUES	**17**
WED	**18**
THUR	**19**
FRI	**20**
SAT	**21**
SUN	**22**
MON	**23**
TUES	**24**
WED	**25**
THUR	**26**
FRI	**27**
SAT	**28**
SUN	**29**
MON	**30**
TUES	**31**

MONDAY 9 AUGUST 1954

Billie opens at the Downbeat Club in San Francisco for a two-week engagement backed by the Vernon Alley Trio.

The *San Francisco Chronicle* of Sunday 15 August reports:

> SINGER BILLIE HOLIDAY flew into San Francisco last Monday morning, rushed to the Downbeat Club at 90 Market, lined up three musicians, rehearsed for five hours on a coffee diet, went back to her hotel for an hour of sleep, and then returned to put on four shows before a house that kept crying for more.
>
> This was the same "Lady Day" who two years ago said, "I want to show San Francisco I can be a good girl." This after her name had appeared in the papers in connection with dope addiction, running out on a contract and numerous hassels with bistro managers.
>
> Helen and John Noga, who run the Downbeat, swear by Billie. "I'll take her any day," says Helen, after recalling all the warnings she received about the smoky-voiced singer, who will be appearing for another week.

SUNDAY 22 AUGUST 1954

Billie closes at the Downbeat Club in San Francisco. Memry Midgett, the intermission pianist at the Downbeat, joins Billie as her accompanist.

From San Francisco, Billie and Memry move on to Los Angeles and before the end of the month is working at the Oasis Club.

It is here that Billie is presented with a special *Down Beat* award as **'one of the all-time great vocalists in jazz.'** Billie had never won a *Down Beat* poll so the magazine devised a special award to recognize her talent.

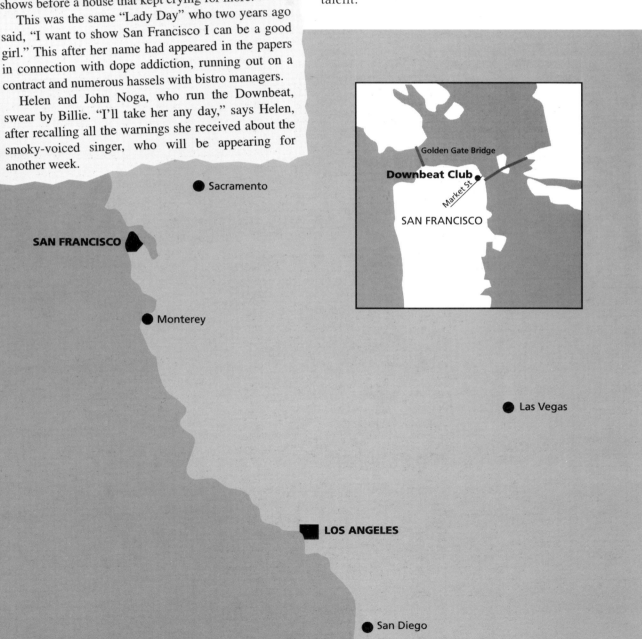

WED	1
THUR	2
FRI	3
SAT	4
SUN	5
MON	6
TUES	7
WED	8
THUR	9
FRI	10
SAT	11
SUN	12
MON	13
TUES	14
WED	15
THUR	16
FRI	17
SAT	18
SUN	19
MON	20
TUES	21
WED	22
THUR	23
FRI	24
SAT	25
SUN	26
MON	27
TUES	28
WED	29
THUR	30

FRIDAY 3 SEPTEMBER 1954

Recording session as Billie Holiday and her Orchestra for Verve at Capitol Studios in Los Angeles. Norman Granz brings in Bobby Tucker for the session.

BILLIE HOLIDAY (vocal), HARRY EDISON (t), WILLIE SMITH (as), BOBBY TUCKER (p), BARNEY KESSEL (g), RED CALLENDER (b), CHICO HAMILTON (d)

Love Me Or Leave Me / P.S. I Love You / Too Marvellous For Words / Softly / I Cried For You / I Thought About You (Billie and Tucker only) / What A Little Moonlight Can Do / Willow Weep For Me / Stormy Blues

18 or 19 SEPTEMBER 1954

Billie closes at the Oasis Club in Los Angeles and flies back to New York.

SATURDAY 25 SEPTEMBER 1954

Billie is part of the new Jazz at the Philharmonic troupe, the Birdland All Stars, which opens its fall tour at Carnegie Hall in New York City. Much of the concert is recorded.

Count Basie Orchestra: *Lullaby Of Birdland / You For Me / Blues Backstage / Perdido*

Charlie Parker: *The Song Is You / My Funny Valentine / Cool Blues*

Count Basie Orchestra: *The Teenager / Two Franks*

BILLIE HOLIDAY (vocal) and the Count Basie Orchestra: THAD JONES, REUNALD JONES, WENDELL CULLEY, JOE NEWMAN (t), BILL HUGHES, HENRY COKER, BENNY POWELL (tb), MARSHALL ROYAL (cl/as), ERNIE WILKINS (as/ts), FRANK WESS (fl/ts), FRANK FOSTER (ts), CHARLIE FOWLKES (bs), MEMRY MIDGETT (p), FREDDIE GREEN (g), EDDIE JONES (b), GUS JOHNSON (d)

All Of Me / Tain't Nobody's Business If I Do / Lover Come Back To Me / My Man / Them There Eyes / Lover Man

Count Basie Orchestra: *Sure Thing*

Count Basie Orchestra with Lester Young: *Pennies From Heaven / Jumpin' At The Woodside / Stompin' At The Savoy*

Sarah Vaughan: *Perdido / S'Wonderful / Easy To Remember / East Of The Sun / How Important Can It Be? / Make Yourself Comfortable / That Old Devil Moon / Polka Dots And Moonbeams / Saturday / Time / Tenderly / Don't Blame Me / Medley: I Ain't Mad At You, Summertime*

Count Basie Orchestra: *Lullaby Of Birdland / One O'Clock Jump*

The Modern Jazz Quartet and the Bill Davis Trio are also on the bill.

Reviewing the concert in *Down Beat*, Hannah Altbush says:

> ... For Miss Holiday, too, it seemed to be somewhat of an off night. Part of the Basie band and her own accompanist backed Billie in excellent arrangements of *Lover, My Man, Lover Man*, and several other songs.

SUNDAY 26 SEPTEMBER 1954

Billie and the Birdland All Stars appear in Boston.

FRI	**1**	MON	**1**	WED	**1**
SAT	**2**	TUES	**2**	THUR	**2**
SUN	**3**	WED	**3**	FRI	**3**
MON	**4**	THUR	**4**	SAT	**4**
TUES	**5**	FRI	**5**	SUN	**5**
WED	**6**	SAT	**6**	MON	**6**
THUR	**7**	SUN	**7**	TUES	**7**
FRI	**8**	MON	**8**	WED	**8**
SAT	**9**	TUES	**9**	THUR	**9**
SUN	**10**	WED	**10**	FRI	**10**
MON	**11**	THUR	**11**	SAT	**11**
TUES	**12**	FRI	**12**	SUN	**12**
WED	**13**	SAT	**13**	MON	**13**
THUR	**14**	SUN	**14**	TUES	**14**
FRI	**15**	MON	**15**	WED	**15**
SAT	**16**	TUES	**16**	THUR	**16**
SUN	**17**	WED	**17**	FRI	**17**
MON	**18**	THUR	**18**	SAT	**18**
TUES	**19**	FRI	**19**	SUN	**19**
WED	**20**	SAT	**20**	MON	**20**
THUR	**21**	SUN	**21**	TUES	**21**
FRI	**22**	MON	**22**	WED	**22**
SAT	**23**	TUES	**23**	THUR	**23**
SUN	**24**	WED	**24**	FRI	**24**
MON	**25**	THUR	**25**	SAT	**25**
TUES	**26**	FRI	**26**	SUN	**26**
WED	**27**	SAT	**27**	MON	**27**
THUR	**28**	SUN	**28**	TUES	**28**
FRI	**29**	MON	**29**	WED	**29**
SAT	**30**	TUES	**30**	THUR	**30**
SUN	**31**			FRI	**31**

WEDNESDAY 6 OCTOBER 1954

Down Beat reports: Billie Holiday is playing dates in Alaska this month.

WEDNESDAY 20 OCTOBER 1954

Down Beat reviews Billie's latest album release:

BILLIE HOLIDAY
Love For Sale / Moonglow / Everything I Have Is Yours / If The Moon Turns Green / Autumn In New York / How Deep Is The Ocean / What A Little Moonlight Can Do / I Cried For You
Rating: ***

Miss Holiday is accompanied on her third Clef LP by Oscar Peterson, Flip Phillips, Charlie Shavers, Barney Kessel, Ray Brown, Alvin Stoller, Herb Ellis, and Ed Shaughnessy. The set is an experience in mounting pleasure that cannot do anything but increase still further no matter how often the LP is replayed. I would underline especially the rocking ease of *Moonglow* and Mr. Peterson's ride on *Moonlight*. It is good, by the way, to have another version of that tune.

As for comparing it with earlier Teddy Wilson-Billie sessions, what's the point? Count your blessings in having both—and that's my general attitude on this bootless business of separating Billie into time periods. Speaking of time, Billie's beat and variations thereon never cease to be among the seven wonders of jazz. **(Clef LP MGC-161)**

NOVEMBER 1954

Billie appears at Storyville in Boston over Thanksgiving, accompanied by Buck Clayton's Band.
She tells the *Down Beat* reviewer that her autobiography is in preparation. Writing the book for her is a *New York Post* reporter, Bill Dufty, who had married Billie's unpaid secretary/friend, Maely Bartholomew.

TUESDAY 30 NOVEMBER 1954

Billie opens at the Metropolitan Theatre, Philadelphia for a one-week engagement.

4 DECEMBER 1954

Billie closes at the Metropolitan Theatre, Philadelphia.

WEDNESDAY 15 DECEMBER 1954

Billie opens at the Rodeo Stage Lounge, 1240 E47th Street in Chicago for the Christmas season.

SAT	**1**	TUES	**1**
SUN	**2**	WED	**2**
MON	**3**	THUR	**3**
TUES	**4**	FRI	**4**
WED	**5**	SAT	**5**
THUR	**6**	SUN	**6**
FRI	**7**	MON	**7**
SAT	**8**	TUES	**8**
SUN	**9**	WED	**9**
MON	**10**	THUR	**10**
TUES	**11**	FRI	**11**
WED	**12**	SAT	**12**
THUR	**13**	SUN	**13**
FRI	**14**	MON	**14**
SAT	**15**	TUES	**15**
SUN	**16**	WED	**16**
MON	**17**	THUR	**17**
TUES	**18**	FRI	**18**
WED	**19**	SAT	**19**
THUR	**20**	SUN	**20**
FRI	**21**	MON	**21**
SAT	**22**	TUES	**22**
SUN	**23**	WED	**23**
MON	**24**	THUR	**24**
TUES	**25**	FRI	**25**
WED	**26**	SAT	**26**
THUR	**27**	SUN	**27**
FRI	**28**	MON	**28**
SAT	**29**		
SUN	**30**		
MON	**31**		

SUNDAY 2 JANUARY 1955

Billie closes at the Rodeo Stage Lounge.

WEDNESDAY 12 JANUARY 1955

Billie writes to Tallulah Bankhead after Bankhead makes it known that she will sue if she is mentioned in Billie's autobiography:

Dear Miss Bankhead:

I thought I was a friend of yours. That's why there was nothing in my book that was unfriendly to you, unkind or libelous. Because I didn't want to drag you I tried six times last month to talk to you on the damn phone, and tell you about the book just as a matter of courtesy. That bitch you have who impersonates you kept telling me to call back and when I did it was the same deal until I gave up.

But while I was working out of town, you didn't mind talking to Doubleday and suggesting behind my damn back that I had flipped and/or made up those little mentions of you in my book.

Baby, Cliff Allan and Billy Heywood are still around. My maid who was with me at the Strand isn't dead either. There are plenty of others around who remember how you carried on so you almost got me fired out of the place. And if you want to get shitty, we can make it a big shitty party. We can all get funky together.

I don't know whether you've got one of those damn lawyers telling you what to do or not. But I'm writing this to give you a chance to answer back quick and apologize to me and to Doubleday. Read my book over again. I understand they sent you a duplicate manuscript. There's nothing in it to hurt you. If you think so, let's talk about it like I wanted to last month. It's going to press right now so there is no time for monkeying around.

Straighten up and fly right, Banky. Nobody's trying to drag you.

TUESDAY 8 FEBRUARY 1955

Billie appears on the Steve Allen Tonight Show on NBC Television, broadcast between 11.30pm and 1.00am. Billie is accompanied by Carl Drinkard on piano and the house band directed by Skitch Henderson.
My Man / Them There Eyes / Lover Man

MONDAY 14 FEBRUARY 1955

Recording session for Verve at the Fine Sound Studios in New York City. The session is arranged and produced by Leroy Lovett.
BILLIE HOLIDAY (vocal), CHARLIE SHAVERS (t), TONY SCOTT (cl), BUDD JOHNSON (ts), CARL DRINKARD, BILLY TAYLOR (p), BILLY BAUER (g), LEONARD GASKIN (b), COZY COLE (d)
Say It Isn't So / I've Got My Love To Keep Me Warm / I Wished On The Moon / Always / Everything Happens To Me / Do Nothing Till You Hear From Me / Ain't Misbehavin'

During the session a row breaks out between Carl Drinkard and Leonard Gaskin. Billie gets involved and she fires Drinkard on the spot. Billy Taylor takes over the rest of the session.

Holiday Waxes

New York—After a long period away from the recording studios, Billie Holiday cut four sides in a six-hour session one night recently. She was backed by Tony Scott, Charlie Shavers, Budd Johnson, Leonard Gaskin, Billy Bauer, Cozy Cole, and Billy Taylor. Arrangements were by Scott, Buster Harding and Leroy Lovett, who directed the date. Among the tunes cut were *Always* and *Do Nothing Till You Hear from Me.*

TUES	**1**	FRI	**1**	SUN	**1**
WED	**2**	SAT	**2**	MON	**2**
THUR	**3**	SUN	**3**	TUES	**3**
FRI	**4**	MON	**4**	WED	**4**
SAT	**5**	TUES	**5**	THUR	**5**
SUN	**6**	WED	**6**	FRI	**6**
MON	**7**	THUR	**7**	SAT	**7**
TUES	**8**	FRI	**8**	SUN	**8**
WED	**9**	SAT	**9**	MON	**9**
THUR	**10**	SUN	**10**	TUES	**10**
FRI	**11**	MON	**11**	WED	**11**
SAT	**12**	TUES	**12**	THUR	**12**
SUN	**13**	WED	**13**	FRI	**13**
MON	**14**	THUR	**14**	SAT	**14**
TUES	**15**	FRI	**15**	SUN	**15**
WED	**16**	SAT	**16**	MON	**16**
THUR	**17**	SUN	**17**	TUES	**17**
FRI	**18**	MON	**18**	WED	**18**
SAT	**19**	TUES	**19**	THUR	**19**
SUN	**20**	WED	**20**	FRI	**20**
MON	**21**	THUR	**21**	SAT	**21**
TUES	**22**	FRI	**22**	SUN	**22**
WED	**23**	SAT	**23**	MON	**23**
THUR	**24**	SUN	**24**	TUES	**24**
FRI	**25**	MON	**25**	WED	**25**
SAT	**26**	TUES	**26**	THUR	**26**
SUN	**27**	WED	**27**	FRI	**27**
MON	**28**	THUR	**28**	SAT	**28**
TUES	**29**	FRI	**29**	SUN	**29**
WED	**30**	SAT	**30**	MON	**30**
THUR	**31**			TUES	**31**

SATURDAY 12 MARCH 1955
Charlie Parker dies.

SATURDAY 2 APRIL 1955
Billie appears at a benefit concert for Charlie Parker at Carnegie Hall. The concert runs from midnight to 4am and features Sarah Vaughan, Dinah Washington, Pearl Bailey, Lester Young, Billy Eckstine, Herb Jeffries, Sammy Davis Jr, Mary Lou Williams, Hazel Scott, Lennie Tristano, Stan Getz, Charlie Shavers, Thelonious Monk, Gerry Mulligan and Baby Lawrence. Leonard Feather, Jazzbo Collins and Barry Ulanov are masters of ceremonies. Billie has the honour of closing the show.

THURSDAY 7 APRIL 1955
Billie's 40th birthday.

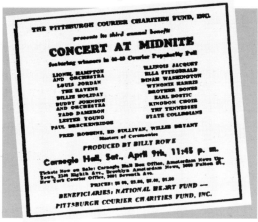

SATURDAY 9 APRIL 1955
Billie appears at the 3rd Annual Benefit Concert for Pittsburgh Courier Charities Fund in Concert at Midnite at Carnegie Hall. Also appearing are the Lionel Hampton Band, Louis Jordan, The Ravens, Buddy Johnson Orchestra, Tadd Dameron, Lester Young, Paul Breckenridge, Illinois Jacquet, Ella Fitzgerald, Dinah Washington. Wynonie Harris, Brother Bones, Earl Bostic, Kingdom Choir and The Tennessee State Collegians.

MONDAY 25 APRIL 1955
Billie opens at Pep's in Philadelphia with Milt Buckner's Band for a one-week engagement.

SATURDAY 30 APRIL 1955
Billie closes at Pep's in Philadelphia.

WEDNESDAY 4 MAY 1955
Down Beat gives Billie's new album 5 stars.

FRIDAY 6 MAY 1955
Billie appears at the Lighthouse Jazz & Variety Concert for the New York Association for the Blind at Carnegie Hall. The concert is split into two parts – the 'Variety Hour' and a 'Spirituals to Jazz' Hour. The jazz part of the show features Billie, Count Basie Orchestra, Buddy Rich, Clifford Brown & Max Roach, Sister Rosetta Tharpe & Marie Knight, Lester Young and Alex Kallao. Part of the concert is recorded by Norman Granz:

Count Basie Orchestra: *Blee Blop Blues / Basie English / Soft Drink / Flute Juice / April In Paris / Oh! Lady Be Good / Fancy Meeting You*

Billie Holiday (vocal), Buck Clayton (t), Lester Young (ts), Count Basie (org), Bobby Tucker (p), Eddie Jones (b), Buddy Rich (d) *Stormy Weather*

WED	**1**	FRI	**1**
THUR	**2**	SAT	**2**
FRI	**3**	SUN	**3**
SAT	**4**	MON	**4**
SUN	**5**	TUES	**5**
MON	**6**	WED	**6**
TUES	**7**	THUR	**7**
WED	**8**	FRI	**8**
THUR	**9**	SAT	**9**
FRI	**10**	SUN	**10**
SAT	**11**	MON	**11**
SUN	**12**	TUES	**12**
MON	**13**	WED	**13**
TUES	**14**	THUR	**14**
WED	**15**	FRI	**15**
THUR	**16**	SAT	**16**
FRI	**17**	SUN	**17**
SAT	**18**	MON	**18**
SUN	**19**	TUES	**19**
MON	**20**	WED	**20**
TUES	**21**	THUR	**21**
WED	**22**	FRI	**22**
THUR	**23**	SAT	**23**
FRI	**24**	SUN	**24**
SAT	**25**	MON	**25**
SUN	**26**	TUES	**26**
MON	**27**	WED	**27**
TUES	**28**	THUR	**28**
WED	**29**	FRI	**29**
THUR	**30**	SAT	**30**
		SUN	**31**

WEDNESDAY 1 JUNE 1955
Billie opens at the Vanity Fair in Miami for a 3-night engagement.

FRIDAY 3 JUNE 1955
Billie closes at the Vanity Fair in Miami.

Billie claims to have lost her passport somewhere during the flight from Miami to Boston.

MONDAY 6 JUNE 1955
Billie opens at the Hi-Hat Club in Boston for a one-week engagement.

SUNDAY 12 JUNE 1955
Billie closes at the Hi-Hat in Boston.

WEDNESDAY 29 JUNE 1955
Down Beat reviews Billie's new single:

> **BILLIE HOLIDAY**
> ***** **Willow, Weep for Me**
> ***** **Stormy Blues**
> Billie still can cut all the jazz singers in the world in depth of emotion—when she feels it. And she did when she made these two sides on the coast in September of last year. Her superb yet unobtrusive accompaniment is by Harry Edison, Willie Smith, Bobby Tucker, Barney Kessel, Red Callender, and Chico Hamilton. The best side is Billie's own blues with fine commentary by Edison and an apt blues intro by Smith. Good recording quality. This kind of coupling could bring back 78s in jazz. (**Clef 89141**)

MONDAY 19 JULY 1955
Jeff Kruger, a London agent, writes to Billie via Bill Dufty offering her work in Great Britain.

FRIDAY 23 JULY 1955
Bill Dufty replies to Kruger on Billie's behalf, asking for more details.

MONDAY 26 JULY 1955
Jeff Kruger writes again:

Dear Billie,

Further to my letter dated 19th July written to you by hand from Paris, I have fixed the following dates which are definite and just await your confirmation that you will be arriving so that I can sign same and finalise all deals.

Please treat this matter as urgent and I must hear from you by return of post giving me confirmation to go ahead and finalise contracts and to issue same for your signature and confirm that commission will be payable to this office and forward publicity material immediately.

The minimum figures you will get for any one week in Europe will be 500$ clear, and that is only at this stage, and I can certainly fill in many more dates but at least this guarantees you work week ending August 21st right through to the middle of October, so this should make your trip worthwhile.

Please do not let me down and I look forward to seeing you middle of August.

Week ending August 21st – Belgium.
Week ending August 28th – France.
Week ending September 4th – England.
Week ending September 11th – England.
Week ending September 18th, 25th, October 2nd and 9th – Paris.

Don't forget to wire or phone me immediately upon receipt of this letter.
Kindest regards.
Yours sincerely,
KRUGER ENTERPRISES (LONDON) LTD:
JEFFREY S. KRUGER.

WEDNESDAY 28 JULY 1955
Jeff Kruger cables Billie:
ARRIVE LONDON BY AUGUST 17 7 WEEKS WORK GUARANTEED MINIMUM 550 DOLLARS PLUS WEEK LETTER SENT 26TH CONFIRM ACCEPTANCE WRITING IMMEDIATELY
=JEFF KRUGER=

SATURDAY 31 JULY 1955
Bill Dufty writes to Kruger on Billie's behalf:
Dear Jeffrey:

I have your letter of July 26 and I am replying immediately to say I am still confused.

The dates you have marked off as definite seem mighty indefinite to me. You mention the country but what else, whether it is clubs, concerts, one nighters, you don't seem to specify?

And your mention of the figure of "$500 a week clear" as a minimum baffles me, too. Clear of what? Commission, travel, or what?

I am sure you understand, for instance, that unless I misunderstand and your letter means clear of transportation, it would take the five weeks of bookings you have mentioned just to clear transportation for myself and an accompanist.

That's why I am confused.

I'm still anxious to come but I'm sure you'll understand I need this pinned down somewhat more definitely before I can commit myself.

Love,
Billie Holiday

MON	**1**
TUES	**2**
WED	**3**
THUR	**4**
FRI	**5**
SAT	**6**
SUN	**7**
MON	**8**
TUES	**9**
WED	**10**
THUR	**11**
FRI	**12**
SAT	**13**
SUN	**14**
MON	**15**
TUES	**16**
WED	**17**
THUR	**18**
FRI	**19**
SAT	**20**
SUN	**21**
MON	**22**
TUES	**23**
WED	**24**
THUR	**25**
FRI	**26**
SAT	**27**
SUN	**28**
MON	**29**
TUES	**30**
WED	**31**

FRIDAY 5 AUGUST 1955
Jeff Kruger cables Billie:

> WHATS HOLDING UP CONFIRMATION TOUR
> FIXED COMMENCE NOW SEPTEMBER 1ST YOU
> MUST CONTACT ME DATES ALREADY
> PUBLICISED PLEASE DONT LET ME DOWN
> JEFF KRUGER

Bill Dufty cables a reply on Billie's behalf:

> THANKS TROUBLE BUT DETAILS TOUR UTTERLY
> UNACCEPTABLE AS OUTLINED COMPELLED
> OTHER ARRANGEMENTS REGRETS
> REGARDS BILLIE HOLIDAY

SUNDAY 7 AUGUST 1955
Bill Dufty writes to Billie outlining the negotiations with Kruger, concluding:
This is for your information in case you talk to him on the phone. I'm keeping the originals instead of sending to you just to make sure nothing gets lost of your answers.

AUGUST 1955
Billie opens at the Crescendo Club on Sunset Strip in Hollywood for a two-week engagement.
She is photographed at the club with Julie London and Walter Winchell.
Between sets she calls at the Garden of Allah where Jess Stacy is playing piano.

WEDNESDAY 17 AUGUST 1955
Billie writes to William Dufty from the Alta Cienega Motel in Los Angeles, complaining of how Joe Glaser had lost her a $5400 appearance on the Steve Allen TV show.

FRIDAY 19 AUGUST 1955
Billie appears at a Hollywood Bowl Concert before rushing back to sing her sets at the Crescendo.
Also appearing on the concert are Dave Brubeck, Buddy De Franco, Andre Previn, Shelly Manne and Shorty Rogers' Giants.

Billie Holiday, an added starter on Leonard Bernstein's jazz symposium at Hollywood Bowl, doubled with her first Sunset Strip stand with a run at the Crescendo.

MON	**1**
TUES	**2**
WED	**3**
THUR	**4**
FRI	**5**
SAT	**6**
SUN	**7**
MON	**8**
TUES	**9**
WED	**10**
THUR	**11**
FRI	**12**
SAT	**13**
SUN	**14**
MON	**15**
TUES	**16**
WED	**17**
THUR	**18**
FRI	**19**
SAT	**20**
SUN	**21**
MON	**22**
TUES	**23**
WED	**24**
THUR	**25**
FRI	**26**
SAT	**27**
SUN	**28**
MON	**29**
TUES	**30**
WED	**31**

MONDAY 22 AUGUST 1955

Billie rehearses for her Norman Granz recording sessions with pianist Jimmy Rowles at the home of Artie Shapiro. Artie Shapiro records the rehearsal:
BILLIE HOLIDAY (vocal), JIMMY ROWLES (p), ARTIE SHAPIRO (b)
Nice Work If You Can Get It / Discussion: Nice Work If You Can Get It / Mandy Is Two / Prelude To A Kiss / I Must Have That Man / Jeepers Creepers / Jeepers Creepers / Discussion: Jeepers Creepers / Discussion: Jeepers Creepers / Please Don't Talk About Me When I'm Gone / Please Don't Talk About Me When I'm Gone / Discussion: Moonlight In Vermont / Misery / Restless / Moonlight In Vermont / Everything Happens To Me / Discussion / I Don't Want To Cry Anymore / I Don't Want To Cry Anymore / Discussion: I Don't Want To Cry Anymore / Everything Happens To Me / Discussion / When You Are Away, Dear / Discussion / It Had To Be You / The Mood That I'm In / Gone With The Wind / I Got It Bad And That Ain't Good / Discussion / A Sunbonnet Blue /A Ghost Of A Chance / Discussion / I'm Walking Through Heaven With You / Discussion / Just Friends / The Nearness Of You / Discussion / It's Too Hot For Words /They Say / I Won't Believe It
The rehearsal lasts for about an hour and a half.

TUESDAY 23 AUGUST 1955

Recording session for Norman Granz at the Radio Recorders Studios in Los Angeles.
BILLIE HOLIDAY (vocal), HARRY EDISON (t), BENNY CARTER (as), JIMMY ROWLES (p), BARNEY KESSEL (g), JOHN SIMMONS (b), LARRY BUNKER (d)
I Don't Want To Cry Anymore (false start) / I Don't Want To Cry Anymore / Prelude To A Kiss (false start) / Prelude To A Kiss (breakdown) / Prelude To A Kiss / A Ghost Of A Chance / When Your Lover Has Gone (breakdown) / When Your Lover Has Gone (breakdown) / When Your Lover Has Gone / Gone With The Wind / Please Don't Talk About Me When I'm Gone / It Had To Be You / Nice Work If You Can Get It

THURSDAY 25 AUGUST 1955

Recording session for Norman Granz at the Radio Recorders Studios in Los Angeles.
BILLIE HOLIDAY (vocal), HARRY EDISON (t), BENNY CARTER (as), JIMMY ROWLES (p/celeste), BARNEY KESSEL (g), JOHN SIMMONS (b), LARRY BUNKER (d)
Come Rain Or Come Shine / I Gotta Right To Sing The Blues / What's New / A Fine Romance (breakdown) / A Fine Romance / A Fine Romance (false start) / A Fine Romance (breakdown) / A Fine Romance (breakdown) / A Fine Romance (false start) / A Fine Romance (breakdown) / A Fine Romance / I Hadn't Anyone 'Till You / I Get A Kick Out Of You / Everything I Have Is Yours / Isn't This A Lovely Day

THUR	1
FRI	2
SAT	3
SUN	4
MON	5
TUES	6
WED	7
THUR	8
FRI	9
SAT	10
SUN	11
MON	12
TUES	13
WED	14
THUR	15
FRI	16
SAT	17
SUN	18
MON	19
TUES	20
WED	21
THUR	22
FRI	23
SAT	24
SUN	25
MON	26
TUES	27
WED	28
THUR	29
FRI	30

WEDNESDAY 7 SEPTEMBER 1955
The Passport Office of the Department of State write to Billie acknowledging her reporting the loss of her passport.

THURSDAY 15 SEPTEMBER 1955
A letter is sent on Billie's behalf to the Passport Office:

Gentlemen:

I have your letter of September 7, with reference to my notification of your office on the loss of my passport.

I am happy to inform you that after I had executed an affidavit on the circumstances, and made enquiries at each spot which I had covered on my recent tour, my passport was happily found and returned to me.

I want to thank you for your consideration in this matter and so inform you of its recovery.

Cordially,

Eleanor Gough McKay
Billie Holiday
160-15 76th Avenue
Flushing Heights
Long Island, New York

FRIDAY 16 SEPTEMBER 1955
Billie opens at the Apollo Theatre in Harlem for a one-week engagement in the revue 'Atlantic City Follies'. Also on the bill are Jimmy Tyler & his Band, The Five Encores, Slappy White, The Fouche Dancers, The Wallace Brothers, Candido, Hortense Allen & her Dancing Boys and Girls and Gorgeous Models.

WEDNESDAY 21 SEPTEMBER 1955
The Amateur Hour at the Apollo is broadcast via station WMCA.

THURSDAY 22 SEPTEMBER 1955
Billie closes at the Apollo Theatre.

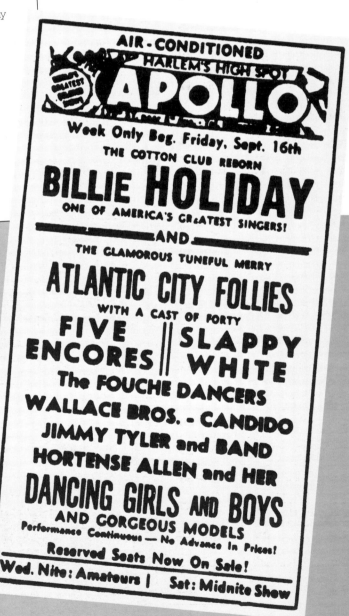

SAT	**1**	TUES	**1**	THUR	**1**
SUN	**2**	WED	**2**	FRI	**2**
MON	**3**	THUR	**3**	SAT	**3**
TUES	**4**	FRI	**4**	SUN	**4**
WED	**5**	SAT	**5**	MON	**5**
THUR	**6**	SUN	**6**	TUES	**6**
FRI	**7**	MON	**7**	WED	**7**
SAT	**8**	TUES	**8**	THUR	**8**
SUN	**9**	WED	**9**	FRI	**9**
MON	**10**	THUR	**10**	SAT	**10**
TUES	**11**	FRI	**11**	SUN	**11**
WED	**12**	SAT	**12**	MON	**12**
THUR	**13**	SUN	**13**	TUES	**13**
FRI	**14**	MON	**14**	WED	**14**
SAT	**15**	TUES	**15**	THUR	**15**
SUN	**16**	WED	**16**	FRI	**16**
MON	**17**	THUR	**17**	SAT	**17**
TUES	**18**	FRI	**18**	SUN	**18**
WED	**19**	SAT	**19**	MON	**19**
THUR	**20**	SUN	**20**	TUES	**20**
FRI	**21**	MON	**21**	WED	**21**
SAT	**22**	TUES	**22**	THUR	**22**
SUN	**23**	WED	**23**	FRI	**23**
MON	**24**	THUR	**24**	SAT	**24**
TUES	**25**	FRI	**25**	SUN	**25**
WED	**26**	SAT	**26**	MON	**26**
THUR	**27**	SUN	**27**	TUES	**27**
FRI	**28**	MON	**28**	WED	**28**
SAT	**29**	TUES	**29**	THUR	**29**
SUN	**30**	WED	**30**	FRI	**30**
MON	**31**			SAT	**31**

OCTOBER 1955
Billie is in Philadelphia at the beginning of October.

WEDNESDAY 5 OCTOBER 1955
Billie appears in Atlanta, Georgia as part of a tour that takes her to the end of the year. During the tour she visits New Orleans, the Regal Theatre in Chicago, the Howard Theatre in Washington and Las Vegas

19 NOVEMBER 1955
Billie writes to Reverend Norman O'Connor:
'My new album for Granz is out and it's called 'Music for Torchin' ... Who knows it may get a good review from Deadbeat. If it does I hope you'll like it anyway.
My book is about to go to the printers. We are still haggling over a couple of places where I want to libel a couple of people and the Publishers and Lawyers think I'd better not. We may have to go to arbitration.'

WEDNESDAY 30 NOVEMBER 1955
Down Beat duly reviews *Music for Torchin'* and gives it the maximum five stars:

BILLIE HOLIDAY
It Had to be You / Come Rain or Come Shine / I Don't Want to Cry Anymore / Ghost of a Chance / A Fine Romance / Gone With the Wind / I Get a Kick Out of You / Isn't It a Lovely Day
Rating: *****
Music for Torchin' was recorded on the west coast in August of this year with the tasteful, relaxed backing of Benny Carter, Harry Edison, Jimmy Rowles, Larry Bunker, John Simmons, and Barney Kessel.

As for the singing, I suppose that the nostalgics will repeat automatically that this isn't the Billie of 15 and 20 years ago. Of course it isn't. Nobody stays the same, least of all in the art of self-expression. This is a Billie who has experienced a lot of pain and some joy in the years between and a Billie whose life-perspective has changed, as does everyone's, with increasing years. She sings more reflectively and less hopefully but with no less depth and warmth. When she's right—and she's absorbingly right on these sides—no one yet is able to touch Billie as the most emotionally striking singer in jazz, 20 years ago or today. Totally recommended.
(Clef 12" LP MGC-669)

SUN	1	WED	1
MON	2	THUR	2
TUES	3	FRI	3
WED	4	SAT	4
THUR	5	SUN	5
FRI	6	MON	6
SAT	7	TUES	7
SUN	8	WED	8
MON	9	THUR	9
TUES	10	FRI	10
WED	11	SAT	11
THUR	12	SUN	12
FRI	13	MON	13
SAT	14	TUES	14
SUN	15	WED	15
MON	16	THUR	16
TUES	17	FRI	17
WED	18	SAT	18
THUR	19	SUN	19
FRI	20	MON	20
SAT	21	TUES	21
SUN	22	WED	22
MON	23	THUR	23
TUES	24	FRI	24
WED	25	SAT	25
THUR	26	SUN	26
FRI	27	MON	27
SAT	28	TUES	28
SUN	29	WED	29
MON	30		
TUES	31		

FRIDAY 10 FEBRUARY 1956

Billie appears on the Steve Allen Tonight Show, a NBC TV show broadcast from New York between 11.30pm and 1.00am. Billie is accompanied by the Skitch Henderson Orchestra with Corky Hale on piano. Between singing *Please Don't Talk About Me When I'm Gone* and *Ghost Of A Chance,* she is interviewed by Steve Allen.

MONDAY 13 FEBRUARY 1956

Billie opens at the Club Pablo in Washington for a one-week engagement with Corky Hale on piano.

WEDNESDAY 15 FEBRUARY 1956

Billie is interviewed by Willis Conover for Voice of America from the VoA studios in Washington:

Conover: Billie Holiday, about whom at least one critic has said, "If you want to know what jazz is about, listen to Billie Holiday." She's been named by more jazz fans and by more musicians, more consistently and for the longest time, as the greatest jazz singer. Stylistically, from Billie Holiday came Anita O'Day and then June Christy and Chris Connor.
I'd like to ask Billie: From whom did Billie Holiday's voice come?

Holiday: I think I copied my style from Louis Armstrong. Because – I always liked the big volume and the big sound that Bessie Smith got when she sang. But – uh – when I was quite young I heard a record Louis Armstrong made called *The West End Blues*, and – he doesn't say any words, you know? – and I thought, "This is wonderful," you know? And I liked the feeling he got from it. So I wanted Louis Armstrong's feeling and I wanted the big volume that Bessie Smith got. But I found it didn't work with me, because I didn't have a big voice, you know? So, anyway, between the two of 'em, I sort of *[smiling]* got Billie Holiday.

Conover: That's very interesting – that the source of so much instrumental music was also the source of such great vocal music as yours: Louis Armstrong. What other musicians have had some sort of influence upon the development of your singing style?

Holiday: Well, I like Lester Young. I always liked – uh – well, Lester came much later in my life, but I liked Lester's feeling. You know, everyone, when he first started, thought: This man, his *tone*, is too *thin*, you know? A tenor sax, y'know. Everybody thinks it has to be real big; and Lester used to go out of his mind getting reeds, you know, to sound *big* like Chu Berry, and – he was very popular in those days – and I told him, "It doesn't *matter*, because," I said, "you have a *beautiful* tone," I says, "and *you watch*. After a while *every*body's going to be *copy*ing you." And it came to *be*, you know?

And then, uh – well, I made my first record with Benny. And … Benny came to a little club in Harlem, to hear me – the Log Cabin. At that time he was not "Benny Goodman," he was just another musician. *[Laughs]* He worked in a *studio* band, and – down at NBC – and he came up one night and he just thought I was wonderful. So he had a recording date under his own name, and John Hammond – you must have heard of him; he's a music critic. And they thought I was *it*, for the vocalist. And the funniest thing – *[Laughs]* I got there and I was afraid to sing in the mike. Because I never saw a microphone before. And I says, "Why do I have to sing in *that* thing? Why can't I just sing like I do at the club? I was scared to death of it. And, uh, Buck and Bubbles – Buck played the piano on that date. Can you imagine – all those *studio* men and Buck, he can't read a note, *[laughing]* he played the piano! Well, that's the way Benny *is*, he likes *music*. You don't have to read, or write, or *any*thing, you just *play* it, *you* know? So Buck says, "You're not going to let these people think you're a *square*, are you?" He says, "Come *on*, *sing* it!" And I sang. *Your Mother's Son-in-Law*, and on the other side was *Riffin' the Scotch.*

Conover: Let's see, you were fifteen years old then, weren't you?

Holiday: No, I was *four*teen. *[Laughs]*

Conover: I beg your pardon. Well, which of your records, Billie, give you more pleasure today – or perhaps I should rephrase that: What different kinds of pleasure do you get from the earlier recordings *and* from the more recent records that you've made?

Holiday: Well, I get a big bang out of *Your Mother's Son-in-Law*. It sounds like I'm doing *comedy! [Laughing]* My voice sounded so funny and high – on there; and I sounded like I'm about three years old! To me, anyhow. But, uh – I don't like any of my records, to be truthful with you. Because it's always something that you *should* have done; or you should have waited *here*; or you should have held that note *longer*; or you should have phrased – well, *you* know how it is. So you're never really satisfied with your records. But the things that I like *most* – I think the things I've done with strings. Or the ones – the real *blues* ones, you know, like *Summertime*. Y'know the ones with no music at all, you know, where we just relaxed? Like the things we did with Teddy Wilson and then Benny and Roy Eldrige. We had – I was with Count Basie's band at the time, and we had been on the road – about three months, doing one-nighters; you know, and that's pretty rough. And we had *no* time to rehearse or anything, and we walked right in the studio – no *music*, and we made six great sides, you know. Those are the kind I like.

Conover: Billie, you've recorded so many songs … Which of the songs that you have recorded did you compose yourself?

Holiday: Oh, I did *Billie's Blues* and *Fine and Mellow*, and, uh –. Oh, let me tell you how I did *Fine and Mellow*. I was working in the Café Society, downtown in the Village; and we get up there to make these records and all of a sudden we needed one more side. So I says, "*I* know. Let's do a blues, and let's make the

WED	**1**
THUR	**2**
FRI	**3**
SAT	**4**
SUN	**5**
MON	**6**
TUES	**7**
WED	**8**
THUR	**9**
FRI	**10**
SAT	**11**
SUN	**12**
MON	**13**
TUES	**14**
WED	**15**
THUR	**16**
FRI	**17**
SAT	**18**
SUN	**19**
MON	**20**
TUES	**21**
WED	**22**
THUR	**23**
FRI	**24**
SAT	**25**
SUN	**26**
MON	**27**
TUES	**28**
WED	**29**

introduction like an organ grinder; you know *[sings]* dah-dah, *dah*-dah, dah."You know. And, uh – *right* there I made it all up. Right in the studio.

And I did *Don't Explain* and oh, what else? A few more, I can't think of 'em *[laughs]*.

But *Don't Explain* had, uh – I did that with a fellow named Razaf, and he helped me with the lyrics. But, gee, I was – I'm very proud of that because I think it's a pretty tune, and as a rule I can only write *blues*, you know. So I thought *Don't Explain* was the end for me *[laughs modestly]*.

Oh – and I did *God Bless the Child* … don't let me forget that one, because I wrote that one for my mother. And how it came *about*, I asked Mother for some money. And she flatly *refused* me. So I said, "That's all right. God bless the child that's got his own!" I walked out, y'know, and, uh – it sort of stuck in my mind. And my piano player and I were foolin' around the next day; I says, "You know, that's a good title for a song." I says, "Maybe we'll have to make it kind of *religious*." So he says, *"No-o-o!"* So we – I write out the words and we get the melody and we wrote the *song. [Laughs]* So I carried it to Marks –the publishing? – he thought it was wonderful, and right away he published it.

So that's how we got *God Bless the Child*.

Conover: Are these your favourite records, of those you've made, Billie?

Holiday: No-o-o …! *[Laughs]* No. Uh, the things – uh, like I told you – the things that I made that *I* like never got popular. Like *Deep Song*? You probably never heard of it. *[Laughing]* It's a Decca. *It* never got popular … *You're My Thrill* – I think it's got a beautiful background, the strings, and the oboe, and – it never got popular …

Like Benny Goodman always says, uh – like this *Some Other Spring* I did. This song, nothing ever happened to it; and it's the most beautiful thing I ever heard in my life. Teddy Wilson – Irene Wilson, his wife, wrote it. And, uh – she got inspired when, the night we were all playing up there, Benny Webster and Benny Carter and myself and John Kirby-the-bass-player? We were at her apartment having a jam session there, and she had made some red beans and rice that night. *[Laughs]* And we were just sittin' around playing, and she got inspired and wrote the tune – but like Benny *says*: *"That's* not gonna – nothing's gonna happen with the tune: it's too *beautiful!"* And he just didn't make sense to us, y'know; but he was right. He says, "Maybe in years to *come*."

Now, for instance, like *Yesterdays* – that's a tune that I recorded, and I *loved* it. But Benny was right, because, uh – well, what was the show? *Roberta*? It came from *Roberta*, I think. But anyway, *I Only Have Eyes For You*, that was popular – all the other tunes. *Yesterdays*, the most beautiful song *in* the show, is just starting to get popular *now*! So, maybe Benny was right.

Conover: What other songs that you *haven't* recorded would you like to record some day, Billie?

Holiday: Well, I don't know, I, uh –. I tell you a song I'd like to sing, and it doesn't have any lyrics to it, I don't think, and that's *Our Waltz* – David Rose. *You* know, things like that. Something nobody else does.

Conover: Well, let's get away from the musical end of Billie Holiday for just a second, and ask how the name Lady Day came about?

Holiday: Well, now, that came about when Lester and I were in Count Basie's band, and Lester named me

Lady Day, and he named my mother, The Duchess, and there was Count Basie, so we were the Royal Family. *[Laughs]*

Conover: I see. Well, how did the gardenia in the Billie Holiday hairdo become Billie's trademark?

Holiday: Well, I've always loved gardenias. And one night I got *very, very* – how would you say it? … well, I guess … uh, uh … well, *I* don't know, there's a word for it. Anyway, I just wouldn't go on. I couldn't go on. I couldn't sing without my gardenia. *[Laughs]* So, it became a trademark; and I just thought I couldn't sing if I didn't have a gardenia in my hair.

And they had to be *fresh. [Laughs]*

Conover: You're no longer wearing the gardenia, these days, though.

Holiday: Well, no, I, uh, got over that. It was just a childish thing.

Conover: Lady Day. Billie Holiday, our in-person guest today on the Voice of America Jazz Hour. Thank you very much, Billie.

Holiday: Thank *you* Willis, for having me here.

SUNDAY 19 FEBRUARY 1956
Billie closes at the Club Pablo in Washington.

MONDAY 20 FEBRUARY 1956
Billie opens at the Showboat in Philadelphia for a two-week engagement.

THURSDAY 23 FEBRUARY 1956
At 3am, Billie and Louis McKay are arrested after a raid on their hotel room. Billie is charged with possessing narcotics, and McKay with possessing a pistol without a permit. Billie is released on bail at 5pm in time to make the evening show at the Showboat.

Billie Holiday Out On Bail

Philadelphia—Billie Holiday and her husband-manager, Louis McKay, were released in $7,500 bail pending a possible grand jury trial after their arrest Feb. 23 on narcotics charge. Billie completed her engagement at the Showboat to large crowds, and then went into a sanitarium for a short time to take a cure. At presstime, she was due to continue fulfilling other engagements, including a March 21 week at the Orchid room in Kansas City and two weeks at Chicago's Birdland March 28. Billie's autobiography, *Lady Sings the Blues*, is due from Doubleday, at last reports, in late May or June.

Billie was arrested in 1947 in Philadelphia on a narcotics charge after which she spent a year and a day at the United States hospital in Lexington, Ky.

Billie and Louis in court in Philadelphia charged with possessing narcotics.

THUR	1	SUN	1
FRI	2	MON	2
SAT	3	TUES	3
SUN	4	WED	4
MON	5	THUR	5
TUES	6	FRI	6
WED	7	SAT	7
THUR	8	SUN	8
FRI	9	MON	9
SAT	10	TUES	10
SUN	11	WED	11
MON	12	THUR	12
TUES	13	FRI	13
WED	14	SAT	14
THUR	15	SUN	15
FRI	16	MON	16
SAT	17	TUES	17
SUN	18	WED	18
MON	19	THUR	19
TUES	20	FRI	20
WED	21	SAT	21
THUR	22	SUN	22
FRI	23	MON	23
SAT	24	TUES	24
SUN	25	WED	25
MON	26	THUR	26
TUES	27	FRI	27
WED	28	SAT	28
THUR	29	SUN	29
FRI	30	MON	30
SAT	31		

FRIDAY 2 MARCH 1956
Billie appears at a concert in Philadelphia.

SUNDAY 4 MARCH 1956
Billie closes at the Showboat in Philadelphia.

MONDAY 5 MARCH 1956
Billie returns to New York and enters a clinic.

WEDNESDAY 21 MARCH 1956
Billie opens at the Orchid Room in Kansas City for a one-week engagement.

TUESDAY 27 MARCH 1956
Billie closes at the Orchid Room in Kansas City

WEDNESDAY 28 MARCH 1956
Billie opens at Budland, 6412 Cottage Grove, Chicago for a two-week engagement opposite Ben Webster. The club had opened a few weeks previously as Birdland, but had to change the name when the famous New York club of the same name threatened to sue.

SATURDAY 7 APRIL 1956
Billie's 41st birthday

SUNDAY 8 APRIL 1956
Billie cables Maely Dufty from Cleveland at 9.20 am:
PLEASE CALL ME HENDERSON 11500
EXTENTION 173 FRANTIC =
LADY DAY BILLIE HOLLIDAY =

TUESDAY 10 APRIL 1956
Billie closes at Budland in Chicago, but is held over by public demand, possibly for another two weeks.

FRIDAY 27 APRIL 1956
Billie and Ben Webster are featured at the Trianon Ballroom in Chicago.

From Chicago, Billie moves on to Cleveland where she appears at the House of Jazz. From there she goes to Philadelphia to appear at Bill Gerson's Pep's Bar opposite Paul Quinichette and his Band.

TUES	**1**
WED	**2**
THUR	**3**
FRI	**4**
SAT	**5**
SUN	**6**
MON	**7**
TUES	**8**
WED	**9**
THUR	**10**
FRI	**11**
SAT	**12**
SUN	**13**
MON	**14**
TUES	**15**
WED	**16**
THUR	**17**
FRI	**18**
SAT	**19**
SUN	**20**
MON	**21**
TUES	**22**
WED	**23**
THUR	**24**
FRI	**25**
SAT	**26**
SUN	**27**
MON	**28**
TUES	**29**
WED	**30**
THUR	**31**

WEDNESDAY 30 MAY 1956

Billie rchcarses at William Dufty's home in New York City for the forthcoming Norman Granz recording sessions. According to Tony Scott there were three hours of tape recordings made, but only about a third have surfaced so far.

BILLIE HOLIDAY (vocal), TONY SCOTT (p)

Discussion: Misery / Israel / Misery / Discussion / I Must Have That Man / Discussion / Strange Fruit / Discussion: God Bless The Child / Discussion / God Bless The Child / God Bless The Child / Discussion / God Bless The Child / One Never Knows, Does One? / Discussion / BeerBarrel Polka / Some Of These Days / A Yiddishe Momma / A Yiddishe Momma / Discussion / Lady's Back In Town / Discussion / Discussion / One Never Knows, Does One? / Discussion / Unknown title

In the *Down Beat* Blindfold Test, singer Jeri Southern has this to say of Billie's Clef recording of *Come Rain or Come Shine*:

BILLIE IS MY IDEA OF A JAZZ SINGER, WHATEVER THAT MEANS. SOME PEOPLE TELL ME THAT I AM, BUT I'M NOT. BILLIE SINGS WITH SUCH HONESTY, LIKE "THIS IS THE WAY I FEEL, AND IF IT SELLS TWO RECORDS THAT'S ALL RIGHT WITH ME." I LIKE THAT LITTLE WAY SHE HAS OF SOMETIMES SOUNDING LIKE "I HATE YOU," Y'KNOW? I REALLY WOULD RATHER HEAR BILLIE SING SADDER SONGS THAN THIS, BUT IT'S A GREAT RECORD. I'LL GIVE IT FIVE STARS.

The English Sunday newspaper 'The People' serialises Billie's story under the title 'Body And Soul'.

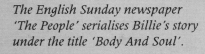

FRI	1	SUN	1
SAT	2	MON	2
SUN	3	TUES	3
MON	4	WED	4
TUES	5	THUR	5
WED	6	FRI	6
THUR	7	SAT	7
FRI	8	SUN	8
SAT	9	MON	9
SUN	10	TUES	10
MON	11	WED	11
TUES	12	THUR	12
WED	13	FRI	13
THUR	14	SAT	14
FRI	15	SUN	15
SAT	16	MON	16
SUN	17	TUES	17
MON	18	WED	18
TUES	19	THUR	19
WED	20	FRI	20
THUR	21	SAT	21
FRI	22	SUN	22
SAT	23	MON	23
SUN	24	TUES	24
MON	25	WED	25
TUES	26	THUR	26
WED	27	FRI	27
THUR	28	SAT	28
FRI	29	SUN	29
SAT	30	MON	30
		TUES	31

WEDNESDAY 6 JUNE 1956

Recording session for Norman Granz at the Fine Sound Studios in New York City. Norman Granz is away on tour in Europe, and the session is conducted by Tony Scott.
BILLIE HOLIDAY (vocal), TONY SCOTT (cl/arr), CHARLIE SHAVERS (t), PAUL QUINICHETTE (ts), WYNTON KELLY (p), KENNY BURRELL (g), AARON BELL (b), LENNIE McBROWNE (d)
Trav'lin Light / I Must Have That Man / Some Other Spring (2 takes) / *Lady Sings The Blues*

THURSDAY 7 JUNE 1956

Recording session for Norman Granz at the Fine Sound Studios in New York City. Norman Granz is still away on tour in Europe, and the session is conducted by Tony Scott.
BILLIE HOLIDAY (vocal), TONY SCOTT (cl/arr), CHARLIE SHAVERS (t), PAUL QUINICHETTE (ts), WYNTON KELLY (p), KENNY BURRELL (g), AARON BELL (b), LENNIE McBROWNE (d)
Strange Fruit / God Bless The Child / Good Morning Heartache / No Good Man

FRIDAY 29 JUNE 1956

Billie opens at the Club 204, 204 E58th Street in Chicago.
Louis McKay buys a share of the club, and names one of the rooms The Holiday Room.

JULY 1956

Publication of 'Lady Sings The Blues'

THURSDAY 12 JULY 1956

Billie closes at Club 204 in Chicago.

THURSDAY 19 JULY 1956

Billie opens at the Dunes Hotel, Las Vegas, for a two-week engagement. Corky Hale is her new accompanist.

MONDAY 23 JULY 1956

Billie sends a postcard to William and Maely Dufty from Las Vegas:
Hi! Bill & Maely now don't faint yes it's me writing. Gee I miss you kids. Hows my God son Kiss him for me. Hey hows the book going there. You cant get it out this way and its sold out in Chicago. If you can send me a copy as I havent read it yet ha ha. Louis sends regard
love Lady Day Billie Holiday

TUESDAY 24 JULY 1956

Louis McKay sends a postcard to William and Maely Dufty from Las Vegas:
Hi Bill. Just open here for two weeks – open L.A. for two – Frisco for two – Seattle for two and back home to good old N.Y. See you soon. Louis and Billie Holiday McKay.

SUN **1**
MON **2**
TUES **3**
WED **4**
THUR **5**
FRI **6**
SAT **7**
SUN **8**
MON **9**
TUES **10**
WED **11**
THUR **12**
FRI **13**
SAT **14**
SUN **15**
MON **16**
TUES **17**
WED **18**
THUR **19**
FRI **20**
SAT **21**
SUN **22**
MON **23**
TUES **24**
WED **25**
THUR **26**
FRI **27**
SAT **28**
SUN **29**
MON **30**
TUES **31**

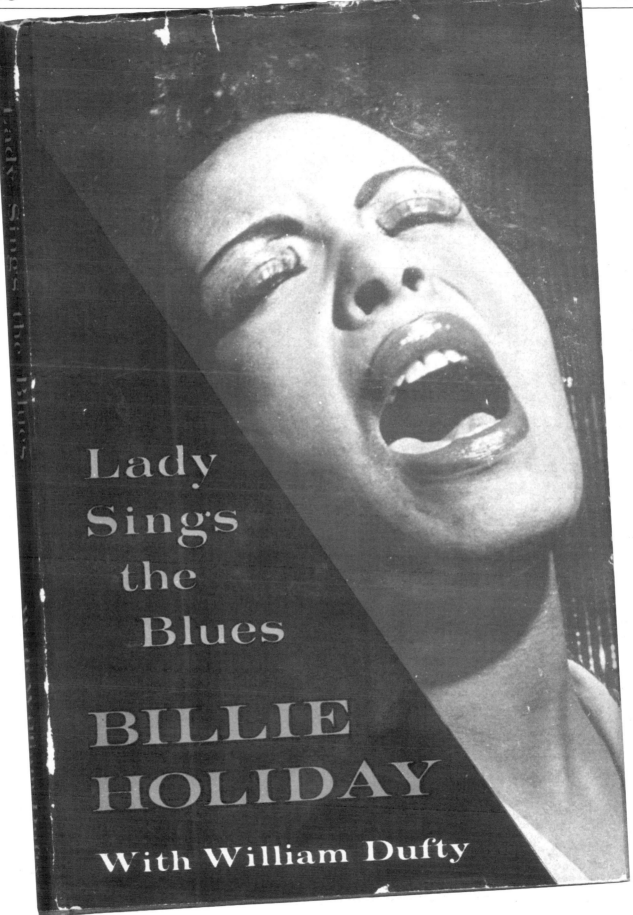

Lady Sings the Blues

BILLIE HOLIDAY

With William Dufty

WED	1
THUR	2
FRI	3
SAT	4
SUN	5
MON	6
TUES	7
WED	8
THUR	9
FRI	10
SAT	11
SUN	12
MON	13
TUES	14
WED	15
THUR	16
FRI	17
SAT	18
SUN	19
MON	20
TUES	21
WED	22
THUR	23
FRI	24
SAT	25
SUN	26
MON	27
TUES	28
WED	29
THUR	30
FRI	31

WEDNESDAY 1 AUGUST 1956

Billie closes at the Dunes Hotel, Las Vegas.

THURSDAY 2 AUGUST 1956

Billie opens at Jazz City in Hollywood for a two-week engagement. She draws the biggest-ever opening night crowd, including Jose Ferrer and Rosemary Clooney, to the club.

WEDNESDAY 8 AUGUST 1956

Down Beat reviews *Lady Sings the Blues*:

Lady Sings the Blues (Doubleday, $3.75, 250 pp.) is Billie Holiday's autobiography. And she tries to get the reader on her side of the mirror so don't expect a three-dimensional view of the subject ... The book's prose is certainly lucid and candid and opens with characteristic toughness: "Mom and pop were just a couple of kids when they got married. He was 18, she was 16, and I was 3."
... But most important is the fact that we have an assessment of Holiday by Holiday. It's not a full portrait, but it will help those who want to understand how her music became what it is—the most hurt and hurting singing in jazz.

'Lady Sings The Blues' Is Tough, Revealing Story

Billie Holiday

Philly Nesuhi?

Bechet Swap For Whittle Reported

'High Fidelity Suite' LP Due For Release In Fall

TUESDAY 14 AUGUST 1956

Recording session for Norman Granz at the Radio Recorders Studios in Los Angeles. Norman Granz is the producer.
BILLIE HOLIDAY (vocal), HARRY EDISON (t), BEN WEBSTER (ts), JIMMY ROWLES (p), BARNEY KESSEL (g), JOE MONDRAGON (b), ALVIN STOLLER (d)
Do Nothin' Till You Hear From Me / Cheek To Cheek / Ill Wind / Speak Low

WEDNESDAY 15 AUGUST 1956

Billie closes at Jazz City.

SATURDAY 18 AUGUST 1956

Recording session for Norman Granz at the Radio Recorders Studios in Los Angeles. Norman Granz is the producer.
BILLIE HOLIDAY (vocal), HARRY EDISON (t), BEN WEBSTER (ts), JIMMY ROWLES (p), BARNEY KESSEL (g), RED MITCHELL (b), ALVIN STOLLER (d)
We'll Be Together Again / All Or Nothing At All / Sophisticated Lady / April In Paris

WED	**1**
THUR	**2**
FRI	**3**
SAT	**4**
SUN	**5**
MON	**6**
TUES	**7**
WED	**8**
THUR	**9**
FRI	**10**
SAT	**11**
SUN	**12**
MON	**13**
TUES	**14**
WED	**15**
THUR	**16**
FRI	**17**
SAT	**18**
SUN	**19**
MON	**20**
TUES	**21**
WED	**22**
THUR	**23**
FRI	**24**
SAT	**25**
SUN	**26**
MON	**27**
TUES	**28**
WED	**29**
THUR	**30**
FRI	**31**

While in Los Angeles, Billie appears on the *Stars of Jazz* TV programme (*above*).

THURSDAY 23 AUGUST 1956
Billie returns to New York City.

FRIDAY 24 AUGUST 1956
The first Annual New York Jazz Festival gets under way at Randalls Island Stadium.

SATURDAY 25 AUGUST 1956
Billie appears at the New York Jazz Festival. Also on the Saturday night bill are Lionel Hampton & his Orchestra, Dave Brubeck Quartet, Gerry Mulligan Quartet, Chet Baker, Chris Connor, Art Blakey's Jazz Messengers, Lee Konitz, Coleman Hawkins, Buck Clayton, Billy Taylor Trio and Wild Bill Davison's All Stars.

WEDNESDAY 29 AUGUST 1956
Billie appears on Bandstand USA, a radio programme broadcast from the Red Hill Inn, Pennsauken, New Jersey.
BILLIE HOLIDAY (vocal), UNKNOWN (p), UNKNOWN (b), UNKNOWN (d)
Willow Weep For Me / I Only Have Eyes For You / My Man / Please Don't Talk About Me When I'm Gone

SAT **1**	MON **1**	THUR **1**
SUN **2**	TUES **2**	FRI **2**
MON **3**	WED **3**	SAT **3**
TUES **4**	THUR **4**	SUN **4**
WED **5**	FRI **5**	MON **5**
THUR **6**	SAT **6**	TUES **6**
FRI **7**	SUN **7**	WED **7**
SAT **8**	MON **8**	THUR **8**
SUN **9**	TUES **9**	FRI **9**
MON **10**	WED **10**	SAT **10**
TUES **11**	THUR **11**	SUN **11**
WED **12**	FRI **12**	MON **12**
THUR **13**	SAT **13**	TUES **13**
FRI **14**	SUN **14**	WED **14**
SAT **15**	MON **15**	THUR **15**
SUN **16**	TUES **16**	FRI **16**
MON **17**	WED **17**	SAT **17**
TUES **18**	THUR **18**	SUN **18**
WED **19**	FRI **19**	MON **19**
THUR **20**	SAT **20**	TUES **20**
FRI **21**	SUN **21**	WED **21**
SAT **22**	MON **22**	THUR **22**
SUN **23**	TUES **23**	FRI **23**
MON **24**	WED **24**	SAT **24**
TUES **25**	THUR **25**	SUN **25**
WED **26**	FRI **26**	MON **26**
THUR **27**	SAT **27**	TUES **27**
FRI **28**	SUN **28**	WED **28**
SAT **29**	MON **29**	THUR **29**
SUN **30**	TUES **30**	FRI **30**
	WED **31**	

MONDAY 3 SEPTEMBER 1956
Billie opens at the Cotton Club in Cleveland for a one-week engagement.

SUNDAY 9 SEPTEMBER 1956
Billie closes at the Cotton Club in Cleveland.

THURSDAY 13 SEPTEMBER 1956
Billie appears on a TV broadcast.
BILLIE HOLIDAY (vocal), UNKNOWN (p), UNKNOWN (b), UNKNOWN (d)
Please Don't Talk About Me When I'm Gone / I Love My Man / My Man

SATURDAY 27 OCTOBER 1956
Billie broadcasts from Olivia Davis' Patio Lounge, in Washington.
BILLIE HOLIDAY (vocal), UNKNOWN (p), UNKNOWN (b), ED PHYFE (d)
Nice Work If You Can Get It / God Bless The Child / Please Don't Talk About Me When I'm Gone / Don't Explain

MONDAY 29 OCTOBER 1956
Billie appears on Bandstand TV programme.

WEDNESDAY 31 OCTOBER 1956
Billie appears at a Grand Rally for the Eisenhower/Nixon Election Campaign in front of the Hotel Theresa in Harlem. Duke Ellington's Orchestra also appear.

MONDAY 5 NOVEMBER 1956
Art Tatum dies.

WEDNESDAY 7 NOVEMBER 1956
Billie appears in Concert with Stan Kenton.

THURSDAY 8 NOVEMBER 1956
Billie spends the day in the New York television studios, promoting her book and the forthcoming Carnegie Hall Concert. She appears on three separate programmes:
NIGHT BEAT, (ABC).
Billie is interviewed by Mike Wallace who asks: 'Why do so many jazz greats seem to die so early?'
Well, Mike, the only way I can answer that question is … we try to live 100 days in one day, and we try to please so many people, we try to… I myself, I wanna bend this note and bend that note, and sing this way, and sing that way and get all the feeling in… and eat all the good food and travel all the… all in one day… you can't do it!
PEACOCK ALLEY (WABD-TV)
Billie is interviewed by Tex McCleary and she explains what is going to happen at Carnegie Hall on Saturday night:
Yes… it's going to be narrated; Gil is going to narrate it, and er… he does a chapter and after each chapter I sing a song.
STEVE ALLEN TONIGHT SHOW (NBC)
11.30pm. Billie, accompanied by Carl Drinkard and the house band directed by Skitch Henderson, sings:
I Loves You Porgy

Billie at rehearsals for the 'Lady Sings The Blues' Concert at Carnegie Hall.

THUR	**1**
FRI	**2**
SAT	**3**
SUN	**4**
MON	**5**
TUES	**6**
WED	**7**
THUR	**8**
FRI	**9**
SAT	**10**
SUN	**11**
MON	**12**
TUES	**13**
WED	**14**
THUR	**15**
FRI	**16**
SAT	**17**
SUN	**18**
MON	**19**
TUES	**20**
WED	**21**
THUR	**22**
FRI	**23**
SAT	**24**
SUN	**25**
MON	**26**
TUES	**27**
WED	**28**
THUR	**29**
FRI	**30**

SATURDAY 10 NOVEMBER 1956

Billie appears in concert at Carnegie Hall in two shows, starting at 8.00pm and midnight.
Chico Hamilton Quintet:
PAUL HORN (fl/cl/ts), FRED KATZ (cello), JOHN PISANO (g), CARSON SMITH (b), CHICO HAMILTON (d)
I Want To Be Happy / A Fine Day / The Morning After / Buddy Boo / Reflections / Blue Sands / Mr Jo Jones / Chanel No.5

FIRST INTERVAL
BILLIE HOLIDAY (vocal), ROY ELDRIDGE (t), COLEMAN HAWKINS (ts), TONY SCOTT (cl), CARL DRINKARD (p), KENNY BURRELL (g), CARSON SMITH (b), CHICO HAMILTON (d), GILBERT MILLSTEIN (narrator)
Lady Sings The Blues (with narration) / *Lady Sings The Blues / Ain't Nobody's Business If I Do / God Bless The Child / Travelin' Light* (with narration) / *Miss Brown To You* / narration / *Billie's Blues / Too Marvellous For Words / Body And Soul* / narration / *Don't Explain / Them There Eyes*
SECOND INTERVAL
BILLIE HOLIDAY (vocal), BUCK CLAYTON (t), AL COHN (ts), TONY SCOTT (cl), CARL DRINKARD (p), KENNY BURRELL (g), CARSON SMITH (b), CHICO HAMILTON (d), GILBERT MILLSTEIN (narrator)
Yesterdays / Please Don't Talk About Me When I'm Gone / I'll Be Seeing You / narration / *My Man / I Cried For You / Fine And Mellow / I Cover The Waterfront / What A Little Moonlight Can Do / Lover Man / I Only Have Eyes For You / Strange Fruit / Easy Living / I Loves You Porgy*

Afro-American:

Billie Holiday stirs Carnegie Hall patrons

NEW YORK—Billie Holiday returned to New York for the first time in three years last Saturday, and her Carnegie Hall recital held the patrons spellbound.

Singing the numbers that have been most closely associated with her long and checkered career, Billie told her life story in her inimitable style – told it in song while Gilbert Millstein of the New York Times reviewed it in prose.

Mr. Millstein read passages from her autobiography "Lady Sings the Blues," while Miss Holiday went through her selections.

MISS HOLIDAY delivered about two dozen numbers, the repertory covering her top hits of the past 20 years.

Her unflagging stamina over the 60-minute span was surprising to some who once witnessed her almost barely able to get through a couple of numbers a few years back.

And her projection was superlative, whether doing a light rhythm number like "What A Little Moonlight Can Do" or such more demanding standards as "My Man" or "Strange Fruit," Miss Holiday's hit.

MISS HOLIDAY was given topflight backing by a crew of top jazzmen who included Coleman Hawkins, Buck Clayton, Roy Eldridge, Al Cohn, Tony Scott, Kenny Burrell and Carl Drinkard.

All played in a muted, swinging tempo that gave the best type of showcase to the singer who, this time at least, didn't need any fortissimo passages to override any vocal deficiencies.

Nat Hentoff, writing in *Down Beat*:

The audience was hers before she sang, greeting her and saying goodbye with heavy applause, and at one time the musicians too, applauded. It was a night when Billie was on top, the best jazz singer alive.

SAT **1**

SUN **2**

MON **3**

TUES **4**

WED **5**

THUR **6**

FRI **7**

SAT **8**

SUN **9**

MON **10**

TUES **11**

WED **12**

THUR **13**

FRI **14**

SAT **15**

SUN **16**

MON **17**

TUES **18**

WED **19**

THUR **20**

FRI **21**

SAT **22**

SUN **23**

MON **24**

TUES **25**

WED **26**

THUR **27**

FRI **28**

SAT **29**

SUN **30**

MON **31**

DECEMBER 1956

Billie appears at the Ball & Chain, a new jazz cellar near the University of Miami campus, Coral Gables, in Miami for two weeks at beginning of December opposite the Australian Jazz Quartet.

FRIDAY 21 DECEMBER 1956

Billie opens at Jazz City in Hollywood for a two-week engagement opposite the Pete Jolly Trio.

MONDAY 24 DECEMBER 1956

Billie's former manager/lover, John Levy, dies of a blood clot on the brain in Long Island College Hospital in New York, aged 48.

Billie sends a telegram to Bill & Maely Dufty from Los Angeles:
DONT TELL BEVIN THERE IS NO SANTA CLAUSE. MERRY CHRISTMAS=BILL HOLLIDAY=
Bill Dufty replies:

Dear Lady and Louis:

We got our Christmas laugh from your wire. And there's news for you. He's 3 feet tall and 2 years old so he's telling us now.

I also got a release from the Shakespeare Festival at Stratford Ontario announcing that Holiday is going to sing for two nights in July, between Lady `Macbeth and Mrs. Othello. I think this is marvelous. They can keep Newport. This Ontario Festival is it, among the summer bookings. My sister has a summer place across the river from Detroit. We're already figuring to go up there for a week with the baby so we can drive over and catch both shows. They have a big place in the country on the Lake. Maybe we can all make it there together for a few days.

Andy told us he had cleared the fine print of the movie deal and the contracts were on their way. I haven't seen them but I just wanted to say it will be the thrill of my life if this movie deal goes through. I knew it was the right thing the night of the Carnegie Concert when the Cowans sat with us and we talked after the performance. I knew that Cowans was the man. He got the message of the concert when he said "What is this Girl doing at Carnegie Hall, she should be doing her own two-a-day at the Palace like Judy Garland."

But even more so. This was the first guy who had faced the basic reason why there can't be honest movies about people who stay brown all year round. Loot. Because, it is said, a third of the box office gross of any movie comes from the South, everybody has to trim and trim. Cowan starts with that. He says it's not true, except for cowboy pictures. He starts out with the premise that you write the South off. You tell the people down there that they aren't ready for this movie yet. And when they are, it can be shown down there. In the meantime, he works on the basis that the southern gross can be made up by Europe. And he starts out, also, on the basis, that if he raises the capital for this movie from the exhibitors, the movie house operators, then he's guaranteed of showings up north, no matter how "controversial" it turns out to be. This is a grown-up way of doing business. If the damn politicians only had this much sense - just to ignore the south - they wouldn't be in the mess they are.

I've had to talk with a lot of people about the book. Cowan is the first one, outside of the publishers in Sweden in the people in England who wrote about it, who dug what the hell it was all about. And let's face it, after Doubleday and their damn lawyers were through chopping the hell out of it, it took someone who could read between the lines to be able to dig anything.

Arthur Dailey brought me over a book one night last week. It's a British thing called "The Negro In Films" by Peter Noble. It's a history of all the pictures, both English and American, made since 1902 that had Negro actors in them. Everything from "Birth of a Nation" to "New Orleans". It has a blacklist a mile long of producers, directors, writers and actors who had something to do with all the crummy pictures that have been made. I hope I'm right, sweetheart, and I think I am, that after Cowan has done your life story in this movie, this cat is going to have to do a new ending for this book. And a happy ending too. If I'm not, I want you to keep this letter and make me eat it next year.

Love - Bill

TUES	**1**	FRI	**1**
WED	**2**	SAT	**2**
THUR	**3**	SUN	**3**
FRI	**4**	MON	**4**
SAT	**5**	TUES	**5**
SUN	**6**	WED	**6**
MON	**7**	THUR	**7**
TUES	**8**	FRI	**8**
WED	**9**	SAT	**9**
THUR	**10**	SUN	**10**
FRI	**11**	MON	**11**
SAT	**12**	TUES	**12**
SUN	**13**	WED	**13**
MON	**14**	THUR	**14**
TUES	**15**	FRI	**15**
WED	**16**	SAT	**16**
THUR	**17**	SUN	**17**
FRI	**18**	MON	**18**
SAT	**19**	TUES	**19**
SUN	**20**	WED	**20**
MON	**21**	THUR	**21**
TUES	**22**	FRI	**22**
WED	**23**	SAT	**23**
THUR	**24**	SUN	**24**
FRI	**25**	MON	**25**
SAT	**26**	TUES	**26**
SUN	**27**	WED	**27**
MON	**28**	THUR	**28**
TUES	**29**		
WED	**30**		
THUR	**31**		

THURSDAY 3 JANUARY 1957

Billie closes at Jazz City in Hollywood.

Earlier in the day, Billie records for Verve at the Capitol Studios in Los Angeles. Norman Granz is the producer.
BILLIE HOLIDAY (vocal), HARRY EDISON (t), BEN WEBSTER (ts), JIMMY ROWLES (p), BARNEY KESSEL (g), RED MITCHELL (b), ALVIN STOLLER (d)
I Wished On The Moon / Moonlight In Vermont / A Foggy Day

FRIDAY 4 JANUARY 1957

Billie records for Verve at the Capitol Studios in Los Angeles. Norman Granz is the producer.
BILLIE HOLIDAY (vocal), HARRY EDISON (t), BEN WEBSTER (ts), JIMMY ROWLES (p), BARNEY KESSEL (g), RED MITCHELL (b), ALVIN STOLLER (d)
I Didn't Know What Time It Was / Just One Of Those Things (2 takes) */ Comes Love* (2 takes, 2 false starts)

MONDAY 7 JANUARY 1957

Billie records for Verve at the Capitol Studios in Los Angeles. Norman Granz is the producer.
BILLIE HOLIDAY (vocal), HARRY EDISON (t), BEN WEBSTER (ts), JIMMY ROWLES (p), BARNEY KESSEL (g), RED MITCHELL (b), ALVIN STOLLER (d)
Day In, Day Out / Darn That Dream / But Not For Me / Body And Soul

TUESDAY 8 JANUARY 1957

Billie records for Verve at the Capitol Studios in Los Angeles. Norman Granz is the producer.
BILLIE HOLIDAY (vocal), HARRY EDISON (t), BEN WEBSTER (ts), JIMMY ROWLES (p), BARNEY KESSEL (g), RED MITCHELL (b), ALVIN STOLLER (d)
Stars Fell On Alabama (2 takes) */ Say It Isn't So* (2 takes) */ Our Love Is Here To Stay* (1 false start) */ One For My Baby* (2 takes, 1 false start)

WEDNESDAY 9 JANUARY 1957

Billie records for Verve at the Capitol Studios in Los Angeles. Norman Granz is the producer.
BILLIE HOLIDAY (vocal), HARRY EDISON (t), BEN WEBSTER (ts), JIMMY ROWLES (p), BARNEY KESSEL (g), RED MITCHELL (b), probably LARRY BUNKER (d)
They Can't Take That Away From Me / Embraceable You / Let's Call The Whole Thing Off / Gee Baby, Ain't I Good To You

FRIDAY 11 JANUARY 1957

Billie opens at the Blackhawk Restaurant in San Francisco for a three-day engagement.

SUNDAY 13 JANUARY 1957

Billie closes at the Blackhawk Restaurant in San Francisco.

FRIDAY 18 JANUARY 1957

Billie opens at the Interlude, her first Sunset Strip engagement in Hollywood.

THURSDAY 31 JANUARY 1957

Billie closes at the Interlude.

THURSDAY 14 FEBRUARY 1957

Billie opens at Fack's II in San Francisco for a two-week engagement.

WEDNESDAY 27 FEBRUARY 1957

Billie closes at Fack's.

3 albums came out of these 5 sessions – *Songs For Distingué Lovers, Body and Soul* and *All or Nothing at All.*

FRI	1	MON	1	WED	1
SAT	2	TUES	2	THUR	2
SUN	3	WED	3	FRI	3
MON	4	THUR	4	SAT	4
TUES	5	FRI	5	SUN	5
WED	6	SAT	6	MON	6
THUR	7	SUN	7	TUES	7
FRI	8	MON	8	WED	8
SAT	9	TUES	9	THUR	9
SUN	10	WED	10	FRI	10
MON	11	THUR	11	SAT	11
TUES	12	FRI	12	SUN	12
WED	13	SAT	13	MON	13
THUR	14	SUN	14	TUES	14
FRI	15	MON	15	WED	15
SAT	16	TUES	16	THUR	16
SUN	17	WED	17	FRI	17
MON	18	THUR	18	SAT	18
TUES	19	FRI	19	SUN	19
WED	20	SAT	20	MON	20
THUR	21	SUN	21	TUES	21
FRI	22	MON	22	WED	22
SAT	23	TUES	23	THUR	23
SUN	24	WED	24	FRI	24
MON	25	THUR	25	SAT	25
TUES	26	FRI	26	SUN	26
WED	27	SAT	27	MON	27
THUR	28	SUN	28	TUES	28
FRI	29	MON	29	WED	29
SAT	30	TUES	30	THUR	30
SUN	31			FRI	31

MONDAY 11 MARCH 1957

Billie opens at Mister Kelly's in Chicago for a two-week engagement with Carl Drinkard on piano.

During the second week of the engagement, Billie writes to Bill and Maely Dufty:

Hi Bill and Maely
Well I dont know if you people have been digging But my Book is Just about a bitch did you see that shit that man from my birthplace Baltimore Wrote He even said my Mom and dad were stinkers for having me I haven't said anything to Louie as yet but you can believe me I am sick of the whole goddamn thing you tell people the truth and you stink I didn't hurt anyone in that book but myself oh the guys name is Redding from Afro American Baltimore paper. Please have Bill to look into this for me or I will take other means to take care of him he needs a lesson hope you can understand my beat up writing. Now you know why I dont. How is my God Son Kiss him for me God knows I hope when he gets to be a man he wont have to go through this kind of shit When I get to New York I will read this letter for you I am at the St. Clair Hotel. Please write or call me
Miss you love you
Billie Holiday
PS Working at Mr Kelley until Sunday leaving Tuesday for Mexico to get married
Mr Kelly 1028 No Bush St
Now you know why I don't write I can't
Lady

SUNDAY 25 MARCH 1957

Billie closes at Mister Kelly's in Chicago.

MONDAY 26 MARCH 1957

Billie shops for a wedding gown.

TUESDAY 27 MARCH 1957

Billie and Louis set off for Juarez in Mexico.

WEDNESDAY 28 MARCH 1957

Billie and Louis McKay are married in Juarez at 11.30am in a civil ceremony.

SUNDAY 7 APRIL 1957

Billie's 42nd birthday

THURSDAY 2 MAY 1957

Billie opens at Pep's Musical Bar in Philadelphia for a one-week engagement opposite Paul Quinichette. Mal Waldron becomes her accompanist.

Mal Waldron: *'She found herself needing a pianist at short notice when she fell out with Carl Drinkard. Maely Dufty, who was sort of managing her, asked Julian Euell, the bass player, if he knew a piano player. He recommended me and I played a week at Pep's Musical Bar with her and ended up staying with her two and a half years.'*

WEDNESDAY 8 MAY 1957

Billie closes at Pep's in Philadelphia.

Billie moves on to Detroit for a one-week engagement at the Flame Show Bar, followed by two weeks at the Bandstand in Philadelphia opposite Paul Quinichette.

Billie and Louis have started using Earle Warren Zaidins as their attorney. When Norman Granz doesn't renew Billie's recording contract, they look around for another record company. A meeting is arranged with Riverside Records, but Zaidins blows the deal by demanding a $4000 advance.

SAT	1
SUN	2
MON	3
TUES	4
WED	5
THUR	6
FRI	7
SAT	8
SUN	9
MON	10
TUES	11
WED	12
THUR	13
FRI	14
SAT	15
SUN	16
MON	17
TUES	18
WED	19
THUR	20
FRI	21
SAT	22
SUN	23
MON	24
TUES	25
WED	26
THUR	27
FRI	28
SAT	29
SUN	30

SUNDAY 2 JUNE 1957

During the weekend, Louis McKay discovers that Billie has been secretly using drugs on money supplied by Zaidins, and is again hooked. After a violent row he packs a suitcase into his car and heads for the West Coast.

TUESDAY 11 JUNE 1957

Billie appears at Loew's Sheridan Theatre at 7th Avenue and 12th Street in Greenwich Village, New York.

SATURDAY 15 JUNE 1957

Billie appears again at Loew's Sheridan Theatre at 7th Avenue and 12th Street in Greenwich Village, New York.

The midnight concert *Music for Night People* is part of the Greenwich Village Jazz Festival and also features the Modern Jazz Quartet, Charlie Mingus Quintet and the Randy Weston Trio.

TUESDAY 18 JUNE 1957

Billie opens at Club Tijuana in Baltimore for a one-week engagement.

MONDAY 24 JUNE 1957

Billie closes at Club Tijuana in Baltimore.

MON	**1**
TUES	**2**
WED	**3**
THUR	**4**
FRI	**5**
SAT	**6**
SUN	**7**
MON	**8**
TUES	**9**
WED	**10**
THUR	**11**
FRI	**12**
SAT	**13**
SUN	**14**
MON	**15**
TUES	**16**
WED	**17**
THUR	**18**
FRI	**19**
SAT	**20**
SUN	**21**
MON	**22**
TUES	**23**
WED	**24**
THUR	**25**
FRI	**26**
SAT	**27**
SUN	**28**
MON	**29**
TUES	**30**
WED	**31**

SATURDAY 6 JULY 1957

Billie appears at the Newport Jazz Festival at
Freebody Park, Newport, Rhode Island.
The Saturday evening programme features:
Turk Murphy and his Band
Chris Connor with Stan Free (piano)
Dave Brubeck Quartet
Teddy Wilson Group with Gerry Mulligan
Gerry Mulligan Quartet
BILLIE HOLIDAY (vocal), MAL WALDRON (p), JOE
BENJAMIN (b), JO JONES (d) JOHNNY MERCER, WILLIS
CONOVER (MCs)
*Nice Work If You Can Get It / Willow Weep For Me / My
Man / Lover Come Back To Me / Lady Sings The Blues /
What A Little Moonlight Can Do*
Dizzy Gillespie Orchestra
Eartha Kitt Dance Group
Mary Lou Williams with Dizzy Gillespie Orchestra

Down Beat reviews Billie's performance:
Her thin, crackling voice quivered through the set in
semi-recitative style.

Billie's set is recorded and released with Ella
Fitzgerald's set as *Ella Fitzgerald and Billie Holiday at
Newport*. It is Billie's final album for Verve.

MON	1
TUES	2
WED	3
THUR	4
FRI	5
SAT	6
SUN	7
MON	8
TUES	9
WED	10
THUR	11
FRI	12
SAT	13
SUN	14
MON	15
TUES	16
WED	17
THUR	18
FRI	19
SAT	20
SUN	21
MON	22
TUES	23
WED	24
THUR	25
FRI	26
SAT	27
SUN	28
MON	29
TUES	30
WED	31

Banned Billie OK for Park

By WILLIAM PEPER

Billie Holiday, the great jazz singer appearing in the show at Central Park, has been denied permission to sing in New York nightclubs since 1949 because of her several arrests for narcotics addiction. Miss Holiday feels that the whole thing is a bit illogical.

"I'm allowed to sing in the park, where children can hear me," she said, "but I'm banned from nightclubs. I think it's pretty silly."

For the past seven years the singer has been able to appear here only at one-night concerts, so it is a relief for her to be able to work for two whole weeks in the park.

"I think maybe the police department is going to let me have the permit this fall," she said. "I sure hope so. I'm tired of travelling. It would be nice to settle down in New York for awhile."

(All nightclub performers must have a card from the police in order to perform in New York City.)

On to Ontario

After she finishes this week at the Theater Under the Stars in Central Park, Miss Holiday is going to sing in the jazz festival at Stratford, Ontario. After that she will begin work on a movie of her autobiography, "Lady Sings the Blues."

"I'm going to record the soundtrack for the picture in September," she said. "I don't know who is going to play the part. I understand they're trying to get a white girl to play it.

"They wanted Ava Gardner but couldn't get her.

She has contracts or something. But even if they get a white actress, the character she plays will still be colored. If they change that, there's no story."

Lester Cowan will produce the film for United Artists release.

'I Told Everything'

Some book reviewers have complained that Miss Holiday sounded too bitter in her autobiography. Of that, she said, "I can't help it. I just told what happened to me. A lot of my life has been bitter. You ought to read what they left out of the book. I told everything, but they had to cut some of it."

The veteran singer was asked what she thought of the modern jazz that has developed in recent years. "I couldn't give you an opinion because I just don't understand it. It's too much for me."

The jazz show has proved the most successful one the park theater has had so far. Miss Holiday is being held over a second week, but the rest of the bill will change tomorrow night when the Modern Jazz Quartet, Dinah Washington, Stan Getz, Kai Winding and Buddy Rich take over.

Producers Michael Grace and Chris F. Anderson are planning another line-up of jazz artists for a third week.

The *World Telegraph* of Tuesday 30 July runs a piece on Billie.

WEDNESDAY 24 JULY 1957
Billie opens in a week-long series of concerts in the open air in Central Park, New York. JAZZ UNDER THE STARS at 8.30 each evening of the week in the Wollman Memorial Theatre in Central Park, featuring Billie Holiday, George Shearing Quintet, Erroll Garner, Gerry Mulligan Quartet, Lester Young, Miles Davis, Jo Jones and Sonny Stitt, compered by Al 'Jazzbo' Collins and Jean Shepherd.

WEDNESDAY 31 JULY 1957
Billie is held over for another week of concerts in the open air in Central Park, New York. JAZZ UNDER THE STARS at 8.30 each evening of the week in the Wollman Memorial Theatre in Central Park, featuring Billie Holiday, Dinah Washington, Buddy Rich vs Jo Jones, Kai Winding Septet, Jimmy Giuffre Trio, Stan Getz and the Modern Jazz Quartet.

THUR	**1**	SUN	**1**
FRI	**2**	MON	**2**
SAT	**3**	TUES	**3**
SUN	**4**	WED	**4**
MON	**5**	THUR	**5**
TUES	**6**	FRI	**6**
WED	**7**	SAT	**7**
THUR	**8**	SUN	**8**
FRI	**9**	MON	**9**
SAT	**10**	TUES	**10**
SUN	**11**	WED	**11**
MON	**12**	THUR	**12**
TUES	**13**	FRI	**13**
WED	**14**	SAT	**14**
THUR	**15**	SUN	**15**
FRI	**16**	MON	**16**
SAT	**17**	TUES	**17**
SUN	**18**	WED	**18**
MON	**19**	THUR	**19**
TUES	**20**	FRI	**20**
WED	**21**	SAT	**21**
THUR	**22**	SUN	**22**
FRI	**23**	MON	**23**
SAT	**24**	TUES	**24**
SUN	**25**	WED	**25**
MON	**26**	THUR	**26**
TUES	**27**	FRI	**27**
WED	**28**	SAT	**28**
THUR	**29**	SUN	**29**
FRI	**30**	MON	**30**
SAT	**31**		

FRIDAY 2 AUGUST 1957

Billie and Mal Waldron sit in at the Five Spot until 4am.

TUESDAY 6 AUGUST 1957

Billie completes her second week of JAZZ UNDER THE STARS concerts in Central Park, New York.

FRIDAY 9 AUGUST 1957

Billie appears at the Shakespeare Festival in Stratford, Ontario, Canada.

SATURDAY 10 AUGUST 1957

Billie appears at the Shakespeare Festival in Stratford, Ontario, Canada, then does a week at the Town Tavern in Toronto.

FRIDAY 23 AUGUST 1956

The second Annual New York Jazz Festival gets under way at Randalls Island.

SATURDAY 24 AUGUST 1956

Billie appears at the New York Jazz Festival. Also on the Saturday night bill are J. C. Higginbotham, Johnny Richards Orchestra, Gigi Gryce-Donald Byrd Jazz Lab, Randy Weston, Bud Powell, Max Roach Quintet and Anita O'Day.

Down Beat says:

> Festival producer Friedman introduced Billie Holiday, who sang a nine-tune set, including *Nice Work If You Can Get It; God Bless the Child; Too Marvellous for Words; Easy Living; Lover, Come Back to Me* and the inevitable *Lady Sings the Blues.*
>
> Her singing here was a distinct improvement over recent outings. Lady's voice had more body and tone than I recall in at least a year. Her phrasing and ability to create a mood never had been less than great, but her vocal texture was a genuine cause for celebration.

WEDNESDAY 28 AUGUST 1957

Billie opens in another week-long series of concerts in the open air in Central Park, New York. JAZZ UNDER THE STARS, returned by popular demand, at 8.30 each evening of the week in the Wollman Memorial Theatre in Central Park, featuring Billie Holiday, George Shearing Sextet, Erroll Garner Trio, Lionel Hampton Orchestra and the Dave Brubeck Quartet, compered by Jack Lazare and Jean Shepherd.

TUESDAY 3 SEPTEMBER 1957

Billie completes the week of JAZZ UNDER THE STARS concerts in Central Park, New York.

SUNDAY 22 SEPTEMBER 1957

Billie is one of the featured guests on the "Woolworth Hour" radio show at 1pm. She shares the "Best in Music" period with opera star Eleanor Steber and concert baritone Philip Moore.

OCTOBER / NOVEMBER **1957**

Los Angeles / New York City

TUES	**1**	FRI	**1**
WED	**2**	SAT	**2**
THUR	**3**	SUN	**3**
FRI	**4**	MON	**4**
SAT	**5**	TUES	**5**
SUN	**6**	WED	**6**
MON	**7**	THUR	**7**
TUES	**8**	FRI	**8**
WED	**9**	SAT	**9**
THUR	**10**	SUN	**10**
FRI	**11**	MON	**11**
SAT	**12**	TUES	**12**
SUN	**13**	WED	**13**
MON	**14**	THUR	**14**
TUES	**15**	FRI	**15**
WED	**16**	SAT	**16**
THUR	**17**	SUN	**17**
FRI	**18**	MON	**18**
SAT	**19**	TUES	**19**
SUN	**20**	WED	**20**
MON	**21**	THUR	**21**
TUES	**22**	FRI	**22**
WED	**23**	SAT	**23**
THUR	**24**	SUN	**24**
FRI	**25**	MON	**25**
SAT	**26**	TUES	**26**
SUN	**27**	WED	**27**
MON	**28**	THUR	**28**
TUES	**29**	FRI	**29**
WED	**30**	SAT	**30**
THUR	**31**		

OCTOBER 1957
Billie at The Avant Garde in Hollywood with Red Norvo. Billie becomes ill during the engagement and is forced to return to New York. McKay remains in Hollywood.

SATURDAY 9 NOVEMBER 1957
Billie appears at the Greenwich Village Jazz Festival at Loew's Sheridan. Also on the bill are the Modern Jazz Quartet, Charlie Mingus Quintet, Randy Weston Trio and Barbara Lea.

FRIDAY 29 NOVEMBER 1957
Billie appears at a benefit concert THANKSGIVING JAZZ AT CARNEGIE HALL for the Morningside Community Centre. Also appearing are Dizzy Gillespie and his Orchestra, Thelonious Monk with John Coltrane, Sonny Rollins, Chet Baker, Zoot Sims Quartet and Ray Charles. There are two concerts, at 8.30 pm and midnight. Billie sings seven songs accompanied by Mal Waldron.

189

SUN	1
MON	2
TUES	3
WED	4
THUR	5
FRI	6
SAT	7
SUN	8
MON	9
TUES	10
WED	11
THUR	12
FRI	13
SAT	14
SUN	15
MON	16
TUES	17
WED	18
THUR	19
FRI	20
SAT	21
SUN	22
MON	23
TUES	24
WED	25
THUR	26
FRI	27
SAT	28
SUN	29
MON	30
TUES	31

THURSDAY 5 DECEMBER 1957
Rehearsal at CBS Television
Studios in New York City for a
TV programme to be broadcast
on Sunday.
Henry 'Red' Allen All Stars:
Wild Man Blues / Rosetta
Mal Waldron piano solo:
Nervous
Count Basie All Stars: *I Left My
Baby / Dickie's Dream*
BILLIE HOLIDAY (vocal), DOC
CHEATHAM (t), LESTER YOUNG,
COLEMAN HAWKINS, BEN WEBSTER
(ts), VIC DICKENSON (tb), MAL
WALDRON (p), DANNY BARKER
(g), JIM ATLAS (b), JO JONES (d):
Fine and Mellow
Jimmy Giuffre & Pee Wee
Russell: *Blues*

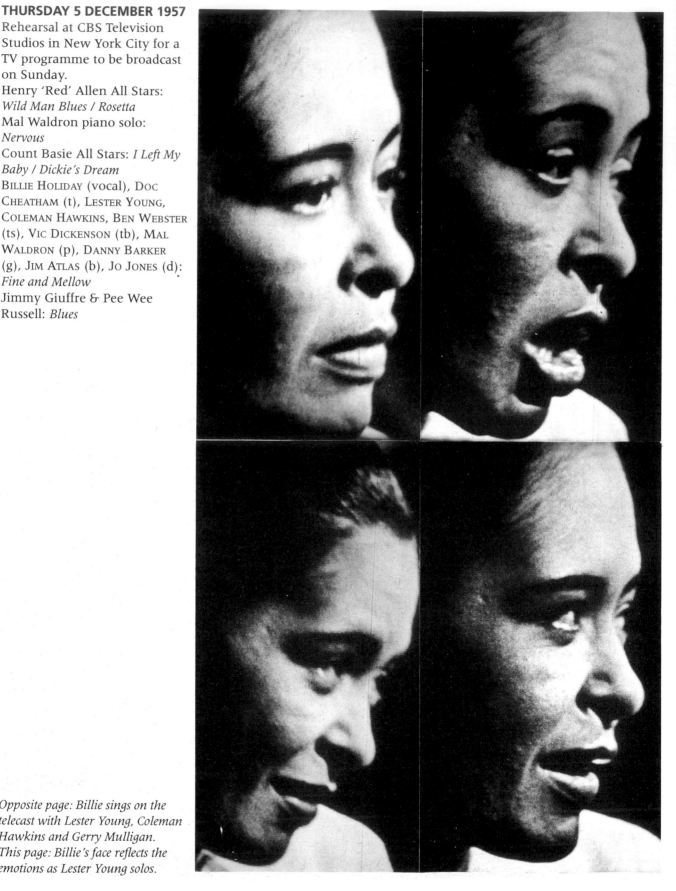

*Opposite page: Billie sings on the
telecast with Lester Young, Coleman
Hawkins and Gerry Mulligan.
This page: Billie's face reflects the
emotions as Lester Young solos.*

SUN	1
MON	2
TUES	3
WED	4
THUR	5
FRI	6
SAT	7
SUN	8
MON	9
TUES	10
WED	11
THUR	12
FRI	13
SAT	14
SUN	15
MON	16
TUES	17
WED	18
THUR	19
FRI	20
SAT	21
SUN	22
MON	23
TUES	24
WED	25
THUR	26
FRI	27
SAT	28
SUN	29
MON	30
TUES	31

SUNDAY 8 DECEMBER 1957

Billie takes part in the live telecast of THE SOUND OF JAZZ, a CBS Television Programme sponsored by Timex in their 'Seven Lively Arts' series at CBS Studio 58 in New York City.

The programme is introduced by John Crosby and produced by John Houseman, assisted by Nat Hentoff and Whitney Balliett.

Count Basie All Stars:

ROY ELDRIDGE, JOE NEWMAN, DOC CHEATHAM, EMMETT BERRY, JOE WILDER (t), VIC DICKENSON, DICKIE WELLS, BENNY MORTON (tb), EARL WARREN (as), BEN WEBSTER, COLEMAN HAWKINS (ts), GERRY MULLIGAN (bs), COUNT BASIE (p), FREDDIE GREEN (g), EDDIE JONES (b), JO JONES (d)

Open All Night / Blues

Henry 'Red' Allen All Stars:

HENRY 'RED' ALLEN (t), REX STEWART (c), PEE WEE RUSSELL (cl), COLEMAN HAWKINS (ts), VIC DICKENSON (tb), NAT PIERCE (p), DANNY BARKER (g), MILT HINTON (b), JO JONES (d)

Wild Man Blues / Rosetta

FIRST INTERVAL

THELONIOUS MONK (p), AHMED ABDUL-MALIK (b), OSIE JOHNSON (d)

Blue Monk

Count Basie All Stars:

I Left My Baby (JIMMY RUSHING vocal) / *Dickie's Dream*

SECOND INTERVAL

Billie Holiday and Mal Waldron All Stars.

BILLIE HOLIDAY (vocal), ROY ELDRIDGE, DOC CHEATHAM (t), LESTER YOUNG, COLEMAN HAWKINS, BEN WEBSTER (ts), GERRY MULLIGAN (bs), MAL WALDRON (p), DANNY BARKER (g), MILT HINTON (b), OSIE JOHNSON (d)

Fine and Mellow

Jimmy Giuffre Trio:

JIMMY GIUFFRE (cl/ts/bs), JIM HALL (g), JIM ATLAS (b)

The Train and the River

JIMMY GIUFFRE, PEE WEE RUSSELL (cl), DANNY BARKER (g), MILT HINTON (b), OSIE JOHNSON (d)

Blues

COUNT BASIE (p), FREDDIE GREEN (g), EDDIE JONES (b), JO JONES (d)

Blues

WED	**1**	SAT	**1**
THUR	**2**	SUN	**2**
FRI	**3**	MON	**3**
SAT	**4**	TUES	**4**
SUN	**5**	WED	**5**
MON	**6**	THUR	**6**
TUES	**7**	FRI	**7**
WED	**8**	SAT	**8**
THUR	**9**	SUN	**9**
FRI	**10**	MON	**10**
SAT	**11**	TUES	**11**
SUN	**12**	WED	**12**
MON	**13**	THUR	**13**
TUES	**14**	FRI	**14**
WED	**15**	SAT	**15**
THUR	**16**	SUN	**16**
FRI	**17**	MON	**17**
SAT	**18**	TUES	**18**
SUN	**19**	WED	**19**
MON	**20**	THUR	**20**
TUES	**21**	FRI	**21**
WED	**22**	SAT	**22**
THUR	**23**	SUN	**23**
FRI	**24**	MON	**24**
SAT	**25**	TUES	**25**
SUN	**26**	WED	**26**
MON	**27**	THUR	**27**
TUES	**28**	FRI	**28**
WED	**29**		
THUR	**30**		
FRI	**31**		

JANUARY 1958

Billie appears at the Apollo Theatre in Harlem for the last time.

TUESDAY 18 FEBRUARY 1958

Recording session in New York City for Columbia, accompanied by Ray Ellis and his Orchestra and an unknown choir.
BILLIE HOLIDAY (vocal), MEL DAVIS (t), ED POWELL, ROMEO PENQUE, TOM PARSHLEY, PHIL BODNER (reeds), URBIE GREEN, JACK GREEN (tb), TOMMY MITCHELL (bass tb), GEORGE OCHNER, MILTON LOMASK, EMMANUEL GREEN, HARRY KATZMANN, DAVID SARCER, SAMUEL RAND, LEO KRUCZEK, HARRY MEINIKOFF, HARRY HOFFMAN, DAVID NEWMAN (vln), SID BRECHER, RICHARD DICHLER (vla), DAVID SOYER, MAURICE BROWN (cello), JANET PUTMAN (harp), BOBBY ROSENGARDEN (xyl), MAL WALDRON (p), BARRY GALBRAITH (g), MILT HINTON (b), OSIE JOHNSON (d)
You Don't Know What Love Is / I'll Be Around / For Heaven's Sake / But Beautiful

WEDNESDAY 19 FEBRUARY 1958

Recording session in New York City for Columbia, accompanied by Ray Ellis and his Orchestra and an unknown choir.
BILLIE HOLIDAY (vocal), ED POWELL, ROMEO PENQUE, TOM PARSHLEY, PHIL BODNER (reeds), URBIE GREEN, JACK GREEN (tb), TOMMY MITCHELL (bass tb), GEORGE OCHNER, EUGENE BERGEN, EMMANUEL GREEN, HARRY KATZMANN, DAVID SARCER, SAMUEL RAND, LEO KRUCZEK, HARRY MEINIKOFF, HARRY HOFFMAN, DAVID NEWMAN (vln), SID BRECHER, RICHARD DICHLER (vla), DAVID SOYER, AL SHULMAN (cello), JANET PUTMAN (harp), BOBBY ROSENGARDEN (xyl), MAL WALDRON (p), BARRY GALBRAITH (g), MILT HINTON (b), OSIE JOHNSON (d)
For All We Know / It's Easy To Remember / I'm A Fool To Want You (2 takes)

SAT	**1**
SUN	**2**
MON	**3**
TUES	**4**
WED	**5**
THUR	**6**
FRI	**7**
SAT	**8**
SUN	**9**
MON	**10**
TUES	**11**
WED	**12**
THUR	**13**
FRI	**14**
SAT	**15**
SUN	**16**
MON	**17**
TUES	**18**
WED	**19**
THUR	**20**
FRI	**21**
SAT	**22**
SUN	**23**
MON	**24**
TUES	**25**
WED	**26**
THUR	**27**
FRI	**28**

THURSDAY 20 FEBRUARY 1958

Recording session in New York City for Columbia, accompanied by Ray Ellis and his Orchestra.
BILLIE HOLIDAY (vocal), MEL DAVIS (t), ED POWELL, ROMEO PENQUE, TOM PARSHLEY, PHIL BODNER (reeds), URBIE GREEN, J J JOHNSON (tb), TOMMY MITCHELL (bass tb), GEORGE OCHNER, EUGENE BERGEN, MAX CAHN, FELIX GIGLIO, HARRY KATZMANN, DAVID SARCER, SAMUEL RAND, LEO KRUCZEK, HARRY HOFFMAN, DAVID NEWMAN (vln), SID BRECHER, RICHARD DICHLER (vla), DAVID SOYER, MAURICE BROWN (cello), JANET PUTMAN (harp), BRADLEY SPINNEY (xyl), MAL WALDRON (p), BARRY GALBRAITH (g), MILT HINTON (b), DON LAMOND (d)
The End Of A Love Affair (2 takes) / *Glad To Be Unhappy* / *You've Changed* / *I Get Along Without You Very Well* / *Violets For Your Furs*

Billie Holiday waxes LP for MGM label

NEW YORK, Wednesday. — Billie Holiday has just completed an album for MGM Records in New York. Ray Ellis made the arrangements and conducted the orchestra that featured, on some numbers, a 12-piece string section.

Instrumental soloists on the date included Al Cohn, Harry Edison, Joe Wilder, Jimmy Cleveland and Gene Quill. The rhythm section was Hank Jones (piano), Barry Galbraith (guitar), Milt Hinton (bass) and Osie Johnson (drums).

As in the Columbia LP she made last year, Billie recorded songs she has never before put on wax.

SAT **1**	TUES **1**	THUR **1**
SUN **2**	WED **2**	FRI **2**
MON **3**	THUR **3**	SAT **3**
TUES **4**	FRI **4**	SUN **4**
WED **5**	SAT **5**	MON **5**
THUR **6**	SUN **6**	TUES **6**
FRI **7**	MON **7**	WED **7**
SAT **8**	TUES **8**	THUR **8**
SUN **9**	WED **9**	FRI **9**
MON **10**	THUR **10**	SAT **10**
TUES **11**	FRI **11**	SUN **11**
WED **12**	SAT **12**	MON **12**
THUR **13**	SUN **13**	TUES **13**
FRI **14**	MON **14**	WED **14**
SAT **15**	TUES **15**	THUR **15**
SUN **16**	WED **16**	FRI **16**
MON **17**	THUR **17**	SAT **17**
TUES **18**	FRI **18**	SUN **18**
WED **19**	SAT **19**	MON **19**
THUR **20**	SUN **20**	TUES **20**
FRI **21**	MON **21**	WED **21**
SAT **22**	TUES **22**	THUR **22**
SUN **23**	WED **23**	FRI **23**
MON **24**	THUR **24**	SAT **24**
TUES **25**	FRI **25**	SUN **25**
WED **26**	SAT **26**	MON **26**
THUR **27**	SUN **27**	TUES **27**
FRI **28**	MON **28**	WED **28**
SAT **29**	TUES **29**	THUR **29**
SUN **30**	WED **30**	FRI **30**
MON **31**		SAT **31**

Jobs are beginning to dry up for Billie, and much of March and April is taken up with speculation on who should portray Billie in her proposed film biography. On the strength of her performance in *Show Boat*, Ava Gardner was sought by Hollywood, to Billie's disgust.

MONDAY 7 APRIL 1958
Billie's 43rd birthday.

MONDAY 26 MAY 1958
In the *New York Journal-American*, Dorothy Kilgallen reports on yet another classic example of Hollywood casting techniques:

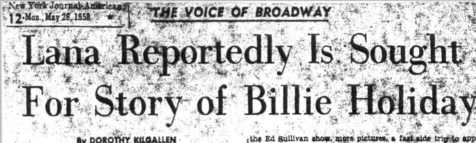

New York Journal-American
12-Mon., May 26, 1958

THE VOICE OF BROADWAY

Lana Reportedly Is Sought For Story of Billie Holiday

By DOROTHY KILGALLEN
Broadway Bulletin Board

CASTING rumors on the Billie Holiday film biography get sillier and sillier. Some months ago Ava Gardner was sought for the leading role, but apparently she wasn't available—or Miss Holiday wouldn't okay her—and now the producer reportedly is trying to get Lana Turner . . . Singer Matt Dennis and his Virginia are knitting tiny garments for the second time . . . The Hal Roach studios are on the verge of a sale to an East Coast group well known to Wall Street.

Prince Philip's latest kick is painting, and he's progressed to the point of doing a study of the Queen reading papers at her desk. Those privileged to glimpse His Royal Highness' work say he's not quite in Winston Churchill's class yet . . . Actress Susan Magness may be

the Ed Sullivan show, more pictures, a fast side trip to appear on Dean Martin's telethon, back to the Sullivan theatre for makeup, dress rehearsal, the telecast, then a wild dash down Broadway to the Latin Quarter, just in time for the first show there.

SUGAR RAY ROBINSON, a certified jazz world guide, planned to take his wife and Doris Day and her husband on a whirlwind tour of 12 hip spots the other night—his itinerary included the East Side, West Side and Greenwich Village—but Doris was so intrigued by the music at the Roundtable they just stayed glued there for three hours, and Ray had to cancel all the other reservations.

Mort Sahl, whose ex-bride just married one of his best friends, appears to be recovering from the blow with the aid of Susan Cabot, a pretty actress. Susan obviously has a penchant for comedians; she used to date Jules Munshin . . . Bobby Cone's first novel, set in a resort with a remarkable resemblance to Fire Island, has a marvelously appropriate title: "The Lobster Quadrill"

THURSDAY 29 MAY 1958
Billie appears on Art Ford's Jazz Party, broadcast simultaneously on radio and TV via station WNTA channel 13 from Newark, New Jersey, 9.00 p.m. to 10.30 p.m.
Jimmy McPartland (c/vocal), Bob Wilber (cl/ts), Bud Freeman (ts), Tyree Glenn (tb/vib), Dick Cary (p/t), Chuck Wayne (g), Vinnie Burke (b), Harry Leon (d):
Blues (theme) / *Basin Street Blues* / *Royal Garden Blues* / *What's New* / *All Of Me* (Abbey Lincoln vocal) / *Crazy Rhythm* / *Three Little Words* / *Don't Blame Me* (Abbey Lincoln vocal) / *I Can't Believe That You're In Love With Me* / *St James Infirmary* / *Chimes Blues*

BILLIE HOLIDAY (vocal), TYREE GLENN (vib), MAL WALDRON (p), CHUCK WAYNE (g), VINNIE BURKE (b), HARRY LEON (d):
You've Changed
JIMMY McPARTLAND (c) or DICK CARY (t) added:
I Love My Man / When Your Lover Has Gone
Original personnel:
Bugle Call Rag / Basin Street Blues (theme)

SUN **1**	TUES **1**	FRI **1**
MON **2**	WED **2**	SAT **2**
TUES **3**	THUR **3**	SUN **3**
WED **4**	FRI **4**	MON **4**
THUR **5**	SAT **5**	TUES **5**
FRI **6**	SUN **6**	WED **6**
SAT **7**	MON **7**	THUR **7**
SUN **8**	TUES **8**	FRI **8**
MON **9**	WED **9**	SAT **9**
TUES **10**	THUR **10**	SUN **10**
WED **11**	FRI **11**	MON **11**
THUR **12**	SAT **12**	TUES **12**
FRI **13**	SUN **13**	WED **13**
SAT **14**	MON **14**	THUR **14**
SUN **15**	TUES **15**	FRI **15**
MON **16**	WED **16**	SAT **16**
TUES **17**	THUR **17**	SUN **17**
WED **18**	FRI **18**	MON **18**
THUR **19**	SAT **19**	TUES **19**
FRI **20**	SUN **20**	WED **20**
SAT **21**	MON **21**	THUR **21**
SUN **22**	TUES **22**	FRI **22**
MON **23**	WED **23**	SAT **23**
TUES **24**	THUR **24**	SUN **24**
WED **25**	FRI **25**	MON **25**
THUR **26**	SAT **26**	TUES **26**
FRI **27**	SUN **27**	WED **27**
SAT **28**	MON **28**	THUR **28**
SUN **29**	TUES **29**	FRI **29**
MON **30**	WED **30**	SAT **30**
	THUR **31**	SUN **31**

SATURDAY 21 JUNE 1958

Billie appears in a midnight concert, Jazz in Greenwich Village at Loew's Sheridan Theatre , Seventh Avenue & 12th Street. Dave Brubeck and Paul Desmond are also on the bill.

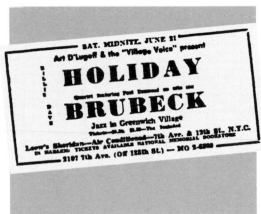

WEDNESDAY 9 JULY 1958

Billie writes a letter to Brian Knight, an English record collector:
I've recorded an album called 'Lady in Satin' for Columbia recently, and I think it is one of the best I've done. Will record a swing album for them soon.

THURSDAY 10 JULY 1958

Billie appears on Art Ford's Jazz Party, broadcast simultaneously on radio and TV via station WNTA channel 13 from Newark, New Jersey, 9.00 p.m. to 10.30 p.m.
Buck Clayton (t), Hank D'Amico (cl), Georgie Auld (ts), Tyree Glenn (tb), Harry Sheppard (vib), Marty Napoleon (p), Mary Osborne (g), Vinnie Burke (b), Osie Johnson (d):
Basin Street Blues / Jumping With Symphony Sid
BILLIE HOLIDAY (vocal), GEORGIE AULD (ts), MAL WALDRON (p), MARY OSBORNE (g), VINNIE BURKE (b), OSIE JOHNSON (d):
Foolin' Myself
Original personnel:
I Got It Bad And That Ain't Good / Perdido
Jackie Cooper replaces Osie Johnson (d):
It Don't Mean A Thing / I Surrender Dear / I Found A New Baby
BILLIE HOLIDAY (vocal), GEORGIE AULD (ts), MAL WALDRON (p), MARY OSBORNE (g), VINNIE BURKE (b), JACKIE COOPER (d):
Easy To Remember

Buck Clayton (t), Hank D'Amico (cl), Georgie Auld (ts), Tyree Glenn (tb), Harry Sheppard (vib), Marty Napoleon (p), Mary Osborne (g), Vinnie Burke (b), Jackie Cooper (d):
I've Got The World On A String
Osie Johnson replaces Jackie Cooper (d):
Sophisticated Lady / Unknown Title
BILLIE HOLIDAY (vocal), GEORGIE AULD (ts), MAL WALDRON (p), MARY OSBORNE (g), VINNIE BURKE (b), OSIE JOHNSON (d):
What A Little Moonlight Can Do
Original personnel:
Body And Soul / One O'Clock Jump

THURSDAY 17 JULY 1958

Billie appears on Art Ford's Jazz Party, broadcast simultaneously on radio and TV via station WNTA channel 13 from Newark, New Jersey, 9.00 p.m. to 10.30 p.m.
Charlie Shavers, Buck Clayton (t), Georgie Auld (ts), Tyree Glenn (tb), Harry Sheppard (vib), Marty Napoleon (p), Mary Osborne (g), Vinnie Burke (b), Osie Johnson (d):
Basin Street Blues / C Jam Blues
BILLIE HOLIDAY (vocal), CHARLIE SHAVERS, BUCK CLAYTON (t), GEORGIE AULD (ts), TYREE GLENN (tb), HARRY SHEPPARD (vib), MAL WALDRON (p), MARY OSBORNE (g), VINNIE BURKE (b), OSIE JOHNSON (d):
Moanin' Low
Original personnel:
Embraceable You / Sunday / Robbin's Nest / The Man I Love / 'S Wonderful
BILLIE HOLIDAY (vocal), HARRY SHEPPARD (vib), MAL WALDRON (p), MARY OSBORNE (g), VINNIE BURKE (b), OSIE JOHNSON (d):
Don't Explain
Original personnel:
This Can't Be Love / Airmail Special / I Can't Get Started
BILLIE HOLIDAY (vocal), BUCK CLAYTON (t), GEORGIE AULD (ts), MAL WALDRON (p), MARY OSBORNE (g), VINNIE BURKE (b), OSIE JOHNSON (d):
When Your Lover Has Gone
Original personnel:
Flying Home

MON **1**

TUES **2**

WED **3**

THUR **4**

FRI **5**

SAT **6**

SUN **7**

MON **8**

TUES **9**

WED **10**

THUR **11**

FRI **12**

SAT **13**

SUN **14**

MON **15**

TUES **16**

WED **17**

THUR **18**

FRI **19**

SAT **20**

SUN **21**

MON **22**

TUES **23**

WED **24**

THUR **25**

FRI **26**

SAT **27**

SUN **28**

MON **29**

TUES **30**

TUESDAY 9 SEPTEMBER 1958

Billie appears in the Persian Room of the Plaza Hotel in New York at a party thrown by Columbia Records. Also appearing are Duke Ellington and his Orchestra, Miles Davis Quintet and Jimmy Rushing. Billie is backed by BUCK CLAYTON (t), MAL WALDRON (p), JIMMY WOODE (b), SAM WOODYARD (d)
Don't Explain / When Your Lover Has Gone

Alfred Duckett reviews the evening in his Showbiz column in the *New York Age*:

You're guest at a party in the Persian Room of the Plaza Hotel. The party is hosted by Columbia Records. With several hundred others – music reviewers, columnists, disk jockeys, feature writers and critics – you sit and sip a bourbon, munch on pretzels and potato chips and listen ...

You listen to suave Duke Ellington and his powerful, driving, clean-sounding big band. You listen to the remarkable, aggressive creations of the Miles Davis group. You listen to big Jimmy Rushing riding the blues.

Then Irving Townsend, a charming guy who is a Columbia veep, introduces Billie Holiday.

Billie goes to the stand. Your mind swiftly filters memories. The first time you ever heard Billie Holiday – at a dance – years back. She was young and fresh and lovely. She was golden brown with a voice that strangely reminded you of corn husks – a voice that was wispy and powerful and able to conjure up sheer sex. Clean, delightful sex. You remember how clean she rode a beat. You remember how joyously she balled the blues. You remember her utter power with lyrics of great social impact like "Strange Fruit." Down the years – as Billie Holiday goes to the stand ... you listen.

You listen.

You listen to all the discordant notes which have made their harsh way into the song of Billie Holiday. The headlines, the scandal, the whispers. "She's through," they said of Billie. "She'll never come back." "Have you heard ...?" "Did you read...?"

You listen. And look. You don't see the picture-book Billie Holiday of the past years. You don't see a lush, lovely woman with the kind of figure that used to make men stare. She's slimmer. She has some of the tragedy of the years written on her face. But she is still beautiful to you – and you look and you listen and you hope.

You listen.

Billie swings into a song. Swings into it like a good automobile gets into motion. In high and with a rhythm like a strong, high powered limousine. There seems – along the route – a hesitant quality but you remember that the hint of hesitancy is a bit of her old technique. Is it your imagination that tells you something is lacking? Is it your imagination – conditioned by the headlines, the whispers and the rumours – that says this isn't Billie Holiday, but a ghost of Billie creating the old illusion.

A radio man sitting beside you leans over to whisper: "I don't think Billie can sing any more."

He says it, without spite, with regret. You stare at him. Then, it isn't only you? It isn't only your imagination?

Billie finishes her song. The applause is big. She does another number. The applause is big. It grows bigger. She is about to leave the stage but the audience wants her back. If this is an illusion, the audience loves illusion.

Billie sings breathily the first few bars of her third song, "Hush now! Don't Explain." She is interrupted by an avalanche of hand-clapping approval. She gets into the song and something chemical, something magic happens between Billie Holiday and her audience. There is no illusion about the way her honey voice drips through, strains through – clear, dripping with heat and astride that beat which is hers exclusively. There is no illusion. She snaps her fingers once – in a break – and what happens to the audience with the snap of that finger is the measure of her genius. For she has snapped everyone in the hushed awed room out of one mood level into another. As she finishes up, the musicians on the bandstand – the musicians who are accompanying her – are watching her with great respect and great appreciation.

You listen – and you hear a magnificent performance. You listen and you listen and you hear – an authentic artist.

You listen. Your heart listens – and you know that great art and great artists, you just don't explain.

Right: Jimmy Rushing singing with the Duke Ellington Orchestra at the Persian Room of the Plaza Hotel in New York City.

MON	**1**
TUES	**2**
WED	**3**
THUR	**4**
FRI	**5**
SAT	**6**
SUN	**7**
MON	**8**
TUES	**9**
WED	**10**
THUR	**11**
FRI	**12**
SAT	**13**
SUN	**14**
MON	**15**
TUES	**16**
WED	**17**
THUR	**18**
FRI	**19**
SAT	**20**
SUN	**21**
MON	**22**
TUES	**23**
WED	**24**
THUR	**25**
FRI	**26**
SAT	**27**
SUN	**28**
MON	**29**
TUES	**30**

SUNDAY 13 SEPTEMBER 1958

Billie appears at Town Hall, New York in a concert billed as an ALL STAR JAZZ SHOW & FAREWELL PARTY to Billie Holiday prior to European Tour. Also appearing are Eddie Condon, Jo Jones Trio, J.C. Higginbotham, Buck Clayton, Hal Singer, Conrad Janis, Max Kaminsky, Freddie Moore, Bobby Hackett and Freddy Price and his Big 10 Piece Jazz Band. 'Jazzbo' Collins is MC. There are two shows, at 8.00 and 11.00 pm.

John S. Wilson in the NY Times:

Billie Holiday Sings With Old Magic In 'All-Star Jazz Show' at Town Hall

Halfway through a so-called "All Star Jazz Show" at Town Hall on Saturday evening, Billie Holiday walked out on the stage somewhat hesitantly and dragged her way through a slow, slow ballad.

Then, as drummer Jo Jones picked up the tempo a bit and Buck Clayton's muted trumpet muttered soothingly behind her, she eased into a swinging version of "When Your Lover Has Gone" and some of the old Holiday magic began to peep through.

This magic has been hard to come by for Miss Holiday in recent years. But it grew and grew at Town Hall until it seemed to fill the stage as she moved confidently through a short set that included "Don't Explain" and two of her very early successes, "Miss Brown To You" and "What A Little Moonlight Can Do."

By the time she wound up with "Billie's Blues," she was singing with more assurance, skill and spirit than this listener has heard from her in years.

Fore and aft of Miss Holiday, the "All Star Jazz Show" was played by grab-bag groups of assorted musicians who laid down a deadly murk through which only the trumpets of Mr. Clayton and Max Kaminsky and Bobby Hackett's cornet penetrated clean, clear and unsullied.

THURSDAY 25 SEPTEMBER 1958

Billie appears on Dave Garroway's 'Today' show on NBC television from 7–10 a.m. singing *My Funny Valentine*.

FRIDAY 26 SEPTEMBER 1958

Billie appears in a Seven Ages of Jazz Concert at the Oakdale Musical Theatre, Wallingford, Connecticut. The concert is sponsored by Ben Segal and Bob Hall, produced and narrated by Leonard Feather as part of a three day festival.

The concert features Buck Clayton, Don Elliott, Coleman Hawkins, Georgie Auld, Tyree Glenn, Willie 'The Lion' Smith, Dick Hyman, Milt Hinton, Don Lamond, Brownie McGhee, Maxine Sullivan and Billie Holiday.

For Billie's segment she is backed by *Buck Clayton* (trumpet), *Mal Waldron* (piano), *Milt Hinton* (bass) and *Don Lamond* (drums).

I Wished On The Moon / Lover Man

TUESDAY 30 SEPTEMBER 1958

Billie opens at the Blackhawk Club in San Francisco for a one-week engagement opposite Leroy Vinnegar's Band.

Dr Herbert Henderson says: *She was ill with cirrhosis of the liver, caused by excessive drinking. Alcohol was resorted to in order that she would have no desire for heroin. She had lost much weight and should have been in a hospital instead of a night club. When I heard her sing – it was pathetic.*

WED	**1**
THUR	**2**
FRI	**3**
SAT	**4**
SUN	**5**
MON	**6**
TUES	**7**
WED	**8**
THUR	**9**
FRI	**10**
SAT	**11**
SUN	**12**
MON	**13**
TUES	**14**
WED	**15**
THUR	**16**
FRI	**17**
SAT	**18**
SUN	**19**
MON	**20**
TUES	**21**
WED	**22**
THUR	**23**
FRI	**24**
SAT	**25**
SUN	**26**
MON	**27**
TUES	**28**
WED	**29**
THUR	**30**
FRI	**31**

SATURDAY 4 OCTOBER 1958
Billie closes at the Blackhawk Club in San Francisco.

SUNDAY 5 OCTOBER 1958
Billie appears at the final night of the First Annual Monterey Jazz Festival in Monterey, California.
BILLIE HOLIDAY (vocal), BUDDY DE FRANCO (cl), BENNY CARTER (as), GERRY MULLIGAN (bs), MAL WALDRON (p), EDDIE KHAN (b), DICK BERK (d), MORT SAHL (mc)
Tain't Nobody's Business If I Do / Willow Weep For Me / When Your Lover Has Gone / God Bless The Child / I Only Have Eyes For You / Good Morning Heartache / Them There Eyes / Billie's Blues / What A Little Moonlight Can Do / Trav'lin' Light / Lover Come Back To Me

MONDAY 6 OCTOBER 1958
Ralph Gleason reports seeing Billie preparing to leave for her next engagement:
I saw her sitting stiffly in the lobby of the San Carlos Hotel in Monterey, the morning after the festival finale. The jazz musicians tried to ignore her. Finally, in that hoarse whisper that could still (after 30 years of terrifying abuse) send shivers down your spine, she asked, 'Where are you boys goin'?' And when no one answered, she answered herself. 'They got me openin' in Vegas tonight.'

Billie on stage at Monterey with Eddie Khan, Gerry Mulligan, Buddy De Franco and Benny Carter.

WEDNESDAY 15 OCTOBER 1958
Billie signs a management agreement which makes George Treadwell her personal manager. Joe Glaser remains her booking agent.

SATURDAY 18 OCTOBER 1958
The *Melody Maker* reports that Billie has filed for her final decree from her ex-manager Louis McKay.

SAT	1	MON	1
SUN	2	TUES	2
MON	3	WED	3
TUES	4	THUR	4
WED	5	FRI	5
THUR	6	SAT	6
FRI	7	SUN	7
SAT	8	MON	8
SUN	9	TUES	9
MON	10	WED	10
TUES	11	THUR	11
WED	12	FRI	12
THUR	13	SAT	13
FRI	14	SUN	14
SAT	15	MON	15
SUN	16	TUES	16
MON	17	WED	17
TUES	18	THUR	18
WED	19	FRI	19
THUR	20	SAT	20
FRI	21	SUN	21
SAT	22	MON	22
SUN	23	TUES	23
MON	24	WED	24
TUES	25	THUR	25
WED	26	FRI	26
THUR	27	SAT	27
FRI	28	SUN	28
SAT	29	MON	29
SUN	30	TUES	30
		WED	31

Billie's European trip gets off to a bad start in Italy. She is booked for a one-week engagement at the Smeraldo Theatre in Milan, but is pulled out after only two appearances.

The *Melody Maker* reports:

BILLIE HOLIDAY ASKED TO QUIT

Milan, Wednesday—Billie Holiday was forced to withdraw from the bill at the Smeraldo Theatre last week after only two appearances.

Starring in a mixed company of pop singers, comedians, acrobats and impressionists, her uncommercial style failed to please an obviously "commercial" audience. The booing and hissing at second house left the management no alternative but to ask her to forgo the remainder of the week.

Now a private concert for the Milan Hot Club has been fixed and negotiations are in progress for TV appearances.

The private concert is organised by film producer Mario Fatoria, and is held in a small hall in the famous La Scala Opera House.

SATURDAY 8 NOVEMBER 1958
Billie writes to her friend Alice Vrbsky from Milan. Alice has been taking care of Billie, and remains a constant friend to the end.

TUESDAY 11 NOVEMBER 1958
Billie arrives in Paris and sends a telegram to Max Jones in London:
AT HOTEL DE PARIS TILL THUR EVENING
LOVE BILLIE HOLIDAY.

WEDNESDAY 12 NOVEMBER 1958
Max Jones telephones Billie who asks, 'Why aren't you here?'
In the evening Billie appears at the Olympia in Paris on the same bill as Jimmy Rushing. Again the audiences are unsympathetic and promoter Bruno Coquatrix pulls out of the rest of the tour. Billie is stranded and is forced into performing at the Mars Club for a percentage of the door money.

WEDNESDAY 15 NOVEMBER 1958
Max Jones writes in *Melody Maker*:

I telephoned Paris on Wednesday to welcome Billie Holiday back to Europe and express the hope that we might see her in London before long.

She wants very much to come here, I gathered, but doesn't know when she'll have the time. "After three days in Paris we go to Italy, then back for a week in Paris," she told me. The "we" applies to Billie and her pianist, Mal Waldron.

What about the report that she is considering settling in England? "I'm writing to you," Billie said. "I'll give you the whole story then." And there the matter had to rest.

'They call me an artist in Britain,' says Billie Holiday

BILLIE HOLIDAY wants to come to London and stay in London. She told me so when I visited her backstage at the Olympia music hall...

Left: Jimmy Rushing and Billie backstage at the Olympia Theatre in Paris.

THUR	**1**	SUN	**1**
FRI	**2**	MON	**2**
SAT	**3**	TUES	**3**
SUN	**4**	WED	**4**
MON	**5**	THUR	**5**
TUES	**6**	FRI	**6**
WED	**7**	SAT	**7**
THUR	**8**	SUN	**8**
FRI	**9**	MON	**9**
SAT	**10**	TUES	**10**
SUN	**11**	WED	**11**
MON	**12**	THUR	**12**
TUES	**13**	FRI	**13**
WED	**14**	SAT	**14**
THUR	**15**	SUN	**15**
FRI	**16**	MON	**16**
SAT	**17**	TUES	**17**
SUN	**18**	WED	**18**
MON	**19**	THUR	**19**
TUES	**20**	FRI	**20**
WED	**21**	SAT	**21**
THUR	**22**	SUN	**22**
FRI	**23**	MON	**23**
SAT	**24**	TUES	**24**
SUN	**25**	WED	**25**
MON	**26**	THUR	**26**
TUES	**27**	FRI	**27**
WED	**28**	SAT	**28**
THUR	**29**		
FRI	**30**		
SAT	**31**		

THURSDAY 8 JANUARY 1959

Down Beat reviews a Decca album:

BILLIE HOLIDAY
LOVER MAN—Decca DL 8702: *Lover Man; That Old Devil Called Love; My Man; You're My Thrill; Crazy He Calls Me; Weep No More; There Is No Greater Love; This Is Heaven To Me; Solitude; Porgy; Girls Were Made to Take Care of Boys; Please Tell Me Now.*
Some quite good Billie, singing material ranging from fine to mawkish, backed by generally drab groups. The voice and the inimitable Holiday feeling manage to shine through. With only trio backing, she breathes life into *My Man* and *Porgy*. Vocal group backing on *Weep No More* and *Girls* is dreadful.

WEDNESDAY 14 JANUARY 1959

Billie receives a telephone call from Inspector McVeigh requesting her to appear at the Customs House the following afternoon for questioning. Billie contacts William Dufty, who calls a lawyer friend of his, Flo Kennedy, of Wilkes & Kennedy, to act on Billie's behalf.

THURSDAY 15 JANUARY 1959

Billie, accompanied by her attorney, Flo Kennedy, is questioned at the New York Customs House by two Treasury Agents, Martin McVeigh and Mario Cozzi. It seems she is in violation of the Narcotics Control Act of 1956 which provides that "no citizen of the U.S. shall depart from the U.S. if he is addicted to or uses narcotics as defined in the Internal Revenue Code of 1954 unless such person registers with Customs prior to departure and upon his return to this country. Penalty for failure to register will subject the offender to fine and imprisonment." The statute also covers "anyone convicted of violation of the narcotic or marijuana laws of the U.S. or any state, the penalty for which is imprisonment for more than one year." Billie's 1947 conviction had been for a year and a day which meant that she had infringed the 1956 Act and could be sent to prison.
The matter is referred to the U.S. Attorney for the Eastern District of New York at the next session.
Billie is terrified at the thought of returning to jail, and begins drinking heavily.

THURSDAY 12 FEBRUARY 1959

Billie attends the informal hearing before the U.S. Attorney in Brooklyn. After an hour and a half of pleading the government declines to prosecute and Billie is free. She heads for the nearest bar to celebrate.

Billie appears on the cover of the February issue of Metronome.

SUN	**1**
MON	**2**
TUES	**3**
WED	**4**
THUR	**5**
FRI	**6**
SAT	**7**
SUN	**8**
MON	**9**
TUES	**10**
WED	**11**
THUR	**12**
FRI	**13**
SAT	**14**
SUN	**15**
MON	**16**
TUES	**17**
WED	**18**
THUR	**19**
FRI	**20**
SAT	**21**
SUN	**22**
MON	**23**
TUES	**24**
WED	**25**
THUR	**26**
FRI	**27**
SAT	**28**

SUNDAY 22 FEBRUARY 1959
Billie flies into London.

MONDAY 23 FEBRUARY 1959
Billie records the TV programme 'Chelsea at Nine' for ATV at the Chelsea Palace Studios:
BILLIE HOLIDAY (vocal), MAL WALDRON (piano), THE PETER KNIGHT ORCHESTRA
I Loves You Porgy / Please Don't Talk About Me When I'm Gone (vocal & piano only) / *Strange Fruit*
Max & Betty Jones, along with Beryl Bryden and Yolande Bavan, are there throughout the day to lend support. Beryl takes the photographs that you see here. Later, Max Jones takes Billie to the 100 Club to see Alex Welsh and Beryl Bryden. They arrive just before 11pm and, as the club is not licensed for alcohol, they soon move on to the Cottage Club.

TUESDAY 24 FEBRUARY 1959
Billie mails a postcard to Alice Vrbsky from Hampstead in London:
Hi Alice Well I made it hope you receive this card before me the trip was crazy six hours Kiss Pepe Regards to family Lady Day

WEDNESDAY 25 FEBRUARY 1959
Billie flies back to NYC.

Above: Billie looks stunning in this photograph by Beryl Bryden, taken backstage at the Chelsea Palace Studios. Left: Billie performing for the cameras.

SUN	1
MON	2
TUES	3
WED	4
THUR	5
FRI	6
SAT	7
SUN	8
MON	9
TUES	10
WED	11
THUR	12
FRI	13
SAT	14
SUN	15
MON	16
TUES	17
WED	18
THUR	19
FRI	20
SAT	21
SUN	22
MON	23
TUES	24
WED	25
THUR	26
FRI	27
SAT	28
SUN	29
MON	30
TUES	31

TUESDAY 3 MARCH 1959

Recording session at the Metropolitan Recording Studio in New York City for Verve, accompanied by Ray Ellis and his Orchestra.

BILLIE HOLIDAY (vocal), ROMEO PENQUE (reeds), JIMMY CLEVELAND (tb), HANK JONES (p, celeste), KENNY BURRELL (g), JOE BENJAMIN (b), OSIE JOHNSON (d), JANET PUTNAM (harp), four unknown strings, RAY ELLIS (conductor/arranger)

All The Way / It's Not For Me To Say / I'll Never Smile Again / Just One More Chance The session continues through the night into the early hours of Wednesday.

WEDNESDAY 4 MARCH 1959

Recording session at the Metropolitan Recording Studio in New York City for Verve, accompanied by Ray Ellis and his Orchestra.

BILLIE HOLIDAY (vocal), HARRY EDISON (t), GENE QUILL (as), JIMMY CLEVELAND (tb), HANK JONES (p), BARRY GALBRAITH (g), MILT HINTON (b), OSIE JOHNSON (d), unknown harp and twelve strings, RAY ELLIS (conductor/arranger)

When It's Sleepy Time Down South / Don't Worry 'Bout Me / Sometimes I'm Happy / You Took Advantage Of Me The session continues through the night into the early hours of Thursday.

WEDNESDAY 11 MARCH 1959

Recording session at the Metropolitan Recording Studio in New York City for Verve, accompanied by Ray Ellis and his Orchestra.

BILLIE HOLIDAY (vocal), HARRY EDISON (t), JOE WILDER (t), AL COHN (ts), DANNY BANK (bs), BILLY BYERS (tb), HANK JONES (p), BARRY GALBRAITH (g), MILT HINTON (b), OSIE JOHNSON (d), RAY ELLIS (conductor/arranger)

There'll Be Some Changes Made / 'Deed I Do / All Of You / Baby Won't You Please Come Home

Billie alone in her apartment, the way she spends much of the last months of her life, watching cartoons on TV, cared for by Alice Vrbsky and Frankie Freedom. Only a few friends, notably Annie Ross, bother to visit.

WED	**1**
THUR	**2**
FRI	**3**
SAT	**4**
SUN	**5**
MON	**6**
TUES	**7**
WED	**8**
THUR	**9**
FRI	**10**
SAT	**11**
SUN	**12**
MON	**13**
TUES	**14**
WED	**15**
THUR	**16**
FRI	**17**
SAT	**18**
SUN	**19**
MON	**20**
TUES	**21**
WED	**22**
THUR	**23**
FRI	**24**
SAT	**25**
SUN	**26**
MON	**27**
TUES	**28**
WED	**29**
THUR	**30**

TUESDAY 7 APRIL 1959

Billie celebrates her 44th birthday with a party. The party lasts all night, winding up at Birdland.

Melody Maker reports:

"A few old friends of Lady Day gathered to wish her luck in her small, comfortable ground-floor apartment near Central Park," writes Leonard Feather.

In the kitchen, Annie Ross helped prepare the drinks. In the living room, Bill Dufty (co-author of Billie's book 'Lady Sings The Blues') talked to Barrie Thorne of the BBC's New York office.

"Across the room a stereophonic phonograph played Lady's just-completed MGM album. Among the listeners were Jo Jones and Ed Lewis, two of Billie's colleagues from the Basie band in which she was the girl vocalist 21 years ago.

"Ed, a little-publicised anchor man of the early Basie brass section, works now as a motorman on the subway, but still gigs with his own group.

"Jo, reminiscing about Lester Young, said: 'What really killed Pres was Herschel Evans's death. They were enemies on the bandstand, but the truth is they were the closest of friends. Lester practically didn't drink or smoke until around the time Herschel died, in 1939.'"

BILLIE HOLIDAY talked to Feather of her recent past – and future.

"Evidently," says Leonard, "she was in a romantic mood when she spoke to you of settling in England – a news item that has been repeated in several New York gossip columns.

"The fact is that, despite all her problems on this side of the Atlantic, Billie isn't going to pull up her roots after all these years. She has a three-year lease on the apartment, and has no plans to sublet it.

"Billie, looking sharp in a leopard-skin blouse and skin-tight toreador pants, said: 'It was about time I had myself a party. This is the first birthday I've really celebrated in 15 years.'"

MONDAY 20 APRIL 1959

Billie opens a one-week engagement at Storyville in Boston, accompanied by Mal Waldron (p), Champ Jones (b) and Roy Haynes (d).
During the week Billie broadcasts from the club via station WMEX.
BILLIE HOLIDAY (vocal), MAL WALDRON (piano), CHAMP JONES (bass), ROY HAYNES (drums)
Nice Work If You Can Get It / Willow Weep For Me / When Your Lover Has Gone / Billie's Blues / Too Marvellous For Words / Lover Come Back To Me

SUNDAY 26 APRIL 1959

Billie concludes a successful engagement at Storyville in Boston.

Billie follows the Boston engagement with two weeks at Lowell, Massachusetts. She also appears at an All-Star concert at the Philadelphia Academy of Art.

FRI	**1**
SAT	**2**
SUN	**3**
MON	**4**
TUES	**5**
WED	**6**
THUR	**7**
FRI	**8**
SAT	**9**
SUN	**10**
MON	**11**
TUES	**12**
WED	**13**
THUR	**14**
FRI	**15**
SAT	**16**
SUN	**17**
MON	**18**
TUES	**19**
WED	**20**
THUR	**21**
FRI	**22**
SAT	**23**
SUN	**24**
MON	**25**
TUES	**26**
WED	**27**
THUR	**28**
FRI	**29**
SAT	**30**
SUN	**31**

MONDAY 25 MAY 1959

Billie appears at a benefit concert at the Phoenix Theatre in Greenwich Village, New York City. Leonard Feather and Steve Allen are the MCs. Feather is shocked by Billie's appearance, and, noticing his expression, Billie says: *What's the matter Leonard? You seen a ghost or something?*

TUESDAY 26 MAY 1959

Leonard Feather expresses his concern to Joe Glaser and, together, they try to persuade Billie to cancel her opening in Montreal next week and to go into hospital. Billie refuses.

SUNDAY 31 MAY 1959

Billie collapses while being served a bowl of oatmeal and custard by her friend, Frankie Freedom. He calls her doctor, Dr Eric Caminer, who arranges for her to be admitted to Knickerbocker Hospital. She is admitted at 3.40 in the afternoon, but when she is diagnosed as a drug addict she is transferred to the Metropolitan Hospital. Billie is admitted at 5.30 pm. Dr. Caminer arrives, finds her still unattended, and demands that she is found a bed. Eventually she is examined and put into an oxygen tent in Room 6A on the 12th floor.

MON	**1**
TUES	**2**
WED	**3**
THUR	**4**
FRI	**5**
SAT	**6**
SUN	**7**
MON	**8**
TUES	**9**
WED	**10**
THUR	**11**
FRI	**12**
SAT	**13**
SUN	**14**
MON	**15**
TUES	**16**
WED	**17**
THUR	**18**
FRI	**19**
SAT	**20**
SUN	**21**
MON	**22**
TUES	**23**
WED	**24**
THUR	**25**
FRI	**26**
SAT	**27**
SUN	**28**
MON	**29**
TUES	**30**

TUESDAY 2 JUNE 1959

Dr Caminer says: *Billie was in very bad shape yesterday, but her condition is improving, although still critical. She is in an oxygen tent.*

WEDNESDAY 3 JUNE 1959

Metropolitan Hospital officials confirm that Billie's illness has no connection with alcohol addiction or drugs. After 72 hours in the hospital, receiving no drugs whatsoever, Billie shows absolutely no symptoms of withdrawal. Earle Zaidins is a frequent visitor, and on one occasion he persuades Billie, ill as she is, to sign with Shaw Artists Inc.

THURSDAY 4 JUNE 1959

Bill Dufty in the *New York Post*:

Billie sat up in her sunny Metropolitan Hospital room today, sniffing bouquets from Ella, Lena and Sinatra, Basie, Belafonte and Bankhead, grinning at the Page One stories forecasting her demise and says philosophically to a crony, "Some damnbody is always trying to embalm me."

"They'll call this another comeback," she predicted, "and I've been nowhere but across town."

MONDAY 8 JUNE 1959

New York (UPI)—Singer Billie Holiday remained in critical condition today in Metropolitan Hospital. Dr. Ferdinand Piazza, senior medical superintendent said, "She is not making very much progress."
Miss Holiday was hospitalized two weeks ago with a heart condition and hepatitis.

THURSDAY 11 JUNE 1959

Nurse Figueroa finds some white powder in a Kleenex box beside Billie's bed. She reports the find, the police are informed and the powder is taken to the hospital lab for analysis.

FRIDAY 12 JUNE 1959

Police raid Billie's hospital room and place a guard on her door. Two detectives interview Billie and then announce that she has been arrested for possession of heroin. Her comic books, records and phonograph are confiscated.

SATURDAY 13 JUNE 1959

A writ of habeas corpus obtained by Billie's attorney, Don Wilkes, to remove police guard from Billie's room. It is signed by Justice Markewich and a hearing is set for Tuesday.

TUESDAY 16 JUNE 1959

The writ of habeas corpus is granted and the police guard is removed from Billie's room.

SUNDAY 21 JUNE 1959

Two detectives fingerprint Billie in her hospital bed.

Billie Caught With Heroin in Hospital

By SIDNEY KLINE

Billie Holiday, 46, whose throaty blues songs brought her fame and wealth that were later dissipated by apparently incurable dope addiction, was arrested on her bed of pain in Metropolitan Hospital yesterday—on charges of illegal possession of heroin.
Critically ill of hepatitis, anemia and a heart condition, and confined to the hospital since May 31, Lady Day somehow still managed to obtain a quantity of the

Drop Police Acting Ranks

Police Commissioner Kennedy

Billie Holiday Critical, Under Oxygen

Singer Billie Holiday remained in critical condition today in Metropolitan Hospital suffering from a severe liver ailment.
Friends said her physician, Dr. Eric Caminer, had been ... her to enter a hospital for months, but ...

BILLI...

Billie Holiday—Did Old Addiction Cause a Hospital Runaround?

By WILLIAM DUFTY

Billie Holiday sat up in her sunny Metropolitan Hospital room today, sniffing bouquets from Ella, Lena and Sinatra, Basie, Belafonte and Bankhead, grinning at the Page One stories forecasting her demise and saying philosophically to a crony, "Some damnbody is always trying to embalm me."
"They'll call this another comeback," she predicted, "and I've been nowhere but across town."
Nobody has yet told "Lady Day" how close she came Sunday to making a one-way trip. Meanwhile, friends were steaming over reports, confirmed by her physician, Dr. Eric Caminer, that the unconscious, incognito, "Lady Day" shuttled from one hospital to another after cursory and hasty diagnosis as a drug addict. She lay on a stretcher in two hospitals for almost three hours Sunday waiting for emergency treatment for the liver ailment (complicated by cardiac failure) that induced her coma.
Yesterday Metropolitan Hospital officials confirmed the original diagnosis of her physicians that her illness had no connection with alcohol addiction or drugs. After 72 hours in the hospital, receiving no drugs whatsoever, Miss Holiday has shown absolutely no symptoms of withdrawal.

The heretofore unexplained hospital shuttle began shortly after 2 p.m. Sunday when "Lady Day" collapsed while her protege and pal—singer Frankie Freedom, 23, was serving her a brunch of custard and oatmeal prescribed by her doctors.
"She was fighting with me and wouldn't let me take her to the hospital in a cab," said Freedom. "She was holding out to go to a private hospital on Monday. Then she went into a coma."
Freedom called Dr. Caminer, who rushed to the singer's apartment at 26 W. 87th St., immediately called police for an ambulance and arranged by phone for her admittance to Knickerbocker Hospital.
Freedom rode the ambulance with her to the Knickerbocker emergency room where he waited "damn near an hour" for some sign that the unconscious singer was getting medical attention.
"When they assured me they could take care of her," said Freedom, "I left to phone her manager and her husband."

A Faulty Diagnosis

Knickerbocker emergency room records show Miss Holiday arrived at 3:40 p.m. after diagnosis as a case of "drug addiction and

Continued on Page 64

BILLIE HOLIDAY

3 — NEW YORK POST, THURSDAY, JUNE 4, 1959

WED	1
THUR	2
FRI	3
SAT	4
SUN	5
MON	6
TUES	7
WED	8
THUR	9
FRI	10
SAT	11
SUN	12
MON	13
TUES	14
WED	15
THUR	16
FRI	17
SAT	18
SUN	19
MON	20
TUES	21
WED	22
THUR	23
FRI	24
SAT	25
SUN	26
MON	27
TUES	28
WED	29
THUR	30
FRI	31

WEDNESDAY 8 JULY 1959

Billie signs a contract with Vinod International Films to appear in a movie, *No Honor Among Thieves.* Joe Glaser visits and explains the situation regarding her signing with Shaw Artists Inc. Billie is mortified, and tries to ring Milt Shaw. When she is unable to contact him, she writes, asking him to return the 'so-called' contract that she 'apparently signed' while sick. The letter threatens legal steps unless the contract is returned within twenty-four hours. There is no reply from Shaw.

FRIDAY 10 JULY 1959

Doctors allow Billie to receive gifts of candy, ice cream or fruit, but no salty foods.

SATURDAY 11 JULY 1959

Billie's heart begins to falter.

WEDNESDAY 15 JULY 1959

Billie receives the last rites of the Roman Catholic Church. Louis McKay mounts a vigil at her bedside.

THURSDAY 16 JULY 1959

Louis McKay remains at Billie's bedside.

FRIDAY 17 JULY 1959

In the early hours of the morning, at 2.40 am, Louis McKay briefly breaks his vigil to telephone his mother. At 3.10 am, while Louis is out of the room, Billie dies.

Billie Holiday Dies After Relapse; First Lady of the Blues Was 44

NEW YORK POST, FRIDAY, JULY 17, 1959

By WILLIAM DUFTY

Billie Holiday died at 3:10 this morning in Metropolitan Hospital as simply and regally as she had lived.

She was young—only 44; yet, as she was quick to point out, neither of her parents lived that long.

She was beautiful; no one who saw her exquisite brown head against the hospital white pillow would dare talk of her loveliness in bygone days.

She was poor; she had 70 cents in the bank, $750 in $50 bills taped to her leg and, with a $50,000 movie contract for her life story waiting for her signature, she was holding out for double or nothing.

She was brave; at the slightest rattle of the oxygen tent, she lunged forward, dukes up, and barked out sharp orders, commanding those about her to slow down to her tempo: "Don't be in such a hurry."

She was regal; intrigue marital, musical and political swirled about her bedside; cops and doctors took their turn as her wardens, but she was undisturbed by it all.

She was triumphant; for 15 years the government had paraded her through a whirligig of courts, jail, bail as a horrible example of something called a drug addict; in the end she turned the tables on all of them.

She was proud; she had attained worldwide acclaim as the greatest jazz singer of all time and that was that.

And she was alone.

When her fighting heart gave out at 3:10 this morning, only her special nurse and this reporter were at her bedside.

Billie fought like a tiger to leave Metropolitan Hospital on her feet. Her 46-day stand in Room 6A12 was the longest engagement she had played anywhere—except for the Strand Theater on Broadway in 1948 with Count Basie. She had gained almost 30 pounds by last Sunday when complications set in. Her longtime manager, Joe Glaser, made arrangements for her transfer to a private hospital; Billie waited for the doctors' OK which never came.

She had a hat-full of plans for the future; she had started with me on another book; we finished one chapter, and sold it Monday to a magazine. She took the advance cash in fifties and taped them to her leg; on Tuesday evening she fastened a gardenia in her hair and signed a contract to appear in a new movie to be shot in New York this fall.

Indian producer-director Vino Pathak and screenplay author George Morris discussed the film

Continued on Page 26

BILLIE HOLIDAY

WED	1
THUR	2
FRI	3
SAT	4
SUN	5
MON	6
TUES	7
WED	8
THUR	9
FRI	10
SAT	11
SUN	12
MON	13
TUES	14
WED	15
THUR	16
FRI	17
SAT	18
SUN	19
MON	20
TUES	21
WED	22
THUR	23
FRI	24
SAT	25
SUN	26
MON	27
TUES	28
WED	29
THUR	30
FRI	31

TUESDAY 21 JULY 1959

Billie's funeral takes place at St. Paul the Apostle Roman Catholic Church, Columbus Avenue and Fifty-ninth Street, attended by 3,000 persons. The *New York Times* reports:

The influential jazz singer, known as Lady Day, was mourned at a solemn requiem mass, sung by the church's choir of ten voices. About 500 of the mourners, who could not be accommodated inside the packed church, stood on the sidewalks.

Six pallbearers carried the body in a heavy bronze coffin into the church. The singer was buried in her favourite pink lace stage gown and pink gloves.

More than 10,000 persons had viewed the body at the Universal Funeral Chapel, Lexington Avenue and Fifty-second Street.

Among the mourners were Miss Holiday's husband, Louis McKay, and her half-sister, Kay Kelly.

Many persons prominent in the entertainment and musical world also attended the rites. They included Benny Goodman, Gene Krupa, Henry (Red) Allen, Joe Williams, Frankie Freedom, Roy Eldridge, Tony Scott, Leonard Feather, John Hammond, Charlie Shavers, Jo Jones and Joe Glaser.

Burial was in St. Raymond's Cemetery in the Bronx.

Jazz Greats Attend Funeral for Billie

By ALFRED T. HENDRICKS

With quiet dignity, the greats of the jazz world said goodby today to one of their own.

For Billie Holiday, an artist who sang some of the purest notes in improvised sound, there was no music save the traditional unaccompanied Latin chants of a 10-voice Catholic choir.

The morning ritual deviated only once, but in the direction of another tradition. On its way from St. Paul's the Apostle Church at 60th St. and Columbus Av., to St. Raymond's Cemetery in The Bronx, the funeral procession detoured eastward to 110th St. and snaked slowly through Harlem.

Few Are Aware

There had been no advance notice of this and few of the passersby in the street were aware of its meaning. It was as much Billie Holiday's farewell as Harlem's.

woman who had excited attention all her life. At the end of the service, the streams of people pouring from the church created a traffic jam. It took 10 policemen to get the cars moving down Columbus Av. again.

40 Pallbearers

Among the 40 honorary pallbearers were Benny Goodman, Gene Krupa, Teddy Wilson, Juanita Hall, Mary Lou Williams, Tony Scott and Bobby Tucker.

Also, Billie's accompanist, Al Waldron, Don Shirley, C...

LADY DAY RECORDS, INC.   SA-DAY MUSIC PUBLISHERS

LOUIS McKAY
8 EAST 48TH STREET
SUITE 2E
—
PLAZA 9-3223

ADMINISTRATOR,   PRESIDENT,
ESTATE OF ELEANORA McKAY   BILLIE HOLIDAY ASSOCIATES
A/K/A BILLIE HOLIDAY